THE PROSTITUTES' PADRE

TOM CULLEN

The Prostitutes' Padre

The story of the notorious
Rector of Stiffkey

THE BODLEY HEAD
LONDON SYDNEY
TORONTO

To
Ellenore Bogigian
and
Robert W. Kenny

© Tom Cullen 1975
ISBN 0 370 10285 1
Printed in Great Britain for
The Bodley Head Ltd
9 Bow Street, London WC2E 7AL
by Unwin Brothers Ltd, Woking, Surrey
Set in Monotype Imprint
by Gloucester Typesetting Co. Ltd
First published 1975

CONTENTS

Acknowledgments

In acknowledging the generous help given to him in the preparation of this biography the author would like to single out first of all Nugent Davidson, who was most kind and patient in answering questions concerning his father's life; Mrs Ruth Roach, of Quebec, Canada, the rector's grand-daughter, who let the author quote from a letter her mother had written, and who furnished the photograph of Molly Davidson; and the late J. Rowland Sales, who first advanced the theory that the rector was a victim of multiple personality, and who thus opened up a new vista to the biographer.

The author would also like to thank the Worshipful H. J. Ellison, V.R.D., M.A., Chancellor of the Diocese of Norwich, and B. O. L. Prior, T.D., Registrar and Legal Secretary to the Bishop of Norwich, for permission to see the verbatim transcripts and other papers pertaining to the rector's trial; Roger North, J.P., for permission to see the notes his father, the Worshipful J. Keppel North, took during the trial; Miss Jean M. Kennedy, B.A., archivist, the Norfolk and Norwich Record Office; Philip Hepworth, M.A., F.L.A., librarian, Norwich Central Library; Dr M. Barratt, assistant librarian, Bodleian Library, Oxford; Dr J. R. Maddicott, librarian and archivist, Exeter College, Oxford; and F. H. G. Percy, M.A., historian, Whitgift School, Croydon, for research assistance given. A debt of gratitude is due to Tom and Elizabeth Van Dycke for having read the book in manuscript.

Among the villagers who have given freely of their reminiscences concerning the Rev Harold Davidson are Mrs Marjorie Atkinson, Mrs Norah Bayfield, of Stiffkey, Norfolk; and Mrs May Eales of Morston, Norfolk. Thanks are due also to Tom Berentemsel, Mrs Laura Brackley, Harold Chilcott, Stuart Douglass, Dr Letitia Fairfield, Bruce Hamilton, Mrs Diana Hamond, Anthony Heath, the Rev J. E. Ironside, Charles Landstone, Charles Lewsen, Mrs Bessie L. Lord, Dennis Mayes, J. P. Oldroyd, the Rev Edward Powell, the Rev W. L. W. Randall, Bert Ross, Thomas R. Shiner,

[7]

ACKNOWLEDGMENTS

the Rev Philip Steer, John Tatham, Mrs Kathleen Ward, David
Wood, and David Wright.

UNCLE HAROLD

'. . . man is not truly one, but truly two. I say two, because the state of my knowledge does not pass beyond that point. Others will follow, others will out-strip me on the same lines; and I hazard the guess that man will be ultimately known for a mere polity of multifarious, incongruous and independent denizens.'

ROBERT LOUIS STEVENSON
The Strange Case of Dr Jekyll and Mr Hyde

I

Will the Real Harold Davidson...

Finding someone in Stiffkey, Norfolk who has an unkind word to say for the village's one-time rector, the Rev Harold Francis Davidson, is like finding a strict Baptist who will put in a good word for sin. Quite simply Davidson, who was unfrocked in the early 1930s for immoral conduct, is regarded as a saint by the 378 inhabitants of this decaying Domesday village where William the Conqueror was once lord of the manor. Express a contrary view and the villagers are immediately up in arms, as I discovered on a recent visit. The same fierce loyalty is to be encountered in certain working-class circles when Edward VIII and the abdication are mentioned, all because Edward, after visiting a mining village in the black Rhondda, muttered 'something must be done'. No doubt Davidson, too, muttered 'something must be done' when he first set eyes on Stiffkey. If so, he soon forgot about it in the mad whirl of saving girls in London whom he deemed to be dangling perilously, if they had not already fallen into the abyss.

The loyalty, however, remains . . . Typical of the older generation whom I talked to is Mrs Marjorie Atkinson, daughter of a Stiffkey churchwarden in Davidson's day, and herself organist at the parish church ('As Mr Davidson was always late for church services I had to play voluntaries to keep the congregation from growing restless'). 'The rector was always a perfect gentleman so far as I was concerned,' Mrs Atkinson relates. 'Many a Sunday night he would escort me home after the evening service, but he never tried to get familiar.' 'More sinned against than sinning,' chimes in Mrs May Louisa Eales, whose mother Sarah Bean was churchwarden at Morston, the other half of Davidson's plural living. 'Mr Davidson was especially kind to old people,' says Mrs Eales, whose son, now warden of the Blakeney Point bird sanctuary, was baptised by Davidson. 'He was always giving the elderly half-crowns, which was a considerable sum in those days.' 'As to what the rector did when he was in London, we knew nothing about that,' Mrs Eales concludes. 'Mr Davidson used to say, "Do as I preach, and not as I do." '

Davidson's long vigil in a barrel on Blackpool's Golden Mile, and the fact that he was fatally mauled by a lion when he entered its cage to preach at Skegness Amusement Park, have done much to propagate the legend of his martyrdom. But even in his lifetime one had only to mention Davidson's name for fierce matrons, not all of them his parishioners, to spring out of the ground to proclaim his saintliness. They surrounded him wherever he went, these stout Boadiceas with the cloche hats planted firmly on their heads. It was Davidson's fate to be forever pursued by domineering women, and to be forever fleeing from them. That was partly the trouble, for his interests lay elsewhere. The rector of Stiffkey had eyes only for girls of quite tender years, nymphets who were still malleable and whose character he hoped to help form.

*　　*　　*

What, one wonders, would these Boadiceas have thought had they seen the Rev Harold Davidson, as he could have been seen six days a week, fifty-two weeks in the year, trotting down Greek Street in Soho. The first thing they might have noticed was that Davidson had left off his dog collar, for he considered this a hindrance to the type of missionary work on which he was engaged. Then, too, they might have remarked a springiness in his step, a gladness in his eye, that were missing when he was at Stiffkey 110 miles away. Davidson, who did not achieve notoriety until he was fifty-six, was a small (5 ft. 3 in.), dapper, quicksilver figure of a man, with piercing blue eyes, a straight nose, and a chin which showed no sign of sagging (he liked to be seen in profile). The reason he looked ten years younger as he made his rounds was that Soho, not Stiffkey, was his spiritual home.

'Untidy, full of Greeks, Ishmaelites, cats, Italians, tomatoes, restaurants, organs, coloured stuffs, queer names, people looking out of upper windows,' is the way that Soho is dismissed in *The Forsyte Saga*, Galsworthy writing that 'it dwells remote from the British Body Politic.' Untidy Soho may have been, and even un-British, but Davidson loved every inch of it, including the cats, Greeks, Ishmaelites, and, above all, the ladies in the upper windows (they were not just looking, Mr Galsworthy; they were rattling their keys). To these latter the rector of Stiffkey would doff his grey homburg and make a sweeping bow.

Parsons of any sort were a rarity in the Soho of the twenties. (A standing joke among the prostitutes who congregated in Old Compton Street was, 'The only time we see the Church of England is when the rent collector calls,' for it was common knowledge that the Church Commissioners owned much of the property in central London on which brothels stood.) But the Rev Harold Davidson was a *rara avis* by any standard. To begin with, he never tried to preach to the girls, most of whom were young enough to be his daughters. 'He would buy us a meal instead of shoving religion down our throats,' as one girl expressed it. Then he was so peculiar, telling the girls how he had been on the stage for ten years before becoming a preacher, and how he had played Charley's Aunt among other rôles, then breaking into an impromptu tap dance as if to prove it.

But it was Davidson's physical courage that had impressed Soho the most. More than once the flyweight preacher had stood up to ponces armed with flick-knives, who told him to lay off their bread-winners. Similarly, without flinching, he had confronted Dixie Din, a professional strongman, who had threatened to bash in the face of one of the girls. The story of how the pocket-size parson had out-faced Dixie Din, who made a kerbside living bending iron bars and wriggling out of chains, made the rounds, earning for Davidson more respect than any amount of Bible-thumping would have done.

'For years I have been known as the Prostitutes' Padre,' Davidson wrote to his Father in God, the Lord Bishop of Norwich, adding that it was 'the proudest title that a true priest of Christ can hold'. 'I believe with all my soul,' the rector continued, 'that if He were born again in London in the present day He would be found constantly walking in Piccadilly . . . His attitude towards the woman taken in adultery and still more his close personal friendship with the notorious harlot of Magdala . . . have always been my inspiration.'

*   *   *

The Prostitutes' Padre? But does this not cancel out the plaster saint image of Davidson which his followers, the Women's Institute types, retain?

[13]

'They sound like two different persons,' I protested to the late J. Rowland Sales, a lifelong friend of Davidson's. 'Surely someone must have got it wrong.'

'You were right the first time,' Sales replied. 'They were two different persons.'

J. Rowland Sales, who died in August, 1972, at the age of 83, had the distinction of having acted as press agent to 'three of the biggest rogues of the twentieth century', to use his own descriptive tag. As a lad of nineteen he had been hired as secretary by J. Maundy Gregory, then a theatrical impresario, but soon to achieve fame as the man who sold knighthoods and baronetcies under Lloyd George. Then during the 1914–18 war Sales stage-managed Horatio Bottomley on one of his recruiting drives (Bottomley charged £50 extra for invoking God in his appeal to young men to fight for king and country). Finally, Sales handled the rector of Stiffkey's lecture tour at local cinemas after the latter's trial. Though he included Davidson in his rogues' gallery, Sales thought of his friend as being more of a madman than a rogue. 'Davidson was so excitable, so impetuous,' Sales explained. 'If he took up anything he got carried away. Yet he was the kindest-hearted man I have ever known—the Davidson whom I call "Uncle Harold", at any rate. He would do anything for you if you were in distress.'

A big man who always wore polka-dot bow-ties, Sales, who was over eighty when I met him, still went daily to his office at Aldersgate in the City. Here he engaged in property deals involving the conversion of cinemas into bingo halls. However, it was at Sales' flat in the Haymarket above the Regency shopfront of Fribourg and Treyer, the tobacconists, that we met; and as we talked I could glimpse through the window Piccadilly Circus and the statue of Eros, which originally had nothing to do with Love's archer, but was supposed to represent the Angel of Christian Charity and was erected in honour of the seventh Earl of Shaftesbury. Somehow this aluminium statue seemed peculiarly appropriate to our discussions, for was not the rector of Stiffkey forever confusing eros with agape? The flat itself was tiny, and with its Rose du Barry colour scheme suggested a cardinal's cabinet.

Picking up the thread of the conversation I said jokingly, 'Next you'll be telling me that there was another Davidson, an impostor running round London blackening the reputation of the good rector of Stiffkey.'

[14]

'There was at least one other impostor, as you call it, though I reckon that there were two,' Sales replied. Then after talking in conundrums, Davidson's one-time manager got down to cases. Davidson had at least three distinct personalities, according to Sales, each with its own foibles and fantasies. In other words, Davidson suffered from a severe personality disorder known to psychiatrists as dissociation, or multiple personality. Sales, who had known Davidson for over twenty years, had arrived at this conclusion after close observation of his friend during that time, and being interested, he had read up on the subject.

The one whom Sales called Uncle Harold was the original Davidson, I gathered, the earnest if ineffectual do-gooder, who was regarded as a saint by Stiffkey and by Soho alike. 'Eccentric perhaps, but he wouldn't hurt a flea,' was the way Sales put it. But there were other Davidsons as well, less benign creatures, who manifested themselves from time to time, according to Sales. There was Little Jimmy, for example.

'Little Jimmy was the nickname his parishioners gave to Davidson,' Sales explained. 'It was intended as a term of endearment, for obviously the villagers were tickled not only by Davidson's diminutive size—there wasn't a woman in Stiffkey who could not have picked him up with one hand, they used to boast—but also by his pixie manner.' To the Stiffkeyites Little Jimmy was like Puck, who 'frights the maidens of the villagery'; but his friend used the sobriquet in a different sense to designate the dark, mischievous, purely destructive side of Davidson's nature. Little Jimmy was permanently at war with Uncle Harold. Sales was able to distinguish a third personality in Davidson's make-up whom he called the Bunco Kid, 'bunco' being American slang for swindler; but the Bunco Kid remained in the shadows most of the time, according to Sales.

The transition from one personality to another could be as startling as it was abrupt, according to Sales. 'I remember once sitting with Davidson in a Lyons teashop,' my host recalled, 'and he was telling me the pathetic story of an elderly couple whom he had found sleeping under a hedge near Stiffkey. They were farm workers who had been evicted from their tied cottage. And as he told how he had taken the couple in, fed them, and given them shelter, Davidson's voice trembled, his eyes filled with tears, and I fully expected him to break into sobs. But no, just at that moment he espied a waitress whom he had never seen before, and his whole bearing changed.'

Davidson's face did not undergo one of those shuddering transformations described by Robert Louis Stevenson in his tale about Dr Jekyll and Mr Hyde, his friend declared. 'But his eyes brightened, and his voice, which normally was high-pitched, grating, took on a vulgar and insinuating tone.' And here his friend mimicked the rector in his Little Jimmy persona as he approached the waitress, ' "Excuse me, Miss, but you must be the sister of Jessie Matthews. You look enough like her to be her twin, only prettier; but then I expect that lots of people have told you that." ' 'Aside from being a brunette, the girl bore not the slightest resemblance to Jessie Matthews,' Sales added. 'As for me, I buried my face in my newspaper and pretended that I was not with him. Meanwhile, Davidson promised the girl he would try to get her a walk-on part in a new revue due to open in London. The maddest part is that having made the promise he rushed out of the teashop bent on hounding some poor producer into giving the girl a job.'

*　　*　　*

The fundamental mistake made by the Church authorities in the Stiffkey case, according to Sales, was in failing to recognise that Davidson was a highly disturbed personality, and as such a suitable case for treatment. Instead of putting him on trial before a consistory court charged with offences against public morality under the 1892 Clergy Discipline Act, his bishop should have recommended Davidson to a Harley Street specialist, his friend maintained. The analyst's couch, rather than the witness-box, was the proper place for the rector to rid himself of his obsessions.

Specifically, the rector, a married man with four children, was accused of having committed adultery over a period of ten years with a 'woman named'; and of having accosted various females in hotel lobbies, pursued them down the labyrinth of the London Underground, cornered them in telephone booths, and, finally, with having embraced them publicly in such exotic places as Chinese restaurants, all of which added up to 'systematically misbehaving himself with young women', in the prosecutor's words on the opening day of the trial, March 29, 1932.

Certainly, Davidson's methods of moral uplift were unorthodox

by Church of England standards. For example, he would not have
dreamt of reforming the professional prostitutes with whom he
came into contact daily in Soho. He had too much respect for their
integrity. He would have agreed wholeheartedly with the British
Social Biology Council's definition of prostitution as 'a way of
living consciously chosen because it suits a woman's personality in
particular circumstances'.[1]

No, Davidson's main concern was for the amateur prostitute, the
young girl, usually just up from the country, who was going on the
game for the first time. Usually she had hitch-hiked to London in
hopes of finding a job; but in London of the depression twenties
job opportunities were even scarcer than in the provinces, and
often, in sheer desperation, she would take to the streets.

Such an amateur was Rose Ellis, aged twenty, who might be
termed the proto-girl in Davidson's life. 'She had eyes as though
she had seen trouble,' Rose's landlady described her at Davidson's
trial. 'She did not look a fresh young girl by any means. She looked
like a girl who had known what sorrow is.' Given to fits of hysteria,
Rose had twice tried to commit suicide, the last attempt occurring
after she discovered that she had been tricked into a bigamous
marriage with an Australian named Malone, who had a wife and
four children in the outback. After that Rose had taken to drink
and prostitution in that order, and had ended up with syphilis.
Davidson paid for Rose's room and board while he arranged for
medical care and tried to find work for her, and they ended up
close friends. This was the woman the rector was accused of having
committed adultery with over a 10-year period.

*   *   *

Some of the girls whom the Rev Harold Davidson tried to help
were very young and very attractive. 'I like to get girls from 14 to
20,' he once confessed, adding that these were 'the most impres-
sionable ages in young girls who are going to be the mothers of the
future generation.' But girls of such tender years (some would
qualify today as teeny-boppers) should not have their heads filled
with notions of motherhood, according to the Bishop of Norwich

---

[1] *Women of the Streets: A Sociological Study of the Common Prostitute.*
Edited by C. H. Rolph. London: Secker and Warburg, 1955.

[17]

and his legal adviser. The fact that the rector concentrated on teenagers became a crucial issue at his trial.

Not fourteen, but sixteen when he met her was Gwendoline Barbara Harris, the ultimate girl in Davidson's life. Her appearance at the Stiffkey trial as star witness against Davidson gave the proceedings that dash of sex and glamour which guaranteed maximum press coverage. 'A slim, attractive girl with the face of a child, lips that Burne-Jones often painted, and large expressive eyes,' is the way a *Daily Herald* reporter saw Barbara. But Barbara's indebtedness was to Max Factor, not to the Pre-Raphaelite Brotherhood. Davidson's defence counsel, in his opening statement, was to describe her as 'this soiled plaything of the very scum of humanity'.

Seduced at the age of fifteen, Barbara had been taken into care by the Church Army, only to abscond from their hostel at the earliest opportunity. When Davidson met her she was out of work and broke. The rector had not only paid her rent and got her jobs, but had tried to improve her mind. 'Do balance things by reading some really good literature dealing with fine noble characters of men and women,' he had urged shortly after they met. For starters the rector then gave her a translation from the French entitled *Damaged Goods*.

Once when Davidson had called to tea, Barbara and a Hindu boyfriend sat up in bed in their pyjamas to receive him. When Barbara asked him how he liked her pyjamas, the rector allegedly replied, 'I prefer you without them.' Asked at his trial if such *déshabillé* did not suggest that the couple were living together, Davidson replied, 'Not at all. She might have taken him a cup of tea, or been sitting in there before she went to bed in her own room.' 'Pyjamas are perfectly respectable clothing,' he added. 'I know people of the highest character who sit round in pyjamas.'

The Rev Harold Davidson had tried to rape her, not once, but on nearly every occasion they were alone together, Barbara would testify. She was always having to fend him off—a claim all the more astounding in that her lovers ranged from the Hindu mentioned above to a member of the Junior Constitutional Club. The rector went so far as to offer to divorce his wife and to leave his children if Barbara would marry him, she maintained.

Accusations such as these made the Stiffkey trial headline news overnight and Davidson himself 'as celebrated as Al Capone'. The

rector and his antics took people's minds off breadlines, hunger
marches, and the dole, or so editors reasoned. He likewise chased
from the front pages those other bogies, the collapse of the Weimar
republic and the rise of Adolf Hitler.

AMAZING CHARGES AGAINST RECTOR

GIRL'S STORY OF BEING LOCKED IN ROOM:
'I BLACKED HIS EYE'

RECTOR'S MIDNIGHT CALL ON WAITRESS

SAYS SHE SAW RECTOR KISSING BARBARA

ARTIST'S MODEL FOR WHOM RECTOR TOOK ROOM

KISSES AS CRIMES: RECTOR'S DEFENCE OPENS

RECTOR'S TRIPS TO PARIS:
'I TOOK MANY GIRLS THERE,' SAYS MR DAVIDSON

RECTOR'S PROTEST: 'GOSSIP BY EVIL-MINDED PEOPLE'

MR DAVIDSON AND PICTURE WITH GIRL:
'I WAS TRAPPED INTO IT'

'MISS D' TELLS HOW SHAWL SLIPPED

Stiffkey's incumbent was good news in the same way that ex-
R.A.F. pilot Jim Mollison was good news when he crash-landed at
Capetown after flying 6,255 miles solo, then climbed from the
plane's wreckage into the waiting arms of Amy Johnson. It was the
year of the yo-yo, a craze imported from America, and in their
resilience both Mollison and Davidson reminded more than one
reporter of that ubiquitous toy.

His friend J. Rowland Sales would say that it was Little Jimmy
who inspired the headlines. Sales used the image of a barometer
house as a model for Davidson's multi-phasic personality, having
borrowed this metaphor from Dr Morton Prince. Thus when
Uncle Harold popped out of the weather house Little Jimmy
stayed inside, and it meant that the weather was set fair, but when
Little Jimmy popped out it was time to put up the storm shutters
for gale-force winds lay ahead.

*   *   *

The more I delved into the Rev Harold Davidson's background the more I became convinced that J. Rowland Sales was on the right track, that here indeed was a genuine case of multiple personality. Such cases are comparatively rare, only seventy-six such having been reported in medical literature during the period from 1917 to 1944.[1] Moreover, multiple personality appears to be a turn-of-the-century disorder, judging by the cases reported at the end of the 19th century and the beginning of the 20th, or before the theories of Dr Sigmund Freud had been widely popularised. The earliest case on record is that of Mary Reynolds, who was born in Pennsylvania in 1793. Melancholic and shy, Mary at the age of eighteen began to have 'fits' of a hysterical nature, one of which left her blind and deaf for a period of five weeks. Some time later she awoke as a new personality, 'a gay, hysterical, mischievous woman, fond of jests and subject to absurd beliefs or delusive convictions'.

Multiple personality, traditionally viewed as a form of hysteria, has been defined by Dr Arnold Ludwig and his colleagues as referring to 'the presence of one or more alter personalities, each presumably possessing differing sets of values and behaviours one from another and from the "primary" personality, and each claiming varying degrees of amnesia or disinterest for one another.'[2] They go on to point out: 'The appearance of these alter personalities may be on a "co-conscious" basis (i.e. simultaneously coexistent with the primary personality and aware of its thoughts and feelings) or separate consciousness basis (i.e. alternating presence of the primary and alter personalities with little or no awareness or concern for the feelings and thoughts of each other), or both.'

The majority of cases reported are dual personalities. An early exception was Mollie Fancher, a clairvoyant variously billed as 'The Brooklyn Enigma', and 'The Psychological Marvel of the 19th century', whose five personalities were given the fanciful names of Sunbeam, Idol, Rosebud, Pearl and Ruby. The record-holder to date, however, is the Wisconsin woman known pseudonymously

---

[1] W. S. Taylor and M. F. Martin. 'Multiple Personality.' *The Journal of Abnormal and Social Psychology*, Vol. 39, No. 3, July, 1944.

[2] *Archives of General Psychiatry*, Vol. 26, April, 1972. 'The Objective Study of a Multiple Personality.' By Arnold M. Ludwig, M.D., Jeffrey M. Brandsma, M.D., Cornelia B. Wilbur, M.D., Fernando Bentfield, M.D., and Douglas H. Jameson, M.D.

as 'Sybil Isabel Dorsett', who, we are told, encapsulates no fewer than sixteen personalities, two of them male (penis envy turned to penis identification?).[1]

Clergymen, it would appear, are especially prone to the disorder, sexual repression and religious fanaticism entering into the picture. One such clergyman was the Rev Ansel Bourne, of Greene, Rhode Island, whose case was studied by Prof William James. On January 17, 1887 Bourne drew $551 from a Providence bank intending to buy a plot of land. He awoke in Norristown, Pa, two months later to find that he had opened a candy store under the name of A. J. Brown. He had no recollection of why or how he had wandered from his home. Another clerical victim of dissociation was the Rev Thomas Hanna who, after falling from his carriage onto his head, developed a lively alter personality noted for his proficiency on the banjo. If Sales' theory is a correct one, the Rev Harold Davidson is a lively addition to this gallery of clerical types.

*   *   *

The multiple personality theory as a rationale for Davidson's eccentric behaviour is not as startling as it might appear at first blush. Dr Ludwig and his colleagues maintain that 'all individuals, to some extent, can be "different" people under different circumstances, depending upon their emotional needs and the external situational demands.' 'Perhaps it is not too presumptuous to assume that all individuals, no matter how well adjusted, have at least a touch of multiple personality within them.'[2]

Dr Morton Prince says much the same thing. 'Dissociated and multiple personalities,' he writes, 'are not novel freak phenomena, but are only exaggerations of the normal. They are caricatures, so to speak, of the normal.'[3] In fact it was after reading Dr Prince's study of the celebrated Miss Christine Beauchamp that I became convinced that dissociation was the only possible explanation for the Rev Harold Davidson's strange behaviour. But if this were true then Davidson's trial would be the acid test. How did he behave in

---

[1] Flora Rheta Schreiber. *Sybil.* New York: Warner Paperback Library, 1974.

[2] *Op. cit.*

[3] Morton Prince, M.D. 'The psychogenesis of Multiple Personality.' *The Journal of Abnormal Psychology*, Vol. XIV, No. 4, October, 1919.

the witness-box? Did Davidson's various alter personalities remain quiescent while he was testifying? Or did they come and go like fast-scudding clouds chasing each other across the sky?

The latter was the case, according to J. Rowland Sales, who attended the trial sessions at Church House. 'Sometimes Little Jimmy would appear,' Sales explained, 'to bait the diocesan chancellor who presided at the trial. He would taunt the chancellor by doing a tap-dance in the witness-box, or by rolling up his trouser-leg to show the chancellor where he kept his folding money.' 'At other times in the midst of Little Jimmy's act the real Harold Davidson—the one I call Uncle Harold—would break through to cry out in anguish, "Nobody understands me,' or "I am the victim of evil-minded people," or again, "My whole life's work lies in ruins." The chopping and changing from one personality to another was uncanny,' Sales concluded.

Davidson's one-time manager believed that Uncle Harold was genuinely amnesic concerning certain episodes in his life for which Little Jimmy was responsible ('An expression of amazed disbelief would cross Uncle Harold's face as Little Jimmy's escapades were ascribed to him'). As for that other secondary personality, the Bunco Kid, he, too, made an appearance, according to Sales. In fact at the Stiffkey trial, as will be seen, the barometer house resembled more a weather-vane in a high wind as the Rev Harold Davidson's various personalities, sometimes singly, sometimes as 'co-conscious' entities, came out 'to laugh and grin and dance in their skin by the light of the moon'.

ROSE

'When all was over, Don Quixote ask'd one of
the Nymphs, who it was that compos'd the
entertainment? She answer'd, that it was a certain Clergyman who liv'd in their Town, that
had rare Talent that way.'
CERVANTES, *Don Quixote*, Part II, Book III

2

Genesis

'Elegant', 'impeccable', 'classic', these are some of the adjectives which psychotherapists apply to Dr Morton Prince's 563-page case history of Miss Beauchamp, which, as a study of multiple personality, has never been surpassed in the seventy years since it was written, in the opinion of many.[1] Christine Beauchamp, the subject of this pioneer study, was a 23-year-old student of Boston, Massachusetts, and 'a neurasthenic of an extreme type' when she first came to Dr Prince in 1898. For the next seven years Dr Prince, a Harvard professor of abnormal psychology, had her under observation, noting her chameleon-like changes. For Christine was not one, but three personalities, each with its own distinctive views, habits, experiences, and memories. For convenience the Harvard professor labelled the trio as the Realist, Sally, and the Saint, the last most closely corresponding to the original Miss Beauchamp, who gave herself holier-than-thou airs.

Of these 'somnambulistic personages' who inhabited Christine the one known as Sally was by far the most intriguing. Dr Prince writes that Sally was 'such a bizarre character . . . that the transformation from one of the other personalities to herself is one of the most striking and dramatic features of the case.' Elsewhere the professor described Sally as 'a mischievous delightful child, loving the outdoor breezy life, free from all ideas of responsibility and care.' In other words Sally represented a reversion to childhood—to the complexes and reactions of that period—on Christine's part.

Sally was unique in another respect in that she alone of the secondary personalities knew about their previous lives. Only Sally was 'co-conscious', to use a term coined by Dr Prince; that is, only she knew what the others were thinking at any given time, and she used this knowledge to play merry hell with their lives. She kept

[1] Morton Prince, M.D. *The Dissociation of a Personality*. New York: Longmans, Green, and Company, 1906.

the other selves awake at night with her childish prattle (she claimed never to sleep). By means of automatic writing she sent them insulting notes. She even hallucinated the Saint into thinking she saw spiders, snakes and toads. February, 1900 saw Miss Beauchamp in a sad state of disarray: the Saint was trying to join a convent, the Realist had taken laudanum in an unsuccessful suicide bid, while Sally jeered from the sidelines.

It was the total absence of fear in Sally's make-up which put me in mind of the Rev Harold Davidson and of his doppelganger Little Jimmy. Dr Prince instances not only Sally's handling of spiders and snakes, creatures which were abhorrent to the Saint, but such examples as Sally 'climbing out on the eaves of the roof and preparing to jump from the fifth-storey window, without apparently experiencing the slightest fear'.[1] Davidson had an abnormal fear of animals, even of his wife's dogs; yet he was absolutely fearless when it came to standing up to a ponce armed with a flick-knife, or to a professional strongman, it will be recalled.

But as I read Dr Prince's study it was when it dealt with Sally's genesis that I was most struck by the resemblance of this elfin personality to Little Jimmy. Sally represented the 'play instinct' in rebellion. She was in revolt against the more serious side of Miss Beauchamp's nature, and against the pressures on her from outside to conform. 'Even her fondness for and habit of teasing and mischief, much to the discomfiture of her other selves, was merely an expression of this (i.e. the play) instinct,' Dr Prince writes.[2] But it was because the play instinct was repressed that Sally suddenly emerged to bedevil Miss Beauchamp.

Something very similar must have happened in the case of Harold Francis Davidson, who was born in Sholing, a suburb of Southampton, on July 14, 1875. Little Jimmy must have manifested himself at a very early age in response to the play instinct being suppressed, for all spontaneity and joyous feeling were crushed out of the youthful Davidson by his strict Victorian upbringing.

*　　*　　*

[1] Morton Prince, M.D. 'Miss Beauchamp, The Psychogenesis of Multiple Personality.' *Journal of Abnormal Psychology*, Vol. XV, June–September, 1920.
[2] *Ibid.*

When Harold's father, the Rev Francis Davidson, came to Sholing (pop. 1,200) as vicar in 1866, this dreary suburb contained a lawless element which may have derived from its proximity to the marshland known as Botany Bay, then used as a staging area for convicts being transported to Australia. Convicts and gipsies—for Sholing (which means 'Wood by the Shore' in Old English) was winter quarters for the romanies who picked hops in Kent in the summer. The more law-abiding inhabitants worked as coal heavers at the Southampton docks, but even these had little time for 'soul savers', as they contemptuously referred to parsons. Thus the Davidson family were not only condemned to genteel poverty (the living was worth no more than £120 per annum), but found themselves totally isolated in a decaying community. This the Rev Francis Davidson endured for forty-eight years, preaching each Sunday to a half-empty church.

Like his son, the Rev Francis Davidson was a tiny man, but with a luxuriant beard that gave him the appearance of a gnome as he made the rounds of his parish on a tricycle. The gnome, however, made up in courage what he lacked in stature. 'He never hesitated to point out to drunken husbands the error of their ways,' writes the Rev Harry Marsh, Sholing's vicar from 1960 to 1971. 'It happened occasionally that one of the drunken husbands threatened to throw the vicar in the pond,' he adds, 'but this doesn't seem to have intimidated Francis Davidson at all.'[1] As for his religious views, Davidson *père* was broad evangelical, he being of those who equate faith with good works. 'The Rev Francis Davidson was most generous to tramps,' writes a former parishioner. 'He was never known to turn anyone away from his door, no matter how unlikely his story.'

Twenty-seven members of the Davidson family were in Holy Orders, and his father was determined that Harold should be the twenty-eighth. The boy's vocation therefore was taken for granted, and he was brought up as one of God's anointed. He was not allowed to play with the coal heavers' sons, nor with the numerous progeny of the gipsies, for fear that these 'little ruffians' would somehow contaminate him. Harold's mother counted for little in

---

[1] For this and other information concerning Davidson *père* I am indebted to the pamphlet compiled by the Rev Harry Marsh on the occasion of St Mary's, Sholing celebrating its centenary.

these decisions for the simple reason that she was stricken with puerperal fever after the birth of Harold's sister Alice, and took to her bed an invalid to remain there the rest of her life.

At the age of six Harold Davidson was enrolled as a day pupil at Banister Court School in Southampton, which was founded primarily for the sons of officers of the Peninsular and Oriental Line. Here he made friends with Ernest Du Domaine, who played the fiddle, and with J. Maundy Gregory, who was a fiddler of a different sort.[1] But even Banister Court was considered too rough for young Harold. Indeed, from contemporary descriptions Banister Court sounds like a forcing house for juvenile delinquents. In rugby, for example, the boys were encouraged to kick one another in the scrimmages ('You were not supposed to have played well unless your legs were well marked,' remarks Christopher Ellaby, nephew of the school's founder, in the *Banister Court Magazine*). Masters played rugby alongside the boys, and Cummings, one of the former, broke a leg while playing in a school match, and afterwards 'was never really of much use', adds Ellaby, who himself tore a tendon while playing against a rival team called the Pirates.

Whether or not it was to spare him from being maimed for life, young Harold was whisked away from Banister Court, and in January, 1890 enrolled at Whitgift School in Croydon, where his two maiden aunts, Gertrude and Alice Hodgskin, lived. They were the second important influence in his life.

Maiden aunts such as the Hodgskin sisters were a feature of middle-class Victorian life. Creatures with wills of iron and astounding longevity, they sublimated their 'darker feelings' by alternately spoiling and bossing their male kinsfolk, always in the kindliest way imaginable. In particular, Aunt Gertrude, who was born in 1857, the year of the Indian Mutiny, indulged a strong taste for dynastic cannibalism by staying with her adored nephew long after he had married and had become the rector of Stiffkey; and in turn, by having his children, her great-nieces and great-nephews, stay with her in Windsor, where she eventually retired. Thus from an early age Harold Davidson's world was a matriarchal

[1] Maundy Gregory became notorious for selling knighthoods and baronetcies under Lloyd George. But before that he and Davidson went into partnership in 1908 in a revival of the musical *Dorothy*, a theatrical venture in which Davidson lost his socks. The full story is told in the author's *Maundy Gregory, Purveyor of Honours*.

one. 'He was smothered by sublimated sex, deafened by the rustle of crinoline,' is the way J. Rowland Sales expressed it.

*   *   *

The Whitgift Foundation was created in 1596 by Queen Elizabeth's 'little black husband', as she playfully called Archbishop Whitgift of Canterbury. Originally it consisted of a fee-paying grammar school, an Elizabethan 'hospital for aged pensioners', and a middle school for 'children of the parish of Croydon of the poorer sort'. The grammar school, in which Davidson was enrolled, catered for superior tradesmen's sons who were thought to be too good for the elementary schools, but not clever enough for King Edward's School.

From the outset Davidson had no time for study, his interests being all extracurricular. He wrote a chess column for the school magazine, captained the cycling club, played cricket for the first XI (this despite an unwillingness to stand up to fast bowling). He also appears to have been the recipient of an extraordinary amount of indulgence on the part of his masters, for it was his boast that he was never on time for class more than five or six times a term. (His lack of punctuality may have been inherited from his father, whose churchwarden, after watching the gnome's vain efforts to catch up with a funeral cortege, remarked, 'The only funeral the vicar won't be late for will be his own.')

Whitgift saw the late flowering of Little Jimmy, the hobgoblin that was born of Davidson's repressive upbringing, and that was at war with all that was serious-minded. Something similar happened in the case of Miss Beauchamp who, when she came to school age, was torn by the conflict between the play instinct as represented by Sally, and a hunger for learning on the part of the Saint who, we are told by Dr Prince, spent most of her time 'curled up in the garret . . . with her books and day-dreams and visions'. Thanks to the mischievous Sally, the Saint found herself playing truant against her will, and being punished for it by being made to stand in front of her class with a dunce's cap on her head.

In Davidson's case the rebellion was against his father's determination that he should win a scholarship to university in order to study for Holy Orders (there was no question of the Rev Francis Davidson paying for the boy's tuition out of his meagre stipend).

[29]

The scholarship in turn was dependent upon young Harold doing well in his examinations, which was where Little Jimmy came in. Little Jimmy saw that his alter ego not only did poorly in the exams, but that he got temporarily sidetracked in his choice of career. For Davidson suddenly developed a craze for the theatre, decided that he wanted nothing so much as to become a stage comic.

Davidson's enthusiasm for the stage was spurred by his friendship with another Whitgift boy, Leon Quartermaine, who was destined to make a name for himself as a Shakespearean actor.[1] In February, 1894 they appeared together in a farce, *Sent to the Tower*, Davidson taking the part of Perkyn Pudifoot, a pastry cook. In the second part of the programme Davidson did a solo turn reciting the comic monologues of George Grossmith. In March, 1895, barely seven months after he had left school, the *Whitgift Magazine* announced that H. F. Davidson 'who has already met with some success in the provinces' was to make his London debut at Steinway Hall, Lower Seymour Street, on Tuesday, March 26, 1895 at 8 p.m. 'We understand,' the announcement stated, 'that the recital will be over in time to enable any Croydon friends who may wish to encourage the young reciter by their presence to catch the 10.5 train from Victoria.' Little Jimmy was letting no grass grow under his feet.

*　　*　　*

'As an entertainer I belong to the era before jazz, bridge, and Noël Coward,' Davidson once told a reporter, to which catalogue he might have added Mah-Jongg, cocktail parties, and the Bright Young Things. Indeed, there is nothing today which even approximates to the 'drawing-room entertainer', or 'society performer', as he was sometimes called, the narrow genre of the theatrical profession to which Davidson belonged. The closest thing today would be the stand-up comic playing the working men's clubs in the north, with one vital difference. Whereas today's stand-up comic depends upon 'blue' jokes to get his laughs, the drawing-room entertainer's humour was free of all suggestiveness. 'Ours is the

---

[1] Quartermaine also appeared in modern plays, playing Osborne in the Broadway production of *Journey's End*.

only performance of a dramatic nature that the Catholic clergy are allowed to attend,' boasted Richard Corney Grain, one of the drollest of the society performers, who deemed it a great compliment when a bishop remarked after witnessing his performance, 'Mr Grain, I have not only been amused, I have been edified.'

The drawing-room entertainer bloomed briefly at the end of the 19th century in answer to the demand of a rising middle class which was neither cultured nor resourceful, but which wanted desperately to be diverted. Instead of hiring a string quartet or a coloratura soprano, as the landed gentry did for their routs, these parvenus engaged the services of Albert Chevalier to sing 'It's the Nasty Way 'e Ses it', and 'The Future Mrs 'Awkins', and George ('Gee Gee') Grossmith to give his comic recitations. Harold Davidson did not belong to this league, but he did well in the provinces playing masonic lodges and the Literary and Mechanics' Institutes which were the forerunners of today's working-men's clubs. But it was as 'Charley's Aunt' ('I'm Charley's Aunt from Brazil where the nuts come from') in a touring production of that farce that young Davidson scored his greatest hit. There have been many notable 'aunts' down the years from W. S. Penley to Ray Bolger, and not forgetting Arthur Askey, but physically at least Davidson was ideal for the rôle. One can picture the future rector of Stiffkey got up in fichu and mittens, and with corkscrew curls pinned to his bonnet, being chased round the piano, by Mr Spettigue, or, in a sly aside, convulsing his audience with, 'I say, what devils we women are!'

*　　*　　*

Little Jimmy did not have things all his own way. The free and easy life Little Jimmy had chosen as a drawing-room entertainer had brought him into sharp conflict with that other Davidson, Uncle Harold, who was very much the creature of his father's and Aunt Gertrude's upbringing. Depending upon which of his personalities happened to be out of the barometer house at the time, Davidson indulged in mild forms of dissipation, or did volunteer social work ('Whenever I was on tour I used to call on the vicar of the town we were in and find out the names of old people who liked to be visited and have the Bible read to them,' he told a reporter, in explanation of the latter occupation). But then such antipodal behaviour is not unusual in victims of multiple personality. In

[31]

switching from the Saint to Sally, for example, Miss Beauchamp
sometimes 'indulges tastes which a moment before would have
been abhorrent to her ideals, and undoes or destroys what she had
laboriously planned,' as Dr Prince points out.[1]

Two events strengthened Uncle Harold in his ascendancy over
Little Jimmy. The first, which occurred shortly after Davidson had
started out as an actor, was like one of those flashes of lightning
that illumine a whole unsuspected landscape. But let Davidson tell
it in his own words. 'I was walking along the Thames Embank-
ment,' he writes, 'in a very thick London fog . . . when I was lucky
enough to rescue a girl 16½ years old who had tried to jump into the
river for the purpose of self-destruction. She turned out to be a girl
who had run away from her home in a little village near Cambridge
ten days before, hoping to get a job of work in London, and had
met with tragically unhappy experiences, after the money she had
brought away from home with her was spent.' 'Her pitiful story
made a tremendous impression upon me,' adds Davidson, who
gave the girl her fare home and a letter to take to her mother. 'I
have ever since, whenever I had any spare time in town, kept my
eyes open for opportunities to help that type of girl, namely, the
country girl stranded on the alluring streets of London.'[2]

Whether or not the 19-year-old Davidson then realised it, he had
found his life's mission. Davidson himself is sketchy about the
details—whether he fished the girl from the Thames, or merely
dissuaded her from jumping into the river—but one thing is certain: one is witnessing the birth of a myth. Thereafter every girl
Davidson met in London, no matter how much she might have
been marked by the asphalt jungle, was a 'country girl' in his eyes,
and as such in dire peril of succumbing to the 'allure of the streets'.
Also, *mirabile dictu*, such girls tended to be sixteen, the golden
mean. So far as Davidson was concerned, girls simply ceased to
grow at the age of sixteen.

*   *   *

The second event, which occurred later, but which was not un-
connected with the Thames rescue, was Davidson's decision to

[1] *Dissociation of a Personality*.
[2] Harold F. Davidson. *The Reason Why*. London: Deane Printing
Works, 1934.

study for Holy Orders at Exeter College, Oxford, and thus to resume a course of action which had been interrupted by the vagaries of Little Jimmy. In this he was assisted by the Rev Basil Wilberforce, son of the Bishop of Oxford, grandson of the abolitionist, William Wilberforce, and himself a friend of the Davidson family. As a leading exponent of teetotalism, Basil Wilberforce had taken an interest in Harold Davidson ever since the latter had signed the temperance pledge.

Young Harold for his part was inspired by the example of Wilberforce in extending the hand of fellowship to the most wretched in society. Thus, in July, 1899 Wilberforce, who was then chaplain of the House of Commons, sought unsuccessfully a reprieve for Mary Ann Ansell, an 18-year-old servant girl, due to be hanged for poisoning her sister, an inmate of a lunatic asylum. Quite obviously there was insanity in the family, but the girl was executed despite Wilberforce's plea to the Home Secretary. 'On the day fixed for the execution,' writes his biographer, 'Wilberforce and his wife went early in the morning to the house in north London where the girl's parents lived. When the fatal hour approached, Wilberforce, kneeling in the midst of the weeping family, conducted a service of intercession for the departing spirit.'[1]

Wilberforce, who was an alumnus of Exeter College, where he had taken his doctorate, was able to be of practical help in getting Davidson, despite his lack of academic qualifications, admitted to Exeter College starting with the Michaelmas term, 1898.

It took Davidson five years instead of the customary three to get his bachelor's degree, one reason being that while keeping terms he continued to accept theatrical engagements in order to finance his studies, having received special permission from the college rector to do this. Thus he packed a copy of Tacitus or Cicero with him in his make-up kit, along with the grease-paint, the spirit gum, the crepe hair. Another reason for the delay was the reappearance of Little Jimmy. Reginald Kennedy-Cox, Davidson's closest friend at Oxford, paints a picture of Little Jimmy at his maddest in describing how the imp on one occasion bearded the Vice-Chancellor about some trivial matter. 'The Vice-Chancellor was racked with excruciating pains of gout, quite the wrong time to interview him,'

[1] G. W. E. Russell. *Basil Wilberforce: A Memoir*. London: John Murray, 1917.

Kennedy-Cox writes, 'but with his usual ill-chosen judgment my friend slipped by the Vice-Chancellor's butler and ran up to the invalid's bed.'[1]

Little Jimmy also made sure that Davidson was ploughed in exams by seeing that he turned up late for them. 'He would insist upon ending his half-finished examination papers with an elaborate and detailed invitation to his examiners to come to tea with him in his rooms,' Kennedy-Cox writes. There they would be able 'to satisfy themselves as to his knowledge upon the subjects which he had been much too late to tackle'.[2] Having failed to pass Classical Moderations on his first try, Davidson was given a year's grace; but doing no better the second time he was asked in March, 1901 to remove his name from the books at Exeter. Thereupon he moved to Grindle's Hall, a forcing house for backward students, many of them Oxford Blues, who could not pass exams.

Quite obviously Davidson's contemporaries (fellow undergraduates at Exeter included the poet Alfred Noyes and a future Lord Justice of Appeal, Herbert du Parcq) regarded him as an oddball, his isolation being heightened by the fact that he was at least five years older than the majority of them. Davidson did achieve some extracurricular distinction by becoming president of the Oxford Chess Club, and captaining an Oxford–Cambridge Chess team which beat a combined American universities' team during his final year; but he laboured under one insuperable social disability. His teetotalism put him beyond the pale. Not only did it bar him from such Exeter dining clubs as the Leonids and the Adelphi, but it excluded him from much else of college social life besides.

'The Bad Men went up to London and womanised,' writes Compton Mackenzie, another of Davidson's contemporaries at Oxford. 'The Good Eggs went up to London and got drunk; and if they womanised no one must know anything about it.'[3] Harold Davidson fell between two stools, for his abstention applied to women as well (jokes about 'Harold's Harmless Harem' referred to photographs of stage beauties, many of them autographed, which

[1] Reginald Kennedy-Cox. *An Autobiography*. London: Hodder and Stoughton, 1931.
[2] *Ibid.*
[3] Compton Mackenzie. *Sinister Street*. London: Martin Secker, 1913.

he had pinned up on the walls of his digs in Walton Street). Davidson did nothing about his love life that is until Miss Horniman's
theatrical company played Oxford, and he met Molly Cassandra
Saurin, who was a member of that company.[1]

They met through Kennedy-Cox, who as a leading light of the
Oxford University Dramatic Society, entertained such celebrities
as passed through Oxford (Fred Terry, W. S. Penley, and Albert
Chevalier were frequent guests at his King Edward Street digs).
Davidson was greatly taken with Molly's beauty. Molly for her
part appears to have been dazzled by Davidson's charm if not by
his intellect ('Mr Davidson is a very clever man,' she was to say
later, adding, 'He has made but poor use of the keen brain he
possesses'). They became engaged while Davidson still had two
more years to study for his degree.

They were to wait six years before marrying, six stormy years
during which Molly, her Irish temper getting the better of her,
broke off the engagement more than once. 'Had it not been for
Aunt Gertrude, whom I adored, I would never have married your
father,' Mrs Davidson used to tell her son Nugent. 'Aunt Gertrude
talked me into it.' Aunt Gertrude, that dynastic carnivore, talked
long and earnestly to her nephew as well, one may be sure. The
hitch was partly due to the Bishop of Oxford's reluctance to ordain
Davidson priest, he having failed both the intermediate and final
examinations on his first try.

The Rev Harold Davidson's first curacy was Holy Trinity,
Windsor, where he was also assistant chaplain to the Household
Cavalry stationed at Combermere Barracks (there appears to be no
foundation for the suggestion made by one of my correspondents
that Davidson began his rescue work here by consoling the cavalry-
men's cast-off girl friends). In 1905 he was transferred as assistant
curate to St Martin's-in-the-Fields, London, where 'his high purpose, his ardent enthusiasm, and his social gifts' attracted notice in
the parish magazine. Then in May, 1906, in strange circumstances
which will be related presently, he was presented to the living of

---

[1] Annie Horniman (1860–1937), the daughter of a wealthy tea merchant,
backed the first commercial production of Shaw's *Arms and the Man* in
1894. Ten years later she joined W. B. Yeats and Lady Gregory in founding the Abbey Theatre, Dublin. But she is best known as the founder of
the Gaiety Theatre in Manchester, where Sybil Thorndike and Lewis
Casson, among others, got their first start.

Stiffkey in Norfolk. At last he was free to take Molly for his bride, which he did in October, 1906. After a honeymoon in Paris, Davidson brought Molly home to the village with which his name will ever be linked.

3

Stiffkey Blues

Stiffkey must be one of the few villages in England that cannot boast a single pub, though there were three in the Rev Harold Davidson's day, the last to close its doors being The Townshend Arms. The local, with its warmth and conviviality, is usually at the heart of village life. But not so at Stiffkey. Those of its 378 inhabitants who are thirsty must trudge four miles to The Anchor in neighbouring Morston for their pint. Stiffkey has deteriorated in other ways. Did its clocks, one wonders, stop running on the twenty-first day of October, 1932 when the man who had been its rector for twenty-six years was 'removed, deposed and degraded' from his offices?

Stiffkey's flint and beach-stone cottages with their red-tiled roofs straggle along either side of the A149, but the visitor is not encouraged to tarry to admire them. Should he do so he risks being sideswiped by motorists whizzing by on their way to Wells-Next-the-Sea, for Stiffkey has no proper footpaths. No main drains nor street-lighting either, so far as I could make out. Stiffkey is a withdrawn, inward-looking community, a village of secrets. 'The East Anglian is, of all the inhabitants of these islands, most wanting in native courtesy,' writes the Rev Augustus Jessopp, who was rector of a Norfolk parish for over thirty years, and who could almost have had Stiffkey in mind.[1] How much of the East Anglian's boorishness is due to his Viking ancestry Jessopp does not venture to speculate, but he adds that 'a wrong, real or imagined, rankles within him [the Norfolk peasant] through a lifetime'.

In the case of Stiffkey the grievance which its inhabitants nurture is real enough, as I discovered in talking to an old-timer in The Hero of Norfolk pub near Burnham Thorpe, where Nelson was born.

[1] Augustus Jessopp, D.D. *The Trials of a Country Parson*. London: T. Fisher Unwin, 1890.

'Stiffkey is the village where the women wear the pants,' the old-timer, a retired postman, informed me, letting the secret out of the bag. 'It's the original home of women's lib,' he pursued. Apparently the women of Stiffkey burnt their camisoles long before Germaine Greer was born, or bras were even invented; and that is why the village has been made the butt of so many jokes. Stiffkey's matri-archal set-up grew out of cockle-gathering, which was the village's sole means of livelihood, but which was considered to be women's work. So while their menfolk stayed at home and smoked their clay pipes, the women waded out into the saltings with their baskets to gather that variety of succulent bivalves known as 'Stewkey Blues'. ('Stewkey', incidentally, refers only to the cockles, not to the vil-lage, whose name 'Stiffkey' is pronounced exactly as it is spelt, according to the people who live there.)

Big, strapping amazons they were, these cocklers with their petticoats hitched up round their waists and their bare legs mottled by the biting winds, according to William A. Dutt, a traveller in Norfolk at the turn of the century. 'They collect such heavy loads of shellfish that they can hardly carry them . . . staggering under their weight,' he writes. The cocklers apparently resented Peeping Toms, for Dutt observes, possibly from first-hand experience, that 'a too-inquisitive male intruder sometimes meets with a rather dis-comfiting reception.' Revisiting Stiffkey in 1932, the year of David-son's trial, Dutt recalls that 'the inhabitants of Stiffkey have been accused of being a degenerate folk, more especially some of the men, who are said to be content to live on the hard-won earnings of their wives and daughters.'[1]

It was Davidson's bad luck, I reflected, to have landed in the midst of a matriarchy—Davidson, who had not only been brought up by domineering women, but had married one. Paradoxically, the harder he tried to flee from such matriarchs the more he appeared to be rushing into their arms.

* * *

Stiffkey hugs its secrets to itself closely, and none more closely than the story of how Harold Davidson got the rectorship. Not

[1] William A. Dutt. *The Norfolk and Suffolk Coast.* London: T. Fisher Unwin, 1909. *Highways and Byways in East Anglia.* London: Macmillan and Company, 1932.

surprisingly, it was through a woman that he got the living, but
Gladys Sutherst was no local amazon with hands roughened from
cockle-gathering. No, Gladys was a stage-struck, 18-year-old
beauty with ambitions. The fact that she was stage-struck in itself
was enough to bring Gladys to Davidson's notice—was he not the
self-appointed father confessor of showgirls?—but he knew her
father, Thomas Sutherst, a company promoter from Yorkshire who
had gone bankrupt owing £250,000 in debts. (Some idea of
Sutherst's probity may be gleaned from the fact that a jury, without
leaving the jury-box, found in favour of an editor whom Sutherst
sued for libel for calling him a 'financial juggler', 'consummate
scoundrel', and 'unmitigated rascal'.)

As for Gladys's ambitions, early in 1905 she made up her mind
to marry the 6th Marquess Townshend, who was twenty years her
senior, but who came from one of England's most distinguished
families (a Townshend had sailed with Drake against the Spanish
Armada, another had been present at the Siege of Cadiz). The joke
was that the marquess, who was land poor, thought that in Gladys
he would be marrying a millionaire's daughter (the marquess actually paid a marriage broker £2,500 for his introduction to Miss
Sutherst). To complicate matters, the nobleman's family threatened
to have him certified as insane if he went through with the marriage.

Into this delicate situation which had all of the elements of high
Restoration comedy stepped the Rev Harold Davidson, who was
then only an assistant curate. Whether Davidson acted as peace-
maker between the marquess and his family, or encouraged the
former to defy the latter, is not clear. What is clear is that on August
9, 1905 Davidson united the marquess and Miss Sutherst in marriage at St Martin's-in-the-Fields, London. Davidson got his reward when in May, 1906 he was presented to the plural living of
Stiffkey with Morston, which was in the gift of the marquess. The
Stiffkey/Morston living was worth £503 per annum, later increased
to £800 during Davidson's incumbency, and included the rectory
and 60 acres of glebe. This was very handsome indeed. In 1939
nearly half of the Church of England's 12,719 livings in England
and Wales were worth less than £400 per annum, and as late as
1962 many C. of E. clergymen were subsisting on £600 a year,
which was less than a bus driver's wages.[1]

---

[1] C. L. Mowat. *Britain Between the Wars, 1918–1940* (1955); and
Anthony Sampson. *Anatomy of Britain* (1962).

In August, 1906, or exactly one year after his marriage, the 6th marquess, after a hearing before a lunacy commission, was found to be technically sane, but incapable of managing his own affairs, which were taken out of his hands. Commenting editorially on the scandalous nature of the lunacy proceedings, *The Times* had this to say: '. . . a reader of the reports of the proceedings might well have been at a loss to know whether the Court was not sitting in bankruptcy, or as an ancillary to the Divorce Court, or as a Court of morals.'[1]

The Rev Harold Davidson's rôle in this murky affair is difficult to fathom. Compton Mackenzie writes of the newly-minted rector calling on him in London in a carriage and pair with a footman on the box, and announcing, 'I'm helping Lady Townshend,' which would indicate that Davidson was firmly in Gladys's camp. ('I cannot recall a more surprising sight than that minute parson bobbing about in that landau with a marquess's coronet on it,' Mackenzie adds.) On the other hand, a letter from Davidson to the 6th marquess dated January 5, 1906 and read at the latter's sanity hearing indicates that Davidson offered his services as mediator in an effort to patch up the marriage. 'As you know, your wedding was the first I ever solemnised,' writes Davidson. 'My anxiety that it would be happy and in every way successful is thus increased.' Davidson might almost have had his own stormy courtship in mind in discoursing about 'the small differences that often arise in the process of dovetailing together into one two characters that have hitherto developed on separate lines.' As a mark of her favour the Marchioness Townshend was one of the witnesses who signed the register on October 9, 1906 when Davidson married Molly Saurin with Dr Arthur Winnington-Ingram, the Lord Bishop of London, officiating.

*　　*　　*

A repository of secrets Stiffkey was and is, yet what could have

---

[1] Of the principals involved Thomas Sutherst was among the 1,198 passengers and crew who went down with the *Lusitania* when the Cunarder was torpedoed by a German U-boat in May, 1915. The 6th Marquess Townshend, who shared Charles II's passion for collecting clocks, died in November, 1921. (On the day of his death all twenty-six clocks at Raynham Hall, the Townshend family seat, were said to have stopped.)

been less secretive than life at the rectory during the Rev Harold Davidon's incumbency? Although screened from the road by shrubbery, the 20-room, flintstone rectory with its severe neo-classical front was an open book to the villagers, who never ceased to marvel at the strange goings-on inside it.[1] 'There were never fewer than thirteen people staying at the house, and sometimes there were double that number,' Nugent Davidson tells me, adding, 'None of the doors was ever locked, which meant that people could walk in and out of your room at any time, and frequently did, without knocking.' This lack of privacy was confirmed to me by J. Rowland Sales, who spent a week-end at the rectory and found that while none of its windows had curtains, some had broken panes through which rags had been stuffed to keep out the cold. One of the guests kept rabbits in his room, according to Sales.

Paying guests included Ernest Du Domaine, Davidson's school chum from Banister Court days, who, now a retired colonel in the Canadian Army and a widower, camped out in one wing of the rectory with his two sons. But the rectory was populated mostly by non-paying transients, strays whom Davidson had picked up in one capacity or another. Typical was Mrs Felice Allman, whom Davidson met at a London tea party, and on the strength of a few minutes of conversation invited to Stiffkey to recuperate from a bout of influenza. Mrs Allman stayed six weeks. As Davidson became more and more engrossed in his work as the Prostitutes' Padre the rectory came to resemble a nature cure for fallen women.

Brooding over this bizarre menage was Molly Davidson, who came from the Irish landed gentry as she never tired of reminding listeners. Molly's father was Michael J. J. Saurin, a wealthy land-owner and a justice of the peace in West Meath; and as a girl she had been accustomed to ordering servants about on her father's estates at Harristown, Garballaugh, and Mullafin. When she came of age she was presented at the Court of St James. In the studio

---

As for Gladys, the Marchioness Townshend, she remarried, became the Lady Mayoress of Lynn and later was elected the first woman president of the Royal Norfolk Agricultural Association.

[1] In later years the rectory served as residence for the Suffragan Bishop of Lynn until in June, 1973 it was sold at auction for £81,000. Its present owner is Aubrey Buxton, a director of Anglia TV, and an authority on wild life.

photograph taken on this occasion Molly, with the three ostrich plumes pinned to her hair, looks somewhat like a startled cockatoo, yet it is apparent that she was a real beauty. Her hair was ash blonde, though the photograph makes it appear darker, her eyes of a deep blue, and she had that fresh pink-and-white complexion for which the Irish are noted. 'Mother retained her beauty even in old age,' Nugent tells me. 'Her face was scarcely wrinkled.'

'I'll be a good mother to Mr Davidson's children, but I won't be a country parson's wife,' Molly used to say, from which it may be inferred that she held herself aloof from the villagers. As for the children, they arrived at two-yearly intervals starting with Sheilagh in 1907, and followed by Nugent, Patricia, and Arnold. As soon as they were old enough, the girls were packed off to a convent in Cheltenham at Molly's expense (she had a small inheritance from her father), while the boys won choral scholarships, Nugent to Magdalen College, Oxford, Arnold to Christ Church, Cambridge. This meant that the children missed out on the bitter quarrels between their parents.

For Molly was possessed of a fiery temper, inherited from her father, which made life difficult for those round her. 'When mother was annoyed with us children she would say, "Your grandfather would have horse-whipped a groom for much less," ' Nugent recalls. In particular, the Rev Harold Davidson roused Molly's fury by his rock-like placidity, born of the conviction that he was always right. 'It is useless,' Molly once remarked, 'to tell a lunatic who says that he is a poached egg that he is not one, for he will exhaust your logic and outstrip your reasoning powers.' All of which did not prevent her from engaging in arguments of the poached egg variety. As Molly was hard of hearing guests who were staying at the rectory when a quarrel occurred were soon privy to the nature of it ('Mother had this peculiarity that the moment you started talking to her she would switch off her hearing aid,' Nugent explains).

Mostly the quarrels were about 'lame cats', as Molly called them ('My mission is to help lame dogs over stiles,' the rector would insist, but Molly thought 'lame cats' more appropriate). Specifically, Molly objected to the rectory being run as a Fresh Air Farm for Lame Cats. Other than to put them to work in the scullery, Molly refused to have anything to do with these waifs whom Davidson brought home, 'the vilest dregs of humanity', as she called them. 'No man can associate with such dregs without having some of the vileness rub off on himself,' she would tell the rector. 'The rottenness permeates the mind, destroying all that is healthy and clean,' she would insist. To all of which the unruffled rector would reply, 'Christ did it—He was known to associate with publicans and sinners.' 'Yes, but you are not Christ,' Mrs Davidson would remind her husband, having read his lips. Then she would switch on her hearing aid, which would begin to sputter as a signal that the argument was finished.

* * *

It was partly to avoid such bickering that the Rev Harold Davidson took to spending six days out of seven in London, usually catching the last train for Wells-Next-the-Sea on Saturday night, and often arriving at Stiffkey with barely time to slip into a surplice before taking matins. The villagers used to joke that it was best not to die on a Monday, especially in summer, for one's remains could get pretty high by the time the rector arrived the following weekend to officiate at the funeral. And not only burials, but marriages and baptisms awaited the rector's pleasure. Similarly I was told that the only time Davidson ever spent seven consecutive days in his parish was during the general strike in May, 1926, and that was because the trains were not running.

And so, armed with a permissive licence from his bishop to do pastoral work outside his parish, Davidson invaded the capital. At first he confined his social work to underprivileged boys in London's East End, organising a Newsboys' Club, whose objects were 'to safeguard boys living in criminal surroundings', and 'to discourage boys from vicious habits and associates', then turning his attention to apprentice lads as being in danger of having their morals undermined.

Davidson's most notable contribution in this field, however, was as a trustee of the London Dockland Settlement founded by his friend Reginald Kennedy-Cox. 'My first real helper down at the Docks was the result of his introduction,' writes Kennedy-Cox, paying tribute to Davidson as 'a man with a heart of gold, outstanding ability, boundless energy, and overwhelming sympathy.'[1]

[1] *Op. cit.*

[43]

Davidson not only found helpers for the dockland work, but money as well. 'I got Lord Crewe to act with me, and then I roped in Lord Beatty,' he boasted later, referring to the Marquess of Crewe, who held Cabinet posts in pre-World War I governments, and to Earl Beatty, who commanded the Grand Fleet during the 1914–18 war. According to Nugent Davidson, his father's zeal attracted the notice of Queen Mary, who was interested in the Dockland Settlement. 'Whenever Queen Mary visited the settlement she always made it a point to ask Kennedy-Cox, "And how is our little rector getting on?" ' Nugents tells me. 'This continued even after father had been brought to trial.'

But London, so far as Davidson was concerned, was not confined to free boots and blanket societies, and to outings in Epping Forest for snotty-nosed boys. The bright lights of West London's theatre-land, which Davidson had known as a stage-struck youth, soon beckoned to him. And here he entered an entirely different world. It was a world of Gaiety girls, Savoy revivals, pantomime at the Drury Lane, and ballet at the Alhambra, for the Edwardian theatre was then in its heyday. It was the world, too, of Pinero Shaw and Ibsen, and of Mrs Patrick Campbell, who reigned as the undisputed queen of tragedy. Reacting to such stimuli, Davidson gradually dropped his interest in the apprentice lads, and began to haunt stage doors as a chaplain accredited to the Actors' Church Union.

In its early days the Actors' Church Union was criticised, not without cause, as affording 'artistically-minded curates' an excuse to 'take tea openly with a pretty woman'. Indeed, visiting pretty women backstage in order to look after their spiritual welfare appears to have been the principal activity of A.C.U. chaplains in the beginning, the record for such visitations being held by one Rev W. E. Kingsbury who, from 1906 to 1912, held tête-à-têtes with 1,847 actresses in their dressing-rooms, according to his own reckoning.[1] It was a record easily shattered by the Rev Harold Davidson, whose calling card soon became familiar to every stage doorman.

But it was not only on spiritual matters that Davidson went backstage; he went behind scenes in order to feast his eyes on

---

[1] Donald Hole. *The Church and the Stage*. London: The Faith Press, Ltd., 1934.

pretty girls in various stages of undress, according to Bert Ross, historian of the British Music Hall Society. 'He would ogle the girls as they stripped for a quick change,' Ross tells me. 'He was caught doing this more than once, and was actually barred from some theatres.'

Although the incident belongs to a later period, Bruce Hamilton, now living in Brighton, tells me that when his sister Diana Hamilton was playing in *Outward Bound* at the Garrick she was puzzled by a middle-aged clergyman who used to visit her in her dressing-room. 'She described him as rather endearing, but a bit of a nuisance because he didn't seem to take hints when it was time for him to go.' It was not until the Stiffkey scandal broke that she recognised the clergyman from press photographs as Davidson.

The rector sometimes stood in the wings practically onstage, much to the intense annoyance of stage managers and electricians, according to Kennedy-Cox. 'One would view from the audience . . . a clearly defined and rather odd clerical shadow reflected by strong limelight, and marring perhaps a particularly beautiful scene,' Kennedy-Cox writes.

Was it Davidson who cast the shadow, one wonders, or was it Little Jimmy, that repressed play instinct? It was the doppelganger, it will be recalled, who had dictated Davidson's choice of the theatre as a career in the first instance, and Little Jimmy had never been happy either in the pulpit at Stiffkey or among the do-gooders in London's dockland. With the outbreak of the 1914–18 war, Davidson volunteered to serve as a chaplain with the Royal Navy, as much to evade nagging at home as anything, and Little Jimmy came out of the barometer house for a prolonged stay.

*　　*　　*

'I am probably the only officer serving with the Royal Navy in the 1914–18 war who got consistently bad reports from all his commanding officers,' Davidson told Kennedy-Cox, though whether he said it gleefully or with regret is not recorded. Davidson was more effective in destroying naval morale than a whole wolf pack of German U-boats, according to his skipper aboard H.M.S. *Gibraltar*, depot ship for the 10th Cruiser Squadron based in the Shetlands. In particular the rector's habit of holding a church parade every time a cruiser came in to coal, whether it was midday or midnight, infuriated the captain. In vain it was explained to Davidson that there was a war on, and that ships must be ready to weigh anchor at a moment's notice—Davidson (or more likely it was Little Jimmy) simply appealed over the captain's head to Vice-Admiral Sir Reginald Tupper, K.C.B., C.V.O., otherwise known as 'Holy Reggie', who gave him backing. When the *Gibraltar*'s duty officers sought to spike Davidson's guns by refusing his requests for motor launches ('Sorry, padre, none available') again he went running to Holy Reggie. When Davidson finally was transferred to H.M.S. *Fox*, flagship of the Red Sea Patrol, the *Gibraltar*'s complement were convinced that they were seeing the back of Kaiser Bill's deadliest anti-personnel weapon. ('I'm afraid I did make myself a bit of a nuisance,' Davidson later declared, in what must rank as one of his more masterly understatements.)

One other episode belongs to this period in Davidson's life, and that was the night that Little Jimmy played a joke on Uncle Harold, and got him arrested in a raid on a brothel in Cairo. Uncle Harold had gone there in tracking down a diseased whore who was wreaking havoc with his men, but Little Jimmy arranged it so that his visit should coincide with a raid on the bagnio. 'Of course I was able to explain everything,' Davidson later told a reporter. 'The fact remains that malicious people can say: "The padre of the *Fox* was raided in a disorderly house." '[1] After the flesh-pots of Egypt dodging submarines in the North Atlantic aboard H.M.S. *Leviathan*, in which Davidson finished the war, must have seemed like child's play.

*   *   *

Demobbed on March 11, 1919, Davidson returned home to find his wife in an advanced state of pregnancy. Three months later Molly Davidson gave birth to a daughter of whom the rector was not the father. The paternity of the youngest Davidson child would have no place in this narrative had not the prosecution made it an issue at the rector's trial, allegedly in breach of confidence. Davidson maintained that he had confided the secret to Henry Dashwood, the Bishop of Norwich's legal adviser, on the understanding

---

[1] *The Daily Mirror*, February 2, 1932.

that it would be kept out of the trial. Indeed, Dashwood's memorandum of the meeting between himself and the rector, which took
place on January 1, 1932, mentions, 'Mr Davidson told me he was
not the father of his youngest child . . .' 'His wife told him the
father was a man who had been killed in the war' the memo continues 'but he himself suspected a local Colonel. The Bishop of
London and Dr Lyttelton were the only people who knew this.
The Bishop of Norwich did not.'[1] (There were several retired
colonels living in the vicinity of Stiffkey, including Colonel Du
Domaine, Davidson's boyhood friend, who, of course, lived at the
rectory.)

Concerning that meeting with the bishop's solicitor Davidson in
the witness-box declared, 'He [Dashwood] put his hand in mine—
and this is the unforgivable thing about this case—and swore that
unless I mentioned it as an excuse for my being away so much it
[the child's paternity] would never be brought up.' (Dashwood, as
a witness, in turn denied that any such undertaking had been
given.) 'This is the only bitter feeling I have in this case,' the rector
concluded, 'that this poor child should have to read about it in the
papers.'

In a state of shock, Davidson's first impulse was to flee as far
away from Stiffkey as possible; namely, to India, where a one-year
appointment as British chaplain at the hilltop station of Simla was
going begging. He went so far as to secure the services of the Rev
A. Blair, an S.P.G. missionary, as locum at Stiffkey. When the
Simla appointment fell through Davidson found himself not only
deprived of his living, but having to fork out £150 to the Rev Mr
Blair to avoid a breach of contract. The missionary stuck to the
Stiffkey rectory like a barnacle.

Molly's infidelity marked the final breakdown of the marriage,
though relations between the couple had been strained for a number of years. For the sake of the children they did not separate now,
but thereafter the marriage was one in name only, as the villagers
soon realised. The taxi-driver who came to collect Davidson for the
London-bound train early on Monday mornings could see through
the curtainless window the rector asleep on a couch in his study.

---

[1] Dr Edward Lyttelton was the headmaster first of Haileybury, then of
Eton. Davidson named as a third person who knew his secret a Mr
Wordsworth, who had acted as solicitor in arranging his marriage settle-
ment.

The news soon spread through the village that Davidson was not sleeping with his wife, as did the rumour that the youngest child was not his, but a cuckoo in the nest.

*   *   *

Just when it seems as though the bottom has dropped out of one's life, and that things could not possibly be worse, it happens frequently that one meets someone who is even more miserable than oneself, and right away one begins to feel better. This happened to the Rev Harold Davidson late one Friday night in September, 1920, as he was hurrying across Leicester Square en route to Liverpool Street Station to catch the last train for Norwich.

Leicester Square at 11 p.m. nightly except Sundays underwent a transformation which was as miraculous as it was sudden. At one moment the square itself would be dead, all life being confined inside those twin pleasure domes which overlooked it, the Alhambra, where George Robey reigned supreme, and the Empire, notorious for its promenade behind the dress circle where women paraded with 'the slow but dignified gait of caged tigresses', in the words of one observer. The next moment the doors of the theatres would be flung open, a river of people gush out, and taxis appear from nowhere to swoop on the theatre-goers like gulls among herrings.

No tigress, but more a sex kitten, was Rose Ellis, whom the Rev Harold Davidson spotted in the throng coming from the direction of Daly's in Cranbourn Street. She was not pretty. Her mouth was too tiny, and she wore her hair in a fringe to disguise the fact that her forehead was low. But Davidson found something appealing about her slight, thinly-clad figure. She reminded him of one of the waifs whom the Actors' Church Union took in—girls who came up to London to get a job in the chorus, and who ended up serving in cheap all-night cafes. Their paths colliding, the rector stopped her. 'I asked her what she was doing so late in that rather objectionable part of London,' he later declared, and Rose explained that she was broke and had nowhere to stay.

The girl looked no more than sixteen, the talismanic age, and 'rather delicate', or so the rector thought. Rose Ellis in point of fact was twenty, and just starting out on the game. The delicacy in her appearance was due partly to the fact that she had been missing a few meals, for Rosie as a prostitute was hopeless. To begin with she was not very bright ('half-witted' and 'mentally defective' is the way Davidson described her in less charitable moments) ,which in the context meant that she let her customers rob her blind. What little money she managed to put by went on drink. Small wonder that the rector called her 'my despair'.

Being in a hurry to catch his train Davidson gave Rose 15s. to get a room, and arranged to meet her at a Lyons' teashop the following Monday. It was the beginning of a friendship which was to have far-reaching consequences for both, for in each case misery and loneliness had sought and found its level in the other partner to that brief, chance encounter in Leicester Square.

4

The Bunco Kid

Dr Morton Prince would seem to rule out the possibility of a Jekyll–Hyde combination existing in one person; that is, of evil alternating with good in the form of secondary personalities. 'The splitting of personality,' he writes, 'is along intellectual and temperamental, not along ethical lines . . . Each personality is incapable of doing evil to others.' And yet there have been notable exceptions. One such was 'Emile X', whose case was reported by Dr Adrian Proust, the distinguished physician and father of Marcel Proust. 'Emile X' in one persona was a respectable lawyer; in another, he was a gambler, swindler, and thief. Even more spectacular was the case of John George Sörgel, an epileptic born in Bavaria, who in 1824 hacked a wood-cutter to death with an axe and then drank his blood in the belief that it would cure 'the falling sickness'. When in his right mind Sörgel was a 'simple, kind-hearted pious lad', given to reading the Bible; but when his alter personality took possession he became violent and unmanageable. Far from feigning his insanity, 'None but a Garrick could have acted madness with such fearful truth and nature,' the examining judge found in committing him to an asylum.[1]

The Bunco Kid, the name that J. Rowland Sales gave to the third personality which manifested itself in the Rev Harold Davidson, was no Sörgel, nor even an 'Emile X', though he had much more in common with the latter. By the same token the Bunco Kid could not be described as benign or 'incapable of doing evil to others'. He was a con-man in his own right, and the confederate of a swindler.

How does an alter personality such as the Bunco Kid emerge? Does it spring upon the scene 'fully armed and brandishing a sharp javelin', like Athene issuing from the forehead of Zeus? Or is it the

---

[1] Anselm von Fuerbach. *Narratives of Remarkable Criminal Trials.* London: John Murray, 1846.

the product of a long germination process? Both, says Dr Morton Prince. The germ of such a personality is usually present in the form of dissociated ideas splitting off in childhood. But for it to take the form of a new entity capable of independent action a severe emotional shock of some sort (what Dr Prince calls a 'psychic catastrophe') is usually necessary.

In Davidson's case the emotional shock which gave rise to the Bunco Kid was the discovery that he had been cuckolded, according to J. Rowland Sales, who renewed his friendship with the rector at this time. Although both were alter personalities, the Bunco Kid had little in common with Little Jimmy, Sales pointed out. Little Jimmy was irrational, impulsive, given to playing tricks on others like a mischievous schoolboy. The Bunco Kid, on the other hand, was as unscrupulous as he was sly, and had a strong sado-masochistic streak in his make-up. The only quality these two shared was their destructiveness: both had dedicated themselves to the ruination of the Rev Harold Davidson.

The Bunco Kid had even less in common with that benevolent creature known as Uncle Harold, whose disdain for money was well-known. 'If father had a thousand pounds anybody, even a stranger, could have it for the asking,' his daughter Sheilagh asserted. 'Often he said he would sooner be swindled by a thousand rogues than refuse one unfortunate man anything it was in his power to give him.' In contrast, the Bunco Kid is so closely identified with a rogue named Arthur John Gordon, who entered Davidson's life at this point, that it is hard to separate the two.

*   *   *

'If Gordon had not existed Harold Davidson would have had to invent him,' J. Rowland Sales told me on one occasion. But Arthur John Gordon did in fact exist. A Canadian by birth, he passed himself off as a company promoter with an interest in American mining properties and patents, all of which were tied up in escrow, and required considerable outlays of ready cash. A tall, clean-shaven, fast-talking type, Gordon had, by his own estimate, made and lost several fortunes, including the proprietorship of London's first cinema, which he had sold at an £85,000 loss. Gordon in fact was an undischarged bankrupt and on his uppers when Davidson met him, according to Nugent, who took an instant dislike to the

Canadian ('He had those pale blue eyes that never seem to blink,' Nugent explains). All of which did not prevent the Rev Harold Davidson from being taken in completely by the swindler.

Or was he taken in? Was it not that the Bunco Kid wanted desperately hard for Davidson to believe in Gordon's get-rich-quick schemes? In other words—and this is where the sado-masochism comes in—was it not the Bunco Kid's intention that Davidson should be diddled? For diddled he certainly was, to the tune of £5,000, part of which Gordon repaid, only to borrow it back. Not only that, but, thanks to the machinations of the Bunco Kid, Davidson became the diddler as well as the diddled, persuading his own friends to invest money in the Canadian's worthless schemes. ('I was instrumental in introducing further money [i.e. into Gordon's promotions] by giving him business introductions,' was the way Davidson expressed it at his trial.) Among those who thus got taken for thousands of pounds were Harold Edwards, the rector's own solicitor, who collected the tithes at Stiffkey, and the Rev Hugh Boswell Chapman, chaplain of the King's Chapel of the Savoy, London. The Bunco Kid had absolutely no compunction about leading them to the slaughter.

To watch this British version of Butch Cassidy and the Sundance Kid in action one had only to drop in for lunch at the Emerson Club in Buckingham Street off the Strand during the early 1920s. The Emerson Club, which had started life as the New Reform Club, was a secularist, or ethical society composed largely of Fabians in those days. In case it might be wondered what an Anglican clergyman of no pronounced political views was doing in such company, the food served at the Emerson Club was excellent and cheap.[1] Besides, some of the Fabians who dined there were ripe for plucking. The pair made a mistake however in approaching the club's secretary Harry Snell (later, as Baron Snell, one of the first Labour peers), who quickly sized them up as crooks. Among others whom Snell warned not to have dealings with Davidson and his partner was Dr Letitia Fairfield, Senior Medical Officer of Health. 'Harry Snell told me that Davidson and Gordon were

---

[1] Davidson was in fact a Tory, though he disliked Stanley Baldwin intensely. Possibly as a reaction against her husband's Toryism, Molly Davidson was strongly pro-Labour; so much so that in 1929 she actively campaigned for Philip Noel-Baker, the Socialist Member of Parliament for Coventry.

operating a bucket-shop in mining shares,' Dr Fairfield tells me. 'One or two club members had already lost money by investing with them.'

* * *

Diddler and diddled, fleecer and fleeced, Davidson's relationship with Gordon was more complicated than a blind urge for self-destruction on the part of an alter personality. It was founded on a deeply-felt need for male companionship on the part of the rector, whose world was dominated by mother-figures. The only real male friendship Davidson had known was at Oxford, where in his final year, he had shared digs with a poet named C. M. Masterman, whom Compton Mackenzie describes as a 'poor imitation of Baron Corvo'. Masterman, a small man with waxed moustaches, 'believed himself to be a serious poet,' writes Mackenzie, who adds that he 'spent most of his time in bed, while little Davidson fussed over him and took him out for walks at night.'[1] Masterman, according to Mackenzie, could not travel by water for fear of yielding to an impulse to throw himself in. Therefore on one occasion the poet crossed the Channel to Calais concealed in a coffin with Davidson, black armband and all, accompanying the 'remains'. Once past the *douane*, the poet climbed out of the coffin, and the pair continued their journey to Paris. But to return to Gordon, it was a measure of Davidson's desperate need for a counter-balance to the feminine influence in his life that he put up with Gordon's philistinism; for the Canadian's conversation was limited to a small fund of smoking-room stories, whereas the rector had not managed to go through Oxford without some of its cultural heritage rubbing off on him.

Gordon needed Davidson as badly, but for a different reason. Aside from a pecuniary interest in the rector, the promoter needed Davidson as objective proof that he, Gordon, existed, and that it was not just a zombie who stared back at him in the shaving mirror each morning.

In addition, Davidson—or rather the Bunco Kid—used Gordon as a convenient fall guy upon whom he could project all of his shortcomings and failures. Thus in the begging letters he wrote to duchesses the rector gave Gordon as the reason for his financial

[1] Compton Mackenzie. *My Life and Times*: Octave Three, 1900–07. London: Chatto and Windus, 1964.

embarrassment, saying that he was expecting money from the Canadian momentarily. Landladies to whom the rector owed money were fobbed off with a similar excuse, and when Davidson had to borrow money for his daughter Sheilagh's wedding he said that he was temporarily short because he was waiting for a Gordon business deal to go through.

The Bunco Kid even roped Gordon in to acting as co-guardian to Rose Ellis, dangling 'Gordon Gold' in front of the girl in order to raise her financial expectations. Specifically, Rose was promised £550, which represented 10 per cent of the monies Gordon owed Davidson, plus £50 of his own, to open a boarding-house or a second-hand clothing business. The idea of Rose, whom Davidson described as 'mentally undeveloped', making a go of it in a business of her own is only less ludicrous than the idea of her being underwritten by two con-men. However, Rose was not so mentally retarded that she could not see through the offer. 'You are a great bluffer, in fact the biggest I know of so far, leaving Gordon out,' she wrote to Davidson, adding, 'You are both liable to get five years each, and it would be better to think over these things before plunging into the depths of the unknown.' 'I imagine your wife and children should be allowed full consideration,' Rose pointed out, 'before you enter into contact with Gordon to conspire together to get money by false pretences from silly Bank Managers.'

Even as late as 1932, when Davidson stood trial, his faith in Gordon remained unshaken. For the benefit of the court, the rector described his erstwhile partner as living like a pasha, with a flat in Buckingham Palace Mansions, a house in Hove, a suite of offices at the Savoy, and a footman and coachman besides. A quick check reveals that there was no Mr Gordon listed among the forty-four tenants of Buckingham Palace Mansions for the relevant dates. His petition in bankruptcy was filed in Hove in March, 1922, so he may actually have lived at the seaside resort, but rumour has it that he was barred from the Savoy after he had been seen in the lobby filching cigar butts from a sand urn. Undaunted, Davidson testified that he still expected one of Gordon's dream boats to come sailing home ('I am seeing him as soon as the court is over to hear the latest news about the position'). When the prosecution called Gordon a swindler it brought Davidson to his feet in an impassioned outburst. Up to that point the rector had endured with equanimity the suggestion that he himself was an adulterer, a satyr, and a corrupter of youth. But to hear Gordon branded as a swindler, and himself as a swindler's accomplice, this stung Davidson to the quick, and he ended by challenging the prosecution to repeat this accusation outside the courtroom, 'where I will know how to deal with it'.

*　　*　　*

It must not be thought that during all the period of the Gordon–Davidson partnership the Bunco Kid held the stage alone, and that Davidson's other personalities were either dead or dormant. All through this period Uncle Harold was active, going about his rescue work in Soho 'with a single-mindedness which in any other circumstances should have brought him a deanery', in the words of the one commentator. 'I cannot help feeling,' Davidson wrote later, 'that if, say, half the London clergy would, individually, spend a quarter of the time I spent looking after country girls stranded in London . . . instead of wasting their time . . . at gossiping Mothers' Meetings, Parish tea fights, and Society functions, there might not be so many thousands of the poor, misguided girls openly, shamelessly plying their terrible trade.'[1]

The truth was that the British middle-class still had the blinkered attitude towards prostitution which had been handed down by the Victorians, as Davidson fully appreciated. The *bien pensants* still refused to face the truth, that prostitution was, as Bernard Shaw described it, 'organised and exploited as a big international commerce for the profit of capitalists like any other commerce, and very lucrative to great city estates, including Church estates, through the rents of the houses in which it is practised'.[2] Clergymen in particular tended to regard prostitution in terms of isolated transactions between depraved women and licentious males, instead of it being the end-product of a system of 'underpaying, undervaluing, and overworking women', in Shaw's words.

Davidson had no time for the sanctimonious attitudes portrayed in *The Outcast*, a play which pivots on the question whether the hero Geoffrey should marry the reformed prostitute with whom he has been living 'in sin'. It is Miriam, the ex-prostitute, who rejects

---

[1] *The Reason Why.*
[2] Bernard Shaw. Preface to *Mrs Warren's Profession*, 1894.

this solution. 'I will cleave to you as long as you wish, but I won't marry you,' she tells her lover. Why the refusal? Because she considers marriage to be a degrading form of bondage? Because she prizes her freedom? No, not for these, nor for any other reason which in the 1970s might be considered valid. She refuses because marriage is 'for the protection of good women', in Miriam's words. It is their 'reward' for remaining good.

Granted that such sentiments were obnoxious to the Prostitutes' Padre, did he attend the revival of *The Outcast* in 1926 for the purpose of making a scene? Or did Davidson get so carried away by indignation that he decided to make his protest heard? Whatever the reason he waited until the curtain had come down on the last act, then sprang to his feet and began to harangue the audience. The author had got the whole thing wrong, Davidson protested. 'Instead of reviling Miriam we should take her to our bosoms and cherish her,' he cried. For did not Miriam and others like her protect the family by preventing philandering husbands from stealing other men's wives? Were they not bastions against domestic unhappiness? 'She should be treated as our sister and not as an outcast.' False attitudes such as those which the play represented had made Miriam what she was, he concluded. 'And you, by your applause,' he accused, 'have encouraged such attitudes.' But by this time the theatre had emptied, and Davidson found himself addressing the vacant stalls.

The voice was that of Uncle Harold, but the hairy hand—who can doubt it?—was that of Little Jimmy. For Little Jimmy delighted in outraging middle-class morality. The imp had not been idle all the while the Bunco Kid had been in evidence. Among other deeds, Little Jimmy had got Davidson expelled from the Overseas League, whose patron was George V. The rector was asked to resign after members had complained about 'undesirable women' hanging about the club entrance in Park Place, off St James's Street, waiting for Davidson to emerge. Also he was accused of pestering the switchboard girls in the telephone room. 'It is horrible to be stabbed in the back this way,' Davidson objected in a letter to Sir Ernest Birch, the league's chairman, though whether he was complaining about his expulsion, or about the tricks his doppelganger had got up to is not clear.

* * *

[56]

Little Jimmy may have been leading Davidson a merry dance, but it was the Bunco Kid who almost lost the rector his living early in 1925. In February of that year a warrant was issued for Davidson's arrest for non-payment of his quarterly rates, and the rector had to obtain a rule *nisi* (later voided) from the High Court of Justice to prevent the arrest from being carried out. Had Davidson been gaoled, he would have been deprived of his living under the 1892 Clergy Discipline Act, and a new rector appointed to take his place. As it was, he borrowed from money lenders at 250 per cent interest in order to pay the rates arrears, and was soon in trouble with these Shylocks for failure to redeem a promissory note. Altogether Davidson was involved in seven different court actions in the 7-month period ending in October, 1925. The most bizarre of the lawsuits was one for damages which Davidson himself brought against three magistrates of the Walsingham Bench, and which was dismissed as being frivolous. Ironically, in one of these actions Davidson was defended by Roland Oliver, the man who years later was to prosecute him for immorality before a consistory court.

In October, 1925 the rector of Stiffkey could see no other way out of his financial muddle than to file a petition in bankruptcy disclosing gross liabilities of £2,924. After that Davidson's living was halved in order to satisfy his creditors, he being left with something less than £400 with which to maintain his family and to entertain the girls in London. Consequently the Bunco Kid's activities were curtailed considerably.

Not surprisingly therefore when Davidson first discovered that he was being investigated (detectives began snooping round Stiffkey as early as June, 1931) he jumped to the conclusion that it was his finances, not his morals, that were under scrutiny. So strong was this conviction that at his first interview with the Bishop of Norwich's legal adviser, Henry Dashwood, the rector brought Gordon along to explain that their joint dealings had to do with financing the restoration of the churches at Stiffkey and Morston. In a memorandum dated December 31, 1931 Dashwood left his impressions of the Canadian: 'Mr Gordon told me he was a broker in the American market. He had no office, and when I asked where he lived, after slight hesitation he said he could always be found at the Charing Cross Hotel . . . He had no religion and was proposing to repair Mr Davidson's churches not out of any interest in the Church but as a great personal friend of Mr Davidson.' When it was explained that the meeting had nothing to do with church repair Gordon withdrew.

* * *

Moral, not financial, turpitude was the gravamen of the complaint laid against the Rev Harold Davidson. His accuser was Major Philip Hamond, whom many would have said was the very embodiment of moral rectitude. Hamond, who had Viking blood in his veins, had run away from school at Repton to fight with the Norfolk Regiment in the Boer War, had been badly wounded, and had become, at the age of eighteen, the youngest D.S.O. in the British Army. Despite a total disability, Hamond, now promoted to major, had fought in the 1914–18 war, taking part in the first tank battles and in the process winning the M.C. and adding a bar to his D.S.O.[1] After the Great War the major had settled at Morston, where he built his house, Scaldbeck. He became a magistrate on the Holt Bench, churchwarden at Morston, a leading light in the British Legion, Blakeney Branch, and otherwise a pillar of local society.

Davidson's crime in Hamond's eyes was 'slackness', which the major would have been hard put to define other than that it was the opposite of 'tickety-boo'. Did it refer to the rector's lack of punctuality? Sunday after Sunday Morston was treated to the spectacle of Davidson, his surplice billowing out behind, furiously pedalling his bicycle down the road, only to arrive at the church after the last parishioner, tired of waiting, had gone home. (Davidson was always full of excuses: his bicycle had had a puncture, he had been stopped en route by a man whose wife was ill, etc.) Or perhaps 'slackness' referred to the slovenly way in which the rector performed his office. On one occasion when Davidson arrived without the bread and wine ('so few take Communion it hardly seemed worth bothering about') a furious Major Hamond ordered him to turn round and to cycle the four miles back to Stiffkey to fetch them. When Davidson, as chaplain of the British Legion, Blakeney

[1] In World War II Major Hamond was consulted by the British 8th Army about the naming of its tanks, the 8th Army being anxious to preserve its links with the past. Thus tanks that fought at El Alamein bore the names of those which, nearly thirty years earlier, had churned up the mud in Flanders.

Branch, failed to take the Remembrance Day ceremony at the war memorial, telegraphing that he had missed the train from London, Major Hamond's patience neared the breaking point.

It snapped when reports reached him that certain *filles de joie* whom Davidson had invited down to Stiffkey from London had taken to breaking out of the rectory grounds at night to frolic with the local farm hands. Ordinarily the only sound to be heard in the surrounding countryside after dusk was the screech of the barn owl as it swooped on its prey, but now Stiffkey's bosky lanes echoed the sighs and giggles of those who played at love's age-old game, and a villager out walking his dog was apt to encounter shadows that sprang apart at his approach. It was this state of affairs which prompted the major to act. 'My husband had a cousin who was a rural dean,' Mrs Hamond explained when I visited her at Scaldbeck, 'and this cousin advised him how to make a formal complaint against Davidson under Article 2 of the Clergy Discipline Act.'

*　　*　　*

Dr Pollock, the Lord Bishop of Norwich, was sorely perplexed when Major Hamond's complaint landed in the episcopal in-tray. A scholar of Charterhouse and of Trinity College, Cambridge, Dr Pollock had been headmaster of Wellington College for thirteen years before being elevated to the See of Norwich at the personal request of King Edward VII, to whom he had served as chaplain-in-ordinary. As headmaster, Dr Pollock had found it extremely distasteful to administer punishment to refractory boys. The same applied to his attitude towards the clergymen entrusted to his care: he believed in leaving them strictly alone so long as they did not create a public scandal. 'It was no part of a Bishop's true function to run round among his clergy', was Dr Pollock's view, according to his obituary notice in *The Times*.

The trouble was that the Rev Harold Davidson would not leave his Father in God in peace. Davidson, in fact, gave Dr Pollock more trouble than the other 900-odd clergymen in the diocese combined. Thus early in 1931 the bishop had found himself defending Davidson when sitting next to Lady Leicester at dinner at Holkham Hall, her ladyship having poured into his ear the latest tittle-tattle concerning Stiffkey's rector. 'Poor Mr Davidson is much maligned,' Dr Pollock had remarked, cutting Lady Leicester short. 'A much maligned man,' the bishop repeated, shaking his head sadly.[1]

Major Hamond's formal complaint against Davidson alleging immorality, however, sent the bishop scurrying to his library shelves to look up the Clergy Discipline Act of 1892. The act had been passed as a panic measure to rid the Church of England of a few clerical black sheep ('The causes it would affect may not be many, but they are *monstrous*,' Archbishop Benson argued at the time), and had been rarely invoked since its passage. Under the Act's provisions a clergyman was automatically deprived of his living if he was sentenced to prison, made the subject of a bastardy order, or was cited as co-respondent in a successful divorce action. Moral offences for which a clergyman could be brought to trial before a consistory court included drunkenness, riot, idling, gaming, adultery, swearing, ribaldry, and 'other wickedness'—all of which were not particularly helpful so far as the Rev Harold Davidson was concerned.

Dr Pollock could either veto the complaint against Davidson as being vague or frivolous, or order it to be proceeded with. In accepting the advice of his solicitors to proceed against Davidson the bishop was acting in no spirit of petty vindictiveness, according to the Rev Edward Powell, vicar of Belchamp St Paul in Sudbury, who knew Dr Pollock. 'In no sense was Dr Pollock a persecutor,' the vicar writes. 'He was a very gentle person who easily became sentimental.' At the same time Dr Pollock had a legalistic mind, thanks to his family background (his father was senior Master of the Supreme Court and Queen's Remembrancer, while his brother was Master of the Rolls). 'I am pretty sure that when Dr Pollock came to prosecute,' the vicar of Belchamp St Paul concludes, 'it was because he had clear proofs that here was a really "criminous clerk".'

---

[1] The bishop was reluctant to take sides against Davidson because he himself had twice been the subject of scurrilous gossip. The first occasion was when he went into prolonged mourning over the death of his secretary, 'Dear Vy', as she was known. Again, in October, 1928, when the bishop aged 64 married Joan Ryder, who was less than half his age, he had set tongues wagging.

5

A Second Wakeford

Charles Arrow, a retired Chief Inspector of the C.I.D., Scotland Yard, and formerly director of Arrow's Police of Barcelona, prided himself that the detective agency which he ran, with offices at 89 Chancery Lane, was more discreet than most. For example, at Arrow's Detective Agency investigations were never referred to as such, but always as 'inquiries'; hence its operatives were designated as 'inquiry agents', whether they were of the smooth-talking, ingratiating type, or the type who are more at home with an eye glued to a keyhole. All of this did not disguise the fact that the bulk of the agency's inquiries concerned adultery, for Arrow's was one of the first to cash in on the postwar divorce boom (this was in the dark age before mental cruelty, incompatability, desertion, or even insanity were recognised as grounds for divorce).

Not that Charles Arrow did not welcome other inquiries of a 'confidential' nature, such as the assignment handed to him by Lee, Bolton and Lee, the Bishop of Norwich's legal advisers, to shadow the Rev Harold Davidson. Indeed, it was a high compliment to be employed by England's leading firm of ecclesiastical solicitors, and might well lead to other business of a similar nature being thrown Arrow's way. In Arrow's mind new vistas opened up: he could foresee his inquiry agents being regularly employed in trailing errant clergyman, and—who could foretell?—possibly even a bishop or two (the memory of the famous Archdeacon Wakeford case no doubt was fresh in the ex-C.I.D. Inspector's mind).[1] This was why Arrow assigned his ace detective, Christopher John Searle, to interview Rose Ellis late in November, 1931.

[1] In February, 1921 Archdeacon Wakeford was found guilty by a consistory court at Lincoln of having committed adultery at The Bull in Peterborough with 'a woman unknown'. (Wakeford maintained that he had put up at The Bull alone in order to prepare his sermons for Holy Week.) On appeal the Judicial Committee of the Privy Council upheld the findings of the consistory court, but there was a great deal of public

Searle, who came to Arrow's via British Army Intelligence, was nothing if not suave. He possessed that other indispensable attribute of the successful private eye, a nondescript appearance. His face was as smooth and devoid of character as an egg, its ovoid symmetry being somewhat spoiled by ears that jutted out at right angles to his head.

Searle had posed as a representative of a charity organisation in order to wangle an introduction to Rose Ellis, but had soon dropped the charity disguise, explaining that he was a detective assigned to investigate the Rev Harold Davidson. There had been complaints that Davidson had been neglecting both his wife and children and his parish, Searle declared. The purpose of the investigation was to scare the rector into spending more time at Stiffkey instead of gadding about London with women of dubious character. She, Rose Ellis, could assist towards this laudable end by telling all she knew about Davidson. (At this point Mrs Ettie Schwab, a detective colleague whom Searle had brought along with him to the interview, had remarked, after giving Rose a critical inspection, that she was badly in want of a coat to keep out the winter chill; and Searle, coming in on cue, had slipped the girl a crisp new one-pound note as an earnest of future intent.)

Rose showed up promptly on Sunday evening, November 29, for her second interview with Searle, and this time she had an oafish-looking individual, whom she introduced as her fiancé Billy Parsloe, in tow. Searle, who met them at Charing Cross Station as per arrangement, led the way to the saloon bar of the Grand Hotel.

The number of glasses of port which the detective bought Rose became an issue at Davidson's trial. Rose, in an affidavit, maintained that it was seven or eight; Searle said that four was nearer the mark (he himself had drunk only Guinness). Taking the detective at his word, Richard Levy, for the defence, cross-examined him severely as to the propriety of his action.

LEVY. Have you the slightest doubt that four glasses of port upon an empty stomach would be likely to make this girl, to say the least of it, muddled?—I have some doubt.

---

sympathy for the archdeacon, who became a pitiful figure. He died in a poor asylum in 1930 after being ruined financially and in health.

Did you think it proper to ply this girl with port wine while trying to get a statement from her?—I didn't ply her with port wine, and I was not trying to get a statement. I had to sit somewhere, and I could not sit without buying drinks.

LEVY: One reason was to get on good terms with her?—I wanted to keep her happy. (Laughter.)

May I suggest expansive. Is it your view that a good deal of drink loosens the tongue?—It is so.

Expansive Rose certainly was. Her tongue was well loosened as she sat in the saloon bar reminiscing aloud about her friendship with the Rev Harold Davidson.

*　　*　　*

Shortly after their initial encounter in Leicester Square in September, 1920 Davidson had taken Rose to Stiffkey where her employment (over Mrs Davidson's strenuous objections) as a 'lady gardener' created something of a local stir. (The fact that Rose had worked on the land during the 1914–18 war qualified her in Davidson's eyes as a 'country girl', though in the eyes of others she was definitely a city type.) A female horticulturalist was in itself enough of a novelty to set Stiffkey tongues wagging, but Rose took to wearing gaiters as she went about her work of weeding and pruning, and when this became general knowledge the regulars at The Townshend Arms could talk of little else.

In the event Rose found the bucolic life not to her liking, returned to London, where Davidson got her digs in Endsleigh Street with a Mme Augusta Faillie, a jolly, kind-hearted Frenchwoman. More important, the rector took Rose to a doctor in New Cavendish Street, where she was treated for secondary syphilis over the next fifteen months by repeated injections of arsephenamine 606.

Davidson also got Rose a succession of jobs, including a bit part with a touring theatrical company, where she appeared under the name of 'Rosalie Bashford'. But ill and discouraged, Rose clearly was in no condition to hold down a job (Mme Faillie, her landlady, was to testify that she was in a state of hysteria much of the time). Also, Rose had taken to drink again, with the result that teetotaller

[63]

Davidson spent his days diving into bars after her and knocking glasses from her hot little hand. When tipsy, Rose became highly excitable, was given to dashing her handbag into the face of whoever roused her ire. Concluding that Rose was utterly incapable of looking after herself, the rector got in touch with her mother, and persuaded the latter to sign a form of deed making him Rose's guardian, a responsibility which he later shared with the egregious Gordon.

It was as her guardian that Davidson took Rose to Paris with the intention of getting her a job as an *au pair* girl. 'I have taken a great many girls to Paris to jobs,' Davidson boasted at his trial. 'I have an old friend there who runs a school just outside Paris, and I often take girls to domestic service there, so they can pick up French.' And not just *au pairs*. Even before the 1914–18 war Davidson, as a chaplain of the Actors' Church Union, had escorted to Paris dancing girls who had been recruited for the Folies Bergère, making sure that they found accommodation at an approved hostel, and otherwise concerning himself with their moral welfare.[1] Davidson made these trips about once a fortnight, stopping off at his father's vicarage near Southampton, where some of the dancers were induced to join the Girls' Friendly Society, according to Davidson's sister, Mrs Alice Cox. This activity continued on into the 1920s. For example, an examination of Stiffkey church records shows that early in 1924 the services on seven Sundays were taken by a Rev Mr Waldron, vicar of a church in Brixton, during Davidson's absence in Paris on business.

Davidson's Paris operations, when they came out in court, gave rise to the rumour that he was engaged in the white slave traffic. The rumour as embellished by many repetitions was that the rector, posing as a theatrical agent, inserted advertisements in *Stage* asking for girls to audition for a dance act to travel the continent. The more starry-eyed among the applicants would be hired, and sent to some third-rate *boite* in Marseilles, where they would soon be sacked as incompetent hoofers. Broke and stranded in a country whose language they did not understand, such girls soon

[1] These chorus girls, the forerunners of Les Bluebell Girls of today, nearly all came from Yorkshire, and were recruited from two English companies, the Tiller Girls or the Jackson Girls. 'Drink, not prostitution, was their problem,' Dr Letitia Fairfield tells me. 'They were not accustomed to French wine.'

found themselves working in a *pension mimosa*, as the French whimsically call their brothels. Davidson, of course, got his 'cut' for each girl supplied, according to this story.

The rumour was so persistent that Davidson himself alluded to it half-jokingly at his trial. 'I have been gossiped about by evil-minded people in connection with every girl I have helped,' he declared. 'I have been accused of being the agent of the white slave traffic, and one of the suggestions was that I took these girls to my room and then that the mysterious Mr "G" sold them to the Argentine. That was one of the things that was common gossip . . .' (Mr 'G' of course was Gordon.)

Whatever their shortcomings, Gordon and Davidson dealt in bogus mining shares, and not in supplying brothels. Davidson's *au pair* scheme was just another of his hare-brained ideas, conceived no doubt as an excuse for him hopping over to Paris once a fortnight to taste the pleasures of that gay capital. In the case of Rose Ellis the experiment was a failure. Rose had no intention of becoming stranded in France as an *au pair*. She was much too attached to the sights and sounds of London, and gave the rector no peace until he had set her down once again in Piccadilly Circus. Not that life with Rosie was always full of discord. She could be charming and a good companion when she was sober. Being Irish she had a pixie sense of humour as is evidenced by her letters, which she signed 'Eilasor', an anagram of Rosalie. Her friendship with the Rev Harold Davidson was replete with scenes of domesticity, for Rose tried to make herself useful by darning the rector's socks and sorting his papers. Sometimes Rose brought her fiancé along with her to the rector's digs in Euston Road, for in November, 1924 she became engaged to Billy Parsloe. Once Davidson came to Rose's bed-sitter in pain to have her dress a carbuncle with hot compresses and boracic lint.

Rose, mellowed by the port, described these and other homely incidents to the private eye from Arrow's Detective Agency, who slipped her another pound note for her pains. How much else she told him is a matter for conjecture, for the 13-page statement which Searle drew up on the basis of Rose's boozy confidences, and which she signed the following day, was never introduced in evidence at Davidson's trial.

*　　*　　*

For no sooner had she left Arrow's offices after signing the statement than Rose's conscience began to prick her. To a friend she wrote: 'Foolishly I made a mistake under considerable temptation, which has placed a mutual friend of ours in a terrible position, and most unjustly so.' She was to tell reporters later: 'Mr Davidson is absolutely innocent of the charges that have been made against him. He has done nothing but kindness to me, and I am grateful.'

When his former ward, remorse-stricken, told Davidson what she had done, the latter pretended to treat it all as a joke. Referring to the forty shillings Rose had received from Searle, the rector quipped, 'You are ten up on Judas—he only got thirty pieces of silver.' That Davidson was worried, however, is evident from the letter he sent to the Bishop of Norwich shortly after seeing Rose, in which such harsh words as 'bribery', 'corruption' and 'blackmail' were used. Without naming her, Davidson told Dr Pollock how Rose Ellis had been approached by detectives who had 'bribed her with money and drugged her with alcohol' in order to get her to make a statement. 'She says that they [the detectives] put things down in quite a different way to what she meant them,' Davidson averred. 'If she is called up publicly she will say that the temptation of the money made her do it, and that they made her so drunk that she did not know half the time what she was saying.'

'The ecclesiastical mind has been guilty in past history of some very underhanded methods,' Davidson accused, adding that he found it hard in the present instance to believe it had stooped so low. 'I have been actively engaged in rescue work for 38 years,' he pointed out. 'This is the first time I have ever experienced anything even approaching the suggestion of blackmail.' Davidson knew perfectly well who was behind the investigation into his private life, but, feigning ignorance, he ended his letter with typical bluster: 'Evidently there must be somebody with money to waste at the back of it [the investigation], but, whoever it may be, I shall take the most drastic action to terminate their activities.'

*　　*　　*

With this pre-emptive shot—fired across the bishop's bow, as it were—the battle of Davidson v Norwich was actively engaged. From the outset the strategy decided upon by the Church Party (if

one may so identify the bishop and his advisers) was clear: Davidson must be forced at all costs to resign his living and to submit to
the bishop's discipline. That way the Church of England would
avoid the scandal of a public trial which could give comfort only to
its enemies. (It was taken for granted that the rector of Stiffkey was
guilty of immoral conduct; never once was the possibility of his
innocence seriously canvassed.)

In the beginning at least there was no question of the Rev
Harold Davidson being deposed. Provided he resigned his living
and submitted himself to the bishop's sentence 'he [the bishop]
undertook . . . that *I should not be Deposed from Holy Orders*', as
Davidson noted in a memorandum of a meeting with Dr Pollock,
which took place at the Athenaeum on January 16, or eight days
after the bishop had already signed the charges against Davidson.
[Davidson's italics.][1] So confident was the Church Party that
Davidson would knuckle under that a Deed of Resignation was
drawn up for his signature when he had called on the bishop's
solicitors at their request earlier in January. To facilitate the
resignation the Church Party was prepared to go to almost any
length. Did Davidson object to the public nature of the deprivation
proceedings? Very well, the bishop would pronounce sentence in
Norwich Cathedral at 8 o'clock in the morning, or at some other
unearthly hour when there were few people about. Did the rector
consider the cathedral too public a venue? In that case his lordship
would pronounce sentence in the library of the episcopal palace. It
was only when Davidson proved obdurate that the Church Party's
attitude towards him hardened.

For whatever else he may have been, the Rev Harold Davidson
was a fighter, and a cunning one at that, as the Church party was to
discover to its discomfort. As a fighter, his first concern was to
secure his flank, which he did by calling his family together in war
council on Sunday, January 10. It was exactly what his father, the
Rev Francis Davidson, would have done under similar circumstances, and it betrayed the rector's Victorian upbringing as no

---

[1] The memorandum containing Davidson's account of the interview
was submitted to the Archbishop of Canterbury on February 1, 1934.
Under a sentence of deprivation it was still possible for a deprived cleric
to function as a priest and even to hold a benefice with the assent of the
bishop concerned, whereas deposition entailed not only loss of all prefer-
ments, but denuding the cleric of Holy Orders.

other action on his part could have done. Present at the pow-wow were Nugent, Patricia, Arnold, and their mother Molly Davidson, whose advice to the rector was the most belligerent of all. 'I should write the Bishop,' Molly counselled, 'that you are so disgusted with the methods employed by his agents, and apparently approved by him, that you have no further use for his Spiritual Guidance.' 'You tender your resignation,' Molly continued, 'and if you have any further trouble with his Lordship or his agents, you hand the whole proceedings to the Press in all its unappetising nakedness.'[1]

His flank thus protected, the Rev Harold Davidson on January 12 fired off another letter to the Bishop of Norwich, this time accusing the latter of 'duplicity'. It was no longer a question of 'someone with money to waste' being behind the conspiracy to oust Davidson from his Stiffkey living. Instead, Davidson told the bishop of his 'horror and distress' upon learning that 'you yourself were ulti- mately responsible for this whole disgraceful business'. 'Do you realise,' he continued, 'what a blow the duplicity of this action of yours would be to the Church . . . if it became publicly known? No single clergyman in your diocese could ever in future trust either your spoken or written word, the word of his Bishop, and Father in God.'

But a few days later, at his interview with the bishop at the Athenaeum, Davidson held out an olive branch to his Father in God, by offering to resign his living immediately providing the bishop substituted a private enquiry for the projected public trial. There was a 'catch' to Davidson's offer, for it was contingent upon the bishop undertaking 'to withdraw the charges pending the private enquiry, and to restore me to my living if I succeeded in satisfying him completely at the private enquiry.'[2] Dr Pollock flatly rejected the proposal, being guided in this decision as in all other decisions affecting the Rev Harold Davidson by his legal adviser, Henry Dashwood, of the solicitors' firm of Lee, Bolton and Lee.

*   *   *

[1] The signed statements of Mrs Davidson and of other members of the family were appended to the letter which the rector wrote to the Bishop of Norwich dated January 12, 1932.
[2] Memorandum to the Archbishop dated February 1, 1934.

Henry Thomas Alexander Dashwood was one of those 'monkish attorneys', as Dickens called them, 'whose existence, in the natural course of things, would have terminated about two hundred years ago'. In other words, in the opaque aquarium world of ecclesiastical jurisprudence Dashwood was a coelocanth, or perhaps a Hydra would be a more accurate description, for Dashwood wore many hats. In addition to being a senior partner of Lee, Bolton and Lee, he was Principal Registrar of the Province of Canterbury, and Registrar of Canterbury Diocese, offices which one might suppose would have kept him fully stretched, but no—he was also Joint Registrar of the Diocese of London.

However, it was simply in his capacity as legal secretary to the Bishop of Norwich that Dashwood was entrusted with the handling of *l'affaire Stiffkey*. Dashwood's was the time-honoured method of inquisitors everywhere in inducing case-hardened criminals to confess; that is, he was alternately threatening and cajoling, hawkish and dove-like in his attitude towards Davidson. Thus in his very first interview with the rector Dashwood began by taking a tough line. 'Mr Davidson, you are in a big hole,' he announced. 'For the sake of your children,' he continued, 'I have asked you to come here so that you do not get deeper.'

But the Rev Harold Davidson was not your common or garden variety of case-hardened criminal, Dashwood decided after observing the rector closely. From the memorandum which Dashwood left of this first meeting it is evident that the solicitor regarded Davidson as a hybrid combining the chattering of the monkey ('He could not stop talking throughout the hour and a half he was with me') with the acquisitiveness of the squirrel ('Mr Davidson brought with him a deep despatch box . . . disclosing a mass of letters, many in envelopes, and some bundles of envelopes. He also seemed to have inexhaustible pockets full of correspondence, etc., and I was struck by the readiness with which he found easily among this debris the letter or photograph suitable to prove the point for the time being he was making').

Not allowing himself to be put off by these impressions, Dashwood patiently explained how Davidson might climb out of the deep hole he had dug for himself. It was really very simple. All the rector had to do was to resign his living and submit to the sentence of the bishop 'whom you trust'. 'In such cases,' Dashwood continued, 'I usually recommend the man concerned to one of two or three solicitors whom I know well, and who trust to my discretion, and after they have seen the person accused, they usually get in touch with me, and I give them the best advice I can in the interests of everybody concerned. He is then urged to submit and avoid public disgrace.'[1]

Thus, if Davidson's version of the interview is correct, the hydra-headed Dashwood, not content with his rôle as prosecutor, insisted upon wearing the hats of judge, jury and defence counsel as well. Charles Dickens, who as a young reporter wrote up the proceedings of the ecclesiastical courts in Doctors' Commons, had the situation sized up when he described the solicitors who practise before such courts thus: 'They are like actors: now a man's a judge, and now he is not a judge: now he's one thing, now he's another . . . but it's always a very pleasant, profitable little affair of private theatricals, presented to an uncommonly select audience.' (*David Copperfield.*)

However, when Davidson ventured to ask Dashwood the nature of the charges being pressed against him, the latter shut up like a clam. 'It is not possible to tell you,' he replied. The rector should examine his conscience as to what he had been doing during the past six months, Dashwood suggested (at a subsequent meeting the solicitor ended by exhorting Davidson to go down on his knees before God). Dashwood's approach at least was more subtle than Graham Heath, another of the Lee, Bolton and Lee partners, whom Davidson saw later. 'We have you cold,' Heath informed the rector in the peremptory tones of a sheriff ordering a cattle rustler to drop his shooting iron and reach for the sky; 'anyhow, you've had a good run for your money.'

*   *   *

In the in-fighting which preceded Davidson's trial the rector's various personalities did not lie doggo. Little Jimmy in particular was obviously in his element, and his hand can be detected behind many of the tricks of showmanship which Davidson resorted to, notably in his handling of the press. Little Jimmy's methods may

[1] 'Why I am Fighting,' by the Rev Harold Davidson. The *Empire News*, February 14, 1932.

not have been 'gentlemanly', but neither were those employed by the Church Party.

The confusion of personalities is evident when Davidson writes Dr Pollock of his 'horror and distress' upon learning of the bishop's complicity. His indignation is genuine enough. This is the authentic voice of Uncle Harold, who goes on in a similar vein to admit, 'I may not have sufficiently followed St Paul's advice to avoid all appearance of evil . . . but there is not one single young person of either sex who can in any way say they have suffered morally by my friendship.'

But then Little Jimmy takes over, and the letter ends with thinly disguised threats aimed at the bishop should his lordship persist in bringing Davidson to trial. 'I shall fight it to the bitter end if forced to fight at all,' the bombastic imp announces, 'and shall subpoena both your Lordship and Mrs Rees-Mogg amongst the very large number of witnesses whom I have decided to call, and in the event of litigation, I reserve my right to make this correspondence public . . .'[1]

This phase of the pre-trial skirmishing was brought to a close by a dramatic episode, if Davidson is to be believed. According to the rector, the Bishop of Norwich suffered a last-minute change of heart, tried to withdraw the charges against him under the 1892 Act and to substitute a lesser charge of indiscipline under a 1926 statute. On Monday, February 1, Dr Pollock cancelled all his engagements and hastened to London with this end in view, only to find that he was too late. The first thing the bishop saw upon leaving Liverpool Street Station were newspaper hoardings proclaiming, RECTOR AND HIS ACCUSERS: 'I WILL FIGHT TO THE BITTER END.' The *Evening News* had broken the story, giving full details of the charges against the rector.

The story of the bishop's change of heart is uncorroborated, but Davidson managed to smuggle a reference to it into his trial, stoutly maintaining that the *Evening News* story had 'stopped the bishop changing the charge'. The following discussion ensued:

---

[1] Davidson in fact threatened to call 481 witnesses, which would have prolonged his trial interminably. At this stage the rector appears to be under the impression that it was Colonel and Mrs Rees-Mogg, from whom he had borrowed £150 without repaying it in May, 1931, who had made the original complaint against him, whereas it was, of course, Major Hamond.

ROLAND OLIVER [for the prosecution]. Please do not talk about things you have no right to talk about.
DAVIDSON. I know it.
OLIVER. He is exercising his imagination.
DAVIDSON. It was told me by the bishop's registrar.
CHANCELLOR NORTH [intervening]. How do you know that?
DAVIDSON. The registrar of the bishop told me.

*　　*　　*

'A Second Wakeford' is the slogan Davidson used for the publicity campaign which he now launched on his own behalf. But Archdeacon Wakeford's pitiful bid for public support had nothing to do with the razzle-dazzle the rector employed to get the public on his side. All the tricks he had learned in ten years of putting himself across the footlights as a stage comic were now brought into play with the result that before the trial began the press was firmly in the Davidson camp, and it remained there throughout the trial. 'Hand the whole proceedings to the Press in all its unappetising nakedness,' Molly Davidson had advised, and this was just what her husband proceeded to do. With the trial set for February 17, the press campaign went into high gear, as the following timetable shows:

> *February 1, 1932:* The London *Evening News* front-pages the coming trial, and gives Davidson's side of the story ['I am alleged to be one of the most immoral men in the world, and I cannot understand it'].
>
> *February 2, 1932:* Under the banner headline RECTOR ACCUSED OF IMMORALITY the *Daily Mirror* devotes its entire front-page to the story with pictures of Bishop and Mrs Pollock, and of Davidson in surplice, and Davidson in the uniform of a naval chaplain ('When I found unfortunate destitute girls in trouble I have often taken them down to Stiffkey, where my wife and I have looked after them until the time came for them to have their babies . . . perhaps some people thought I was the father of all those children').
>
> *February 4, 1932:* WOMAN'S OWN STORY IN RECTOR CASE is the heading of the front-page story in the *Daily Herald* in which Rose Ellis tells how she was 'bribed' by

detectives to make a statement against Davidson ('I was hard up at the time, and I was promised money to make the statement . . . I did not dream of the consequences').

February 5, 1932: Mae Douglas, an actress appearing in Noël Coward's *Cavalcade* at the Theatre Royal, Drury Lane, tells a *Daily Herald* reporter that she has known the Rev Harold Davidson for twenty years, and has never heard anything but good spoken of him.

February 7, 1932: The first instalment of Davidson's life story (for which he was supposed to be paid £750) appears under his by-line in the *Empire News*.

February 17, 1932: Davidson's trial is postponed on application of defence counsel. The venue of the trial is switched from Norwich to London in order to accommodate the large number of witnesses subpoenaed by both sides.

February 22, 1932: The *Daily Herald* and the *Empire News* are fined for contempt of court in an action brought by the Bishop of Norwich to restrain both newspapers from commenting on the Stiffkey case while it is pending.

As may be inferred from the foregoing, 'Operation Wakeford No. 2' was an unqualified success so far as Davidson was concerned. Far from finding the nakedness unappetising, as Molly Davidson seemed to think would be the case, Fleet Street found it toothsome in the extreme. So much so that in its eagerness for more naked details the press quite forgot itself, or rather forgot the august powers of the ecclesiastical courts, whose authority derived from William the Conqueror. A salutary reminder of this might and majesty was supplied by the contempt action which the Bishop of Norwich filed in the King's Bench Division of the High Court of Justice.

'My clients,' declared Norman Birkett, K.C., appearing for the *Daily Herald*, 'had no idea they were offending against the rule of contempt.' Sir Patrick Hastings, K.C., for the *Empire News*, was abject in his apology, readily conceding that the Bishop of Norwich had powers to punish as rigorously as the king's judges, which prompted Mr Justice Mackinnon to inquire facetiously, 'Do you suggest that your editor be excommunicated?' No bulls of excommunication, but fines of £100 and £50 respectively were meted out to the *Empire News* and the *Daily Herald*. As for the Rev

Harold Davidson, who was a co-defendant in the action, he was let off without a fine, but ordered to pay costs.

Meanwhile, although it passed virtually unnoticed at the time, the press story which was to have the gravest consequences for Davidson was the interview given to the *Daily Herald* by Mae Douglas, whom Davidson had helped to launch on a stage career before the First World War. Now happily married, Mae Douglas had asked the rector to do the same thing for her young and pretty daughter. The actress told the *Daily Herald* reporter, who found her backstage at the Drury Lane Theatre, that the Rev Harold Davidson was one of her best friends. 'I first met him when I was a bridesmaid at a wedding at which he officiated,' she explained. 'I was invited to spend the week-end at the rectory, and ever since Mr Davidson has been a good friend to me . . . and now he has become an equally good friend to my young daughter.' 'Perhaps it is enough to say,' the mother concluded, 'that I have been glad to leave her in charge of Mr Davidson on many nights when I have been in the theatre.'

The daughter, Estelle Douglas, was just fifteen, an age which spelt trouble for the rector of Stiffkey.

*   *   *

SUN-BATHING WITHOUT CLOTHES LURES BOTH SEXES proclaimed a headline in the *People* (over 2,800,000 certified sales) for Sunday, February 7, 1932, while elsewhere in the paper under the heading WALK—BUT DO NOT TALK the Archbishop of York extolled the joys of rambling in the countryside. Nudists of either sex were in short supply at St John with St Mary's, Stiffkey, that Sunday morning, but bronzed ramblers with rucksacks on their backs were in evidence, for the *wandervogel* cult imported from Germany was then at its height. Just about every other sort and condition of man thronged the village church, having been transported thither by charabanc from as far afield as Bournemouth.

For his text the Rev Harold Davidson chose I Corinthians xiii, 1 : 'Though I speak with the tongues of men and angels, and have not charity, I am become as a sounding brass, or a tinkling cymbal.' Those who had come expecting Stiffkey's sounding brass to denounce his accusers were disappointed, for the only reference he made to his coming trial was when he invited the congregation to pray 'that God may so rule things . . . that His Church may not suffer unduly from the publicity which must inevitably attach to this case for the next six weeks or so.' Inasmuch as Davidson himself was the author of most of this publicity this may have struck some of his listeners as droll. If so, they gave no sign, for the rector was listened to so raptly that in the hush one reporter professed to hear those tinkling cymbals—the Mons Star, General Service Medal, and Victory Medal—which were pinned to the rector's surplice.

An even greater crowd turned out for the evening service. Curiosity-seekers stood six deep at the back of the church, and even sat on the chancel steps, so that Davidson had difficulty approaching the altar. This time the rector got down to the nitty-gritty of the matter. 'God does not sit all day in empty churches,' he cried in ringing tones. 'God does not wait to minister to a few saved souls—those icebergs of untempted chastity.' Christ during his life on earth had gone among the destitute and the fallen. 'No character in the world's history suffered from misunderstanding and vituperation more than Jesus Christ,' he reminded his congregation. No character, that is, unless—dare one whisper it?—unless it were Harold Francis Davidson, who in the next breath went on to complain that he, too, had been 'misunderstood in the work which I have not specially sought, but which I have never refused when it was thrown my way.' It was all heady stuff, and a cheer burst from the crowd outside when the rector, a mortar-board jammed on his head, issued forth from the church, and promptly lit a sixpenny cigar. CROWDS MOB ACCUSED RECTOR headlined the *Daily Herald* the following morning, while the *Daily Express*, not to be outdone, bannered its story STIFFKEY'S RECTOR CHEERED BY HIS FLOCK.

*　　*　　*

Meanwhile, Nemesis in the person of 17-year-old Barbara Harris was preparing to re-enact the love-chase myth which Robert Graves tells us originated when the nymph-goddess pursued the sacred king through his seasonal changes until she finally devoured him.[1] This time it was not the sacred king in his various

[1] Robert Graves. *The Greek Myths*. London: Penguin Books, 1955.

[75]

guises of hare, fish, bird, and grain of wheat whom the infernal deity sought as the object of her vengeance, but the Rev Harold Davidson as his all-seasonal, all-purposeful self.

'Dear Sir, I am writing about the Rev H. F. Davidson. I have been wanting to do this for a long time—.' Thus on Tuesday, February 9, did Gwendoline (Barbara) Harris begin her letter to the Bishop of Norwich. A fainter heart might have turned back, so exalted was the personage whom she addressed; yet though her bedsitter in Shepherd's Bush must have seemed the antipodes of the bishop's palace at Norwich Barbara persisted, knowing that hers was a righteous cause. She persisted despite spelling mistakes ('accentric', 'restarant', 'frighted'—'I was almost frighted to go out in the evening'—to name but a few) until the words, printed in block letters, filled both sides of seven pages of feint-ruled loose-leaf notebook paper. 'I mentioned it [the letter] to the Rev David-son,' Barbara went on, 'and he told me I would not be believed, and that my word would not stand against his. I am thinking if he is let off he will do just the same, and I am sorry for the girls in the future.' 'A lot of people will stick up for Davidson because they are afraid of their past,' the teenage goddess assured the bishop. 'Others might stand up for him because they believe him to be an accentric [sic] nice old man, as I believed at one time.' 'I know lots of things against him,' she added.

Davidson's defence counsel was to contend that Barbara's hand was guided ouija-board fashion across the pages. But whatever outside help she may have had in the composition of the letter the malice was clearly her own. 'He says he helps women in the streets,' she wrote. 'Do you call girls of fifteen women? Davidson did not help me, even when I was fifteen.' 'It is hard to be good once you have been bad,' she opined. It was an observation to which the Rev Harold Davidson might have assented by intoning a pious 'Amen'.

BARBARA

'One spends one's whole career as a clergyman in fighting for people's souls and very often their bodies. Very often you have to do the body first.'
THE REV HAROLD DAVIDSON

'A clergyman who is given to miscellaneous kissing and embracing of young girls at sight and in public is clearly lacking in balance.'
Truth, July 13, 1932

'It is very hard to be good once you have been bad.'
GWENDOLINE (BARBARA) HARRIS

6

Pestering

Nemesis, the moon-goddess, is usually depicted with a wicked-looking scourge dangling from her girdle as an earnest that she means business. But if Barbara Harris had any such weapon she kept it well out of sight when she arrived at Church House at 10 a.m. on Tuesday, March 29, the opening day of the Rev Harold Davidson's trial. There was nothing about her to suggest retribution, divine or otherwise, as she posed for press photographers on the steps of Church House, a venue more commonly associated with bishops in lawn, missionary blackbirds, and Bible colporteurs than with 'cheesecake' photography. Barbara simpered, she pouted, she purred as the photographers aimed their cameras at her from all angles.

In between 'takes' she studied her face in the mirror of the large vanity case she carried, which contained among other things a flagon of 'Love Charm' perfume ('The enchantresses of old—Cleopatra, Du-Barry—understood its magic power') for which Barbara had sent away to a movie fan magazine. 'Give us a big smile, Barbara,' the press photographers sang out, and the moon-goddess obliged, first moistening her lips. 'Come on, Barbara, show us a bit more leg,' the cameramen pleaded. She lifted her skirt a few inches higher. Then she was gone, darting through the doors of Church House to be lost among those assembling in the Great Hall.

Arriving a few minutes later, the Rev Harold Davidson was cheered by a small band of admirers as he got out of his taxicab. They included some of his women parishioners from Stiffkey, who had taken the early morning train to London. Descendants of those buxom amazons who gathered cockles while their menfolk stayed at home, these Stiffkey matrons were prepared to tell whoever would listen what a saintly man their pastor was, an opinion in which he would most heartily have concurred. Davidson himself obviously was in his element as he bowed and smiled his way through the throng, pausing here and there to give a woman his autograph. 'The face of a scholar and the bearing of a man of the world,' is the way a *Daily Herald* reporter described him; but to some observers Davidson's puckish face and nimble movements suggested those of Fred Astaire, who in partnership with his sister Adèle had long since captured the hearts of London theatre-goers.

Davidson needed no prompting from the photographers. He waved a fat cigar at his followers; he held the cheap, cardboard suitcase that served him as attaché case aloft as though it contained the budget and he was the Chancellor of the Exchequer emerging from No. 11 Downing Street; he shook the hands that were profferred. Once inside the Great Hall the rector was careful to select a seat in full view of the public gallery.

The Great Hall, which normally seated 1,300, had been partitioned by means of a blue velvet hanging for the purposes of the trial, and the ground-floor seating rearranged accordingly. Though it had been converted into a courtroom, the hall retained that churchy smell which is compounded of hymnbook covers, soiled kid gloves and central heating. Still it was to be preferred to the carbolic odour exuded by the Salvation Army dosshouse round the corner in Great Peter Street, if the number of inmates from the latter who crowded the public gallery was any criterion. That and the fact that the Great Hall was heated swelled the daily attendance of these down-and-outers, who queued for seats in the public gallery as soon as they were turned out of the Sally Ann 'spike' each morning. They were like the chorus from *The Beggar's Opera* as from their gallery perch they kept up a running commentary on the actors and the drama being unfolded below.

The Worshipful F. Keppel North, chancellor of the diocese of Norwich, for example, was a type whom these gallery gods instantly recognised and appreciated. Did they not come up against his kind every day in the week in the magistrates' courts of the metropolis? Did he not personify the 'beak' before whom they pleaded guilty to vagrancy, or drunk and disorderly, and who lectured them like a stern father before sentencing them to a week's hard labour? In fact Chancellor North was more at home in dealing, as chairman of the Norfolk Quarter Sessions, with miscreants such as poachers than he was in presiding at a morals trial such as Davidson's. The chancellor had his homelier side as well. W. F. Fellow, now accountant for the Corporation of Church House, but then a junior clerk, was rather shocked to see North arrive at Church House one morning with a hole in the heel of his stocking the size of a half-crown. 'Somehow it made him seem human,' Fellow recalls. Seated under a richly-carved canopy of oak on the dais where the Archbishop of Canterbury presided at Convocation, Chancellor North as the court convened was busy reading a letter he had received in the morning's post signed 'GOD' in large letters with 'by his servant Miss X' scrawled in tiny letters beneath. It was the first of many such crank letters the chancellor was to receive, the most notable being a series which reported that Judas Iscariot was alive and well and incarnate in the person of the Borough Surveyor of Southend-on-Sea.

The barristers were seated at two rows of tables, their dirty grey wigs resembling the foamy crest of a wave that was about to break at the chancellor's feet. They, too, were to become familiar figures to the ragged gallery gods as the Davidson trial got under way. They were to provide much of the drama, the hostility which developed between counsel, Roland Oliver, K.C., representing the Bishop of Norwich, and Richard F. Levy, defending the rector of Stiffkey, going far beyond the call of advocacy.[1] However, there was no hint of animosity when Oliver rose to make his opening statement. Roland Oliver had come into prominence in 1922 as junior Crown prosecutor at the sensational Thompson–Bywaters murder trial at the Old Bailey. Now in his fiftieth year, Oliver's sleek good looks were somewhat marred by the fact that he seldom smiled, a faint frown line creasing his forehead. A humourless man inclined to be pompous, one would have said. Clearly a candidate for a High Court judgeship and a knighthood, which in fact was the way Oliver's career evolved.

In outlining the case against the Rev Harold Davidson the prosecutor lost no time in getting to the heart of the matter. The trial was about sex. 'You see sex running through the whole thing,' Oliver maintained. The five charges brought against Davidson under Section 2 of the 1892 Clergy Discipline Act boiled down to

[1] Oliver was ably seconded by Walter Monckton, the future Cabinet minister, who was to serve as King Edward VIII's legal adviser at the time of the abdication; and by Humphrey King, who was then chancellor of the dioceses of Sheffield, Chester, and Carlisle. As for Levy's juniors, E. Ryder Richardson became recorder of Stoke-on-Trent, while K. J. P. Barraclough, the only one of the trial counsel still alive, became a magistrate,

the fact the rector had for years in London been 'systematically misbehaving himself with young women'. By 'young women' the prosecutor made it clear that he meant from the age of fifteen onwards. The question before the court was whether the rector's association with these young women was of an innocent or a guilty character. It was an association, the bishop's counsel contended, which involved Davidson in escorting these young women to theatres and cinema shows, in paying for their lodgings as well as their meals and taxicab rides, and this at a time when the rector was an undischarged bankrupt with a wife and four children to support.

Those of the beggars' army who attended the trial in the expectation of hearing something gamey would not go away disappointed, the prosecutor intimated. For Roland Oliver saw sex rearing its sinful head wherever the rector was to be descried, whether it was in a bedsitter in Shepherd's Bush ('a curious place to proselytise young women'), a Chinese restaurant in Bloomsbury where Davidson was accused of embracing a young woman, an actress's flat ('What was a clergyman doing with a key to an actress's flat?') or in the Paris hotel where Davidson took Rose Ellis ('a strange place to take a rescued prostitute'). The mere contemplation of so much concupiscence made beads of sweat break out on Oliver's forehead, for he mopped his brow copiously as he sat down.

*   *   *

Barbara Harris was the first witness called by the prosecution, but because her evidence turned out to be so crucial to the prosecution's case, Davidson's fate hanging upon her word, it will be dealt with in a separate chapter at the sacrifice of strict chronological order. The other prosecution witnesses fell into two categories, waitresses and landladies, with operatives employed by Arrow's Detective Agency fleshing out the case against Davidson.

Favourites of the gallery gods, who constituted the most critical of audiences, were the Hebes who tended the tea urns at the Lyons Corner Houses. Listening to them testify the spectator was plunged into a world of big, mirrored caverns with marble-top

---

and as recently as 1972 served on the Advisory Council on the Misuse of Drugs.

tables, potted palms and string orchestras in gipsy costume playing selections from *The Student Prince*. It was an aseptic world presided over by vestals whom Messrs Joe Lyons and Company in their wisdom had designated as Nippies (apprentice-vestals were known as Trippies) and who wore starched caps with a big, red 'L' embroidered in the centre, and black uniforms with a double row of pearl buttons sewn with red cotton. Now in court without their Nippy uniforms, but in ordinary street clothes, these handmaidens seemed strangely diminished as, one by one, the Winnies and the Dollies, the Phyllises and the Dotties, went into the witness-box to tell of the eccentric clergyman whom they knew as 'the Mormon', and who left theatre tickets under his tea-cup as tips.

Of a different breed were the landladies who were the most numerous of the prosecution witnesses (nine landladies in all testified). With their testimony one entered that hades known as London's bedsitter-land—a sunless, flowerless, cheerless region whose only warmth was generated by shilling-in-the-slot gas meters. It was a region guarded by watchdogs with voices of bronze and many heads which dribbled black venom. The multi-headed phenomenon was encountered especially by tenants who entertained members of the opposite sex in their rooms without leaving the door ajar, while the bronze voice was heard by those who overstayed their occupation of the bathroom. Woe to those who fell behind in their rent—on them was the full force of the black venom discharged.

Yet for all their fearsomeness these landladies were vulnerable, as Richard Levy, Davidson's defence counsel, was quick to perceive. Graven on their flinty hearts were the words 'Fen Ditton', referring to a recent High Court decision which re-defined 'brothel'. No longer was it necessary to prove that premises were used by professional prostitutes in order to prove that they were a brothel. If the premises were kept knowingly 'for the purpose of people having illicit sexual connections there', then the landlady could be had up under Section 13 of the Criminal Law Amendment Act of 1885. In the Stiffkey trial context, if a landlady were to testify that the Rev Harold Davidson was involved in hanky-panky under her very nose, so to speak, she might find herself in the local magistrate's court charged with running a disorderly house.

Taking full advantage of 'Fen Ditton', Levy proceeded to turn around these otherwise hostile witnesses, and to make them score points for the defence, notably Mary Jane Bevan, who kept a rooming-house in Alderney Street, Victoria, where Davidson called on Barbara Harris in August, 1930.[1]

'We are all agreed that your house is a respectably-kept house,' Levy purred. 'You would do nothing to countenance the slightest immorality in your house?' To which Miss Bevan replied, 'Oh, no, and there was none.'

> LEVY. Are you satisfied beyond any doubt that there was no immorality between those two people in the house?—Quite.
>
> If anything had happened to convey to you the slightest indication or suggestion of immorality you would immediately have sent both of these people away?—Certainly.

Not all of the landladies testified for the prosecution. Mrs Jessie Walton, a motherly-looking woman of Scottish extraction, appeared for the defence to tell how Davidson was known as a 'kissing fool' at her boarding-house in Macfarlane Road, Shepherd's Bush. Not only did he kiss her, but he kissed her husband, and the milkman too, Mrs Walton claimed. When Levy sought to explain away his client's habit of bussing all and sundry by citing the biblical injunction, 'Greet him with a holy kiss', his was the only straight face in court.

The reason that Richard Levy knew the psychology of landladies so well, and was so sensitive to their feelings, was that he had lived among such humble folk most of his life. In contrast to Roland Oliver, who came from the stockbroker belt in Kent and was educated at Marlborough and Corpus Christi, Oxford, Levy was born in Hackney and was the product of the local secondary school and London University. Whereas all doors opened easily to Oliver, Levy had had to batter on them until admitted. Indeed, it was not until the 1950s that Levy made his name, and it was as a fighter for workmen's compensation in cases involving such dread industrial diseases as anthrax and pneumoconiosis. Finally, Levy's career was

---

[1] Levy's skill at cross-examination was never seen to better advantage than when in 1950 he defended Donald Hume in the sensational Setty murder trial at the Old Bailey. In October, 1949, the headless, legless torso of Stanley Setty, a black marketeer, was found floating in the marshes off the Thames Estuary. Arrested for Setty's murder, Hume, an ex-RAF pilot, admitted dumping a canvas-wrapped parcel from a plane, but denied

to be crowned with the chairmanship of the Monopolies Commission, a post which he held during the nine years preceding his retirement in 1965. But in 1932 when he was instructed to defend the rector of Stiffkey Levy still had his spurs to win.

* * *

It was when the string of waitresses from the Lyons and A.B.C. restaurants went into the witness-box that the word 'pestering' was first used in connection with the Rev Harold Davidson. 'Pestering' became a catch-all covering every Davidson aberration from his habit of chucking waitresses under the chin to his reading of their palms and predicting that they would become the mothers of large families. So much so that Richard Levy at one point protested, 'The word "pestering" seems like a gramophone record in the mouth of every witness in this case.'[1]

Typical of the 'pesterees' if one may call them that was Dorothy (Dolly) Burn, 21, a pretty blonde in a light blue coat and matching hat, who identified herself as the manageress of a corset shop. In the summer of 1929 when she first encountered the rector she was eighteen and a waitress at Lyons teashop in Walbrook, Dolly testified. 'He followed me about the shop, took hold of my hand,

---

knowing the parcel's contents. The jury disagreed, after which Hume, on his counsel's advice, pleaded guilty to the lesser charge of being an accessory after the fact of murder and was sentenced to twelve years imprisonment. He served just over eight years at Dartmoor. Released on February 1, 1958, he promptly confessed the Setty murder giving the details in a sensational series in the *Sunday Pictorial*. As judgment had been passed and sentence served, there was nothing the police could do about it. A year later Hume, during a bank hold-up in Zurich, murdered a taxi-driver, who had tried to stop his getaway. He is now serving a life sentence in a Swiss prison.

[1] *The Stiffkey Scandals of 1932*, a musical version of Davidson's life, featured a song entitled 'Pestering' (lyrics by David Wood). Sample:

> 'Pestering,
> The latest thing,
> Making a nuisance,
> Every man the same.
> Seduction has flowered,
> Along with Noël Coward,
> Yes, pestering's the latest London game.'

told me I was lovely and ought not to be working as a waitress as I was too good for the job.'

The ex-waitress said that Davidson showed her photographs of actresses, telling her that he used to visit them often to forgive their sins.

WALTER MONCKTON (for the bishop). Have you consulted him about yours?—No, I did not have much to say to him. I used to try to get away from him.

Did he appear to have any money to spend?—Yes, he had notes. He said if ever I wanted to go away for a week-end I could go down to his house. I said I would not.

CHANCELLOR. Why would you not go?—I didn't like him. He used to pester me.

Dolly said that on one occasion Davidson had offered to perform her marriage ceremony, saying, 'You will have eight children.' This revelation was greeted by a burst of laughter in the courtroom in which the rector himself joined. Only Chancellor North saw nothing funny, gavelling for silence with, 'I will not have laughter in this court.'

On another occasion Davidson had followed Dolly downstairs to the girls' dressing room, and the manageress had had to shoo him away.

Cross-examined by Levy the witness agreed that Davidson wanted to be friendly, but his friendliness was not reciprocated. 'I did not like to serve him,' Dolly said. 'I did not like the way he talked to me. He was a nuisance to me and interfered with my work.'

LEVY. He did this in full view of a whole restaurant of people?—Yes.

So far as he was concerned there was nothing to conceal about it? It was in the sight of the whole world?—Yes.

His prophecy that you were too good for the job has turned out to be right. You are now manageress to a corset maker?

At this point there was an interruption. Before the girl could reply a woman in the gallery shouted out, 'She did not get the job through him, either. He made her ill.' The chancellor demanded silence. 'I am her mother,' the woman protested before an usher succeeded in quieting her.

Referring to the occasion when Davidson had followed her into a room that was closed to the public, Levy asked, 'He was not chasing you to a place where you were alone?'

'No, he did not get the chance,' Dolly replied, causing another ripple of laughter to pass through the courtroom.

LEVY. Did he tell you that in some restaurants he had been permitted by the manageress to preach to the girls?—I do not remember.

Dealing with the rector's invitation to the waitress to spend a week-end at Stiffkey, Levy asked, 'There could be no harm in going to a clergyman's house where his wife and children were living, could there?'

DOLLY. I don't know. I would not like to chance it. (Laughter.)

Levy suggested that when Davidson predicted that Dolly would have eight children 'he was telling you that he disapproved of childless marriages, and that it was better for you to have a lot of children?'

DOLLY. I don't know that.
LEVY. Did he ask you to let him meet your young man?—He may have, but I do not remember it.

Four other waitresses testified against Davidson, but the burden of their complaint was the same: the rector was a pest. Winifred (Winnie) Barker, who was employed by the A.B.C. restaurant in Oxford Street, said that Davidson had patted her under the chin, saying, 'You have nice teeth.'

CHANCELLOR. Did you like it?
WINNIE. No, I did not.

Cross-examined, Winnie admitted that it was in connection with her potentialities for the stage that Davidson had appraised her dental work. This was corroborated by Doris White, another

A.B.C. waitress, who said that she had heard Davidson pay compliments to Winnie Barker and had seen him give her cigarettes.

OLIVER. Mr Davidson is not a usual sort of gentleman. Have you ever seen anyone else like him before?

'Never,' Doris said emphatically.

*   *   *

More light comic relief was provided by the operatives from Arrow's Detective Agency, who told the court of their efforts to shadow Davidson, apparently no easy task. 'Mr Davidson is a very difficult man to follow,' Percival Henry Butler, the first of the detectives to testify, explained. 'He is always running, and it is always necessary to get right on top of him. Otherwise you would lose him.'

In comparison, divorce inquiries, the type of work on which Butler was usually employed, were child's play. On a divorce case one knew where one stood, which was usually on a street corner waiting for a light to be extinguished in an upper-storey bedroom window. Whereas with Davidson one never knew when the reverend gentleman might take it into his head to duck into the nearest tube station, and suddenly one would find oneself pounding along the platform in hot pursuit. This happened on Friday, October 30, and when Butler surfaced again after chasing Davidson through the bowels of the London Underground it was to trail his quarry to the Marquis of Cornwallis pub in Marchmont Street, whose proprietor greeted the rector with, 'Hullo, you old thief, how are all the girls?' (The pub landlord when it came his turn to testify denied making this remark.)

The balance of that Friday afternoon had been like one of those Keystone comedies where the film is speeded up, and where everyone appears to be running round in circles like mice chasing their tails. First, Davidson called for Barbara Harris and Betty Beach, a honey-coloured blonde, at Miss Grace's School of Dancing in Soho Square, and took them to the Beta restaurant, where they were joined by his daughter, Patricia Davidson. The rector then excused himself and rushed out and bought a wing collar in Oxford Street, which he put on in the shop; rushed back, collected his party and piled them into a taxicab. The taxi stopped first at the Duke of York's Theatre, where Betty and Patricia got out; then on to the Theatre Royal in Drury Lane, where Davidson was unsuccessful in getting free tickets. Then the rector and Barbara jumped into still another taxicab and were away before Butler could give chase. The detective had no way of knowing it, but Friday, October 30, was typical of the 8,736 aimless days Davidson had spent in London since he had been ordained.

Inglebert Thole had better luck in keeping the rector under observation for eight days in July and for three days in October. On July 29 he saw the rector leave the house in Macfarlane Road arm-in-arm with Barbara Harris and Rose Ellis, and had followed them to the West End where they shopped at Woolworth's, afterwards lunching at a Chinese restaurant in Glasshouse Street. On October 7 Davidson called for Mrs Betty Beach at 4 Melcome Place, near Marylebone Station, and the pair went to the Phoenix Theatre where *Late Night Final* starring Godfrey Tearle was playing. After the performance the rector took Mrs Beach backstage to meet Tearle.

WALTER MONCKTON (for the prosecution). Did you notice whether Mr Davidson smoked cigars?—Continually.
CHANCELLOR. What have cigars got to do with this?
MONCKTON. It has some purpose.
LEVY. I thought it was evidence of immoral intent. (Laughter.) You omitted to tell us how many times Mr Davidson sneezed that day. Did you notice that?
THOLE. Cigars, yes; sneezes, no. (Laughter.)

*   *   *

One of the most formidable prosecution witnesses was Mrs Flora Osborne, otherwise known as Battling Flora, who ran a rooming-house at 26 Barnard Street, Russell Square, where Davidson stayed from 1928 until 1930. Battling Flora was the apotheosis of the landladies who testified at the Stiffkey trial. Hard-drinking, pugnacious, she had been summoned for assaults on tenants, while she herself had summoned Davidson on six different occasions for non-payment of rent. Once in pursuit of the defaulting rector she had climbed through the bathroom window and had seized him just as he was about to undress for his bath ('I got hold of him, and my husband had to come and separate us.') But it was not only his defaulting on the rent that Battling Flora objected to, but his habit of bringing young girls to his room. On one occasion that she knew of the rector had entertained Rose Ellis in his room while he changed into evening dress to go out, but her maid told her that this had happened more than once.

OLIVER. We can't have what anyone said.
MRS OSBORNE (indignantly). You have got to listen to your own maid. If you cannot that is very unfortunate.
OLIVER. Did that incident of changing his clothes happen with any other girls?

But Battling Flora obviously was nettled. If a landlady could not trust the word of her maid whose word could she trust? Unwittingly the prosecutor had touched on a sore point.

MRS OSBORNE. It is all very well for you. I have said what I heard from my maid, and you have told me to be quiet about that.

Oliver then asked her what sort of girls Davidson brought to the house.

MRS OSBORNE. Young girls, girls he told me he was doing rescue work for. I engaged three of them, although I told him I did not think much of them. But I gave them a trial.
OLIVER. What was the final thing when you turned him out?
MRS OSBORNE. It is hard to say. I was always on the warpath with him. I wanted my rent, and did not want those girls coming. I was mistress in my own house. He was a continual nuisance.

Under cross-examination Battling Flora enlarged on the episode when she had climbed through the bathroom window after Davidson. The previous Saturday she had given him a week's notice to vacate his room for failure to pay his rent. At five minutes to midnight the following Saturday, Flora, with blood in her eye, went in search of the artful dodger only to find that he had locked himself in the bathroom and was preparing for his weekly soak. 'I got through the bathroom window and put him out, just as he was taking his coat and vest off,' she told the court. 'This is not a laughing matter,' she protested, as laughter swept the gallery. 'He should have had his luggage packed after my giving him a full week's notice. I said, "Don't forget, Mr Davidson, you leave my house at 12 o'clock." ' And leave her house that night the rector did, though he had to get two policemen to restrain Battling Flora while he packed his bags.

LEVY (cross-examining). You are a little inclined to be quarrelsome?—No, I am all right with people if they pay me my bill.

You had other steps available to get him out?—Yes, but then he will summon you. You can slap undesirable tenants across the face and put them out, but what does it mean to you?

Did you from time to time have the most violent quarrels with your husband?—No more than any other woman in business with her husband.

LEVY (sternly). Answer my question. Did you have the most violent quarrels?—I would not call them violent.

I am not going to mince matters. Did you sometimes drink heavily and become outrageously drunk?—Not outrageously drunk. (Laughter.) I knew Davidson had a grudge against me.

Did you take a cure for drunkenness at his special request?—Yes, I know that is where he had one up against me, but it was not for drunkenness. (Laugher.)

CHANCELLOR. There must be no laughing, or the gallery will be cleared.

LEVY. What was it for, corns?—That I do not think is really called for.

What was it for?

CHANCELLOR. Do you mean the cure?

LEVY. Yes, a cure called Normyl treatment.

MRS OSBORNE. Can I speak to you for five minutes, sir, without being interrupted.

CHANCELLOR. Attend to Mr Levy's questions.

Levy then questioned Battling Flora concerning a summons for assault which one of her tenants, Dr Seymour, had taken out against her.

LEVY. Did you ask Mr Davidson to intercede for you?—Certainly not.

CHANCELLOR. What became of the action?—The summons was called off.

LEVY. Was it not a fact that Mr Davidson at your express request got Dr Seymour to call it off?—No, I arrived at court to answer it.

Did Mr Davidson get the summons withdrawn?—I don't know who it was. I know that the summons was withdrawn. I have had three summonses for assault in my life and each one has been dismissed.

Is it a fact that your husband as the result of one of the quarrels you had with him threatened to go abroad?—He has threatened to go to Gibraltar one hundred and one times and we are still together.

Mrs Osborne added that her husband had to go to a hospital for three months, but she denied that she had asked Davidson to go and visit him. 'Mr Davidson made himself a nuisance with the nurses there,' she said.

LEVY. Didn't you have a dispute with the matron?—Can you have disputes with matrons and nurses there?

LEVY. I should think that you could.

CHANCELLOR. Is it necessary to go quite so elaborately into all this? I think it is quite obvious that the woman does not like Mr Davidson.

LEVY. Another point I want to make is that Mr Davidson is the sort of gentleman who is always helping or trying to help people, and sometimes makes a perfect nuisance of himself.

MRS OSBORNE. Quite right.

He is always getting his finger into the pie?—Yes, but would pester you to death. Threepennyworth of good and a shilling's worth of harm.

CHANCELLOR. Mr Davidson seems to have done many kind things.

LEVY. It is a fact that a maid named Lizzie was taken ill?

MRS OSBORNE. Oh, so that has come. My God! Yes, she was taken ill with appendicitis.

Did not Mr Davidson go and bring an ambulance?—I found

Mr Davidson at 8.30 in the morning still in evening dress. I asked him to get into his clerical clothes and go for an ambulance, and I had to give him five shillings to take a taxi. The only two things he has done in my life were to get something for my nerves and to get an ambulance for Lizzie. He even remembers that. What a charming man!

In reply to the chancellor the witness said that the girls who came to see Davidson were sometimes alone and sometimes in pairs.

CHANCELLOR. Were they girls belonging to the unfortunate class?—They were dressed better than I.

You did not like them?—I did not want to be bothered with them.

Was it because you thought they were girls who were not respectable?—Not at all.

*   *   *

So far the prosecution had produced nothing more damaging against the rector than that he 'pestered' waitresses by chucking them under the chin, admiring their teeth, and telling them that they should be in the front line of a Cochran chorus. Kissing the hand of the waitress who served you might be quixotic, but it was hardly immoral. Similarly with the landladies who testified to Davidson's habit of calling upon his adopted 'nieces' after midnight—it all added up to bohemianism of a frowsty variety rather than to convincing evidence of Davidson 'systematically misbehaving himself with young women'.

But if the defence was beginning to breathe a bit more easily it reckoned without the moon-goddess who, at the opening of this chapter, was seen posing for photographs on the steps of Church House. In the end the case made by Barbara Harris became the case to answer, hers the evidence to impeach if Davidson was to be acquitted. In the end the trial boiled down to the question who was lying, the 56-year-old clergyman or the teenage tart whom he had taken under his wing?

7

Little Miss Judas

Marble Arch has always been a favourite rendezvous for London prostitutes, one reason being its proximity to Hyde Park, which is the scene of an amazing amount and variety of sexual activity, according to police reports. Another reason is that the prostitute who makes her pitch at Marble Arch stands a chance of being picked up by an out-of-town business man stopping at one of the hotels in the vicinity, and of being treated to a steak dinner at one of the better restaurants. The concentration of so many tarts in one spot in turn may have something to do with the presence of so many preachers of the hellfire variety, who hold forth at Speakers' Corner urging sinners to repent.

But the Rev Harold Davidson was off duty the night in August, 1930 he met Barbara Harris; consequently it was in no professional capacity that he stood in the entrance to the Marble Arch tube station watching the passing throng. 'It was the peculiar way she walked that attracted my attention,' the rector was to testify at his trial, and the pressmen covering the trial knew instantly what he meant. 'A practised wiggle,' is the way that J. Rowland Sales described Barbara's walk, adding, 'She walked as though she was conscious that she might be discovered by a talent scout at any moment.' And why not? Did not the movie magazines which Barbara devoured assure her that Hollywood was looking for new talent? Barbara, who was sixteen, knew from reading these magazines that stardom was purely a matter of chance, like holding a winning lottery ticket. By the same token she knew that the movie queens had started life as shop girls like herself, and had climbed to fame, by winning a Charleston contest, like Joan Crawford, or by being glimpsed in the street by a talent scout. And if the Joan Crawfords, the Norma Shearers could do it, why not Barbara Harris? She walked round in a dream of imminent discovery.

The Rev Harold Davidson therefore touched on the one chord which was certain to make Barbara vibrate when he stepped up to her, tipped his hat, and said, 'Excuse me, miss, but has anyone told you how much you look like Mary Brian, the movie actress?' (As though someone had pressed a button, Barbara's mind immediately began a print-out of information fed to it by the fan magazines: Mary Brian, born in Corsicana, Texas; won popularity contest and signed by Paramount; played Wendy in movie version of *Peter Pan*; rumoured engaged to Rudy Vallee and to Jack Oakie, but insists, 'We're just friends.') Not that there was anything hit or miss about the rector's approach. 'Nearly every girl passes through a phase when she wishes to go on the stage or into films—I should say 99 per cent,' as he was to explain later.

So though the Rev Harold Davidson was old enough to be her grandfather (he had left off his dog collar, so she had no means of knowing at this first meeting that he was a clergyman) Barbara went willingly as the rector led the way to Maison Lyons across the street. Eagerly she drank in his words as he told her what a hit she would make in pictures.

Barbara needed all the pipedreams she could get to sustain her, for she came from an appalling family background. She had never known her father, and her mother had a history of mental instability which led to her being locked up in an asylum in Eastbourne. Barbara's brother would have nothing to do with her; her sister Sylvia, who was 4½ years older, was in domestic service, so Barbara had been left to shift for herself. At the age of fifteen she had been seduced by an Indian gentleman, who had infected her with gonorrhea (the Indian gentleman himself got a prison sentence for interfering with a minor). After that Barbara had been taken into care by the Church Army, from whose hostels she had twice run away. At the time Davidson met her Barbara was drifting. She had also had a few minor brushes with the law, having been fined on one occasion for 'obstructing the footpath', the usual charge preferred against prostitutes. Another time she had been remanded to Holloway Prison for a week charged with stealing clothing from the hospital where she was being treated for V.D. (the charge was later dismissed).

*   *   *

The rector's encounter with Barbara at Marble Arch marked the beginning of an association that was to last for nearly eighteen months. During the first three months Davidson was a constant visitor at her rooming-house in Alderney Street, where he introduced himself as Barbara's uncle. Later when she moved to Macfarlane Road he was even more pressing with his attentions. Davidson gave Barbara small sums of money, and sometimes paid her rent, but he soon realised that in undertaking to help her he had landed himself with an albatross. For Barbara was too lazy to get up in the morning and look for work; instead she stopped in bed until noon reading her fan magazines ('All I wanted was to be alone reading,' she would testify).

Having found the key to Barbara's heart, the Rev Harold Davidson at first encouraged her in her fantasies. 'If I wanted her to go out to look for a job,' the rector explained in the witness box, 'I would say, "You look like Greta Garbo", and then arrange a curl in a different way and say, "Now you look like Lilian Harvey." She would be pleased as punch, and then I would say, "Come on, queen of my heart," and she would go out.' Davidson also paid for Barbara's dancing lessons at Miss Grace's academy in Soho. He even introduced her to a comedian in pantomime, but Barbara knew that 'people in a play don't have anything to do with getting jobs unless they are great friends with the director', as she shrewdly pointed out.

As time went on Davidson's energies were diverted more and more into trying to get Barbara a job as a lady's maid. 'I know how you dislike the idea, and I think you are quite plucky to face it,' he commiserated on the eve of Barbara taking up domestic service with Lady Grace Paget-Cooke. 'Anything is better than the uncertain life you had to live for the past two years,' he added. But Barbara was sacked after only a few days when her boyfriends began telephoning her to make dates. Davidson also got Barbara a job as a maid with the Dowager Lady Waechter of Chiddingfold, a slightly dotty friend of his who was interested in helping homeless girls (when Lady Waechter learned that Davidson was to stand trial she wired him, 'You ass stop what can I do to help'). But this, too, did not last long, and Barbara on her own initiative got a job as a saleslady at the toy stall in Marks and Spencer's basement during the Christmas rush season.

In the meanwhile there were stormy scenes with the rector, who was beginning to get on the girl's nerves. On one occasion Barbara threw a fistful of coins in Davidson's face as they stood on the platform of an Underground station; on another, she gave the rector a black eye.

In defence the Rev Harold Davidson would claim that his interest in Barbara was purely altruistic, that he had tried to take her away from the life of vice she had been leading, and that he had introduced her to his wife and children at Stiffkey with this end in view.

RICHARD LEVY (cross-examining for the defence). You were introduced to various other persons for the purpose of taking you out of your surroundings and showing you a little of family life and affection?

BARBARA. What was the good of introducing me once and never taking me again?

LEVY. Was the reason he did not take you again because they all disliked you so much?

BARBARA. I do not know. He used to tell them I had been in Holloway prison.

LEVY. Do you mean to say he would take you to Lady Waechter and say, 'Here's a girl, she has been in Holloway'?

BARBARA. Yes, he used to say I had slept in Hyde Park.

Far from persuading her to change her mode of life, the Rev Harold Davidson was always trying to make love to her, Barbara would contend. 'He begged me to give myself to him body and soul just once,' she would testify. But she never had; instead she had found herself continually repulsing his advances.

On the only occasion they had ever discussed religious matters, Davidson had told Barbara, 'God does not mind sins of the body, but only sins of the soul,' according to the girl. Asked by the defence if the rector had not cited the parable of the Prodigal Son on this occasion, Barbara replied, 'He never mentioned no prodigal son.' Davidson had also told her about Egyptian brothels, where the girls were 'very jolly'. 'It was their religion to do that sort of thing,' he had explained. He also said that he had visited similar places in Paris, and that Barbara 'would do very well' in one of them.

If the Rev Harold Davidson had embarked on a course of seduction, as the prosecution claimed was the case, why did Barbara keep running back to him time after time whenever she was in trouble? It was because she still wanted him to get her a job, the girl replied.

LEVY. Do you usually like to keep friendly with people who try to rape you?
BARBARA. If they come in useful.

*   *   *

Barbara may have been stingy with her favours as far as the rector was concerned, but she dispensed them generously to others during the period Davidson knew her, notably to an Indian police officer, a Scottish wrestler, and an Italian lover who kept her out until 3 a.m. Barbara's romances had as their exotic settings the back rows of one-and-sixpenny balconies in various Bijou and Biograph cinemas, not to mention the Cosy Café in Edgware Road, where the girls sat on the laps of their lorry driver boyfriends.

It speaks volumes for his stormy relationship with Barbara that the rector got on with her boyfriends better than he did with her. In particular, he appears to have hit it off with the Hindu gentleman with whom Barbara went to live in Tolmers Square in November, 1930. The Hindu was in fact a high-ranking police officer from Calcutta who was in London as a delegate to the Round Table conference which had opened in September.

On one occasion the rector was entertained to tea by Barbara and her paramour while the two were in their pyjamas and sitting up in bed. When Davidson was asked how he liked Barbara's new pyjamas he told her, 'I prefer you without them.' This at any rate was Barbara's story.

CHANCELLOR. I suppose that Mr Davidson as a Church of England clergyman would not like to see the girl living with a Hindu.
LEVY. Don't assume too much, sir. According to Mr Davidson what he found was the Hindu wanting to marry the girl.

Being under eighteen, Barbara had to get special permission from the Home Office to accompany the Hindu to Calcutta as his bride, which was where Davidson came into the picture. Barbara had appealed to the rector to intervene with the authorities on her behalf. Before he could do so, however, the Hindu had returned to India, and nothing more was heard from him. At Davidson's trial Barbara was questioned closely about this affair.

LEVY (for the defence). Mr Davidson's desires for you were not so keen and intent as to try to stop you marrying and going to India?
BARBARA. He did not like the idea.
LEVY. But if he was so passionately intent do you suggest that he would have been quite willing that you should marry this man?
ROLAND OLIVER (for the prosecution). I object. The question is in the form of comment.
CHANCELLOR. I should have thought so.
LEVY. I am suggesting throughout that he had no desire to be intimate with you at all?
BARBARA. He had plenty of other girls.
LEVY. That is a scandalous thing to say, Miss Harris. You do not mind what scandalous things you say about him, do you?
BARBARA. No, and he doesn't mind what scandalous things he says about me.

*   *   *

The Rev Harold Davidson got on even better with Barbara's next boyfriend, Dixie Din, a Scotsman who performed strongarm feats on the pavements of South London. Dixie may have bent iron bars and wriggled out of chains with ease, but he was in no position to offer Barbara marriage for the simple reason that he already had a wife and four children. But he took her to the theatres and bought her tea (Barbara was hard-up and living in a hostel in Westminster Bridge Road at the time).

LEVY. It must be quite a remunerative profession to be able to afford theatres and teas?
BARBARA. Sometimes he earned £3 a day.
CHANCELLOR. This sort of people usually have money to spend.
LEVY. Yes, one feels so sorry for them, and then it is found that they have plenty of money. It is enough to make the mouths of several members of the Bar water. (Laughter.)

[99]

A good spender he may have been, but Dixie Din had a fiery temper, which began to manifest itself after a time. It was after the strongman had threatened to 'bash her face in' that Barbara wrote to Davidson once more asking him to intercede. Davidson put on his clerical collar, introduced himself to Dixie as Barbara's uncle, and discovered that the strongman was really quite a nice chap.

Not long after the strongman episode Davidson sent both Barbara and Rose Ellis to Stiffkey (Barbara went along ostensibly to keep Rose company, for the rectory was supposed to be haunted, and Rose, who was full of Irish superstition, did not like to sleep alone). Immediately a misunderstanding arose. Barbara was under the impression she had been sent to Stiffkey as a holiday treat, and not as unpaid help; but Molly Davidson put her to work in the kitchen. Great was Barbara's disillusionment.

LEVY. Did you serve tea in your bathing costume?—Yes, but I had something else on as well, a skirt.

I am not suggesting indecency. I am suggesting you were out frequently?—No, I went down there as a visitor, not as a maid.

Did you have a bed?—I did not. I slept on an invalid's chair.

You had food and shelter?—We had hardly enough food.

Oh, you were starved. You had shelter. Don't you think that was better than living at Macfarlane Road with the attentions of Mr Davidson?—At least I had something to eat at Macfarlane Road.

The defence counsel went on to suggest that the reason why Barbara left all the dirty work in the kitchen for Rose to do was that she did not want to spoil her fingernails. Concerning those nails, they were long and painted red, according to Mrs Lake, her landlady, 'My husband used to chip her about them and said they were more like claws,' Mrs Lake recalled.

Convinced that he had tricked her into going to Stiffkey, Barbara hitch-hiked back to London after a fortnight vowing to scratch the rector's eyes out with her long, red nails, according to two witnesses. In fact the defence tried to make out that Barbara's hatred of the rector dated from this episode, but indications are that it had much deeper roots.

*　　*　　*

Davidson, in point of fact, does not emerge from his friendship with Barbara in a creditable light. Having encouraged Barbara's theatrical ambitions, the rector tried to fob her off with domestic work, in the meantime dangling the lure of 'Gordon Gold' in front of her eyes. Thus, in order to console Barbara for taking a maid's job with Lady Paget-Cooke, Davidson writes to her in August, 1931 that 'the moment Mr Gordon pays up we can get you properly started in something'. (The rector had encouraged Rose Ellis with similar promises, it will be recalled.)

Barbara was much too independent for domestic service, which was a main source of employment for unskilled girls in the depression thirties. She was much too spirited to welcome the prospect of working 14 to 16 hours a day for a mistress who would address her as 'Harris', lock her out of her basement room if she did not return by 10.30 each night, and pay her a slave wage.[1] This was what Davidson and do-gooders of his ilk failed to take into consideration in demanding of the Barbaras in their midst that they should tread the path of virtue.

The do-gooders also failed to recognise that prostitution as a consciously chosen way of life could become for someone as insecure as Barbara a 'stabilising force'. In this respect the British Social Biology Council's survey of prostitution cited earlier came to some surprising conclusions. 'Once a girl has become a professional prostitute,' the council's investigator found, 'she has acquired a profession where she is needed, and needed by men, where she has regular hours and colleagues, and most important of all, where she finds herself in the company of people who are like herself in personality and outlook. She becomes a member of that society of which she had been on the fringe in her state of instability.' Furthermore, to be a successful street-walker demanded 'the same qualities making for success . . . in any other professional sphere— charm, sympathy, intelligence, organising ability, capital.'[2]

When Barbara first met Davidson she had not yet exchanged her amateur status for that of a professional, though plainly she was headed in that direction. It was because the rector threatened to interfere with her way of life and to rob her of her independence

[1] In 1930 the starting wage for girls aged 16 and 17 placed by the Metropolitan Association for Befriending Young Servants (MABYS) was £24 per annum. *The New Survey of London Life and Labour*, 1931.
[2] *Op. cit.*

that Barbara turned on him with the fury of a Little Miss Judas. What good were the dancing lessons, the nebulous promises of 'Gordon Gold' when Barbara was hungry most of the time during the seventeen months she knew Davidson. ('When I was at Mac-farlane Road I lived on bread and cheese and eggs,' she scribbled in the courtroom notes she kept during the trial. 'I only had one set of clothes from him.')

There was another, a psychological element which undoubtedly came into play in turning Barbara against the Rev Harold Davidson. This element too is touched upon in the British Social Biology Council's report on prostitution, which notes: ' . . . the need to debase the male or father figure is relevant to the prostitute's trade just as the opportunity to debase the female or mother figure in the form of a prostitute is for the man.'

That Davidson represented a father figure to Barbara there can be little doubt (she had never known her real father, it will be re-called, nor had she known any home life after the age of eleven). Davidson acknowledged his surrogate rôle in a letter dated October, 1931 in which he wrote, 'I have tried to be a sort of Mother, Father, Brother and Sister to you myself.' In turning against the rector as an interfering old busybody Barbara was really rebelling against the father who had decamped from her life.

Finally, Barbara's desire for notoriety, born of the movie fantasy world in which she lived, should not be discounted as a motive for turning her into Little Miss Judas. Asked by defence counsel whether Barbara had not said she was keen on getting into a mur-der trial, Mrs Alice Lake, her landlady, replied, 'Not a murder trial—she said a big trial.' 'Barbara said that she did not mind her photograph getting into the papers,' Mrs Lake added. 'She wanted something thrilling to happen to her.' 'Something thrilling'—it was the *cri de coeur* of thousands of girls Barbara's age who read the movie fan magazines to divert their minds from the drabness of their uneventful lives.

It was against this background that Barbara Harris went into the witness-box to testify against the Rev Harold Davidson.

*　　*　　*

Almost as soon as Barbara was sworn a note of incongruity was introduced into the proceedings; for Chancellor North, being hard of hearing, had difficulty in following her testimony, which was given in a low-pitched voice. To remedy this situation he invited Barbara to sit closer to him on the dais where in happier times the Archbishop of Canterbury presided. The sight of the 72-year-old chancellor cupping his ear to catch the wisdom of this 17-year-old child of the plucked eyebrows and the clinging satin frock, while bewigged counsel likewise hung on her every word, was like a modern version of 'Susanna and the Elders' done by a painter with a mordant sense of humour.

After leading Barbara through a series of preliminary questions, Roland Oliver, for the prosecution, questioned her about an incident which occurred shortly after she had met Davidson when the rector arrived unexpectedly at Alderney Street at 9 a.m. to find Barbara still in bed in her pyjamas.

OLIVER. When he came in on this morning when you were in bed will you tell us what happened? What did he do?—Well, he pushed me back on the bed.

CHANCELLOR. Were you not lying in the bed?—No, I had just got off the bed.

In your nightgown?—In my pyjamas.

And he pushed you back on to the bed?—Yes.

OLIVER. Did he try to do anything else?—Yes.

Tell us what. I am sorry to trouble you, but we must have this in evidence. What did he do?—He tried to have intercourse with me.

Did you let him?—No.

When you refused, did he say anything?—He said he was sorry afterwards.

CHANCELLOR. When he tried to have intercourse with you, did he do anything to his clothes?—Yes, he said he got them in a mess.

Did he undo his clothes?—No, not at first. He did two or three days afterwards.

Barbara said that she herself was fully dressed and sitting on the bed on the first occasion that Davidson undid his trousers.

OLIVER. What did he do on that occasion?—He did not do anything really. He tried to.

You mean he tried to have connection with you?—Yes.
Did he succeed?—No.
Did he do anything? You said something about his clothes being in a mess?—He relieved himself.
Did that happen once, or more than once?—More than once. It happened two or three times.
You said he kissed you?—Yes.
How often did he kiss you?—He was always kissing me.
Did he ever ask you to do things?—Yes, he asked me to give myself to him body and soul just once.
And you would not?—No.
Did he ever put his hands upon you at all?—Yes.
Where?—All over.
Do you mean when you had your clothes on, or not?—Yes.
You were always dressed, I gather, except that one time?—Yes.
When he put his hands all over you, do you mean really all over you?—Yes.
. . .
How often did he ask you to behave in that way with him at that period when you were at Alderney Street?—Nearly always whenever he was there with me.
He was always doing it?—Yes.
And kissing you?—Yes.
Did you ever let him do it to you?—No.
CHANCELLOR. He never really had connection with you?—No.

Thanks to a censorship which was no less remarkable in that it was self-imposed, Barbara's description of the rector's attempt to rape her was passed over almost in silence by the Fleet Street press (*The Times* went so far as to eliminate all mention of 'kisses and caresses', which the other newspapers used).[1] And not only the press, but in the courtroom itself sexual intercourse was seldom referred to as such, the genteel euphemism 'sexual connection'

[1] An acute observer of the between-the-wars scene writes that newspapers 'primly pulled down their skirts when in danger of revealing certain taboo-words such as adultery, rape, or homosexuality.' 'Lots of people . . . had no idea at all what the Press meant by orgies in Chelsea.' Leslie Baily. *Scrapbook for the Twenties.*

The Reverend Harold Davidson in the
pulpit at Stiffkey. (Photo *Topix*)

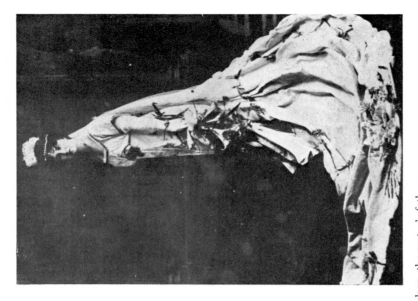

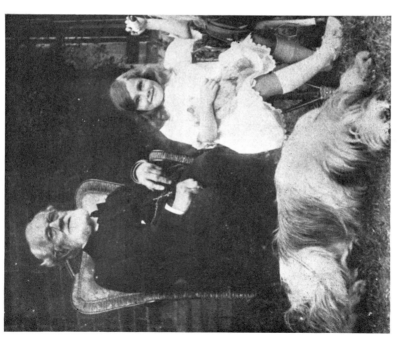

Left: The Reverend Francis Davidson, the rector's father.
Right: Molly Davidson in court dress.

Left: Sheet music of the hit tune from *Dorothy*. Davidson was involved in an unsuccessful revival of the musical, and often used the phrase 'Queen of My Heart' as a term of endearment. (*Raymond Mander and Joe Mitchenson Theatre Collection*.) *Right*: The Nippy. The smart waitresses of Lyons' Corner Houses were favourite objects of Davidson's ambivalent concern.

Above: The Rectory, Stiffkey. *Below:* The rector giving a pyjama party at the Rectory. The girl sitting on the right is Estelle Douglas. (Photo *Syndication International*)

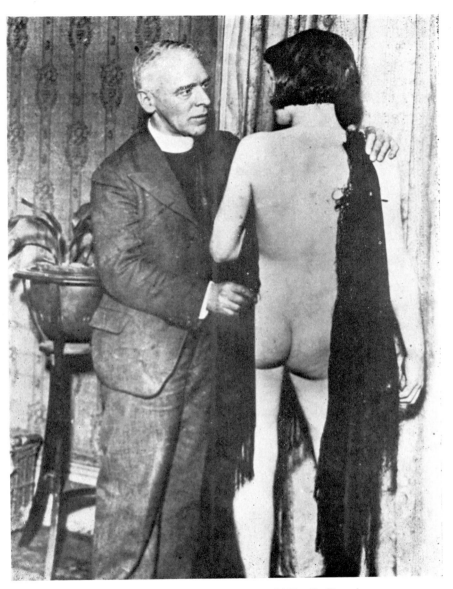

Davidson and the undraped 15-year-old Estelle Douglas.
This photograph was an important piece
of evidence at Davidson's trial.

Rose Ellis.

Barbara Harris.

The Worshipful F. Keppel North, Chancellor of
the Diocese of Norwich.

The trial in progress in the Great Hall of Church House, Westminster. The rector is at the extreme right of the picture with hand cupped to ear. Violet Lowe, a waitress, seen sitting on Chancellor North's left, is giving evidence. (Photo *Topix*)

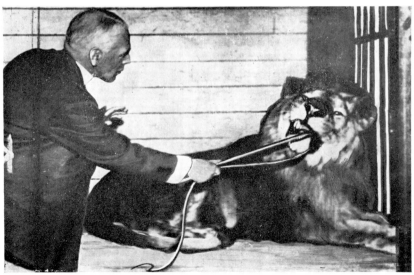

Above: Davidson with the barrel in which he was exhibited at Blackpool. (Photo *Topix*). *Below:* Davidson in a lion's cage at Skegness Amusement Park, July 1937. Shortly after this photograph was taken, Davidson was fatally mauled by the lion. (Photo *Syndication International*)

being preferred by counsel and chancellor alike (the latter abbreviated the expression in his notes to 'con', which might easily be misconstrued by a student of the French language). In describing the attempted rape the press, however, plumped for 'intimacy', a term which once aroused the ire of A. P. Herbert.[1]

Concerning the testimony which follows, although Barbara claimed that the rector kept condoms in a trunk in his room not a word of this appeared in the press, while in court the condoms were referred to as 'preservatives' (the chancellor, ever original, used the abbreviation 'French LL', as though referring to a doctorate degree). Again, the press fought shy of mentioning the appendicitis scar on Davidson's stomach, which Barbara described so vividly. As for the rector's habit of wearing only the top part of his pyjamas, this too was blue-pencilled, which made his subsequent denial that he ever wore pyjamas meaningless to newspaper readers.

*   *   *

The prosecutor's next questions covered the period in Barbara's life when she went to live with her Hindu boyfriend in Tolmers Square; and after he had returned to India, when she had stayed at the hostel in Westminster Bridge Road. Then in June, 1931, being penniless and out of work, she had moved into Davidson's digs at 85 Macfarlane Road with the understanding that the rector would go and live with his sister in Ealing. For a week the arrangement worked, the girl testified, then Davidson began to 'sneak' into the room, saying he had missed his train.

OLIVER. Did you keep the door locked?—Yes.

Why?—To keep him out because he came back one night and came in.

How did he afterwards get in?—He knocked on the window until I opened the door.

CHANCELLOR. Did not other people in the house object to this?—Yes, they complained in the morning.

[1] Referring to the use of 'intimacy' in press reports on divorce cases, Herbert writes: 'Nobody but the English could use such a word for such a purpose. I sometimes think of re-writing the classics in the language of the newspaper law-reports. Paris was "intimate" with Helen of Troy. Thou shalt not commit intimacy. Ha!' *Holy Deadlock.*

OLIVER. You say he slept in the chair?—Yes.

Did he go on sleeping in the chair?—After a few days he slept on top of the bed.

How would he be dressed then?—Fully dressed.

What size bed was it, a single or a double?—It was a rather large double bed.

You say he slept on top of the bed in his clothes. What was the next thing?—He started getting into bed.

Had he his clothes on then?—No.

He took them off?—Yes.

All of them?—Yes.

CHANCELLOR. Do you mean he had nothing at all on?—No.

You mean he was naked?—He had the top of his pyjamas on.

OLIVER. The top of his pyjamas on, and the rest of him quite naked?—Yes.

CHANCELLOR. Were there times when he had not even the top of his pyjamas on?—Yes.

What had you, your pyjamas?—Yes.

OLIVER. Did you ever notice anything about his body?—Yes, a scar.[1]

Where was the scar, and what sort of scar was it?—On his stomach, on the right-hand side.

Did you notice anything about the appearance of it?—It was an oblong scar, and sloped from left to the right downwards, and was dented and puckered.

You are giving the description of something you have seen?—Yes.

How often did you see him naked?—After a time he did it every night.

When he was in bed with you did he leave you alone?—No.

What did he do, or try to do?—He tried to have intercourse with me.

Did you ever let him?—No.

Did you see him use anything at any time?—Yes, French letters.

[1] A propos of Davidson's appendicitis scar, Barbara, under the prosecutor's prodding, repeated in court a joke which the rector had told her, and which was supposed to illustrate his 'indelicate' sense of humour (Oliver called the joke 'indecent'). A Scotsman, sitting with his girl in Hyde Park, asked her if she would like to see where he had been operated

Where did he get them from?—He had them in a trunk by the door.

*　　*　　*

Davidson got Barbara a job as receptionist with a Mr Farmer, a dentist in Euston Square, after which the rector used to ring her up at work to ask her to go out with him in the evening. 'Once he told me over the telephone that I was queen of his heart,' Barbara said. 'Hardly an isolated position,' the prosecutor observed drily. 'I asked him what he had done about all the other girls,' Barbara continued, 'and he said that he had given them all up.'

While Barbara was working for the dentist an arrangement was made whereby she was to sleep at the dentist's surgery on weekday nights, and at 85 Macfarlane Road at weekends when Davidson would be away at Stiffkey. The weekend arrangement broke down, however, when Davidson took to staying late on Saturday nights or arriving by the 3 a.m. mail train on Monday mornings.

OLIVER. What did he do?—He used to get into bed with me.

Dressed or undressed?—Partly dressed.

I do not want to keep asking you these unpleasant questions, but did the time ever come when he left you in peace, or was he always trying to get you?—He was always trying to get me.

The whole time right up to the end?—Yes.

Did he ever ask you how old you were?—No, he knew my age. I told him.

He knew when he first met you that you were only sixteen?—Yes.

Barbara then told of a visit she and the rector had paid to Betty Beach, an aspiring young actress, who was in bed in her nightgown when they arrived. 'Betty got out of bed,' Barbara explained. 'Mr Davidson kissed her and put his arms around her. She showed him what she had been doing at dancing lessons and did some acrobatics, bending backwards and forwards. He said that he was glad she was getting on so well.'

---

on for appendicitis. 'Not here,' the girl replied, whereupon the Scot led her across the park to St George's Hospital, and, pointing to it, said, 'That is the place.' 'I never heard a joke with less joke in it,' the chancellor declared.

That night Davidson took Barbara to *Salome* at the Duke of York's theatre, and afterwards he begged her to come back to Macfarlane Road with him. When she demurred he threatened to commit suicide, according to her testimony. Under this pressure she gave in and went with him.

> OLIVER. Did he ever tell you about his wife?—Yes, he told me that he saw her only once a week, that she did not like him, that he did not like her. He also said that she got jealous because there were so many girls, and that he would get a divorce.
>
> For what?—He said the last child was not his.
>
> Did he say what he would do when he got a divorce?—He said he would marry me.

At this point the irrepressible Rev Harold Davidson either laughed, or made some kind of noise which attracted the attention of the prosecutor who, turning, thought he saw a grin dying on the rector's face. 'Mr Davidson appears to be amused,' the barrister commented acidly, adding, 'I don't think it is right for Mr Davidson to laugh aloud in the presence of this young woman.'

> CHANCELLOR. Most certainly not. I did not see him, but if he did it is a very wrong and disgraceful thing to laugh at things of this sort and I will not allow it.
>
> OLIVER. I saw him sir.
>
> DAVIDSON (half-rising from his seat). I did not laugh.
>
> CHANCELLOR. Mr Oliver tells me he saw you.
>
> OLIVER. He laughed when she said that he told her he would get a divorce and would marry her.
>
> CHANCELLOR. It is a very shocking and scandalous thing—I mean the suggestion—and it is still more shocking and scandalous if a gentleman belonging to his sacred profession treats it with levity.
>
> LEVY (for the defence). I do not think he laughed very loudly if you did not hear it.
>
> DAVIDSON. I did not laugh at Miss Harris's remarks at all.

It was symptomatic of the tension that had built up in the courtroom during Barbara's testimony that what was perhaps an involuntary snort could cause so much commotion.

8

Barbara's Ordeal

LEVY. Miss Harris, for your age you have had a very considerable experience of men?—Yes.

I do not want to put it insultingly, but to get the atmosphere,
have you had relations with many men?—Yes.

White men?—Yes.

Black men?—Yes.

Indians?—Yes.

And men of other kinds?—No.

You had already had such experiences when Mr Davidson
met you in August, 1930?—Yes.

Thus did Richard Levy begin his cross-examination of Barbara
Harris on behalf of the defence. From the beginning Levy was
hard-hitting, relentless, for he realised that if the Rev Harold
Davidson was to establish his innocence Barbara was the witness to
vanquish: her testimony must be impeached, her credibility be
destroyed. In particular doubt must be cast on her story of
attempted rape.

Barbara, for her part, stood up to the ordeal remarkably well.
'Miss Harris bore the long strain with extraordinary calmness,'
in the words of the *Daily Sketch*, which reported, 'Except for an
occasional dropping of the eyelids and a still more occasional
flicker of a smile, her face remained throughout coldly impassive.'
The *Evening Standard* agreed about her impassivity, adding, 'Her
self-possession was that of a woman twice her age.' Her performance earned grudging praise even from the Rev Harold Davidson,
who thought she was 'the best witness under a trying ordeal I have
ever seen'. That beneath the calm exterior the girl may have been
seething is indicated by the notes which she took in court for the
prosecution's benefit. Thus while Levy was accusing her of sleeping with men of many colours Barbara jotted down angrily, 'I only
mixed with middle class and better class men,' with an arrow

pointing to the words 'Junior Constitutional Club' pencilled in the margin.

The barrister next cross-examined Barbara about medical treatment which she had received during the time she knew Davidson. Barbara readily admitted she had told Davidson that she thought she had gonorrhea whether or not she did in fact have the disease.

LEVY. After Mr Davidson had seen your brother in January, 1931 did he not take you to the Hospital for Venereal Disease in Endell Street?—No, not until October, 1931.

I suggest to you he took you there in January, 1931, and that from then onwards you were under constant treatment for venereal disease that you had contracted before you met Mr Davidson at all?—No, I was not under treatment for that.

Be careful, Miss Harris, because this can be tested easily, you know.—The doctor said not.

You see what I am suggesting to you: that you went there in January of 1931, and that you were being treated thereafter two or three times a week for venereal disease?—No.

It is a hospital for venereal disease, is it not?—And kidney and bladder trouble.

(Dr Francis Doble, of the Endell Street hospital, when it came to his turn, testified that Barbara had first come to him in September, 1931 as a potential V.D. case; but that after carrying out various pathological tests he had concluded that she was suffering not from gonorrhea as Barbara had supposed but from leucorrhea, more popularly known as 'the whites', which the dictionary defines as a 'discharge from the vagina resulting from inflammation or congestion of the mucous membrane'. Barbara's testimony therefore was correct, though Levy scored his point immediately afterwards with two deftly-placed questions.)

LEVY. You are asking the court to believe that during the whole period from August, 1930 until recently Mr Davidson was endeavouring to be intimate with you?—Yes.

If it be a fact that during the whole of that time he knew, or thought he knew, that you were suffering from this disease that would obviously be a very dangerous thing to do?—Yes.

Levy's next questions were designed to test Barbara's veracity. For Davidson's version of his initial encounter with Barbara at Marble Arch differed in several respects from that of the girl, who claimed that he had followed her in the street before accosting her and pretending that he had mistaken her for Mary Brian, the film actress. According to Davidson, he had intervened when he saw Barbara at Marble Arch talking to a woman whom he knew to be a procuress.

LEVY. When you first met Mr Davidson were you talking to a woman?—I had said 'Hullo' to a girl. I was in a hurry.

But you were not in such a hurry that you could not stop to have a long conversation with Mr Davidson?—I was going shopping.

Did Mr Davidson come up to you and say, 'Do you know that woman?'—No.

I am suggesting, and Mr Davidson is going to say, that she was a woman he knew as a procuress. Do you know what that means?—I suppose it means the white slave traffic.

And I suggest that he came up to speak to you when you had been speaking to the woman and asked if you knew her, and you replied that you did, and that she had asked you to lend her some money?—No.

Think again. It is a long time ago, and you may have forgotten. Is it not a fact?—No.

He inquired what you were doing in order to find out something about yourself?—He asked me where I was going.

Did you say you were out of work?—He thought I was a typist because I had an attaché case in my hand. That was after he said he thought I was a film star.

The notes which Barbara made in court and which were intended for the prosecution's guidance throw further light on the incident, and tend to support the rector's version of it. 'The woman I spoke to was down and out and I had known her for some time,' Barbara wrote. 'She was filthy and never had any money and was always starving. She would never go on the streets for money and used to borrow money off anyone she knew (man or woman).' One is left wondering why Barbara was not more forthcoming in her answers, but then she was giving nothing away so far as the rector was concerned.

Levy next touched on Barbara's movie mania, but his suggestion that she fancied herself as a prospective film star brought a vehement denial.

Did you not when at Macfarlane Road pose as various film artists?—No.

You would be a very unusual girl if you did not think you were suited for films?—No, I should hate to work for the films.

Why?—I cannot face the cameras.

Judging by the newspapers you seem to have been very successful in facing them yesterday. (Laughter.)

OLIVER (interjecting). I don't think she had much chance to avoid them.

LEVY. This obsession of being a film star colours every conversation you have?—No.

Was not your favourite rôle that of Greta Garbo?—Davidson and everybody else used to say I looked like her.

Was not that because you were always posing as Greta Garbo, and to humour you they said, 'Yes, you look exactly like her'?—No.

At the first mention of Greta Garbo's name Chancellor North glanced up from his notes with a look of utter bewilderment on his face. His son Roger North, who, as consistory court registrar was seated on the chancellor's right side, explained to me what followed: 'I kicked father hard under the table before he had a chance to open his mouth. You see, father had never been to a cinema in his life. Consequently he didn't know Greta Garbo from Mickey Mouse. I wanted to save him the kind of celebrity that was visited upon Lord Chief Justice Coleridge after his famous query, "Who is Miss Connie Gilchrist." '[1]

*　　*　　*

Levy led up to Davidson's version of the alleged attempt to rape

[1] Connie Gilchrist, then at the height of her fame as a Gaiety Girl, was mentioned in a court case over which Lord Coleridge presided. His query is often cited as an example of judicial ignorance.

Barbara through a series of questions designed to bring out the lack of privacy at the Macfarlane Road boarding-house.

LEVY. You have told us of alleged efforts on his, Mr Davidson's, part during this time to be intimate with you?—Yes.

Is it not a fact that upon the door of the room you occupied there was neither lock nor bolt nor key?—There was a lock, but no bolt or key.

There was a lock that would not work, is that right?—Just an ordinary lock.

There was no key to fit it?—No.

So if he were endeavouring, as you say, to force his attentions upon you, he always had to do it with an open door in the sense that it had no lock, and your landlady or anybody else could walk in at any moment?—Yes.

Barbara said that occasionally Davidson put a chair in front of the door of the room which she occupied in Alderney Street, Victoria.

LEVY. You said that sometimes he took the risk of trying to force his attentions on you without any sort of barrier at all, no chair, no barrier, nothing. Do you agree that this would be a very indiscreet thing to do?—Yes, but the stairs were wooden, and they would squeak.

You told us of an occasion when you say he pushed you back on the bed. Is not this what happened, that when he came into the room you suddenly went up to him and kissed him on the lips and forced your tongue into his mouth?—No, it is not true.

And then he pushed you back on to the bed when you did that?—I did not do that. I had not the time to get off the bed.

I suppose it is not an unusual experience for you to kiss men in that way, is it?—Only people whom I have known a very long time, and I have liked.

People with whom you had sexual intercourse?—Yes.

You did not always know them for a very long time, did you?—Yes.

You told us, you know, that they were largely promiscuous. I suggest to you that that is what you did to him, and that he pushed you on the bed because he did not like it?—No.

[113]

And did you throw your legs round him, and did he say, 'What are you doing?' And did you say, 'Making love with my legs'?— I never said anything of the sort and never did anything of the sort.

Levy tried very hard to make Barbara admit that she was highly-sexed, but surprisingly it emerged from her testimony that she was the exact opposite. She was in fact suffering from that occupational hazard of the prostitute, frigidity. As the British Social Biology Council's report points out, 'the prostitute is completely without physical or emotional feeling for the man . . . she views the apparent self-indulgence of the man with distaste'.

I suggest that there is no possible doubt, is there, Miss Harris, that you are a very sensual person?—I do not think that I am.

What is it then that drives you to this intercourse with men if it is not your senses?—I do not know.

If it is not your indulgence, I suggest to you it must be your senses?—I have never done it, really, because I wanted to.

You have done it because you did not want to?—Yes.

What for?—Sometimes I have been forced to do it.

In what way do you mean you have been forced to do it? Do you mean that men have raped you?—No, not exactly.

Then in what way?

CHANCELLOR. Does not she mean she has been forced to do it in order to get money out of men?

LEVY. If she means that she might say it, but she so far has denied it. (To Barbara). Is that what you mean, that you have done it for money?—Only with people I knew.

You said you were forced to do it?—Sometimes I have been friendly with a man for about a year, or half a year, and he started getting brutal, and I thought the best thing to do was to give way and stop a lot of unpleasantness.

Do I understand you are telling us now that you always did this against your will?—Yes.

With all the men whose numbers you cannot remember . . . black men, white men, and so forth? You have always done it against your will?—It was two Indians, I can remember the white men.

How many was it?—It might have been eight or ten.

[114]

Are you suggesting to me that those eight or ten men in effect raped you?—Two of them did not.

And the other eight did, is that it?—Yes.

And it was never your desire? You never wanted to do it? You always disliked it? Is that right?—Yes.

In reply to the chancellor's question as to why she gave in to the men, Barbara said that it was because she 'did not want to offend them'.

* * *

The next set of questions was designed to show that Barbara was indolent, that she made no real effort to get a job. But her answers showed that she was perhaps a little more level-headed than she was given credit for being. She pointed out that she could not get employment without references. As for the Labour Exchange, 'I knew it was no good.'

'When a young woman of your type has been out of work for months, do you think she ought to discriminate in advance whether she would get work or not?'

CHANCELLOR. Mr Levy, is that not a very high moral question?

LEVY. Perhaps we are not dealing with high morals.

CHANCELLOR. I think I can answer that.

LEVY (to Barbara). There is plenty of work in domestic service?
—Yes, but a girl must have uniforms to go there.

A maid's outfit, she said, would cost about £10. A girl would want black frocks and blue frocks, and lots of caps and aprons.

LEVY. Have you ever thought it possible that there might be situations in domestic service which did not require £10 for an outfit?—Yes, I suppose about one in a thousand.

When it was suggested Mr Davidson should come and call on you, did you tell him that your landlady might wonder who he was and might object?—Yes.

And did he say, 'I will make you one of my adopted nieces. I have dozens of them. You can call me Uncle Harold.'?—No.

At the words Uncle Harold there was an outburst of laughter from the seats directly behind the defence counsel which were reserved for barristers. Now it was Levy's turn to complain. 'Things have been said about the gravity of laughing at serious matters of this sort, but I find that a man behind me has been laughing uproariously,' he pointed out.

CHANCELLOR (sternly). I did not notice him. They will have to go out of court if they do.

LEVY. I can understand people who are not used to being in these courts laughing, but when it comes from a professional man who is used to conducting cases I am a little surprised.

CHANCELLOR. I think if he had laughed uproariously I should have noticed it. I hope there will be nothing of this sort. This case is quite difficult, and quite painful enough.

LEVY (to Barbara). There is no possible doubt that Mr Davidson was very kind to you?—Yes, he was.

In your favour be it said that you never sponged upon him, and did not ask him for money except when you absolutely needed it?—No, I never asked anybody for money.

Levy dwelt at some length on the fact that Barbara, despite Davidson annoying her, kept coming back to the rector. For example, when she went to live with the Indian policeman in Tolmers Square it would have been easy for her to make the rector disappear from her life, instead of which she wrote to the rector and invited him round to meet her Hindu boyfriend.

LEVY. You say that you resented what Mr Davidson was trying to do to you, and that you repulsed him. You went away to a place he did not know, and you need never have seen him again in your life?—Yes.

If that were true, why did you communicate with him again? —I still wanted him to get me a job.

You got into touch with him in order to get at Mr Gordon's money. Your scruples were not too fine about that, were they? You would bear his attentions, his handling you, much as you disliked it, in order to get Mr Gordon's money?—Yes, for him to set me up in business.

. . .

Did you say the Indian was a very nice man and you would like Mr Davidson to meet him?—Yes.

You had a brother of thirty-four, yet you wanted Mr Davidson to interview the Indian. Why not your brother?—My brother does not like me.

At this point Barbara changed her testimony to indicate that Davidson had taken a dislike to the Hindu. The defence counsel was quick to pounce upon the apparent contradiction. 'I really must test this,' Levy declared. 'I want to find out whether you are really telling us the truth or not. You said Mr Davidson found the Hindu a very nice man. Now you say he did not like the man. Which is true?'

BARBARA. I said anyone must like him because he was a nice man.

CHANCELLOR. You must not expect too much consistency from a witness such as Miss Harris.

LEVY (to Barbara). When Mr Davidson came to see you there were no signs that you were living together?—He could not help seeing that we were living together. Our clothes were in the room and we were having tea together.

There is nothing wrong with having tea together?—But it was in a bed-sitting room.

It was the only room the Hindu had?—Yes.

There was another Indian in a back room and a girl living with him?—Yes.

Mr Davidson may well have thought that you two girls were living in the back room, and that the two Indians were living in the front room?—No, I told him I was living with the Indian when he first came there. It was obvious.

He was willing that you should marry the Indian?—Yes.

*　　*　　*

When Barbara resumed her testimony after the lunch break Richard Levy was quick to spot that she had changed the emerald green straw hat she had been wearing for a close-fitting black skull cap. 'Forgive me for being personal, Miss Harris,' Levy remarked, 'but I cannot help noticing you have got a different hat on since you

were here this morning. Is it a new one?' But any hopes Levy may
have entertained of starting a hare were dashed when Barbara
denied that it was new.

The closing moments of cross-examination were enlivened by
Barbara's description of how she gave the Rev Harold Davidson a
black eye after he had locked her in his room, facts which had not
been brought out in direct examination. The incident occurred on
the night in October, 1931 when Davidson, according to the girl's
testimony, had threatened to commit suicide unless she spent the
night with him. Earlier in the evening they had been to see *Salome*
at the Duke of York's theatre, and after the theatre Barbara had
gone to Macfarlane Road with the rector for the express purpose of
getting some clothing she had left there.

LEVY. On the way home in the tube did he notice that the time
was late and say, 'Look here, you will miss your last tube. You
had better get out'?—No, he said that afterwards.

Do you say that he said he was prepared to die for love of
you?—No.

Why should he threaten to commit suicide except that he was
prepared to die for love of you?—He said that he would commit
suicide if I did not go home. He said he could not bear to be
alone with his thoughts, and he said that if I did not go home
with him he would get Rosie.

You say he was going to commit suicide or satisfy himself with
Rosie, and that he was going to get Rosie. He thought the other
alternative was an easier one?—Yes.

I suggest this is all nonsense?—No.

Did you put your fingers in your ears and refuse to listen to
him while you were in the tube train? You insisted upon going to
Macfarlane Road in spite of his protests?—Yes, I put my fingers
in my ears. I didn't care what I did.

Barbara said that she intended to walk back from Shepherd's
Bush, but Davidson locked her in his room and would not let her
go.

'That was the time I gave him a black eye,' she added.

CHANCELLOR. You gave him a black eye? This is new.—
Yes.

LEVY. Why did you not bang on the door to attract people's attention?—I did, but nobody came. I did not scream out.

Why have you not mentioned this before?—I was not asked.

Did you mention to Mrs Walton (the landlady) that he forced you to stay against your will?—Yes, I did later.

I suggest that this is a pure fabrication in order to get out of the position you are in?—No.

In the tube he was begging you to go back?—Yes.

Why did he change his position?—He said that he would pay for a taxi home, and I said I would never take a penny from him.

You would not take a taxi fare from him, but you did not hesitate to live for a month in November at his expense in Macfarlane Road?—I was independent.

But if you took a loan from him you could have repaid him?— He would not take it. He always threw it in my face, shouting in buses and trains about the money he gave me.

He is a man with rather a small voice is he not?—He has rather a large voice.

CHANCELLOR. And that is when you gave him a black eye. Was it a real black eye?—Yes, but it went on top not underneath.

So there was a bruise which would show to people?—Yes.

Barbara looked pale and drawn when she stepped down from the dais where she had been sitting beside the chancellor, and took a seat in the body of the hall. She had been in the witness-box a total of 9 hours and 25 minutes, and quite obviously she was exhausted.

* * *

Although Barbara no longer occupied the witness-box her spirit continued to hover over the courtroom as the defence sought to establish the startling proposition that she was the 'kept woman' of the prosecution. Specifically, Lee, Bolton and Lee were accused of having supported Barbara in style for over a month while waiting for the trial to begin. Not only had the solicitors' firm paid Barbara's rent for three weeks while she lived in Shepherd's Bush, but it had continued to keep her when she moved into the hostel where she was staying at the time of the trial, and had given her pocket-money besides. These facts Levy sought to establish in his cross-examination of H. T. A. Dashwood, senior partner of Lee, Bolton and Lee.

When last encountered Dashwood had been urging the Rev Harold Davidson to go down on his knees before God, it will be recalled, (this as a preliminary to the rector signing a Deed of Resignation). Now in the rôle of witness Dashwood exuded the same air of sweet reasonableness, as he told of the series of interviews he had had with Davidson starting on December 21st. Inevitably the paternity question came up. Referring to his second interview with the rector, the solicitor declared, 'He came, as far as I understand, with the express purpose of telling me he was not the father of his youngest child.'

> CHANCELLOR. Why did he tell you that?
> LEVY (interposing). It is quite right he did, but he told Mr Dashwood many things in strictest confidence, and this was one of them.
> OLIVER. It is a terrible thing to produce, but it must be introduced in evidence to corroborate Barbara's story.

When it came Levy's turn to cross-examine he lost no time in intimating that the prosecution had 'bribed' Barbara in order to influence her testimony against Davidson.

> LEVY. Do you think that in a criminal prosecution it is a proper course to give money to people who are going to be witnesses on behalf of the prosecution?—In this case it is absolutely right.
> She would be grateful to you and to those concerned in the prosecution for keeping her, wouldn't she?—Yes.
> Have you promised her she is going to be looked after?—I have asked her what she wishes to do so far as work is concerned. It is very largely a charitable matter.
> Do you think it is wise or desirable to make as an object of your charity a girl who is going to give most important evidence in a case you are about to present to the court?—I can see no better object of charity.
> CHANCELLOR. I do not think that is quite an answer.
> LEVY. Do you think it is a proper course to select as an object of your charity a person who is going to be a vital witness in this case?—Yes, in this case.

You know that from time to time this girl has been largely supported by Mr Davidson?—Yes.

What attitude would you have taken if Mr Davidson had given her money? Would not we have had an outcry here about tampering with witnesses?—Yes.

If he had given half a crown to this girl to keep her from starving it would have been tampering with witnesses?—Yes.

CHANCELLOR. Supposing she had been your witness, Mr Levy.

LEVY. It is a most monstrous and improper thing to have done, in my submission.

Now it was the chancellor's turn to get the rough side of the defence counsel's tongue. The clash occurred when Chancellor North referred to allegations that the defence had attempted to tamper with Barbara. This brought Levy to his feet. 'I protest against what I consider to be a gradual and complete poisoning of your mind in this case,' he declared heatedly. 'There has never been any attempt to tamper with Barbara Harris.' In the face of this denial the chancellor did a hasty climb-down.

CHANCELLOR. It may be that Mr Oliver in opening put this into my head.

LEVY. I should be glad if you would try to keep an open mind.

CHANCELLOR. I shall. I am relying on you by-and-by to clear that away.

LEVY. I do ask you not to accept, of necessity, everything that has been said, because there is a very different point of view.

CHANCELLOR. I do not, after forty years' judicial work of one sort or another.

After this incident Levy renewed his questioning of Dashwood with, 'Do you ever think of going down Piccadilly and seeing people in the gutter—people without any bed or food—to exercise your charity on people there, instead of on Miss Barbara Harris, who was going to give evidence for the prosecution?'

DASHWOOD. My time is otherwise employed.

LEVY. Did you hear Barbara say something to this effect, 'I would do almost anything for money when I wanted it'?—I will take it that she did say it, I do not remember.

[121]

She is a girl who would give her body?—She was a girl who
would give her body.

She was speaking in the present tense. She was confessing that
she was the type of girl who would do anything if she wanted to
make use of people?—I think she was referring to before
January.

Levy said that he would read the passage in Barbara's evidence.

OLIVER. Be good enough to read it all.

LEVY (heatedly). That is another offensive observation. If I do
no read quite enough Mr Oliver can ask me to read further without making an offensive interruption. I resent it.

A moment later, after further interruption, Levy bristled at
Oliver once more. 'Do try to contain your ire for a short time,' he
admonished. 'I am getting rather tired of the continued interruption.'

LEVY (to Dashwood). It would be a monstrous and shocking
thing to do if Mr Davidson had given Barbara the price of a
meal?—It would be open to misunderstanding.

It has been open to misunderstanding in this case. Do you
know that from the time you started supporting this girl the
gravest allegations were being made on affidavit against the conduct of the inquiries of your inquiry agents?—I beg your pardon.

LEVY (sharply). Please pay attention. It is very difficult to have
to repeat every question. I say, do you know the gravest allegations of corruption had been put on affidavit against your inquiry
agents?—You are referring to Rose Ellis?

Yes. Yet at this time you take Barbara under your wing while
the most formal and deliberate protests were being alleged against
monstrous corruption by your agents?

As Dashwood did not reply, Levy produced letters from Rose
Ellis's solicitor protesting to Lee, Bolton, and Lee about the
methods the private detectives hired by the latter firm had used in
pursuing their inquiries.

LEVY. It was alleged that they (the detectives) were going round driving witnesses to make statements?—I know that it was all untrue.

I presume you had been told by the agents themselves that it was untrue. You did not expect them to say it was true?—We knew that they could not have done it.

Knowing what was alleged, did you still think it was proper to give money and support to Barbara?—There was no money at the time. It was paid to the landlady. She did not have any money until she went to the hostel.

Please answer the question. Did you still think it was proper? —Yes.

You thought it proper to give her money to go to cinemas and amuse herself?—The last ten shillings was on March 30.

And the first ten shillings was on March 16. That is £2.15s. in a fortnight, as I said. Please do not introduce silly things like this. It was more money than this girl had ever had before, so far as you know?—I don't know.

Have you ever troubled to inquire?—No.

*　　*　　*

Barbara made one more appearance in the witness-box when she was recalled by the defence on Tuesday, April 5, and questioned about hanky-panky in the Cosy Café in Edgware Road, where she had met Dixie Din, the strongman. It was obvious that the defence had been talking to Dixie, and that he had supplied the information on which the additional questions were based.

LEVY. Did you sit on his knee in the café at one time?—No.

And did you try to undo his clothes?—No.

Understand, Miss Harris, that I am not putting these things to you from my own fancy. You appreciate that, do you not? —Yes.

Just think . . . because you are on oath. Do you swear that you did not sit upon his knee and do this?—No.

You mean you did not do it? You do swear that you did not do it?—Yes. I used to sit next to him.

You were trying to get him to make love to you, were you not, and give you money?—No.

On this occasion when I suggest to you that you sat upon his knee and did this, did he push you away?—I did not do it, so he could not push me away.

Do you remember an occasion when he pushed you away from him, and did you fly back at him and scratch his face?—No.

All this is pure imagination?—Yes.

CHANCELLOR. I suppose they would not let you into the café if you did this sort of thing?

LEVY. I hope you will not form any conclusion about this café. There are cafés where this happens, and where such things are encouraged.

OLIVER. I wonder how long they would last?

CHANCELLOR. I should think, especially with a licensed place, there would be proceedings elsewhere.

LEVY. I don't doubt that in this case there will be, but this was not a licensed café.

After these observations the moon-goddess, symbol of divine retribution, resumed her seat in the back of the courtroom. The press photographers may not have spotted her whip of scorpions when she arrived at Church House, but the Rev Harold Davidson had taken the lash full in the face.

LITTLE JIMMY

'He was fifty. It's the age when clergymen first
begin to be preoccupied with the underclothing
of little school-girls in trains . . .'
ALDOUS HUXLEY, *Chawdron*

'I am in Love, but no more than the Profession
of Knight-Errantry obliges me to be; yet I am
none of this Age's vicious Lovers, but a chaste
Platonick.'
CERVANTES, *Don Quixote*, Part II, Book III

9

Rector in the Box

When the consistory court reconvened on Thursday, May 19, to hear the Rev Harold Davidson's defence the queues for seats in the public gallery were longer than ever.[1] Long before the doors of Church House opened Great Smith Street was black with people at its Westminster end. They stood blinking in the unexpected spring sunshine, the men in the long overcoats from the Salvation Army dosshouse round the corner, their faces leached white by hopelessness. Indeed the news during the six weeks the Stiffkey trial had been adjourned had seemed more depressing than ever. In that interim a French President and a Japanese premier had been assassinated, Hitler had made sweeping gains in Prussia, the £500 million utilities empire of Samuel Insull had crashed. At home the news had been equally sobering. After visiting Tyneside where he found a family of six living in one room the Prince of Wales returned to Fort Belvedere feeling ill ('How could one hope to build a healthy nation on such wretchedness?' he wrote). At Cambridge University two young scientists split the atom, thereby realising the dream of the alchemists, in the words of the *Daily Herald*. The same newspaper was responsible for the headline FASHION SAYS YOU MUST LOOK HALF-STARVED.

Those fashion plates from the dosshouse who queued for seats at Church House in the hope that the spectacle inside would take their minds off their shrunken bellies were not disappointed. Their hero gave a dazzling performance, or should one say performances? For it was soon evident that Davidson was a bundle of performers bound together in one small package. Referring to another such

[1] The court had adjourned on April 7 after the defence had run out of funds, and after Davidson had rejected the prosecution's extraordinary offer of £250 to continue the case. (Although the prosecution was coy about it, the money was to have come from the Church Commissioners.) Meanwhile, on May 15 Lady Waechter opened a defence fund on Davidson's behalf.

multiple personality, Miss Beauchamp, Dr Morton Prince writes, 'The personalities come and go in kaleidoscopic succession, many changes often being made in the course of twenty-four hours.' In the case of the Rev Harold Davidson the changes could occur in a matter of minutes.

It was as Uncle Harold, the avuncular but slightly dotty country clergyman, that Davidson went into the witness-box on Friday, May 20, after Richard Levy had concluded the opening statement for the defence. Taking the Bible in his hand Uncle Harold listened intently as Chancellor North repeated the words of the oath, then kissed the book reverently, and took a seat beside the chancellor on the dais. Levy then ceded his place to junior counsel, E. Ryder Richardson, who began his examination of Davidson by eliciting a vigorous denial from the latter of the charges.

'Have you ever been guilty of immorality?' Richardson asked. The rector replied with an emphatic 'No'.

The next question was: 'Have you lived in adultery with any woman?' Again the answer was 'No'.

RICHARDSON. Have you ever importuned a woman with immoral intent?
DAVIDSON. Never in my life.

The barrister then led Davidson through a brief résumé of his life's history. Not only was his father a clergyman, but twenty-seven of his relatives were men of the cloth, Davidson explained. It had always been his desire to enter the Church, but at first it was impossible for financial reasons. He then told how he had gone on the stage in order to finance his studies at Oxford.

His counsel next questioned Davidson about his sleeping habits.

RICHARDSON. Do you sleep very much?—Very seldom. Two or three hours a night at the outside; very often not at all.
Do you go to bed every night?—Very seldom. I have only been to bed three times since the adjournment.
CHANCELLOR. You mean to say you never go to bed.
DAVIDSON (laughing). I have a bath every morning, but I rarely take my clothes off at night. I promised Mr Richardson I would go to bed last night, but I did not.

Questioned further about his insomnia, the rector replied: 'I sit in a chair and read and write until my pen drops, and then I drop off for an hour, and when I wake I can go straight on with the next word in the sentence. My brain never sleeps. My father was just the same. He did not go to bed three times in the last nine years. He used to sleep like this.' Here Davidson slumped down in the witness chair and laid his head on his hand.

CHANCELLOR. We don't want to see.

Davidson gave his answers in a high-pitched voice. He was extremely voluble, but at times became almost inaudible. Several times he moved his chair, first nearer to the chancellor and then to counsel, and raised a laugh when he apologised to the registrar for sitting with his back to him.

It was when it came to dealing with numbers that Davidson's testimony veered into the realm of surrealism. The rector wrote later: 'I was picking up roughly, as my diaries show, an average of about 150 to 200 girls a year, and taking them to restaurants for a meal and a talk,' thus indicating that in the decade ending in 1932 he had picked up between 1,500 and 2,000 girls. 'Of these,' he added, 'I was able definitely to help into good jobs of work a very large number.'[1]

In the witness-box, however, Davidson scaled down this estimate considerably.

RICHARDSON. How many girls do you think you have spoken to in this way in the last 10 years?
DAVIDSON. I have a list of 500.
RICHARDSON. How many have you helped?
DAVIDSON. Perhaps 200.
RICHARDSON. Not only financially, but with advice?
DAVIDSON. Oh, with advice between 500 and 1,000.

Five hundred or a thousand, the mind boggles in contemplation of so much girlhood.

It was the contention of the Bishop of Norwich and his advisers that Davidson chose only pretty girls, never plain ones, as the

[1] *The Reason Why.*

objects of his charity, to which the rector replied that it was the pretty ones who were in greatest need of his help. The plain ones could fend for themselves.

The girls whom Davidson helped were not only pretty, but they were young, their ages ranging from 15 upwards. The rector countered the implied criticism of himself as a cradle-snatcher by quoting Mirabeau, who, when asked what he would do to create the model French citizen, said that he would begin twenty years before the child was born by educating the woman who was to be its mother. 'That is why I have always striven to inculcate the highest principles into girls between the ages of 14 and 20,' Davidson told the court.

Neither pretty nor green in years was Rose Ellis, who was twenty when Davidson first met her. Questioned about that first meeting with Rose in Leicester Square in September, 1920, Davidson described her as 'one of those delicate-looking girls [who] you are amazed to find can lift huge tables in doing housework.' 'Her muscles are very strong,' the rector added, as though describing a work horse. Strong in the arms, but evidently not in the head, for the rector went on to say that Rose was 'mentally undeveloped'. 'I felt she was very weak and very easily led,' he amplified. To give him some measure of control over Rose, Davidson had a guardianship deed drawn up, signed by her mother, and stamped at Somerset House. Asked to produce this document in court, the rector said he would look for it, but that he had about twenty cases of documents at Stiffkey, and another thirty in London.

Referring to the period in 1922 when he had taken a room for Rose in Endsleigh Street, Davidson said she was known by three different names: Rose Ellis, which was her real name; Rosalie Bashford, which was the stage name she took when he had got her a job with a touring company; and Mrs Malone, which referred to the bigamous, wartime marriage she had entered into with the Australian soldier. At Endsleigh Street the rector had introduced Rose as his secretary-ward. She copied letters and did filing for him. She was a 'little unreliable', but 'exceptionally capable and extraordinarily quick', this mentally-retarded girl.

RICHARDSON. We have heard that you and Rose left to go to Paris. Did you conceal that you were going there?—No, I discussed it with people.

[130]

Did you in fact go?—Yes, and Rose accompanied me.

What was the purpose?—I wanted to get her a job. I have taken a great many girls to Paris to jobs. I have an old friend there who runs a school just outside Paris, and I often take girls to domestic service there so that they can pick up French.

Rose did not like the job, and did not stay. At that time Davidson was interested in many other girls. In fact, he was more interested in them than he was in Rose.

RICHARDSON. And in a similar way?

DAVIDSON. Well, they were girls for whom I had more hope of doing something. She was rather my despair.

*   *   *

If it was Uncle Harold who stepped down from the witness-box on Friday night, at the conclusion of his first day in giving evidence, it was Little Jimmy who entered it on Saturday morning, according to J. Rowland Sales, who attended the hearing. It was the self-destructive hobgoblin's turn to be out of the barometer house. 'Davidson's whole demeanour changed when he went into the witness-box the second day,' Sales told me. 'Overnight he had become mischievous, provocative, as though thumbing his nose at the proceedings. One moment he would be waving to friends on the other side of the courtroom; the next he would be slouched in his seat, staring up at the ceiling in a bored manner. The change was very marked.'

So much so, that even Chancellor North remarked it. 'Sit quiet and don't keep shifting and fidgeting about,' the chancellor admonished Davidson before the latter could even open his mouth. The defendant must keep his hands out of his pockets, the chancellor added, as though correcting a member of the awkward squad on the parade ground.

RICHARDSON. You are asking even more than can be expected from Mr Davidson. I do not think he has ever remained in one position for more than five minutes in his life. I hope you will be tolerant.

CHANCELLOR. Yes, so your learned leader assured me.

RICHARDSON. I hope you are satisfied. I thought you might think there was some wilful malice.
CHANCELLOR. Oh, no.

But wilful malice was Little Jimmy's speciality. Had Davidson been on trial for his life Little Jimmy would have tightened the noose round his neck, for this persona now proceeded to do all in his power to antagonise the Worshipful J. Keppel North. His manner became cocky, his answers impertinent. At times spectators got the impression that they were seeing a comic double, for the more outlandish the rector's replies, the more incredulous did Chancellor North show himself to be.

In particular Little Jimmy reared his head when Davidson was questioned about his friendship with 28-year-old actress Winifred Wayne, whose father was a clergyman, and who herself played leading rôles with Martin Sabine's repertory company (she played the lead in *Daddy Long Legs* in December, 1926). In 1928 Miss Wayne contemplated becoming a Catholic (she later became a nun), and in an effort to dissuade her Davidson got the bright idea of introducing her to the Bishop of Norwich, who was noted for his broad evangelical views. Accordingly, Davidson persuaded his landlady, Battling Flora Osborne, and her husband to drive the actress and himself to Stiffkey, where he hoped to entertain the bishop to tea on the rectory lawn. But everything had gone wrong. First the bishop had begged off this madhatter's teaparty. Then Molly Davidson, who was in her gardening clothes, refused to have her picture taken with the group, and when her husband insisted grabbed a handful of leaves and held them in front of her face. 'But surely that is a boy,' Chancellor North protested when shown the photograph with Molly looking like the scarecrow in *The Wizard of Oz*. When told that it was Mrs Davidson, he inquired, 'Does she always go about like that?'

On the return journey to London in the Osbornes' motorcar Davidson had put his arm round Miss Wayne's waist, according to Battling Flora, who testified to this effect at the trial. It was a situation ready-made for Little Jimmy's genius.

RICHARDSON. Did you put your arm round her waist?—Certainly not. You could not in a motorcar with any comfort, I imagine.

CHANCELLOR. Just think of that answer. Do you mean you did not because you could not? You mean it would have been impossible for you to have done so even if you had wished to do so?
DAVIDSON. Yes, provided one was sitting in a decent position.
RICHARDSON. Were you sitting in anything but a decent position?—Certainly not.

Had you got your arm round her waist?—I could not have had.

I do not want to know whether you could have.—No, I had not.
CHANCELLOR. Mr Richardson knows remarkably well what he is about. So please attend to him just as you would attend to a doctor who has prescribed for you.

Again, the spectator might be forgiven for thinking that he had blundered into a pantomime rehearsal rather than a serious court trial in listening to Little Jimmy descant on the advantages of keeping one's money in one's boots in order to foil pick-pockets. This discourse was prompted by an A.B.C. waitress's testimony that she had seen the rector tuck some notes in his sock.

RICHARDSON. Is it true to say your pockets are generally bulging with photographs and papers?—Yes, I am the despair of my tailor. I had sixteen pockets put into this suit.

Where do you keep your money?—Mostly I keep large sums in my socks down *here* (demonstrating), but I do not want everyone to know that. (Laughter.) What I would do would be this: I would divide £10 up into £5 on each side; I would fold one up in my sock like *this* (demonstrating), and put it in *here*; then roll that up, and then I would put the other £5 on the other side.
CHANCELLOR. Do you mean in the A.B.C. restaurants?—Yes, or anywhere. They used to be rather amused when I had to dive down and fish it out.

You do that in public?—Yes, but not too publicly, because I do not want people to know where it is. It is the last place which a burglar would think of. I have so often had my pockets picked by pickpockets. Anyone who wanted to take it would have to take my boots off.
RICHARDSON. That is rather unconventional, is it not?—I do not know. I have recommended several people to do it. Ladies do

the same, only they keep it higher up *here* (demonstrating) under their garters.

CHANCELLOR. Did you say you had to take your boots off to get your money?—No, anyone who wanted to get it would have to. If you like I will give you a demonstration.

RICHARDSON (hastily). No, we do not wish that.

Little Jimmy agreed with counsel that he was a man of impetuosities. 'I never think whether a thing is advisable or not,' he said. 'I go straight away and do it on the spur of the moment.' On several occasions he had given moral lectures to waitresses in restaurants. He had also given a talk to the Jackson Girls at the Palladium in their dressing-room.

CHANCELLOR. In their dressing-room where they change clothes?—Yes, we of the Actors' Church Union are often behind the scenes.

RICHARDSON. Behind the scenes you see ladies with very little clothes on, do you not?—Yes.

When you spoke to those girls in their dressing-room was there anything indecent or immoral about it?—No, none whatever. I was invited to go by the management.

However, unconventional for a country parson?—But it is not unconventional for the Actors' Church Union. It is our duty. We are in and out of the wings.

Chancellor North's capacity for being shocked seemed limitless. He made the perfect straight man, or 'feed' for Little Jimmy's knockabout comic, as time and again he rose to the latter's bait. Take the matter of Winifred Barker's teeth and of Davidson's professed admiration for them.[1] Little Jimmy was questioned about this.

RICHARDSON. Miss Barker said you patted her under the chin? —I should think that exceedingly unlikely in a public restaurant. I should not in the least hesitate to do it if I wanted to look at her

[1] Davidson's fetishism concerning teeth was alluded to in a song from the musical *The Stiffkey Scandals of 1932* whose lyrics ran, 'When I see a scarlet-painted rosebud/Smiling to uncover strong and healthy teeth.'

teeth. I have often done it if I wanted to look at their teeth, to see if they were even.

CHANCELLOR. Just attend, because I want you to do justice to yourself. Do you really say that you would pull her lips down and look at her teeth?—If a girl was asking me whether she was suitable for film work, supposing her teeth were all completely uneven, I should say, 'No, you had better go to a dentist.'

Would you open her lips and look at her teeth, just as you would a horse?—Yes.

If you wanted to know a horse's age you would look at its teeth?—Yes, in many cases they would be asses for wishing to go on the stage.

Would you do it without her leave?—Certainly not. That is the whole point.

RICHARDSON. Was there anything immoral in looking at her teeth?—Not in the least.

*　　*　　*

Almost perceptibly Little Jimmy faded, and the more responsible Uncle Harold stepped into his shoes as Davidson was examined concerning his friendship for Barbara Harris.

His counsel began by questioning Davidson concerning his first meeting with Barbara in August, 1930. The rector said he was standing outside the Marble Arch Underground station waiting for Mr Gordon when his attention was attracted to Barbara Harris by 'the peculiar way she walked'.

About twenty minutes later Davidson saw Barbara talking to a woman whom he considered undesirable, and as soon as the woman had left the rector went up to Barbara and told her so. This was not an exceptional thing for the rector to do. Over coffee Barbara had then told Davidson that she was out of work, and he, in turn, had promised to help her. 'She told me that if I called at her room her landlady might think it funny,' Davidson added. 'So I said that I had better adopt her as a niece. I had lots of adopted nieces. I usually call myself their adopted uncle. It is an Irish custom I learned from my wife.'

Davidson said that he visited Barbara at her room in Alderney Street five or six times. Sometimes he went half-way up the stairs and called to her, but when he went into her room he never shut the door, nor did he put a chair up against the handle to prevent the landlady from entering.

And so the questioning was brought by easy stages round to the alleged rape attempt at Alderney Street. Here the problem posed— namely the nature of truth—is identical to that posed in the film classic *Rashomon*, which likewise is concerned with rape. In the film the material facts are never in dispute. Something unpleasant has taken place in the woods, but what? No two witnesses are agreed. The same episode is seen through four pairs of eyes—the bride, the groom, a bandit, a wood-cutter who is cast in the rôle of a Peeping Tom. Which version is the correct one? In Barbara's case only two pairs of eyes were involved, but the story the Rev Harold Davidson now told contradicted the girl's in every respect.

Davidson told how he had called at Alderney Street at lunch time one day to find Barbara still in bed when she should have been dressed and ready to go out with him. 'Naturally I was annoyed, especially as she told me she had been drunk the night before, and I suppose my voice showed it,' the rector testified. 'Then she got out of bed and put both arms round me, and twined her legs in a most unpleasant way all round me, and kissed me in a most disgusting and offensive way. I threw her back on the bed and I said, "Do not do that again." '

RICHARDSON. Did she tell you what she was doing?—She used the phrase, 'I am making love with my legs'.

What was your attitude to that incident?—After that I never went to the house again to see her. I apologised for having thrown her back onto the bed before I left, because I did it very roughly perhaps. I said I was sorry.

. . .

Did you ever say you wanted to possess her body and soul?— No, I said I was ready to fight for her body and soul.

Even a remark like that unexplained sounds extraordinary?— One's whole career as a clergyman is fighting for people's souls, and very often their bodies. Very often you have to do the body first.

Did you think she would easily go wrong?—I did not know much about the things in her life at that time. Many of the things I heard for the first time when she was in the witness-box. I was amazed when I heard of her relations with men.

[136]

Davidson was then questioned about the occasion when he called at Tolmers Square at 11 p.m. and, according to Barbara, found her in bed with her Hindu boyfriend. He denied going into the room, nor had he seen Barbara in the presence of the Indian in her pyjamas. He denied saying 'I prefer you with them off'.

RICHARDSON. Have you any pyjamas?—I have not had any for years. Mr Barton (Davidson's solicitor) lent me some the other night.

And therefore it would be false as anything could be to say that you got into bed with Barbara Harris with your pyjama top on and nothing else?—Absolutely, because I have not got any.

Did you ever spend a night in the room with Barbara Harris with the door locked?—Never.

With a trunk up against the door?—Never.

Barbara Harris has told us that you used preventatives in your association with her. Is that true?—No.

She has told us that you kept preventatives for your personal use in your trunk?—No, the only one I had was one I found in her bag. I spoke to her about it, and locked it up in my trunk, and destroyed it a day or two later. It was either one or two.

Have you ever in your life used preventatives?—No.

This is a question which I am instructed to ask you which you may not wish to answer in public: Have you ever had connection with your wife without having prayed first?—I do not think so.

Have you ever had it for any other purpose than for the sacred purpose of procreating children?—No.

(NOTE: In his copy of the trial transcript Chancellor North underscored the answers to the last two questions with red crayon; there are also huge exclamation marks in red crayon in the margin.)

RICHARDSON. Barbara Harris has described in some detail your appendicitis scar, so she says. Has Barbara Harris ever seen your stomach?—Unless she peeped through the bathroom door, as she did through other doors sometimes, I think not.

Has she ever with your knowledge and consent seen your stomach?—Never.

* * *

Next Davidson was questioned about the arrangement he made whereby Barbara could sleep in his room at Macfarlane Road at week-ends while he was away at Stiffkey. He said that his landlady, Mrs Jessie Walton, had agreed to the arrangement, and that she had also agreed that when the rector was there Barbara could sleep with Mrs Walton's daughter, Evelyn.

RICHARDSON. Did Mrs Walton like Barbara?—She was very sorry for her and seemed to like her.

Barbara has described how on five consecutive nights you knocked and banged on your own door so that she had to get up and let you in?—It is absolutely untrue except for one night. I was going to Stiffkey. I missed the 12.10 train, and while I was looking through my bag at the station I realised I had left behind some very important papers. When I returned I found the door of the room locked.

You intended to be out of London that night?—Yes, that was why Barbara Harris was sleeping in my bed.

What did you do to rouse her?—I knocked at the door two or three times. Knowing that she was a very heavy sleeper I went into a room halfway down the stairs, through which, with a stick, I could reach the bedroom window.

How did you know she was a heavy sleeper?—Once or twice when I had got back about 6.30 in the morning I had gone to the room to make myself some tea and nothing seemed to rouse her.

Did you on any occasion at Macfarlane Road get into bed with Barbara Harris?—No, on one occasion I lay on the bed when she was in it when other people were in the room, my son and a little girl.

Did anything immoral take place on that occasion?—Nothing whatsoever.

Under his counsel's prompting Davidson then told about a Miss Taylor whom he had met at one o'clock in the morning on a late-night bus leaving from Lancaster Gate. The rector had got into conversation with Miss Taylor, and ended by inviting her to stop off at Macfarlane Road for a cup of tea.

RICHARDSON. In the middle of the night?—Yes, the bus leaves Lancaster Gate at 12.46 and gets to Shepherd's Bush at 1.05. I knocked up Mrs Walton and asked permission to take Miss Taylor into a vacant room for tea.

Did you go into Barbara Harris' room?—Yes, I had to go in there to get the sugar.

Barbara Harris has told us that the light was out in that room. Is that so?—It was out for a short period.

Why was that?—Because while I went down to make the tea she said she had rather a headache. There was no shade on the lamp, and as there was a strong light from the street-light outside, the room was still lit.

Were you in the room with Miss Taylor with the light out?— Not more than a minute or two, because I went down to leave her alone to rest. I think I gave her some aspirin, if I remember rightly.

Did anything immoral occur between you and Miss Taylor in that room?—Nothing whatsoever.

The prosecution had made much of Davidson calling Barbara 'queen of my heart', so Richardson now sought to repair this bit of damaged fence.

RICHARDSON. Can you tell us the name of one other person you called 'queen of my heart'?

DAVIDSON. There are so many. My landlady, Mrs Walton, for one. It comes from a song, 'You are Queen of My Heart Tonight'.

It is a pity that Richardson did not pursue the matter further, for Davidson had told only half the story. 'Queen of My Heart' was the song hit of the comic opera *Dorothy*, starring Marie Tempest, when it opened at the Gaiety Theatre in 1886; in fact, it was all that saved that show from being a flop. Newsboys whistled it; postmen and milkmen sang it as they made their rounds, so did shop assistants and men-about-town.

But not even 'Queen of My Heart' could save *Dorothy* in December, 1908 when it was revived by Maundy Gregory, with his schoolmate Harold Davidson raising the money from among his friends. The trouble was that Gregory had sticky fingers to which the box-office receipts adhered. When the unpaid musicians went on strike the show suddenly collapsed. Amid the ruins the plaintive voice of Davidson, who had invested £200 of his savings in the venture, could be heard wailing, 'Ruined, ruined—I shall be ruined.' All that the rector managed to salvage from the wreckage was that wisp of a refrain with which he used to serenade his landlady, among others.

*   *   *

It would take a Hogarth or a Rowlandson to do justice to the faces of the gallery gods, the dosshouse inmates who had turned out to hear the Rev Harold Davidson tell his story. Faces etched by hunger, red-eyed from drinking meths, they were like gargoyles as they leaned over the gallery railing to hear the rector testify. As part of the gallery was located directly above the canopied dais on which Chancellor North and the witness were seated, some of these gargoyles had to crane over the top of the canopy to catch a glimpse of what was happening below. This they were content to do for hours on end. Meanwhile the chancellor remained seemingly unaware of the weird tableau above his head. Unseen these gallery gods may have been, but they soon made themselves heard in a noisy demonstration in favour of the rector. It happened when E. Ryder Richardson, for the defence, touched on the delicate matter of the paternity of Davidson's youngest child.

RICHARDSON. Barbara tells the court that you offered to marry her?—Certainly not; how could I?

She told the court you told her about your youngest child?—That is totally and absolutely untrue.

Have you spoken about it to many people?—Very few originally.

Has it become a part of local gossip in Stiffkey?—Yes, as early as 1920.

You had returned home from abroad in October, 1918?—Yes.

Were you living with your wife when you returned?—No, I only saw her for a few hours. I was still on active service, and was not demobilised until March, 1919.

Davidson was then questioned about the interview during which he had told Henry Dashwood 'in strictest confidence' that he was not the father of his youngest child. According to Davidson, the solicitor then swore that the matter would not be brought into the trial unless the rector used it as an excuse for his being absent so much from his parish.

At this point Roland Oliver objected that the matter had not been put to Dashwood when he was cross-examined, but Richardson maintained that the phrase 'in strictest confidence' had been used. While counsel were wrangling over this point Davidson, with a catch in his voice, broke in, 'This is the only bitter feeling I have in this case, that this poor child should have to read about it in the newspaper from your opening statement, Mr Oliver.' At this there arose murmurs of 'Hear, hear' from the back of the court, while cheers broke out in the gallery. Chancellor North at once ordered that the gallery should be cleared, but then changed his mind, and singling out one woman, a sans-culottish creature who had been particularly vociferous in cheering, he ordered, 'Let her leave the court.' The woman rose and walked out, but the rest of the gallery occupants remained seated. After this dramatic scene, Davidson, apparently overcome by the demonstration, asked that the court be adjourned for a few minutes while he recovered.

There was one more passage of arms before the court rose for the day, and this occurred between Chancellor North and the defendant.

CHANCELLOR. Did you introduce Barbara to your daughter?—Of course I did.

Knowing what Barbara was?—Hoping what she might become, I prefer to put it.

Did you introduce Rosalie Ellis?—We are all very fond of her, my children and I.

Do they know what she is?—Yes.

You introduced your daughters?—But why not? How are you going to raise . . .?

CHANCELLOR. Do not ask me questions.

DAVIDSON. If you do not want to make outcasts forever you have to associate them with decent people. The great failure of the Church is that the icebergs of chastity draw their skirts away from them. That is the whole point. They are finer Christians in practice than most other people, I have found.

10

A Time Bomb

With Little Jimmy it was always 'Let me be your little dog until your big dog comes', as Fats Waller would have it. The trouble was that by the time the big dog arrived on the scene, the little dog had decamped, leaving Uncle Harold to clean up the mess it had made. Put in more technical terms Uncle Harold was amnesic most of the time concerning Little Jimmy, while the latter existed co-consciously—i.e. was aware of all that went on in Uncle Harold's mind.

This cleavage of personality had, of course, been noticeable before Davidson's trial. In the wartime raid on the Cairo brothel, for example, who can doubt that it was Little Jimmy, that daemon dedicated to self-destruction, who chose this particular night for Uncle Harold to do his research into vice conditions, and thus to get himself arrested? (Davidson claimed that he was trying to trace a particular whore who was infecting the men on his ship.) It was not until he came to in the Cairo police station that Uncle Harold realised to his horror what had happened. Similarly with the rumpus Little Jimmy created at the performance of *The Outcast*: Uncle Harold awakened to find that his familiar spirit had been haranguing the audience about the play's ending.

It was not until the closing days of Davidson's cross-examination that his two selves—the little dog and the big dog—were brought face to face in the courtroom. Their confrontation, so sudden and unexpected, was to provide one of the dramatic highlights of the long, drawn-out trial. Its effect on Davidson himself was shattering, according to J. Rowland Sales. Meanwhile, when Roland Oliver rose to cross-examine the rector of Stiffkey the latter showed signs of losing his calm. The process of dissociation, noticeable when Davidson gave his evidence in chief, became greatly accelerated now that he was under fire. At times Davidson's mind was crystal clear, as when he corrected Roland Oliver concerning testimony he had given earlier about the waitress Winifred Barker.

OLIVER. You said she had pretty hair, skin, and teeth?
DAVIDSON. I never said skin.
OLIVER. Didn't you?
DAVIDSON. No, I should like the shorthand note to be read.
OLIVER (after referring to the trial transcript). You are quite
right. You did not say skin.
DAVIDSON. I know I am right. It would be better if you believed
me.

At other times Davidson's mind clouded over, such hazy spells
usually masking the presence of Little Jimmy. To J. Rowland
Sales at least, it was evident that Uncle Harold suffered genuine
amnesia concerning Little Jimmy's merry pranks as, prodded by
questions, he tried desperately to recall them. Thus when asked
whether he had told waitress Dolly Burn to telephone him when
she felt lonely, the rector warily replied, 'I have no recollection of
saying it. I may have.'

RICHARDSON. Did you invite her to Stiffkey?—If she said so I
don't doubt I did. I have invited twenty or thirty girls to Stiffkey.
Did you say you liked Miss Burn?—I might have done so. I
like most people. I am very fond of getting to know people.
Do you remember asking her to go out to tea with you?—I
think very probably I did. I often did.

Even when Little Jimmy was testifying Uncle Harold kept
breaking through to cry in anguish, 'My whole career, my life's
work is at stake.' Once, while Oliver was rummaging for some
document, Davidson, in his Uncle Harold persona, began to mut-
ter to himself, 'I have been accused of misconduct with everyone I
have been associated with.' 'I have been misunderstood,' he wailed.
This caused Chancellor North to prick up his ears.

CHANCELLOR. Do you say misconduct? Do you mean in this
case or generally?
DAVIDSON. No, I said misunderstood. I have been gossiped
about by evil-minded people in connection with every young
girl I have helped.

Defence counsel was inclined to blame fatigue for the fugues

Davidson suffered (had not the rector boasted that during the six weeks the court had been adjourned he had been to bed no more than three times?). Indeed, E. Ryder Richardson lectured him sternly about his insomniac habits, saying that he was doing 'great injustice to the court' by not going to bed. In retrospect, it was not sleeplessness that was troubling Davidson, but something buried deep in his consciousness like a time bomb and ticking away.

Before the prosecution could get round to detonating this bomb the third of Davidson's personalities made a brief appearance. It was the Bunco Kid's turn to come out of the barometer house while the other inmates remained inside. In treating cases of multiple personality psychiatrists frequently have used hypnosis to call forth the various secondary personalities. Thus Dr Morton Prince describes how Miss Beauchamp under hypnosis would 'rub her eyelids in an unaccountable way, until of a sudden [Sally], laughing and gay, would burst out of her chrysalis into her butterfly existence'. In the present instance the Bunco Kid popped out in response to the prosecution's probing of Davidson's financial affairs.

*　　*　　*

'Father was the original communist,' his son Nugent tells me. 'He had no sense of private property. He lived by the rule, What's mine is yours, and vice versa.' Davidson's disregard for money, his own and other people's, may have been supreme; but he showed infinite cunning and ingenuity in acquiring it. He belonged to the genus Begging-Letter Writer, species Impoverished Clergyman, preying upon wealthy and titled people such as the Duchess of Devonshire and Sir Abe Bailey, the Transvaal mine owner. That Davidson used the monies thus raised to help his poor, starving girls is the excuse put forward in his defence. But the facts do not always substantiate this. Thus in approaching the Duchess of Devonshire for a £500 loan, to be secured by a life insurance policy for that amount, the rector pleaded that he was overdrawn at the bank, and that 'I have my wife and four children . . . at home practically without coal or food.' (His appeal might sound more convincing had he not been entertaining Barbara Harris at suppers and shows at the time.)

In particular Davidson abused the friendship of Dr Winnington-Ingram, the Lord Bishop of London, whom he used as referend in asking for loans. 'Lord Dulverton kindly said he would consider helping me if you would write him a few lines,' Davidson writes to the bishop in September, 1930 (Dulverton was president of the Imperial Tobacco Company). 'Perhaps you would send me a short letter that I might just show to anyone I find interested, instead of referring them to you,' the rector continues, assuring his friend, 'You can rely on my honour not to abuse this in any way.' But the long-suffering Winnington-Ingram was too fly to fall for this.

Undeterred, Davidson found other ways to make use of the bishop, notably in conning Mrs Rees-Mogg out of £150. Under cross-examination he described the artfully contrived scene with Mrs Rees-Mogg. 'When I was leaving I picked up my bag,' he related, 'and I had the photograph of the Bishop of London in it which I was taking to be framed . . . As I picked up the bag . . . it came unclasped, and all my things shot out on the floor, and his photograph happened to shoot out just at the foot of the lady in question. She stooped down and picked it up, and said, "What a very good photograph." I said, "Yes, he gave it to me the other day." ' Not for nothing had Davidson served his apprenticeship on the stage.

But it was not until the prosecutor mentioned the name of Arthur John Gordon that the Bunco Kid sprang upon the scene fully-armed and ready to do battle in defence of his friend's honour. Again, it was good theatre, and as such it was wildly applauded by Davidson's partisans until Chancellor North sent for the police and ordered the gallery cleared.

Oliver's opening questions elicited the facts that Davidson had first met Gordon in 1919, and that shortly afterwards he had handed over to Gordon 'a lot of shares that I had in a company before the war, and he [Gordon] was going to try and see what he could do with them for me.' By September, 1920 the con-man had swindled the rector out of £4,500.

OLIVER. When did Mr Gordon become bankrupt?—In 1922, I think it was.

Has he been an undischarged bankrupt ever since?—You will be able to ask him when he comes.

I want to know from you?—I do not believe he has. All kinds of funny things have happened about his business. He is very reticent about his business.

At this point the Bunco Kid waxed indignant. Gordon's name was not to have been mentioned at the proceedings, but he was to have been referred to only as 'Mr G'. Now the resultant publicity might at any moment 'completely wreck his [Gordon's] life's reconstructive work'.

OLIVER. His life's reconstructive work did not make much progress during the last ten or twelve years?—He says that it is nearing completion.

I am suggesting that he is a sort of swindler?—You can ask him that.

And that you have acted with him. There is nothing like being frank in such matters.—That is absolutely untrue, and if you dare to say that outside the court I will deal with it.

The prosecutor was asking about shares which Gordon had taken over when the Bunco Kid interposed, 'I am being charged with sexual immorality, not financial immorality. If the Bishop of Norwich will frame another charge I shall be delighted to meet it.'

OLIVER. One thing we have to test is whether you are a truthful person, and these questions are for that purpose.

DAVIDSON. You have just accused me of being a swindler.

The Bunco Kid then turned to Chancellor North and asked if one of the charges could not be amended for this purpose. This brought a burst of applause from the gallery which grew in volume despite cries of 'Silence!' from the chancellor. The clapping continued for an appreciable time, and when it finally subsided the chancellor pointed to one section of the gallery and announced, 'Unless those people who were clapping leave, I will have that part cleared.' Nobody stirred. The request was repeated several times, and still nobody batted an eyelid. It was not until three uniformed police officers appeared that the gallery was cleared. The thirty or so spectators who were ejected did not have far to go, as the Sally Ann hostel was just round the corner.

* * *

By now it should have been obvious to all concerned that in

taking on the Rev Harold Davidson the Church Establishment was dealing with no ordinary mortal. His own counsel admitted that Davidson was 'a troublesome busybody', declaring, 'Not even Mr Oliver will dispute that he is very unusual and eccentric.' But this was precisely what the prosecutor did dispute. Oliver insisted on judging Davidson's behaviour by a hypothetical norm.

OLIVER. You have described Rose Ellis as your ward, your secretary, and to some extent your nurse. You assert she was never your mistress?—Certainly.

If you were to be judged by the standards by which ordinary men are judged would you agree you would be convicted?—No, except by bad men. Not by decent-minded men.

If an ordinary man took rooms or a flat in which a girl lived for three months do you think he would be properly convicted?—Certainly not.

Not even on suspicion?—No man could ever have a flat and put a servant in and go away if that were so.

Do you think if an ordinary man took a room for a girl of about twenty for six months, that his action might be open to the construction that he was keeping her?—Not if the matter were explained to the landlady beforehand as I did. Instead of Rose being at Stiffkey and paid wages she was being provided with lodgings in London and worked for practically nothing.

If an ordinary man took a girl to Paris for a trip do you think it might be misunderstood?—If he took her for a trip it might be, but I did not. I took her to get her a job.

The prosecutor next referred to Davidson having his boils dressed by Rose Ellis, and wondered whether the canons of ordinary, decent behaviour allowed of such services being performed by one who was a secretary-ward.

OLIVER. Is it your view of decency to go to a flat and to get this pretty girl to dress your naked body?

DAVIDSON. You are making the most outrageous suggestion. I never said that.

OLIVER. Was the boil on the buttock of your body? (As the rector delays his answer) Have you to think?

DAVIDSON. Yes, I do not know what the buttock is.

OLIVER. Do you not know?

DAVIDSON. Honestly, I do not.

OLIVER. Mr Davidson!

DAVIDSON. It is a phrase honestly I have never heard. So far as I remember, it is a little below the waist.

OLIVER. Are you serious?

DAVIDSON. Honestly I have never heard it. When it was mentioned the other day I had to ask what it was.

Davidson's protestation that he had never heard the word 'buttock' is difficult to believe (after all, he had spent more than three years in the navy), and one detects the fine hand of Little Jimmy at work.

A moment later the prosecutor was suitably horrified when Davidson testified that he took Rose Ellis to a Dr Peacock to be treated for syphilis.

OLIVER. Did Dr Peacock tell you she was safe?—Yes, he said it was a very mild form indeed.

Without mentioning names was it the same disease which Barbara Harris was supposed to have?—I will write it down for you.

OLIVER (after witness had written on a piece of paper and handed it to him). That is a very attractive thing to take to your home, isn't it?

CHANCELLOR (after looking at the slip of paper). Good gracious! That is the worst form of it, is it not?

DAVIDSON. In this particular case I understand it was what is called secondary.

OLIVER. How long do you say she had it?

DAVIDSON. I do not know. I really did not bother about it. I left it in the hands of the medical man. I paid for the treatment.

CHANCELLOR. Were you asking this girl down to your home?

OLIVER. I suggest you were frequently asking her to your home, associating with her year after year for ten years, and you say why should you bother about her having that?

DAVIDSON. But I understand 85 per cent of the men you meet have it.

CHANCELLOR. 85 per cent?

DAVIDSON. After the war I think 60 per cent to 85 per cent.

OLIVER. I want that answer carefully recorded that 85 per cent of the men in this country have got that disease.

The prosecutor then taxed Davidson with his lack of knowledge concerning venereal disease.

OLIVER. Do you suggest that you, as the 'Prostitutes' Padre', have not made any sort of study of it?—I know very little indeed about it.

It is one of the scourges of that most unfortunate occupation, is it not?—Yes, but I have never discussed it.

You have consecrated your life to helping those people and you know very little about it?—Very little indeed, and I am constantly being pitched into by my friends for my ignorance of it.

Did you say you did not know that that disease [gonorrhea, from which Barbara Harris was thought to be suffering] was horribly dangerous?—No, I honestly did not know. I thought it was comparatively safe in actual contact.

If you were on brothel duty in the Navy, do you suggest you would not have full instructions about the disease?—I did not, as a matter of fact.

* * *

The rector was next handed a coin-in-the-slot, passport-type photograph, measuring $1\frac{1}{2}$ inches by 2 inches, of himself and Betty Beach, the young, married actress with whom he 'habitually associated . . . for immoral purposes', according to the indictment. The rector was dressed for evening, a butterfly collar replacing his clerical collar; and he was leaning his head against the marcelled waves of the pretty blonde actress.

OLIVER. Is that the sort of photograph you used to show to girls in restaurants?—No, they were taken with a view of registering expressions for the cinema. I showed them all to the Bishop of Norwich.

Why have you got to be in a picture for the purpose of registering expressions?—If you are going to act a part you have to act with someone. If the photo was used I should be cut out.

CHANCELLOR. They would have to cut off some of Mrs Beach's hair, too.

OLIVER. Why must you be in the photograph?—It helps them to act. Suppose they are acting the part to my 'father', or to my 'lover'.

Which does the photograph depict you as, the father or the lover?—I should think the villain by the look of me. (Laughter.) It is a most horrible expression, the worst type of villain you could see.

The prosecutor then took up the disputed incident at Alderney Street which Barbara alleged was Davidson's attempt to rape her, and which the latter contended was the reverse.

OLIVER. That was a disgusting assault you say she made upon you if it is true?—It was disgusting to me.

I suggest it is the foulest lie?—It is absolutely true. I doubt whether she did it from the point of view of corruption, I think it was more with the idea of—

A kind old clergyman?—She was trying to coax me. She had been accustomed to that sort of man and that would be her way. Most men possibly liked it.

A kind old clergyman?—I am old of course in years.

From her point of view?—But my manner is rather young, I hope, still.

From her point of view; she is only sixteen, twining her legs round you?—Yes.

Putting her tongue in your mouth?—Very horrible. It nearly made me sick.

Could you imagine a more abandoned little creature, if your evidence is true, or half of it?—She was not abandoned, not in that way. She had some very remarkable qualities of character.

*　　*　　*

Dr Morton Prince, it will be recalled, maintained that the emergence of a secondary personality is usually preceded by a 'psychic catastrophe', which acts as a trigger mechanism. Often the incident may seem trivial to the observer, but it serves as a rolling stone to start the avalanche. In Davidson's case the shock which he was

about to experience did not herald the emergence of a new personality, but rather the lifting of the veil of amnesia which had
obscured the activities of an old friend, Little Jimmy, who had not
been idle on the eve of the rector's trial. Uncle Harold and Little
Jimmy were to confront each other without the protective barrier
of the former's studied unawareness of the latter's existence. The
precipitating factor in this case was a bit of pasteboard no bigger
than a postcard.

When the court re-convened after lunch Roland Oliver had to
search for some time among his papers before producing this bit of
pasteboard, which was a photograph of the Rev Harold Davidson
taken on Easter Monday, March 28, the day before the trial at
Church House opened. Unfortunately for him, the rector was not
alone in the photo. He was posed with a 15-year-old girl.

OLIVER. Mr Davidson, you told me this morning that for stage
purposes you have very frequently been photographed with
young women. Do you remember that?
DAVIDSON. Oh yes, very often.
OLIVER. Did you have any photographs taken with a young
woman on Easter Monday?
DAVIDSON (after pausing as though to recollect). Yes, on Easter
Monday.
OLIVER. Was that in the presence of two gentlemen whose
names I have written upon this piece of blotting paper?
DAVIDSON. Yes.

The two gentlemen, thereafter designated as 'Mr B' and 'Mr C',
were press photographers working as freelances in Fleet Street.

The 15-year-old in the photograph was Estelle Douglas, the
daughter of Mae Douglas, an actress whom Davidson had helped
to get started on her stage career. In the photograph Estelle is
wearing a black fringed Spanish shawl draped so that her left
shoulder is bare. The rector, who has his hand on her right
shoulder to prevent the shawl from slipping and her breast from
being exposed, gazes steadfastly at the girl rather like a tailor
measuring her for a costume. An aspidistra plant is prominent in
the background. On the eve of Davidson's trial Mae Douglas, it
will be recalled, had given an interview to the *Daily Herald* in
which she declared, 'Perhaps it is enough to say that I have been

glad to leave my daughter in charge of Mr Davidson on many nights when I have been in the theatre.'

From Davidson's replies to the questions which followed two things are obvious. One, that the rector had not told his counsel about the photographs (for there were two of them) possibly for the reason already stated that Uncle Harold had conveniently blotted them out of his memory. As a result, Richard Levy and E. Ryder Richardson were ready to give up the case in disgust, according to J. Rowland Sales, who talked to them at the time. Secondly, that the photographs were the handiwork of Little Jimmy. Only the imp, dedicated as he was to seeing the rector destroyed, could have acquiesced to such a suicidal project on the eve of the trial.

In response to questioning, Davidson explained that Mae Douglas was keen to get her daughter 'in pictures', and had asked him to arrange for the photography session, which took place in the actress's flat in her absence. 'I was pushed into the photograph,' he added. 'I did not want to go in.'

CHANCELLOR. Against your will, do you mean?
DAVIDSON. No, I thought if it would help anyone I did not mind.
OLIVER. What were you supposed to be doing? Was it to drape the lady?—No, she was draped. I was to be posing her. It was a perfectly ridiculous idea, but if it would help anybody I did not mind.
Were you posing her?—Posing her for an artistic tableau.
How was she dressed?—She was draped with a shawl.

Davidson having identified it, the prosecutor then handed the photograph to Chancellor North who commented, 'It looks as though she had nothing on at all except what he is putting on.'

Davidson explained that when he took 'Mr B' round to meet Mae Douglas, she asked the photographer to take some pictures of her little girl in a bathing suit—for advertising purposes, as the rector had understood it. Originally the photographs were to have been taken at Stiffkey on Palm Sunday, and Estelle went down to Stiffkey with the rector, the photographer, and three other girls for that purpose. 'Mr B' took some pictures of the girls in their pyjamas, then ran out of plates so that the publicity shots of Estelle had to be postponed until Easter Monday, when the photographer brought along a colleague, 'Mr C'.

DAVIDSON. He [Mr C] suggested a photograph being done in a way that I absolutely could not agree to at all.
OLIVER. What way was that?—He suggested that she should be, well with very little clothing on.

Photographed with you with very little clothing on?—Yes. Of course, I said I could not possibly have that.

Why should he want that?—I do not know. I understand that it was to sell to Mr Searle, who offered £125 for it. I think it was to be a nude photograph.

(Christopher Searle, it will be recalled, was the investigator from Arrow's Detective Agency who bought Rose Ellis glasses of port while he questioned her about her relationship with Davidson.)

CHANCELLOR. A girl of 15?
DAVIDSON. That was suggested to me by two people connected with the press.
OLIVER. Did they take the one they wanted to take?—Not to my knowledge.

Not to your knowledge? What do you mean? How could she be taken with no clothes on without your knowledge?—They did not take one without any clothes on.

At this point Roland Oliver brought off his *coup de théâtre*. Producing a second photograph with a flourish as though he had whipped it out of the folds of his gown, he demanded, 'Was that the one?'

If the photograph which had already been introduced in evidence could be described as 'Before', this second photograph clearly was 'After', though 'After' what one would have been hard pressed to say. This time Estelle, who looks awfully big for her age ('quite a kiddie,' Davidson called her) is standing with her back to the camera; but, alas, the black fringed Spanish shawl has come away from its moorings, exposing that part of the anatomy which Davidson was surprised to learn is called the buttocks. The rector himself is still standing with his hand on Estelle's shoulder, but his eyes have a distinctly glazed look.

'Davidson's face was a study when the prosecutor handed him

this photograph for identification,' J. Rowland Sales told me. 'The horrified disbelief written on it was not feigned,' his friend continued. 'This was Davidson's moment of truth, the moment when he came face to face with his doppelganger, and quite honestly he could not believe what the latter had done.' Whether he believed it or not, Davidson's reaction was that of nearly every man who finds himself in a tight corner, and who needs time to think. He claimed that he had been 'framed'.

DAVIDSON. I am not sure whether the photograph is faked, or what has been done to it.

OLIVER. You can see perfectly well if you look that it has not been faked. You knew that it was taken, and you were expecting it to be produced, were you not?—I understood that Mr Searle had offered £120 or £125 for it.

Never mind about Mr Searle. How can that photograph be taken without your knowledge?—It was.

CHANCELLOR. You are actually there with the girl?—Yes, if you will allow me to explain.

When the Rev Harold Davidson, who had handed the photograph to Chancellor North, leaned over to point something out on the photograph, the latter recoiled as though he had been bitten by an adder.

CHANCELLOR. Keep your distance, Sir. Don't explain it to me. You can explain it to Mr Oliver and see if you can make him believe it.

This brought E. Ryder Richardson to his feet protesting.

RICHARDSON (to chancellor). I wish to draw your attention to the remark that has just fallen from your lips. Even in this matter I hope you will allow Mr Davidson to explain it to you, and not only to Mr Oliver. I hope you will try to understand it as Mr Oliver has done throughout this case.

CHANCELLOR. I am trying to be as much like a machine as I can, but I am only human.

RICHARDSON. I hope you will not only be human, but you will

also be judicial. I ask you to take as much care of this explanation of the point as you have done of every other.

The prosecutor then asked Davidson to hold up the photograph so that those concerned could see it.

DAVIDSON (indignantly). Do you want the public to see it?
OLIVER. I do not care what the public sees. I am not conducting this case for the public, but for the learned chancellor.

As the witness did not hold up the photograph, Oliver came round and stood by the side of Richardson so that the chancellor and both counsel could see it.

OLIVER. Now will you explain the photograph?
DAVIDSON. That piece of robe there, which was quite firmly in my hand at the time before it was dropped, slipped out of my hand accidentally without my knowledge. She was respectably draped so far as I could see. I suggest it was either flicked out of my hand or dropped out. I should never have tolerated such a picture being consciously taken.

The rector, unprompted, then unfolded a tale of conspiracy which was amazing for its ingenuity, if not for its verisimilitude. (It is difficult to determine whether at this point Little Jimmy, taking advantage of Uncle Harold's state of shock, has taken over or whether Uncle Harold is simply hallucinating.) 'I was given a particular warning that I would be trapped about three weeks before,' he began. 'One point was that I would be telephoned by a poor lady of title and asked to go to her house. When I got there I would find . . . that she had removed all her clothes except her dress, and when I got into the house she would remove that and stand before me naked, and then two detectives would step out in the room to discover me in that position. Another way was that they would try to get me photographed in a compromising way, and that is why I got trapped into this.'
Davidson then asked how the photograph came to be in Oliver's possession.

OLIVER. You will ask me nothing.—No, I know! That is the

whole point. If you will tell me who gave you the photograph I will tell you who is guilty. Now that is quite a fair challenge.
CHANCELLOR. You are not to challenge the learned counsel.
OLIVER. On the eve of the trial a photograph like that might in some countries sell for a great deal of money?—No, no, no, there was no money to pass in connection with it. I beg your pardon, but that is a lie, absolutely.

I make a suggestion to you, and you are not entitled to say it is a lie.—I am sorry. It is not true.

I am putting it to you that these are press photographs taken for the purpose of publication?—Can you imagine that I was going to have that published which would prove my guilt before I started? It is too absurd and ridiculous.

Of course, not in this country.—Or anywhere else. I am known in every country in the world. It is a ridiculous and absurd suggestion.

A moment later Davidson declared, 'Anyone who was consciously a party to a photograph of that sort ought to be put in prison.'

OLIVER. If I may say so respectfully, I agree. But nobody would blame the child.—Nor the poor fool of a parson who was trapped into it.

As the court adjourned for the day there was an electric hum of excitement.

* * *

Roland Oliver was quite right in thinking that the photographs had been intended for foreign publication. Messrs 'B' and 'C', thinking to cash in on the rector's notoriety, were planning to sell them on the American market, as it came out in subsequent testimony. For the rector's trial had been getting a big play in the American press ('In one great American city the only English news reported one day recently was news relating to this case,' the Bishop of Malmesbury complained to the Church Assembly). Not only the tabloids, but the *New York Times* carried accounts of the trial.

The Rev Harold Davidson had labelled as 'too absurd and

ridiculous' the notion that he had consented to have published photographs 'which would prove my guilt before I started'. He had gone on to refer to himself as 'the poor fool of a parson who was trapped into it'. But if trapped, who was responsible for the trapping? Not those pillars of cheque-book journalism, Messrs 'B' and 'C'—Davidson in later testimony was at pains to exonerate this pair from having deliberately twitched Estelle's shawl out of his hand ('I would not for the world say that'). But if not these *paparazzi*, who laid the trap?

Nugent Davidson told me what happened just prior to the photograph being taken. 'I had come up to London to stay with father during the trial,' Nugent explained. 'My fiancée and I were told by his solicitor not to let father out of our sight for fear that he might do something foolish, so we kept a strict watch on him.' However, one day Davidson came to his son saying that he had been offered £50 to have his picture taken with Mae Douglas's daughter for newspaper publication ('B' apparently got the idea for the publicity stunt from the interview which Mae Douglas had given to the *Daily Herald*). 'My fiancée and I both told him to have nothing to do with the offer,' Nugent continued, 'even though father pleaded that he needed the money desperately for his defence.' And so the matter was dropped by everyone concerned, with the possible exception of Little Jimmy, until the day before the trial began.

'It was an Easter Monday,' Nugent recalled, 'and father, who had been with us all day, was nervous and in a highly excitable state. Towards evening the three of us, father, my fiancée and I, had stopped at a café near Covent Garden for a snack when father excused himself, saying that he had an errand in the neighbourhood, and that he would be gone only a few minutes. We waited, but father did not return. Then my fiancée and I looked at one another, the same horrifying thought travelling through our heads. We rushed to Mae Douglas's flat, which was in Endell Street, as I recall, and arrived there just as the flash powder went off.'

J. Rowland Sales when I talked to him took up the story from there. Apparently Davidson had no recollection how he got to Mae Douglas's flat. He appears to have blacked out completely, at least so far as the personality known as Uncle Harold was concerned. This black-out is not at all uncommon in cases of multiple personality. Very often on coming to they find that they have strayed from their homes, sometimes to distant cities; and they have complete amnesia for these odysseys until confronted with the evidence of their alter personalities. It was not until he was confronted with the photographs in the courtroom that details of that evening came flooding back to him, or so Davidson told Sales.

*   *   *

When the court convened the following morning, Thursday, May 26, Chancellor North, who had been poring over the photographs of the rector and Estelle Douglas with the aid of a magnifying glass, asked if they were taken by ordinary light or by flashlight. The Rev Harold Davidson said that they were taken at night and by flash powder at Mae Douglas's flat, the original plan to have them taken in a studio at Richmond having been ruled out. 'It is possible that the flashlight made me start,' Davidson declared, 'and that is what made the thing slip. It has obviously slipped or been twitched.'

OLIVER. You did not see anybody twitch it?
DAVIDSON. No, I would not for the world say that.
CHANCELLOR. Why did they place your hand on her shoulder?
DAVIDSON. It was putting it in a little more artistic pose. My fingers may have been clenched and not quite right.
OLIVER. You said yesterday that the lady was to be photographed for advertising a bathing costume. What sort of bathing costume does that represent?—She had a bathing costume on when she came.
She is stark naked there?—Not quite.

The witness testified that originally the shoulder strap of the bathing suit showed beneath the shawl, so he had suggested that Estelle go upstairs and loosen the strap, which she apparently did. After speaking to one of the photographers the girl had gone upstairs a second time, and when she came down the photograph was taken. 'Until I saw it I had not the faintest idea that the bathing costume was not underneath,' the rector maintained.

OLIVER. What had that shawl to do with the bathing costume, that is what I am trying to find out?—I do not know. Perhaps she thought she was going to have a bathing costume photograph taken after the shawl one. The original idea down at Stiffkey was that it was to be in a bathing costume, and then the man suggested that she should be practically naked.

CHANCELLOR. What did you say to that, sir?

DAVIDSON. I took such absolute precautions to prevent it that I insisted on his seeing the mother first.

CHANCELLOR. Not too successfully, surely.

RICHARDSON. Is that a matter of comment, sir, that I am able to reply to?

CHANCELLOR. You are quite right, Mr Richardson, but not now. I am most anxious that you should have before you what is passing in my mind about it.

RICHARDSON. I can see most clearly, sir, what is passing in your mind.

DAVIDSON. You consider me guilty of having that photograph taken. Would a sensible man on the eve of his trial go and have that photograph taken? If so, I should be certified as insane at once.

The chancellor posed the question, If the photograph were taken at the moment the shawl was twitched or fell away, would not the edges of the shawl appear blurred?

DAVIDSON. That is a thing which only an expert photographer can tell.

CHANCELLOR. This has been a good deal on my mind since yesterday.

DAVIDSON. It has been on my mind since it was taken as soon as I heard Mr Searle had offered £125 to buy it.

OLIVER. You know you are not entitled to say that. Were any more photographs taken than those two?—Yes, five.

What did the others depict?—The others were all the same, for all I know. I have only seen two.

Did one of them depict the girl with bare breasts?—No.

Are you sure?—I am certain of that.

Are you sure?—Certainly not to my knowledge.

If you were in that position with her, you would know.— Certainly there was no photograph which I saw of that description.

Never mind what you saw. Did you pose for a photograph with that girl with bared breasts?—Certainly not.

Do you swear that?—Absolutely, unless—

Will you tell me what other photographs were taken besides these two?—As far as I remember they were all quickly posed. The whole thing was done in about ten minutes. There is *that* one. Then there was another one in which she was supposed to be—the whole thing was too utterly ridiculous—with her foot out *there*, and I was arranging her toe.

CHANCELLOR. Had she put on any more clothes for that photograph?

DAVIDSON. As far as I knew, she was perfectly clothed underneath. I believed her to be clothed in her bathing dress, and I did not take off the shawl to look at her. (Pause.) A nice thing if I had! If they had been detectives they would have accused me of doing that.

OLIVER. This girl is standing there with nothing upon her except that shawl, and it is quite obvious that the only means of keeping that shawl upon her was your hand?

DAVIDSON. Yes, that is the mistake that was made. It ought to have been pinned.

Replying to further questions, Davidson declared, 'I am anxious to give you true answers. I had done an exceedingly foolish thing.' 'This was a girl who had been placed in my trust,' he added.

OLIVER. Is that the way you treated her?—That is exactly where the trap came in.

Continuing his explanation, the rector said, 'They first came to me and suggested a photograph which I considered utterly and entirely improper, and although I was almost starving at the time—

OLIVER. What sort of opinion of your character must 'B' and 'C' have had if they suggested you should be photographed with a little protégée of yours naked?

DAVIDSON. They said their opinion of my character was that it was so pure that no one in the world would think anything wrong of it. They said, 'Why not have that photo published so that the world will know the day before your case is taken, and it will proclaim your innocence?'

* * *

There was a near-riot at Church House when the doors were opened after the lunch recess, the hordes seeking admittance getting completely out of hand. For by midday the early editions of the afternoon papers had appeared on the streets with such sensational headlines as NUDE PHOTO BOMBSHELL. This time women outnumbered those gods from the Sally Ann hostel who had turned the gallery into a quasi-exclusive male preserve, and this may have had something to do with the melée which ensued. It began with good-natured pushing and shoving, but by the time the doors had been shut and bolted from the inside several policemen had had their helmets knocked off or pulled down over their eyes, and several women had suffered concussed ribs. None of the injuries was serious enough to require hospital treatment, however; and some of his female admirers, bruised ribs, barked shins and all, were on hand to greet the Rev Harold Davidson when, dazed from his ordeal, he emerged after the court had adjourned.

II

'I Believe Barbara'

The Worshipful F. Keppel North no doubt breathed a sigh of relief when the prosecution concluded its summing up on June 6, and the consistory court was adjourned for one month to give North time to consider his verdict. The trial itself had lasted twenty-five days spread over a period of nine weeks. and this despite the fact that the court had sat on Saturdays in order to speed up the proceedings. Sixty-nine witnesses had been heard, and 1,500,000 words of testimony had been accumulated to fill 2,300 pages of court transcript. Small wonder that Chancellor North was glad to reach his country seat at Rougham, Norfolk (81 families, 240 population) where in tranquillity he could deliberate. For the weary chancellor it meant no more camping out in a London hotel, with all his meals taken in restaurants, and with no one to darn his socks. It meant also no more unruly mobs hammering on the doors of Church House, no more rowdies to clear from the public gallery. In contrast, Rougham had never seemed so peaceful.

In appearance Chancellor North was anything but prepossessing; indeed, he was almost as small as the rector. A Humpty-Dumpty sort of a man, one would say, with cold eyes and a pursed mouth, judging from photographs. Yet F. Keppel North came from one of the most distinguished families in Norfolk. One ancestor had been Privy Councillor to Henry VIII, while another had been Queen Elizabeth's ambassador to France. In his life style Chancellor North was a Trollopian character whose recreations were listed in *Who's Who* as 'cottage improvement, tree planting, and watching cricket', to which catalogue might have been added riding with the West Norfolk Fox Hounds.

'Father was the most fair-minded of men,' Roger North, J.P., informed me as he drove me from King's Lynn to Rougham Hall, the 17th-century seat of the North family. The son, who is seventy-three and Recorder of the Crown Court, recalled two pieces of advice the chancellor had given him, and which had stood him in good stead in his legal career. 'The first was never to be impatient, for you cannot hurry the law,' he explained. 'The second was that if ever I were tempted to be humorous while trying a case to desist. My humour could only be at the expense of the defendant, who would not think it funny.'

If the Worshipful F. Keppel North had a sense of humour he kept it well out of sight during the Rev Harold Davidson's trial. Indeed, he appeared to be constantly surprised by events instead of anticipating them, to be given to what is known in stage jargon as the 'double take', and to miscellaneous 'ohs' and 'ahs' as he contemplated the depths of depravity to which the human spirit could sink. As to his fairness towards Davidson, the chancellor himself, it will be recalled, had pleaded, 'I am trying to be as much like a machine as I can, but I am only human.' Just how human the squire of Rougham could be is indicated in his underscorings of the trial transcripts as he read them over prior to giving his verdict. For example, whenever Davidson in his evidence uses the words 'quite frankly'—and his testimony is peppered with such circumlocutions—the chancellor has set off those words in inverted commas. Similarly the rector's expression, 'to tell the honest truth' is enclosed in single quotes, as though to say 'quite frankly' that there wasn't an honest or truthful bone in the rector's body.

To his credit, the Worshipful F. Keppel North did believe that justice must be seen to be done. He was a firm exponent of the verdict that is arrived at after a hearing in open court, in contrast to Dr Lang, the Archbishop of Canterbury, who would have preferred that Davidson's trial be held *in camera*. 'I believe in publicity,' Chancellor North declared in the course of the trial. 'Serious as the mischief may be of publishing nasty details, it is not nearly so serious as the mischief of secret trials may be.'

Now, as in the quietness of his study at Rougham Hall he pored over the trial transcripts, no doubt he bore the concluding words of the opposing counsel in mind.

* * *

Richard Levy had begun his summing-up for the defence in a typical low-keyed fashion. The Rev Harold Davidson's character was the first thing the court must examine, he maintained. Davidson had been asked whether he wished to be judged by ordinary standards, and had said that he did. 'You might as well ask a lunatic if he were sane,' his counsel observed. 'I do not put it so highly in Mr Davidson's case, but not even Mr Oliver will dispute that he is very unusual and eccentric. You have seen that he is a man completely and utterly indifferent to the way other people judge his behaviour.'

In dealing with the photograph of Estelle Douglas, the defence counsel said that it had been wrongly described as the photograph of a naked woman. 'There is no more showing in that picture than you would see in women dancing in an hotel or on the front page of an art magazine.' Besides, the photograph was an accident, as any fair-minded person could see.

Coming to Barbara Harris, Levy said that of all the hundreds of girls who had been associated with the Rev Harold Davidson she was the only one who had come before the court to say that he had made improper advances to her. 'You are asked to ruin this man's career and his life for all time on the uncorroborated evidence of that girl,' Levy added. If the chancellor believed her evidence then the rector would be 'damned and forever blasted'. Commenting on the prosecution's frequent reference to 'What could poor Barbara do?' the defence counsel said, 'I suggest that what "poor Barbara" might do was to get up before one or two in the afternoon and get an honest job of work.' Levy continued: 'She lay in bed during the day, went to cafés in the evening, and slept with men all night. If she had the slightest respect or decency she would have tried to earn her living in a decent way.' 'Sympathy is rather wasted on this degraded and evil-living girl,' he insisted. 'Yet she is called "poor little Barbara" while decent hard-working people are derided in the witness-box.'

Having begun his 3½-hour summation in a low key Levy ended with a peroration that sounded as though it were intended for a jury rather than for the chancellor's ears. 'If you prefer the voice of scandal and suspicion to the voice of tolerance and understanding,' Levy cried; 'if you prefer evidence from sources that are tainted with vice and falsehood to evidence of people who are decent, and honest, and virtuous . . . then and then only will you find that these charges are proved.' 'If you do,' he concluded, 'I say that this case will leave an indelible stain on the fair name of justice in this country, and will reflect lasting discredit upon those responsible for such a prosecution.'

Roland Oliver, as was expected, had dwelt at length on the Estelle Douglas photograph which he described as 'infamous'. 'On the eve of one of the most notorious trials in my lifetime,' he began, 'this photograph of the rector with a girl without a stitch of clothing on save a shawl was taken. The real reason, I suggest, is that it was to sell as the notorious rector of Stiffkey with one of his girls, in foreign countries.' It was no answer to say it was a mad thing to do. 'In many respects,' Oliver said, 'it would be safe to say Mr Davidson is a madman, but not a madman in law.' The prosecutor described the Rev Harold Davidson's evidence as a 'catalogue of lies', citing thirty-nine instances in which he alleged that the rector had contradicted himself in the witness-box. In contrast, Barbara Harris was a model of truthfulness. 'It is said that she is a bad girl,' Oliver continued. 'From many points of view she is. Any girl of her age who has had affairs with men would be called a bad girl. It might occur to some people with a little sympathy, I ought not to say Christianity, that she never had much chance.'

The prosecutor went so far as to assert that Barbara was not a prostitute in the accepted sense of the word. She had tried to get a little money by doing needlework, and had only stopped in bed mornings because there was no coal and it was too cold to get up. 'These facts surely prove that she was not a prostitute in the sense that she was trying to make money from shameful relations with men,' Oliver declared. But he was less concerned with Barbara's character than he was with whether she was telling the truth. The prosecutor suggested that Barbara had 'a wonderful memory', and after quoting a number of passages from her evidence, commented: 'Would any witness, however clever, have stood under the fire of cross-examination for nearly two days and emerged absolutely untouched? If ever a witness emerged triumphant from that ordeal it was Barbara Harris.'

Concluding his speech, Oliver referred to the peroration in Richard Levy's address in which the defence counsel had said that a verdict against the rector would reflect 'discredit upon the fair name of justice in this country'. 'That was obviously addressed not to you but to the public,' the prosecutor told Chancellor North, 'and it was intended to be an invitation or an incitation to the public to think that the case had never been properly proved or that you had been influenced by prejudice and had not acted fairly upon the evidence.'

*   *   *

There was the usual stir of expectancy when the Norwich Consistory Court convened at Church House at 10.30 a.m. on Friday,
July 8, to hear the chancellor's findings. In their father's absence
Patricia and Nugent Davidson, both of whom had given evidence
on his behalf, sat behind defence counsel. In the final days of the
trial the indictment against the Rev Harold Davidson had been
tidied up by dropping various charges. Betty Beach, named as one
of the 'women of loose character' with whom Davidson was accused
of consorting, had been dismissed from the proceedings, as had
Violet Lowe and a Miss Williams, both waitresses. Likewise
dropped were charges relating to women unknown whom the
rector was accused of accosting in the vestibules of hotels and
within the purlieus of various underground stations.

The chancellor now dealt with the remaining charges after
making plain not only what Davidson was accused of, but what he
was not on trial for. 'I am not trying Mr Davidson for neglecting
his parish,' the chancellor declared. 'For all I have heard here he
may be an excellent parish priest.' 'I am not trying him for any
offence against the bankruptcy laws, obtaining money by false
pretences, conspiracy, perjury, or even the outrage on that child
of fifteen committed on the 28th of last March at which he
admits he was present,' he continued. 'These are relevant only to
the question of whether I can believe Mr Davidson on his oath.'
The chancellor's task was to say whether the prosecution had
established beyond reasonable doubt a case against the rector on
the five offences with which he was charged. 'I bear carefully in
mind that it is not for Mr Davidson to prove his innocence,' he
added.

*   *   *

It was at this point that the Rev Harold Davidson entered the
Great Hall and took a seat alongside his counsel, Richard Levy. He
was dressed in clerical black and carried a silk top hat in his hand
like those Members of Parliament who follow an old-fashioned
tradition by turning up at the House of Commons in top hats on
Budget Day. For once, however, Davidson's entry created no stir,
so intent were the spectators upon hearing judgment pronounced.

[166]

In contrast Davidson, as the chancellor droned on, allowed his eyes to travel upwards to the hammer-beamed ceiling, as though the chancellor's findings concerned someone else, according to the ever observant J. Rowland Sales. Perhaps in the few moments that remained before judgment was pronounced the rector was reviewing in his mind a recent event at Stiffkey. For Little Jimmy had not been idle while the court stood adjourned.

THE RECTOR OF STIFFKEY IN AMAZING SCENES

CHURCH STRUGGLE FOR BIBLE

SECOND CLERGYMAN LEAVES

Thus ran the headlines in the *Daily Telegraph* for Monday, June 13. They referred to angry scenes the previous day when the Rev Harold Davidson had arrived at St John with St Mary to take the evening service only to find that a neighbouring clergyman, the Rev R. H. Cattell of Wareham, had been deputed by the Archdeacon of Lynn to preach in his place. Davidson walked to the lectern, and the two men struggled briefly for possession of the Bible, with Davidson wresting it from his colleague's hands.

'As nothing short of force will prevent Mr Davidson taking part I can see nothing left to do but to withdraw,' the Rev Mr Cattell told the congregation, adding, 'It reduces the service to a farce.' Davidson, his voice trembling, then read the second lesson.

Long before the evening service was due to begin more than 200 people, many of them visitors, had filled the church, according to the *Daily Telegraph*, which described the scenes of near pandemonium when the Rev Mr Cattell was forced to retire from the field. Women shouted and applauded, the newspaper claimed, and it was only Davidson's repeated admonition to 'please, please remember this is a house of God' that finally restored order. The rector then preached, choosing as his text, 'Blessed are the pure in heart, for they shall see God.'

*   *   *

Whether or not the Rev Harold Davidson was to be numbered among that band singled out as blessed for their purity of heart he came to with a jolt, his eyes travelling down from the ceiling, when Chancellor North began reading his findings in the case. The chancellor found Davidson guilty on all five counts of immoral conduct, giving his reasons in each case; and in doing so he went out of his way to brand the rector as a liar and a discredited witness.

'I watched Mr Davidson anxiously in the witness-box for something like four days,' North began, 'and I do not believe him. His evidence in chief was a tissue of falsehoods and, as Mr Oliver has demonstrated, reckless and even deliberate falsehoods. He went down an absolutely discredited witness on whose oath no reliance can be placed.' A little later, the chancellor pointedly declared, 'I cannot accept Mr Davidson's evidence where it is in conflict with anyone else's evidence,' meaning presumably that anyone's word was to be preferred to the rector's.

The Rev Harold Davidson's conviction did not rest solely on the fact that he was an 'awful liar', Chancellor North declared. He then went on to infer guilt from the defence's failure to call Rose Ellis, Mr Gordon, and Mrs Davidson as witnesses. ('Had that evidence left me in doubt Mr Davidson's resolute refusal to call three vital witnesses would have clinched the matter,' was the way the chancellor expressed it). 'Mr Gordon, who runs through this case like a silver thread, has been prayed in aid of the defendant,' the chancellor pointed out. 'When I asked what it was that caused Mr Davidson to spend all his week-days in London, Mr Levy said, "You will hear that Mr Davidson had important business in London. Mr Gordon is no character of fiction. You will see him." But we have not. More important is Mrs Davidson, who from time to time, we are told, received Rose Ellis at her home as a welcome inmate. When the lady was said to be ill the court offered to go to Stiffkey and take her evidence there, but the defence would have none of it.'

As to the defence's failure to put into the witness-box Rose Ellis, who had been subpoenaed by the prosecution, Chancellor North had spoken his mind on this subject earlier in an extraordinary exchange with Richard Levy.

CHANCELLOR. Rose Ellis is alive, and can be called. I want you to consider very carefully whether it is not necessary to call so material a witness. . . . What will be the atmosphere created if the defence does not call her? It will be as brimstone to brown paper.

LEVY. Mr Oliver and I are both agreed that Rose Ellis is a witness upon whom one cannot rely. Mr Oliver has not called her for that reason, and I do not see why I am in a different category from Mr Oliver. I am not going to take the responsibility of calling the girl on behalf of Mr Davidson when I know that she has made contradictory statements.

CHANCELLOR. She ought to be able to give the most valuable corroborative evidence.

LEVY. Then I suggest you call her yourself and obtain a statement from her without either me or Mr Oliver cross-examining her.

The chancellor however declined to take this course of action. Now in giving judgment the chancellor underlined his belief that it was Richard Levy's responsibility to call Rose as a witness, and not Roland Oliver's. 'Had he [Oliver] done so, the first material question he put I should have told her she need not answer because it was likely to lead to penalties under the Perjury Act.' So much for brimstone and brown paper.

Chancellor North, who had been saving Barbara Harris as a *pièce de résistance*, now dealt with this young lady, asserting that the facts concerning the rector's association with Barbara were scarcely in dispute. That association had lasted eighteen months, during a substantial part of which time Barbara and the rector admittedly had slept in the same room—in the same bed, if the girl were to be believed. 'Of course, if Barbara is not speaking the truth, there is an end of the matter,' the chancellor conceded. Was Barbara speaking the truth? 'I sat side by side close to her and watched her manner for three days, while she was examined, cross-examined, recalled, further cross-examined, and further re-examined. I have come to a definite conclusion. I believe Barbara.'

After this ringing affirmation of faith in the word of 'poor little Barbara', there was little left for the chancellor to say or do, except to notify the Bishop of Norwich of his verdict and of the sentences he recommended to be pronounced in respect of each offence. The actual date of the sentencing would be fixed by the bishop himself after the time allowed for appeals had elapsed. Meanwhile the chancellor could and did make an order for costs against the rector of Stiffkey, which his counsel did not oppose.[1] As though obeying a starter's gun, the Rev Harold Davidson snatched his silk hat from the table and ran at full tilt down the long aisle of the Great Hall and out of the door. He hurried down the staircase and in the outer lobby found Richard Levy, who had left the courtroom a few minutes earlier. Grasping his counsel's hand, the rector thanked him for all he had done, then was swallowed by the crowd which had gathered outside to await the result.

*   *   *

Three and a half months were to elapse between Chancellor North's finding the Rev Harold Davidson guilty, and the latter being unfrocked at a bell, book and candle ceremony in Norwich Cathedral. Once more the cautious side of Bishop Pollock's nature had come to the fore. 'We are dealing with an unaccountable person,' Dr Pollock wrote to Walter Monckton the day after Davidson had been found guilty, 'and therefore I feel that it would be wise to defer pronouncing my sentence until the longest time is up during which he can appeal on a question of law.' Davidson did in fact appeal to the Judiciary Committee of the Privy Council, as was his right under the 1892 Clergy Discipline Act. He did much more than that as the following time-table shows:

> *July 10, 1932*—Davidson calls for a complete overhaul of the consistory court system in a sermon preached at the Stiffkey parish church. He goes on to point out that Christ shocked the religious leaders of His time by consorting 'with the lowest, both men and women'. However, when the rector goes in the afternoon to take the service at Morston he finds the doors of the old Saxon church locked.
>
> *July 15, 1932*—The Stiffkey trial is criticised as 'deplorable' and 'tragically ill-advised' in a leading article 2½ columns long in the *Church Times*, which places the blame partly on

---

[1] The trial cost the Church Commissioners £8,205, which was four times what it cost to bring Dr Crippen to justice, as Davidson was fond of observing. In awarding costs against Davidson the chancellor showed himself to be incurably optimistic, for the rector at that moment was being pursued through the courts unsuccessfully for £47 owing in back rent to Battling Flora Osborne.

the Bishop of Norwich's legal advisers ('No experienced criminal solicitor could conceivably have blundered so badly and consistently'). 'A Consistory Court is still, in the eyes of the law, a Court Christian,' the editorial observes. 'We might at least have expected in it a higher tone than we get in the secular Courts. We did not get it.' While admitting that the Rev Harold Davidson's conduct throughout the trial was 'foolish and eccentric', the religious weekly maintains that 'there can be no doubt that he was originally moved by a high Christian impulse, and that he is still regarded by many as the champion of the outcast and the wretched'.

Finally, the *Church Times* criticises Chancellor North for his lack of charity towards the defendant. 'A word of real sympathy by the Judge for the ideal which, at least in the beginning of his career, Mr Davidson had set before himself, would have raised the Church in the opinion of the masses.'

July 18, 1932—Davidson takes five curtain calls when he makes his debut at the Prince's Cinema in Wimbledon as a variety act sandwiched between screenings of Lupe Velez in *The Storm*. 'A thousand people greeted the rector on his arrival at the cinema,' the *Daily Herald* reports, and goes on to quote the rector as saying, 'I am doing this because it is a question of either sponging on my friends or of using what gifts God has given me.'

July 30, 1932—Leave for Davidson to appeal against the findings of Chancellor North on the grounds of errors of fact is refused by the Judiciary Committee of the Privy Council, with Lord Atkin presiding.

August 9, 1932—The Harrogate Sun-bathing Society bars the rector from its nudist camp. When he seeks to join naturists playing medicine ball, Davidson is escorted from the premises. 'I am considering establishing a similar type of thing among my parishioners at Stiffkey,' he tells reporters.

August 10, 1932—A 14-day notice of inhibition signed by the Bishop of Norwich is nailed to the door of the Stiffkey parish church.

August 21, 1932—Davidson's farewell service at Stiffkey. Afterwards Davidson, accompanied by a friend, calls on his old enemy Major Hamond at the latter's home, but is forcibly ejected, the major bringing the toecap of his boot up smartly to the seat of the rector's trousers. In court on October 15 the major pleads guilty to assault, and is fined 40 shillings by the Holt Petty Sessions. ('My husband was inundated with letters of congratulation,' Mrs Diana Hamond told me when I called on her at Morston. 'Some of the letters contained money; others enclosed nails and cleats for the major to attach to his boots.')

October 13, 1932—The Judiciary Committee of the Privy Council refuses Davidson leave to appeal on questions of law, when he appears before it to argue the motion. (Davidson by now had run out of funds with which to pay for a barrister's services.)

October 21, 1932—Sentence of deprivation is pronounced upon Davidson by the Bishop of Norwich.

* * *

At 11.45 a.m. on Friday, October 21 the Rosencrantzes and Guildensterns were present in Norwich's honey-coloured, 12th-century cathedral, as were the Voltimands, the Corneliuses and the Osrics in the persons of archdeacons, percentors, and minor canons. But there was no sign of the Prince of Denmark. Earlier the stage had been set for the last act in the Stiffkey drama when, after closing the main body of the cathedral to the public, officials had arranged wooden folding chairs around a baize-covered table in the tiny Bauchon Chapel. The twelve members of the public had been admitted on a 'first come, first serve' basis. But public and participants alike were growing restive when the diocesan registrar, as if to quell incipient mutiny, rose and read the following telegram addressed to the Bishop of Norwich, which had been handed in at Newmarket at 10.22:

HAVE MOTORED THROUGH NIGHT TO BE PRESENT CATHEDRAL TODAY ELEVEN FORTY FIVE STOP HAVE BEEN SLIGHTLY DELAYED STOP IF LATE PLEASE ALLOW FEW MINUTES GRACE STOP HOPE SEE YOU AND ARCHDEACON ABOUT BUSINESS MATTERS AFTERWARDS.

Hardly had the registrar finished reading the telegram when

distant cheers announced the arrival of a small, mud-bespattered motorcar, out of which jumped the Rev Harold Davidson in a silk top-hat. Not even stopping to acknowledge the applause of his admirers, the rector raced to the Bauchon Chapel, where he seated himself at the table facing the bishop's throne. Preceded by cathedral officials with wands of office, the bishop's cortege then entered the chapel, with Dr Pollock, gorgeous in mitre and cope, and with a gold and silver crozier in his hand, bringing up the rear. 'Oyez, oyez, oyez,' the apparitor called out, 'all persons cited and admonished to appear at this court draw near and answer to your names as you shall be called. God save the King.' Davidson answered 'Here' as his name was called.

'Let us pray,' said the bishop, who then intoned a prayer in which there was prominent mention of 'the traitor Judas', and the pious hope expressed that the Church might be spared 'false apostles' and be guided by 'true pastors, through Jesus Christ our Lord'. It was only when Dr Pollock picked up a manuscript preparatory to pronouncing sentence that it became horribly apparent that the Rev Harold Davidson did not intend to stick to the script. For the rector sprang to his feet with 'May I be allowed to speak before sentence is passed?' The bishop, after a hurried consultation with his legal adviser, H. T. A. Dashwood, assented. 'I wish before you pass sentence to say that I am entirely innocent in the sight of God,' Davidson cried, glaring hard at the bishop. 'It is the Church authorities who are on trial and not myself.' The rector then spoke of his work among the 'lower depths of society', and said that every clergyman should leave the ninety-nine just and seek the one who is lost. 'I shall devote myself to that work as I have done since I was eighteen years of age,' he pledged. 'There is not a single deed I have done which I shall not do again with the help of God. . . .'

As though he had not heard, the bishop picked up the manuscript again, and began to read: '. . . Whereas the judge and chancellor of our consistory court has notified to us that the Rev Harold Francis Davidson, M.A., clerk in Holy Orders . . . has been found guilty of certain immoral conduct, immoral acts, and immoral habits . . . now we, Bertram, by divine permission Bishop of Norwich . . . pronounce decree and declare that the Rev Harold Francis Davidson . . . ought by law to be deprived of all his ecclesiastical promotions in the diocese of Norwich . . . and we do deprive him thereof by this our definitive sentence . . .' Resuming his seat 'we, Bertram' then signed the document to give it legal effect. The irrepressible rector was on his feet immediately to give notice of appeal.

In medieval times a criminous clerk was literally stripped of his garments as deacon and priest, much as a French Army officer might be degraded by having the very buttons of his tunic ripped off in public. Some faint trace of this barbarous custom was to be discerned in the deposition ceremony which the bishop, moving to the High Altar to give it added solemnity, now performed.[1] After kneeling in prayer at the High Altar, the bishop rose and read from a long document, from which it emerged that the ex-rector of Stiffkey had caused 'grave scandal to the Church'. 'Now, therefore, we, Bertram . . . do hereby pronounce decree and declare that the said Rev Harold Francis Davidson being a priest and deacon ought to be entirely removed deposed and degraded from the said offices . . .' In the prayers which followed mention was made of human frailty.

But the said Harold Francis Davidson was still taking his entrance cues from a different play script. With Jack-in-the-box precision he sprang to his feet to announce, 'I am very glad that the deposition service has been added, as this gives me the right to appeal to the Archbishop of Canterbury, which I shall do.' But even as he spoke the bishop's procession had re-formed and was filing slowly, sorrowfully one might say, down the aisle to the vestry. Among the dignitaries who swayed past the impenitent Davidson was the Worshipful F. Keppel North, who, it was noticed, was wearing a full-bottomed wig instead of the truncated version he had favoured at Church House. The black cloth on top of the wig, which was a feature of sentencing in capital cases, had been dispensed with on this occasion, observers were happy to note.

---

[1] The deposition has appeared to many of Davidson's adherents as wholly gratuitous. Archdeacon Wakeford, who was found guilty of adultery, was not deposed, but merely deprived, they point out. Theoretically at least it was possible for a deprived cleric to continue his priestly functions with the Archbishop's permission, and even to hold a new benefice with the assent of the bishop concerned.

Jottings from a Notebook

The following jottings from the author's notebook were written with no eye to publication, but were intended as *aides-mémoire* to research. They consist of notes made of interviews with various persons who knew Davidson, together with the author's own observations on various aspects of his life. They are presented in no particular order in the belief that they may shed additional light on the Rev Harold Davidson's character.

CRIMINAL COURT CRITERIA: 'He is entitled that such an offence shall be proved against him as clearly as if he were subject to prosecution in the ordinary criminal court, and he has to be convicted, if at all, not on grounds of suspicion . . . but only upon such proof as if the charge were an offence against the criminal law.' *The Lord Chancellor, Lord Birkenhead, to the Judicial Committee of the Privy Council which heard Archdeacon Wakeford's appeal in 1921.*

Were the criteria laid down by Lord Birkenhead rigidly adhered to in the case of the Rev Harold Davidson? Did Chancellor North demand such clear proofs of guilt? Sir Ernest Wild, K.C., Recorder of London at the time of the Davidson trial, is quoted as saying that had the case come before him he would have thrown it out for lack of evidence.

*   *   *

ONE WOMAN IN FORTY: Virtually ignored by the defence in its summing up was Detective Christopher Searle's admission, surely the most damaging of the whole trial, that out of forty women interviewed only one claimed that Davidson had misbehaved with her. The relevant testimony was as follows:

RICHARD LEVY. Will you tell me the number of women who have been interviewed in respect of Mr Davidson's conduct?—I can't tell you the number; there were so many.

Roughly, how many?—I probably have interviewed 40 women.

I am not speaking about landladies. How many women with a view of ascertaining whether Mr Davidson had misbehaved with them?—Two.

Only two. That is Miss Harris and Miss Ellis?—Yes.

Finally, Searle agreed that out of all the statements and enquiries made only Rose Ellis had alleged misconduct on Davidson's part. Rose Ellis, as already indicated, made her statement while under the influence of alcohol, repudiated it in a more sober moment, was not called by the prosecution as a witness.

* * *

SEX IN THE HEAD: Davidson suffered from what D. H. Lawrence called 'sex in the head' (writing of those 'emancipated bohemians who swank most about sex,' Lawrence declared, 'the whole thing has been driven up into their heads . . . Their sex is more mental than arithmetic; and as vital physical creatures they are more non-existent than ghosts'). This would explain Davidson's voyeurism in going backstage to ogle the pretty girls as they made their quick changes in a corner. Bert Ross, the historian of the British Music Hall Society, who used to have coffee with Davidson in the Express Dairy in Charing Cross Road, thinks that the rector was simply a Peeping Tom. 'He used to chat up the birds who came into the Express Dairy, then suddenly he would go all coy. I don't think he ever took any of them back to his room.'

* * *

TRAIN-SPOTTER: But all those girls—500, or was it 1,500?—whose names Davidson kept in his diaries, how does one account for them? 'Mr Davidson was a train-spotter,' Mrs Kathleen Ward (née Clarke), of Brookmans Park, Hatfield, tells me when I call on her.

'He was one of those people who spend their lives watching the trains go by. They jot down the numbers of the locomotives, then they shut their little notebooks, go home, and dream that they are the Flying Scotsman.'

[176]

Over a period of years Kathleen Clarke, as she was then, used to encounter Davidson on the L.N.E.R. bound for Norwich, where she was enrolled in a secretarial college (Davidson himself got down at Wymondham to change trains for Wells). Kathleen was only sixteen at the time, and Davidson put himself out to be affable to her and her girl friends, taking an interest in their studies, their beaux, even the crochet work some of the girls brought with them. Had he ever tried to make dates with them? 'Never,' Mrs Ward replies. 'He used to offer us tickets to the London theatres, but none of us could use them. I don't think that any of us had been farther from home than Norwich.'

Sometimes Davidson wore his clerical collar, sometimes not. 'We concluded that Mr Davidson was an actor who doubled as a lay preacher, a notion which he did nothing to discourage. It was only later when we read about him in the newspapers that we learned that he was the Prostitutes' Padre.'

*   *   *

DON'T CALL ME HAROLD: Not all waitresses made heavy weather of Davidson's attentions, according to Mrs Laura Brackley, a retired waitress now in her eighties ('Look how steady me hand is,' she tells me; 'I can still balance a tray'). Mrs Brackley says that she used to chaff the rector when he came into the Express Dairy in Eversholt Street, King's Cross, where she worked. 'Don't call me Harold when I'm in my clerical clothes,' Davidson would admonish, to which Laura would reply, 'As far as I'm concerned, you can take them off.' 'It was only said in fun,' Mrs Brackley, a short, kindly-faced woman with glasses, explains. 'If Mr Davidson bothered the girls too much Mrs Yates, the manageress, would take him by the scruff of the neck and say, "Out you go!" '

*   *   *

LACK OF SPONTANEITY: Nugent Davidson tells me, 'Mother once said that when it came to sex father was far from being spontaneous. They knelt for prayers beside the bed each night before retiring.'

*   *   *

NON-PERFORMER: Davidson's trial was nowhere watched with greater interest than in the women's ward of the Sheffield Street Hospital for Venereal Diseases, according to Dr Letitia Fairfield, who, now nearly ninety, was then Senior Medical Officer of Health with the London County Council. 'Both Rose Ellis and Barbara Harris had been out-patients at the hospital, which was where professional prostitutes were treated,' Dr Fairfield tells me when I call on her at her flat in Chelsea. 'When the trial started matron came to me and said, "The girls are thrilled to bits, for they know all about the rector." ' It seems that Davidson was a standing joke among Soho's street-walkers. The reason? He was a non-performer. 'Davidson was impotent,' Dr Fairfield explains. ' "Of course you wouldn't know about such things, but we ourselves are in no doubt," the girls told matron.'

*   *   *

THE LAST VICTORIAN: Davidson's vices as well as his virtues were Victorian. Had Davidson been born fifty years earlier his efforts to rescue 'soiled doves' would have been applauded instead of condemned. Scarcely a voice was raised against Gladstone ('Old Glad-Eye', the whores called him) when he undertook similar rescue operations among the 'unfortunates' he picked up nightly on the Duke of York Steps. Rather, Gladstone's uplift work was hailed as 'characteristic of his courage and proof of conscious purity', in the words of Sir Wemyss Reid.

As in Davidson's case, Gladstone's rescue mission began at Oxford when as an undergraduate 'Gladstone and a group of other earnest young men swore a solemn oath to devote a tenth of their income to saving society's outcasts.'[1] For the remainder of his life Gladstone's habit when in London was to walk the streets at night alone and armed with a stout stick for protection. 'At first, he liked to wait for prostitutes to accost him,' his biographer tells us. 'But he would often accost women himself, and suggest that they should accompany him home, where he told them that they would be treated with respect by his wife and himself, and that they would

[1] Richard Deacon. *The Private Life of Mr. Gladstone*. London: Frederick Muller, 1965.

[178]

be given food and shelter.'[1] If necessary Gladstone did not hesitate to pursue his quarry into brothels, preferably in the daytime, but 'with a supreme, and almost perverse, disregard of worldly considerations . . .'

As in Davidson's case, Gladstone's quixotic behaviour laid him open to criticism and misunderstanding. 'Gladstone manages to combine his missionary meddling with a keen appreciation of a pretty face,' Henry Labouchere spitefully remarked, adding, 'He has never been known to rescue any of our East End whores.' Finally, Davidson himself was not laggard in acknowledging that Gladstone's example had been an inspiration to him. 'Very many years ago,' he told a reporter, 'Gladstone visited a clergyman friend of my father. I have always remembered what this friend said of Gladstone's attitude towards fallen women, and I made up my mind long ago to help them so far as I could.'[2]

*　　*　　*

WITHIN A BUDDING GROVE: What could be more Victorian than Davidson's predilection for girls of a tender age? 'The nineteenth century was especially replete with gentlemen who had for girl children an overwhelming penchant,' a chronicler of Victorian sexuality points out, adding that 'when these men were respectable such attachments were treated as if they were ordained by God.'[3] One thinks immediately of the Rev Charles L. Dodgson ('Lewis Carroll') punting on the Isis with Alice Liddell and her little friends. The difference was that Dodgson lost interest in girls when they reached the age of puberty ('the awkward stage of transition', as he called it) whereas Davidson's interest was awakened at this point.

*　　*　　*

NYMPHOLEPTS: Both Dodgson and Davidson suffered from nympholepsy, which *The Shorter O.E.D.* defines as 'a state of

[1] Philip Magnus. *Gladstone: A Biography*. London: John Murray, 1954.
[2] *The Daily Herald*, February 3, 1932.
[3] Ronald Pearsall. *The Worm in the Bud*. London: Weidenfeld and Nicolson, 1969.

rapture supposed to be inspired in men by nymphs'. But nympholepsy is also defined as 'desire for the unattainable', or 'violent
enthusiasm for an unattainable ideal'. Was it not precisely because
the nymphets were out of reach that the two reverend gentlemen
were attracted to them? What would Dodgson have done if Alice
had reciprocated his tender feelings, or Davidson if Barbara had
called him 'king of my heart'? Would not both have run a mile?

*   *   *

VIOLET CHRISTIAN: Davidson's reward for 'living dangerously
for God' was the testimonials he received from grateful girls whom
he had helped, he used to say. During his trial the rector read from
the pulpit at Stiffkey a testimonial received by his solicitor from
one Violet Christian who, judging from her name, might well have
strayed from *Pilgrim's Progress*. Reading along Davidson broke
down in sobs when he came to the part where Violet avowed, 'I am
now happily married, thanks to my old friend, but deep down in
my heart I love him for saving me from I know not what.' His
enemies claim that no matter how much Davidson shuffled the
letters in his cheap cardboard suitcase Violet's always came out on
top. They claim further that no one was ever allowed to handle the
letter in order to verify the handwriting and signature, but only to
hear extracts from it read between sobs.

*   *   *

LETTERS TO BARBARA: Inexplicably, the defence made no use of
the letters which the rector wrote to Barbara Harris, and which
were entered as evidence at the trial. I have examined twenty-one
of these letters, none of which could by the remotest stretch of the
imagination be considered a love letter. All are signed 'Your sincere
friend and padre, Harold F. Davidson', and show genuine concern
for Barbara's welfare. The first letter, written August 22, 1931, on
the eve of Barbara taking a maid's job with Lady Paget-Cooke,
radiates confidence in the girl. 'Remember,' the rector writes, 'I
thoroughly believe in you and in your abilities to make good and I
will always help you in any way I possibly can.'

The last of the letters was written and posted from Stiffkey on
Christmas Eve, 1931. 'Get some little Christmas remembrance for

yourself out of the enclosed 5/- Postal Order,' Davidson writes. 'I do pray,' he continues, 'that now you have made a real start on the right road you may have strength and grace to carry on. But do remember that it is only by keeping in constant living touch with Jesus Christ that you can hope for any real happiness and success. My Christmas wish for you is that Christ may be born anew in your heart . . .' This from the man who was alleged to have laughed at Barbara on the only occasion that he had asked her to pray, and whose only piece of spiritual advice to her was said to have been, 'God does not mind the sins of the body, but only those of the soul'.

*   *   *

FASTIDIOUS: 'As for the charges that father had sexual intercourse with Rose Ellis and Barbara Harris,' declares Nugent, 'the fact that Rose had syphilis and that Barbara, too, thought she had V.D. would, if nothing else, have precluded this. Father was terribly fastidious.'

*   *   *

PHENOMENAL MEMORY: Nugent Davidson tells me that his father had a phenomenal memory. At chess, for example, Davidson blindfolded could play five opponents simultaneously and beat them. He taught Nugent to play without a chess board so that they could enjoy a game while travelling up to London together by train. The rector's sermons were hardly ever prepared beforehand, but they were leavened by quotations from the Bible and from Tennyson, Ruskin and Kipling. At home Davidson was a stickler for correct speaking taught his children diction and voice control. One of them, Sheilagh, became an elocution teacher.

*   *   *

ACTOR OF MERIT: Concerning Davidson's ability as an actor there is no need to accept his word. Describing Davidson's post-trial appearance at the Embassy Ice Rink in Birmingham in a skit entitled 'The Sermon of Mother Hubbard', a *Daily Express* reporter writes: 'He adopted the attitude, the gestures and the sing-song intonations associated with such discourses, and gave to the mock sermon so much of sincerity and deep feeling that it was difficult at times to feel that he was not in the pulpit preaching the Gospel.' However, it was in a take-off on the Irving school of melodramatic acting that Davidson excelled, according to the *Daily Express*. 'Spectators saw the Rector of Stiffkey falling over invisible objects and rolling on his back on the platform, picking invisible objects out of his hair, his ears, and his nose. This brought down the house . . .'

When Davidson later appeared at the Prince's Cinema in Wimbledon a critic for the local newspaper wrote: 'But best of all, perhaps, were his brilliant studies of a woman in the intricate process of dressing her hair in the pre-shingle era.' 'There is no need to go to this performance in an attitude of sympathy or solely in search of novelty,' the critic added. 'It deserves to be regarded as a work of art.'

NOTE: The performances described above took place in 1932, or thirty years after Davidson had quit the stage for the priesthood. It is a tribute to his remarkable memory that he was able to recreate at this late date the comic skits in which he had triumphed as a young man.

*　　*　　*

CELEBRITIES: Davidson knew celebrities from every walk of life. Some of these friendships date from Davidson's days on the stage. Nugent remembers that as a little boy he was taken to meet George Bernard Shaw when the Shaws lived at 10 Adelphi Terrace. (As Davidson had toured with Granville Barker it is possible that Barker introduced him to Shaw. Again, the rector was a member of the Emerson Club, which used to meet at Shaw's house.) His friendship with other notables (Field-Marshal Earl Roberts, Earl Beatty, the Duke of Westminster, the Marquess of Crewe, Lord Hugh Cecil) dates from the days when Davidson helped out at the London Dockland Settlement. But what, one wonders, is the story behind the photograph of Sarah Bernhardt inscribed 'To Harold with love', which had pride of place on the desk in Davidson's study?

*　　*　　*

UNWANTED: To his friends Davidson became The Man Who Came to Dinner, the unwanted guest whose footstep on the stair fills his host with dread. Compton Mackenzie tells how Davidson, as a newly-ordained deacon, descended upon the Oxford digs which Mackenzie shared with Harry Gordon-Pirie begging lodging for two nights. Told there was no vacant bed, Davidson elected to curl up under the dining-table. The next morning his hosts, fed up with listening to Davidson rehearse the sermon he was to preach that day, locked him in the lavatory; but he escaped by climbing out of the window and shinnying down a drainpipe. 'He's a proper little monkey,' the landlady exclaimed.

Another who lived in dread of Davidson's knock, which usually occurred round 2 a.m., was the Rev Maurice Davis, vicar of All Saints, Haggerston, in East London. In response to that knock the vicar would pop his head out of the window, espy Davidson looking up at him. 'Let me in, Davis,' the rector would call out. 'I just want a little sleep. Anywhere will do—the study chair.' And Davidson would slump down in the study chair, put his feet on the vicar's desk, and doze until 4.30 a.m. when it was time to catch the first train for Norfolk.

J. Rowland Sales ended by putting Davidson's suitcase outside the door. 'I couldn't stand it any longer,' Sales told me. 'It wasn't his midnight visits I minded so much as the mess he made. He would strew his papers all over the spare bedroom.'

*　　*　　*

WRONG TIME: Nugent Davidson tells me of a visit which his father paid when Nugent and his wife were living in Harrow in a flat five flights up. During the evening the rector kept watching the clock on the mantelpiece, and when it was time for him to catch the last train back to London he hurriedly departed for the Rayner's Lane station. 'Not long afterwards we heard someone pounding up the stairs,' Nugent recalls. 'Father staggered through the door gasping, "Your clock is three minutes fast by the station clock." Then he slammed the door, and we heard him racing down those five flights of stairs. Mad, utterly mad—but that was father.'

FREDDIE

———————

'Then said Daniel unto the king, "O king, live for ever. My God hath sent his angel, and hath shut the lions' mouths, that they have not hurt me; forasmuch as before him innocency was found in me; and also before thee, O king, have I done no hurt." '
The Book of Daniel, 6:21–24

12

The Geek

Harold Davidson lived like a 'geek' for the five remaining years of his life. A 'geek' (from the middle low German *Geck*, meaning 'fool') is a carnival performer who earns his bread by performing feats, usually of a disgusting nature, which no normal person would dream of doing. The circus wild man who bites off the head of a live chicken is a geek. So was 'The Starving Woman of Haslingden', whom Davidson was hired to replace on Blackpool's Golden Mile after her star had begun to wane. Finally, 'The geek has a low status in the carnival and is usu. considered mentally deranged or perverted.' (*Dictionary of American Slang.*)

Davidson began his life as a geek by being exhibited in a barrel at Blackpool. He ended by sharing the billing with a couple of mangy lions at Skegness. In between he rang the changes, being shown in the process of freezing in a refrigerated case, or alternatively, being roasted in a glass oven while an automated demon prodded him in the backside with a pitchfork. Sometimes Davidson was the sole attraction; at other times, he was the sun round whom minor geeks orbited. One such mini-geek was a girl named Barbara over whom the ex-rector of Stiffkey was to keep watch for ten days and nights 'for love of her sister', according to the fair-booth posters. Alas, the Barbara in the adjacent barrel was not 'Little Miss Judas' come to do penance publicly for having betrayed her benefactor. She was a Miss Barbara Cockayne, aged 20, whose name suggests that she was no stranger to show business. On another occasion Davidson's companion was a cousin of Mahatma Gandhi who, clad only in a loin cloth, made himself comfortable on a bed of nails.

For all the need to vary his act from time to time, Davidson felt most at home in the womb-like security of his barrel on the Blackpool promenade, where he squatted like some latter-day Diogenes. Davidson's barrel, however, was more comfortable than Diogenes' tub, it being fitted with an electric light, a cushioned seat, and a chimney up which Davidson blew his cigar smoke. A window cut in the side of the barrel permitted Davidson to chat briefly with visitors as they filed past; or if he were busy the latter could glimpse him with a legal tome on his lap as he prepared a new appeal against the consistory court judgment.

'I should like it to be known that every fibre of my being revolts against the indignity of this procedure,' cried Uncle Harold from the depths of his barrel, and to make sure that the world got the message he caused notices to be posted to the effect: 'The former Rector of Stiffkey has been placed in his present position by the authorities of the Church of England who failed in their Christian duty towards him . . . The lower he sinks, the greater their crime.'

'Hurry! Hurry! Hurry!' cried the doppelganger known as Little Jimmy. 'See the one and only ex-rector of Stiffkey—not even the Archbishop of Canterbury can muzzle him! Hurry! Hurry! Hurry!'

For Little Jimmy and Uncle Harry were still at war. Davidson's basic personality conflict had not been resolved, far from it—but the relationship between the alternating egos had undergone a subtle change, according to J. Rowland Sales. A *modus vivendi* had been worked out between them. 'They had agreed to disagree,' Sales declared. In this Davidson was reminiscent of that other clerical victim of multiple personality, the Rev Thomas Hanna, whose alter personality, a coarse fellow, had learned to play the banjo, much to the clergyman's dismay. Hanna's solution was to embrace them both, the Bible-thumper and the banjo-strummer, evidently acting on the 'if you can't lick 'em, join 'em' principle. As Hanna explained it, 'I decided to take both lives as mine, because of the fear and anxiety that the struggle would be repeated again and again. The mental agony in the struggle of the two lives was too great to endure . . .'[1]

* * *

At first the holiday-makers with their Kiss-Me-Quick hats, their candy floss and sticks of Blackpool rock came in their hundreds for a tuppenny peep at the geek.

[1] Sidis, Boris and Goodhart, Simon P. *Multiple Personality*. London: Sidney Appleton, 1905.

[188]

'Father regarded his appearances at Blackpool as an opportunity to talk to people and to explain his case,' Nugent Davidson tells me. 'His attitude was that the more people he could reach the better.' Uncle Harold's volubility brought him into sharp conflict not only with Little Jimmy, but with Luke Gannon, the flashily-dressed 'Showman King of Blackpool', who was Davidson's impresario. 'Gannon was all for rushing people through the turnstiles so that he could collect more admissions, whereas father didn't like to be cut off in mid-sentence when he was talking to someone.'

Among those whom Davidson detained in explaining the whys and wherefores of his case was Harold Chilcott, of Barry, South Wales, who with his wife paid to see the ex-rector in his barrel. Chilcott writes: 'Davidson brought out from his pocket a bundle of letters which he said he had received from parents of girls he had helped expressing their sincere thanks for what he had done.' In parting Davidson, after asking the Chilcotts if they would accept a quotation from him, wrote the following on a scrap of paper and gave it to them: 'We are all in the gutter, but some of us are looking at the stars.'[1]

As time went on Davidson spent nearly as much time in the local magistrate's court as he did in his barrel, for the Blackpool authorities did not take kindly to 'this raree show', as one newspaper called it. When not being fined for causing a breach of the peace, Davidson was being fined for obstructing the footpath, until finally the editor of the *Sunday Express*, under the heading STUPIDITY THAT ONLY ADVERTISES HIM, urged that a halt be called, warning that 'persecution is the salt of notoriety'. 'The rector of Stiffkey would soon be forgotten if the police and bishops could be persuaded to abandon their booming of his absurdities.'

In July, 1933 Battling Flora Osborne finally caught up with her defaulting tenant, and Davidson was jailed for nine days at Liverpool for £43 in rent arrears, the case having been remitted from London. The task of serving the warrant on Davidson was entrusted to J. P. Oldroyd, now retired and living in Queensland,

---

[1] The quotation is from *Lady Windermere's Fan*. There is a possibility that Davidson appeared in a touring company production of this play. His daughter Sheilagh maintained that Davidson had toured in one of Wilde's plays. Certainly Davidson admired the Irish playwright. As a naval chaplain he was reprimanded by his captain for lending a young officer a copy of *De Profundis*, which the captain was all for burning. 'Would you burn

Australia, but then a young clerk in a Blackpool law firm. Oldroyd writes that Davidson, in dodging him, showed all the agility of a Spring-Heeled Jack, going so far as to climb out of a back window and to slide down a drainpipe while Oldroyd hammered on the front door. Davidson's return to Blackpool after serving his sentence in Liverpool's Walton gaol was in the nature of a Roman triumph. 'An open landau brought him from the station,' Oldroyd recalls. 'The reverend was flanked by two young Negresses who threw flowers to an enthusiastic crowd.'

Uncle Harold relished these courtroom appearances, for did they not provide him with another platform on which to protest his innocence? So much did he enjoy them that when not being sued, Uncle Harold himself took to suing. A case in point was when in August, 1935 Davidson was arrested for 'unlawfully starving himself with intent to commit suicide.' Davidson by then had completed ten days of a projected thirty-five-day fast undertaken 'in order to bring the Archbishop of Canterbury and the Church authorities to their senses'. When arrested the ex-rector, who was described by the *Daily Mail* as 'a haggard, untidy figure beneath tumbled bedclothes', had to be lifted from the glass case in which he was displayed, so weak was he. In court Davidson argued successfully that it was not his fault if his protest had been billed as a 'Fast to Death: Like the late Mayor of Cork.'[1] He had no intention to starve himself to death, considering it more important to remain alive until the 1892 Clergy Discipline Act had been repealed. Acquitted, Davidson promptly sued the Blackpool Corporation for malicious arrest and was awarded £382 in damages by a sympathetic jury.

Curiously, the episode badly dented Davidson's credibility, for the rumour spread that during the ten days he was supposed to be fasting Davidson lived on bananas and grapes that were smuggled to him in his glass cabinet. Thanks to this rumour, attendance fell off sharply. The Lancashire mill hands in the Kiss-Me-Quick hats

---

Shakespeare because he wrote *The Rape of Lucrece*?' Davidson enquired. More to the point he asked, 'Would you refuse to read anything about Lord Nelson because of his love affairs?'

[1] Terence McSwiney, poet, dramatist, Gaelic scholar, Lord Mayor of Cork, died in Brixton prison on October 25, 1920, after fasting for 74 days in protest against his arrest by British troops for I.R.A. activity.

scattered their money freely among Blackpool's sideshow freaks, but they didn't like to be taken for mugs.

Uncle Harold may have basked in the limelight of those court-room dramas, but it was Little Jimmy who got himself arrested at Victoria station in November, 1936, charged with 'trespassing on railway property', which was another way of saying that he had been pestering two 16-year-old girls. Davidson had introduced himself to the girls, one of whom was in charge of a station kiosk, explaining that he was looking for an actress to play a leading rôle in a West End play. If either of them cared to audition for the part he would give her £5 for her pains, he offered. When the ex-rector turned up at Victoria the following day to keep an appointment with the girls he walked straight into the arms of railway police, who had been alerted. In the witness-box at Westminster police court Davidson once again claimed that he had been 'framed', but to no avail—he was fined 40 shillings plus £2.5s. costs, and prompt-ly announced that he would appeal. The Greek superstition was that once one had glimpsed a nymph in a stream or spring one was struck with incurable madness, and remained a nympholept for life.

*   *   *

'Father has tried to play the game of his life as he would a game of chess, planning all his moves ahead,' Davidson's daughter Patricia once remarked. 'This has been his great downfall,' she added, 'because human pawns and pieces have a disturbing way of moving by themselves into another square, and thus upsetting the whole scheme of things.' Nowhere was this rigidity of mind more noticeable than in Davidson's attempts during the last year of his life to get his case re-tried in a civil court. His grand strategy for getting his case re-opened was as mad as the Memorial on which Mr Dick of *David Copperfield* fame worked unceasingly, and into which the troubled thoughts of King Charles the First kept in-truding.

It was to be war on two fronts, or rather a pincer movement, the first prong of which consisted of Davidson suing for libel anyone who dared to brand him as immoral in citing Chancellor North's judgment in *Norwich v Davidson*. Sheilagh Davidson explained the gambit thus in a letter to her daughter Ruth: 'Father always said his only chance of getting justice was to keep his case before the public, keep suing everybody who published anything unsavoury about him, always hoping that somebody would plead the Chancellor's verdict to justify what they had said . . . You see the Chancellor's verdict was not legal in English law. It was a church verdict, and if anyone had pleaded this in defence he would have to answer before a judge and jury and prove whatever Father was objecting to . . . That is why for five years he did all the peculiar things he did in order to speak to people and defend himself in public and gain supporters.'

The notion that a diocesan chancellor's judgment had no validity in English law was one which existed only in Davidson's mind, just as King Charles's head existed only in the addled brain of Mr Dick.

Prong No. 2 was, if anything, more hare-brained than its predecessor. It consisted of Davidson publishing libels against the principals who had figured in his case—notably, Dr Pollock, Chancellor North, H. T. A. Dashwood—in the hopes that at least one of the said principals would be provoked into suing him for slander, and thus permit the re-opening of his case. What Davidson's feverish mind failed to take into account was that none of those libelled was likely to sue when there was no chance of collecting damages from an ex-clergyman who was also an undischarged bankrupt.[1]

Undeterred by such ratiocination, Davidson published 'I Accuse', a mimeographed pamphlet consisting of three sheets of closely-typed foolscap stapled together (the ex-rector could not afford a printer). Beginning with the Archbishop of Canterbury, the ex-rector raked the establishment with his broadside. The archbishop he accused of 'failing to show any spiritual solicitude for my soul, or to administer any Christian comfort', among other lapses. The Bishop of Norwich was guilty of 'duplicity, a lack of charity and of moral rectitude'. Even harsher judgments were reserved for the lesser lights in the case. Chancellor North, for example, was arraigned for 'judicial incapacity, physical disability, rank prejudice and occasional somnolence' (his worship was said to have

---

[1] Estimates of how much Davidson earned in five years at Blackpool range from £5,000 to £20,000. Proof that he earned good money during his first summer season there came unexpectedly when on November 25, 1932 the Official Receiver in Bankruptcy announced a 'first and final' dividend of 4s. 7d. to the pound to be paid to Davidson's creditors. How-

dozed occasionally during the Stiffkey trial). As for Detective Searle and Solicitor Dashwood, the former was accused of 'criminally conspiring with others by means of lying misrepresentation, bribery and corruption', while the latter was indicted for 'active personal participation' in the said conspiracy. Dashwood should be 'struck off the rolls of an honourable profession which he has disgraced', in Davidson's opinion.

None of the above-named being so foolhardy as to walk into the trap he had so carefully set for them, Davidson decided to carry the fight directly to the enemy camp. On November 20, 1936 his frenzied campaign to get his case reopened came to a climax at a meeting of the Church Assembly at Central Hall, Westminster, when Davidson stood up in the public gallery and demanded to be heard 'in the name of justice'. Dr Cosmo Gordon Lang, who then had the abdication crisis on his hands, and who therefore was in no mood to deal with a *trahison des clercs*, sharply rebuked Davidson, telling him that he had no right to speak. There were scattered 'Hear, hears' and a general susurration of approval of the archbishop's ruling as the delegates turned to stare at the ex-cleric. Seeing Uncle Harold thus publicly discomfited, Little Jimmy came to the rescue. For it could only have been the imp who prompted Davidson to cut the string on a bundle of the 'I Accuse' pamphlets which he had placed on the seat beside him, and to shower the pamplets down on the heads of the assembly below in a veritable blizzard of paper. Then as stewards from all parts of the hall converged on him Little Jimmy hurriedly exited from the gallery, raced down the stairs and out the door. The incident rated a few paragraphs in the morning papers.

Altogether the winter of 1936 was the winter of Davidson's discontent. Not only had the grand strategy failed to produce results, but Davidson was in debt, the Blackpool box-office takings having fallen off drastically. The truth was that people were tiring of the ex-rector and his madcap adventures. After the 'Fast to Death' fiasco word got around that he was a fraud as well as being an old bore. Undoubtedly these were considerations which persuaded Davidson to sign with Captain Fred Rye, the owner of a menagerie,

---

ever, the Blackpool season lasted only five months; and after the first few years the ex-rector's pickings were lean. Cigars were his only extravagance, according to his wife Molly.

to appear at Skegness Amusement Park during the 1937 summer season in an act billed as 'A Modern Daniel in a Lion's Den'. Meanwhile, Davidson lay low at South Harrow, where Molly Davidson had bought a small house with money realised on life insurance policies. He made frequent trips to the pawnshop all during that winter, pledging the few articles of value he had managed to save when forced to give up the rectory at Stiffkey. He also cadged money from such old friends as Dr Winnington-Ingram and the Rev Pat McCormick, vicar of St Martin's-in-the-Fields. Thanks to these handouts plus a £50 loan from the Ecclesiastical Commissioners (secured by a first lien on Davidson's future earnings) Davidson was able to eke out the winter months. But only his faith in himself and in the rightness of his cause kept him going.

*   *   *

To appear in a cage with a lion was an act of courage on Davidson's part, for he was deathly afraid of most creatures which walk on four legs. He would not cross a field if he saw a cow munching peacefully in one corner of it, nor would he allow his wife's dogs to come near him. Once his fellow freaks at Blackpool played a mean trick on Davidson by putting a mouse in his barrel. Davidson nearly had hysterics before the sideshow barker, hearing him bang on the staves, let him out of the barrel. One lion was bad enough, but how Davidson let himself be talked into appearing with two jungle beasts—Freddie the lion and its mate Toto—is something of a mystery. Perhaps he was unaware that playing gooseberry in such a *ménage à trois* involved real danger. His friends, however, warned him. 'I said I thought it was a silly thing to do,' Mrs Norah Knotts, a public stenographer to whom Davidson used to dictate his letters, later declared. 'He said he had to have money somehow. He could not continue to live on his friends.' Davidson was cognisant of the danger involved, according to Mrs Knotts. 'He said, "Do you realise I shall be risking my life to pay you and my other creditors?" '

On the other hand, 'daring to be a Daniel' no doubt appealed to Davidson, who took heart from the Old Testament prophet's example. For like Daniel, the seer and interpreter of dreams, was not he, Harold Davidson, a spiritual exile in Babylon? And like Daniel's companions in captivity had not he, too, been tested in the

[194]

burning fiery furnace? Some such thoughts may have distracted Davidson's mind as he prepared to go into the lion's cage at eight o'clock on the evening of Wednesday, July 28. At that hour Skegness Amusement Park was thronged with holiday-makers, many of them early arrivals for the August Bank Holiday, and over a hundred had paid at the turnstiles of Rye's Pavilion to see the 'Modern Daniel' inside. Davidson's act followed an invariable routine. It began outside the cage with the ex-rector giving a 10-minute spiel about the rights and wrongs of his case while the tawny shapes of the lions, who were usually lying down, could be discerned in the background. Then after lambasting Archbishop Lang and Bishop Pollock (Davidson always made it clear that it was the Church leadership, not the Church of England, that he blamed) he would make a little joke. 'It's all very well for you people, you only have to listen to me once,' he would say. 'But what about the poor lions? They hear the same spiel four times a day.' 'One of them had me cornered yesterday,' he would add. 'I don't know what they will do to me tonight.' It was all pretty feeble, but then Davidson was never good at writing his own material.

The cage which housed the lions measured 14 ft by 8 ft and had doors at either end, the righthand door being always padlocked and the key left with Mrs Rye at the box-office. After exchanging his ebony walking stick for a short stock whip Davidson would enter the cage through the door on the left, and either Captain Rye or a girl attendant who was employed as assistant lion-tamer, stood by the door armed with a pole during the two or three minutes the ex-rector was in the den. It was all perfectly safe, according to Captain Rye, who had left his own 8-year-old daughter alone in the cage with Freddie on one occasion. All of which did not prevent things from going horribly wrong shortly after 8 p.m. on Wednesday, July 28.

William Stanley Bliss, a Watford clerk on holiday at Skegness, had taken his wife and their two small children to see the show, and later, at the coroner's inquest, he gave a graphic account of what happened next. Evidently the lions were too docile for Davidson's liking, for no sooner had he entered the cage than he began to stir things up, snapping the whip at the beasts while exhorting them to 'get a move on'. Toto, the lioness, who was lying at the far end of the cage, did not stir. But Freddie, fully aroused, began to stalk his tormentor round the cage. Suddenly the male beast reared on its haunches and struck Davidson with its two front paws knocking him over. 'The lion got the rector by the neck and carried him round the cage like a cat would carry a mouse,' Bliss declared.

For a split second Bliss and the other holiday-makers thought that Davidson's struggle with the big cat was all part of a comic lion-taming act, but the laughter quickly froze in their throats as realisation of the tragedy sank in. Horror-stricken the spectators bolted for the door.

It was Captain Rye's day off. In his absence the pavilion was manned by Mrs Rye, who sold tickets in the box-office; an assistant named Norman Wallace, who had had no experience whatsoever as an animal trainer; and Irene Violet Somner, the girl lion-tamer, who was so near-sighted that she wore thick, horn-rimmed glasses at all times. It was Irene, described by the press as being 'convent-bred', who was the heroine of the occasion. For as soon as Irene saw what had happened, she dashed into the cage and grabbed Freddie by the mane in a vain attempt to make the lion drop its victim. Irene apparently had gone into the cage armed with a pistol which fired blank cartridges, but in the confusion she had dropped the weapon in the sawdust, and being near-sighted could not spot it. She did, however, find a tree branch lying in the cage, and with this she beat Freddie over the head until the lion dropped Davidson in the far corner of the cage. Irene then began shouting, 'Get Mrs Rye! Get the key from Mrs Rye!'

In the meanwhile, Bliss, having shepherded his wife and children to safety, returned with a wooden handle, which he jammed into the lion's mouth, but the handle broke. He then poked an iron rod through the bars, and with the assistance of Patrick Mellin, a showman from a neighbouring fairbooth, who arrived with a 12 ft pole, managed to hold both beasts at bay. For no sooner had Freddie dropped Davidson face downwards in the sawdust than the lioness, which all the while had remained passive, started to come at the ex-rector. Irene dragged Davidson, his head covered in blood, to safety through the righthand door, whose padlock she had unlocked. The girl then fainted.

The Old Testament tells us that Daniel was rescued from the lions' den by an angel of the Lord. Angels, of course, are ageless as well as being without gender. Irene was just sixteen.

*　　*　　*

The rest of the story belongs in the realm of folklore. One of the more piquant bits of apocrypha has it that Davidson, dragged torn and bleeding from the lions' cage, had the presence of mind to give orders, 'Telephone the London newspapers—we still have time to make the first editions.' However, the medical evidence at the coroner's inquest suggests that he was in a deep state of shock when he was rushed to the Skegness Cottage Hospital, where he was found to have a broken bone in his neck and a deep gash behind his left ear, caused by the lion's claws. He died on Friday, July 30, in a diabetic coma induced by his injuries, 'death by misadventure' being the verdict of the coroner's jury. Even while Davidson was still hovering between life and death a huge placard went up outside Captain Rye's Pavilion:

SEE THE LION
THAT MAULED & INJURED THE RECTOR,
AND THE PLUCKY GIRL
WHO WENT TO HIS RESCUE

As a candidate for folklore Davidson has been the subject of numerous limericks, jokes, and songs of the bawdy sort, most of which equate 'Stiffkey' with certain priapic propensities on the rector's part (if Davidson had been the incumbent of a village with a name other than Stiffkey would he be remembered as vividly today?) He sued one gramophone company and collected £350 damages for a scurrilous ditty which, pressed in wax, sold over the counter at Woolworth's. Not all of the verse was of the rugby changing-room variety, as witness the following which circulated in East Anglia in the 1930s, and which is not without a certain charm:

> The lock on my door
>   has a very stiff key,
> And a barrel of oil
>   will not let it go free.
> When the barrel is empty
>   we'll all get inside
> And pretend we're Little Jimmy
>   washed up by the tide.

The posthumous tribute which would have pleased Davidson the most was to be made the hero of two musicals in 1969, though he would have been disappointed that both were commercial flops. *God Made the Little Red Apple* (later retitled *The Vicar of Soho* which first saw the light of day at the Stables Theatre, Manchester, was the collaboration of Stuart Douglass, a socially-committed TV writer, and the late composer Tony Russell, and stressed Davidson's rôle as a social reformer ('If Davidson was a ridiculous figure then the twenties and thirties were ridiculous, defying the logic of historians,' writes Douglass in a programme note). Not content with making Davidson a victim of 'the system', the authors give *Apple* a Brechtian twist by insisting that he was a willing victim ('He wallowed in his isolation . . . He played this game without realising what a nonsense he was perpetuating'). To point up the irony, the girls whom Davidson has helped return in a dream sequence to thank him. One, a reformed prostitute, who has given up her easy earnings for married respectability, now finds herself saddled with a husband out of work and four nippers to feed. Another has found happiness by joining Moseley's Black Shirts, and goes Jew-bashing in London's East End every weekend.

The Stiffkey Scandals of 1932, which folded at the Queen's Theatre, London, after a run of only nine days, is the work of David Wright and David Wood, and also features a dream sequence. It comes when Davidson, having just been found guilty, takes from a brown paper parcel which he has been carrying all evening a pair of black patent leather pumps. After peering furtively round to make sure that he is not observed, he puts on the pumps and proceeds to do a soft shoe number to the tune of 'When My Dream Boat Comes Home'. When *Scandals* was presented on BBC television, *The Daily Telegraph*'s critic found it 'unconvincing'. 'One wonders in the end,' the critic mused, 'whether there was artistic justification for presenting a musical about so sad and peculiar a person . . .'

Sad and peculiar Harold Davidson may have been, but the media will not let him rest in peace. As recently as 1973 when the rectory at Stiffkey was put up for auction his life story was rehashed by the popular press. WHAT THE SCARLET RECTOR LEFT BEHIND, bannered the *People* across five columns, while the *Sunday Express*, not to be outdone, headlined A WOMAN REMEMBERS RECTOR WHO KNEW VICE GIRLS. Small wonder that the Stiffkey villagers turn bitter when reporters come round seeking gossip tit-bits about their former rector. 'The rector has been dead nearly forty years—

why can't they leave him in peace?' Mrs Norah Bayfield, daughter of Davidson's gardener, and now in her late seventies, complained to me. 'Mr Davidson was as innocent as I'm standing here in front of you today,' she said with some vehemence. 'I should know,' she added, 'for I was nursemaid to his children, and in and out of the rectory at all times. I would have known if there had been any hanky-panky going on.'

Mrs Bayfield tends Davidson's grave in the Stiffkey churchyard with loving care, keeping fresh flowers growing on it (when I visited Stiffkey it was planted in lobelia). That grave is soon to become the object of 'organised pilgrimages', if a letter published recently in the *Lynn News and Advertiser* is to be believed. 'The number of pilgrims to the Rector's lonely grave in the churchyard at Stiffkey is growing every year,' the writer declared, adding that 'soon there will be organised pilgrimages from all parts of England and a movement to seek for the Rector, through the Court of Arches, justice and charity, at last.' Evidently the Lynn newspaper took the leg-pull seriously for it headlined the letter across six columns with CULT OF STIFFKEY IS GROWING RAPIDLY.

Time has obliterated Davidson's name from the headstone over his grave, but its inscription, a quotation from Robert Louis Stevenson, is still discernible: 'For on faith in man and genuine love of man all searching after truth must be founded.' Is it by accident, one wonders, that Davidson's headstone is facing the wrong way? Or is it that Davidson, even in death, is defiantly asserting that everyone is out of step except him? Looked at another way, perhaps it is intended that when he rises on Judgment Day the Rev Harold Davidson shall be facing his parishioners as he did so often in the pulpit of St John with St Mary. They are all buried round him, the Suttons, the Elwoods, the Cursons, the Bayfields, whom he baptised, married, and in some cases buried. And when the trumpet sounds no doubt they will be found listening again to their pastor's message of truth based on faith in man and genuine love of man.

GNOSIS AND THE
NEW TESTAMENT

GNOSIS

AND THE

NEW TESTAMENT

R. McL. WILSON, B.D., Ph.D.

*Senior Lecturer in New Testament
Language and Literature,
St. Mary's College,
University of St. Andrews*

1968
BASIL BLACKWELL · OXFORD

631 10650 2

Printed in Great Britain by
Western Printing Services Ltd, Bristol

LONDON BOROU(
PUBLIC LIBRARIES

No. D76145

This book must be RETURNED on or before the last date stamped below unless a renewal has been obtained by personal call, post or telephone, quoting the above number and the date due for return.

L 18-06-76 due 18-7-76 +2 324				

In the case of infectious illness, do not return books to the Library, but inform the Librarian.

Contents

Abbreviations

HTR	Harvard Theological Review
ICC	International Critical Commentary
JEH	Journal of Ecclesiastical History
JTS	Journal of Theological Studies
NTS	New Testament Studies
OLZ	Orientalistische Literaturzeitung
PW	Pauly-Wissowa-Kroll, *Realenzyklopaedie*
RAC	*Reallexikon f. Antike u. Christentum*
RGG	*Die Religion in Geschichte u. Gegenwart*
RoB	Religion och Bibel
ThR	Theologische Rundschau
TLZ	Theologische Literaturzeitung
TU	Texte u. Untersuchungen
TWB	Theologisches Wörterbuch zum NT
Vig.Chr.	Vigiliae Christianae
ZKG	Zeitschrift f. Kirchengeschichte
ZKT	Zeitschrift f. katholische Theologie
ZNW	Zeitschrift f. neutestamentliche Wissenschaft
ZRGG	Zeitschrift f. Religions- u. Geistesgeschichte
ZTK	Zeitschrift f. Theologie u. Kirche

Preface

THIS book had its origin in a series of lectures delivered in the spring of 1965 at a number of universities and colleges in the United States and Canada. My wife and I have the most pleasant memories of our extended tour, and we should like to take this opportunity of expressing our thanks to all those who by the warmth of their welcome and cordial hospitality helped to make our journey so enjoyable. To mention a few however, and ignore the others, would be invidious and ungracious; but the list is frankly too long to print, the more especially if it were extended, as it ought to be, to include not only the institutions but the individuals who received us so warmly. We therefore hope our American and Canadian friends will accept this general expression of our thanks and appreciation.

One name however must be mentioned, that of the late Professor Kendrick Grobel, who was responsible for the initial invitation which enabled me to spend a semester as Visiting Professor at Vanderbilt Divinity School, and who later crowned all the many kindnesses he and Mrs. Grobel showed us by planning and arranging the whole tour for us. It was our one regret that his untimely death just before we set out made it impossible for us to report to him on our return how well his plans had been laid.

For publication, the lectures have been completely revised and considerably expanded. In chapter 5 in particular opportunity has been taken to include some discussion of the significance of each of the documents so far published. The lecture form has however been preserved so far as possible, and detailed technical discussion therefore avoided. References to the relevant literature are supplied in the footnotes, but no attempt has been made at a complete coverage. Detailed analysis of differing points of view would have extended the book far beyond the limits of space available.

An earlier version of chapter 4 appeared as an article in the *Expository Times*, and I have to thank the editor for granting permission for the use of this material here. Dr. Ernest Best and Mr. G. E. McMillan read the manuscript, and have helped to eliminate various weaknesses, but are not of course responsible for any shortcomings which remain. Finally, my thanks are due to Mrs. Isobel Stuart, who efficiently reduced a not always very tidy manuscript to neat and orderly pages of type.

St. Mary's College,   R. McL. Wilson
St. Andrews
January 1967

I

The Gnostic Heresy in the Light of Recent Research and Discovery

In the Kerr Lectures delivered in the University of Glasgow in 1909, Dr. Robert Law observed that the rise and spread of Gnosticism 'forms one of the dimmest chapters in Church history.'[1] Even today it would be too much to say that the obscurity has been altogether removed, the darkness dissipated. We cannot yet trace the whole history of this movement in all its ramifications, or identify the precise influences which were operative at each particular stage of its development. Nevertheless progress has been made. The patient study and research of many scholars, and the discovery of quite substantial quanties of new material, have shed light on many a dark corner and contributed to a fuller and better understanding. But, as so often happens, the removal of one problem has sometimes only given rise to several others. New discoveries have provided the answers to some of our questions, but in their turn they have raised new questions for investigation, questions of dating, questions of relationship to the material already known, or to the other documents contained in these new discoveries themselves, and so on. New methods of research again have prompted the reconsideration of many problems, but the new solutions offered have not always proved entirely satisfactory.[2]

The extent of the progress that has been made may perhaps be most readily seen from a consideration of Francis Legge's *Forerunners and Rivals of Christianity*, which has recently appeared in a second edition.[3] First published in 1915 in two volumes, this is in many ways an excellent book, and no disparagement is

---

[1] Robert Law, *The Tests of Life*, (Edinburgh 1909), p. 26.

[2] For a recent survey see K. Rudolph, 'Stand u. Aufgaben in der Erforschung des Gnostizismus', Tagung f. Allgemeine Religionsgeschichte 1963, Sonderheft der *Wiss. Zeitschr. Jena*, pp. 89 ff.

[3] F. Legge, *Fore-runners and Rivals of Christianity*, (2 vols., Cambridge 1915; reprinted in one vol., New York 1964).

intended when it is used in the present connection. Its author was a scholar, with a truly scholarly and scientific approach—if anything perhaps rather ahead of his time. His descriptions of the actual documents which were available to him are still useful and accurate, and much may be learned from his work. The second edition however is a reprint, unchanged and without revision, of the 1915 book, and therefore suffers from the simple fact that it is fifty years out of date, for much has happened in the interval. In his chapter on Manicheism, for example, Legge refers to the Turfan fragments, at that time a comparatively recent discovery; but he had of course no knowledge of the Coptic Manichean documents which only became available in the thirties.[4] To the Mandeans, again, he makes only passing reference, for he wrote before the 'Mandean fever' of the twenties, and without access even to the earliest Mandean documents to be published; but in some quarters there has been a tendency among modern scholars to treat Mandeism almost as normative for the study of Gnosticism.[5] Thirdly, and here again he was in advance of his time, Legge speaks of pre-Christian Gnostics, although he was well aware that in so doing he was widening the range of the term. Many scholars today would agree, but not all would approve of his choice—the Orphics, the Essenes and Simon Magus.[6]

Simon, of course, is denounced by Irenaeus as 'the father of all heresies', and the question whether he should be included here is to some extent one of definition: was he a Gnostic, and in what sense, before he came into contact with Christianity? And how far can the teachings of the later Simonian sect be attributed to the founder? In the other two cases, however, Legge had to make his bricks with a rather scanty minimum of straw—in the case of the Essenes on the basis of the information

[4] H. J. Polotsky, *Manichäische Homilien*, (Stuttgart 1934); H. J. Polotsky and A. Böhlig, *Kephalaia*, (Stuttgart 1940); C. R. C. Allberry, *A Manichean Psalm-Book*, (Stuttgart 1938). See also Polotsky, art. Manichäismus in *PW* Suppt. VI; Böhlig, *Wiss. Zeitschr. Halle* X.1, (1961), pp. 157 ff. K. Rudolph, *Wiss. Zeitschr. Halle* (Sonderheft 1965), pp. 156 ff.

[5] Cf. Schmithals' criticism of Jonas in *Die Gnosis in Korinth*, (Göttingen 1956), p. 87 n.1.

[6] For Orphism, cf. U. Bianchi, *Numen* 12, (1965), pp. 161 ff.; for Simon, E. Haenchen, *Gott und Mensch*, (Tübingen 1965), pp. 265 ff. [=*ZTK* 49, (1952), pp. 316 ff.].

supplied by Philo and Josephus, with the assistance of a certain amount of imagination. He had of course no knowledge of Qumran, and the scrolls which have shed so much fresh light upon a hitherto almost unknown aspect of Judaism in the New Testament period. In this connection it may be noted that when the Dead Sea Scrolls were first discovered many claimed that this was the library of a Gnostic sect; but these claims soon subsided.[7] As it has been said, nearly all the ingredients of the later Gnosticism are present,[8] yet something still is missing. The Scrolls are important for the study of Gnosticism, as they are important for the New Testament period as a whole, particularly from the point of view of the Jewish background. But here again there is a question of definition, to which we must return. At these three points then, Manicheism, Mandeism and Essenism, we now have at our disposal a mass of documentary evidence, some of it not yet fully evaluated, of which Legge and his contemporaries never knew; and this takes no account of the specifically Gnostic texts which have now become available, or of the research that has been done by many scholars.

Looking back across the years, we can trace a distinct change in the estimates of Gnosticism which have been put forward, from the somewhat contemptuous disparagement of Charles Bigg,[9] who wrote of the Gnostics 'the ordinary Christian controversialist felt that he had nothing to do but set out at unsparing length their tedious pedigrees, in the well-grounded confidence that no-one would care to peruse them a second time', to the more complimentary opinions which saw in them the first real theologians, the men who for all their shortcomings first grappled with the problems of presenting the Gospel in adequate philosophical terms and who by their very errors forced the Church to the elaboration of a more satisfactory solution. Bigg might have paused to consider that Irenaeus and Hippolytus, to name no others, both wrote at considerable length against the Gnostics—which at least suggests that to them this movement was a serious threat; otherwise they would not have put themselves to so much trouble.

But what *is* Gnosticism and who were the Gnostics? As

---

[7] Cf. Wilson, *The Gnostic Problem*, (London 1958), pp. 73 f.
[8] R. M. Grant, *Gnosticism and Early Christianity*, (New York 1959), p. 39.
[9] Charles Bigg, *The Christian Platonists of Alexandria*, (Oxford 1886), p. 28.

Bultmann puts it,[10] Gnosticism 'first appeared and attracted the attention of scholars as a movement within the Christian religion, and for a long time it was regarded as a purely Christian movement, a perversion of the Christian faith into a speculative theology.' The various Gnostic systems described by the early Fathers differ on points of detail, but the basic elements common to them all are (1) a distinction between the unknown and transcendent true God on the one hand and the Demiurge or creator of this world on the other, the latter being commonly identified with the God of the Old Testament; (2) the belief that man in his true nature is essentially akin to the divine, a spark of the heavenly light imprisoned in a material body and subjected in this world to the dominance of the Demiurge and his powers; (3) a myth narrating some kind of pre-mundane fall, to account for man's present state and his yearning for deliverance; and (4) the means, the saving *gnosis*, by which that deliverance is effected and man awakened to the consciousness of his own true nature and heavenly origin. This deliverance, and the eventual return of the imprisoned sparks of light to their heavenly abode, means in time the return of this world to its primordial chaos, and is strenuously opposed at all points by the hostile powers.

Some elements of Gnostic thought are shared by other religious movements also. Moreover, as van Unnik says,[11] 'the Gnostics often applied the principle of "Je prends mon bien où je le trouve" ', taking over and adapting for their own purposes the ideas, the language and sometimes the literature of other faiths. It is this that creates the problem first of defining Gnosticism in such a way as to cover all that is essentially Gnostic, without at the same time including elements common to Gnosticism and to other faiths which are not necessarily essentially Gnostic at all; and secondly of determining the origins and development of this movement, and the influences which were operative in the process. As will become apparent later, it

[10] Rudolf Bultmann, *Primitive Christianity in its Contemporary Setting*, (ET: London 1956), p. 162. The German original has 'die Gnosis', which in this context implies something rather wider than 'Gnosticism' as understood by most English-speaking scholars (see below).

[11] W. C. van Unnik, *Newly Discovered Gnostic Documents*, (ET: London 1960), p. 91.

is not the separate elements in themselves which are Gnostic, but the total synthesis, the system, into which they are combined.

The traditional theory, which in general held its ground from Irenaeus down to the time of Harnack, saw in Gnosticism a Christian heresy, the result of the contamination of the faith by the muddy waters of Greek philosophy. Thus Harnack in a famous phrase spoke of 'the acute hellenisation of Christianity.'[12] Plotinus, one must suspect, would have demurred—for him the contamination was the adulteration of the pure stream of Platonic philosophy by the new-fangled Christian faith. From Harnack's point of view the whole history of early Christianity, from the beginnings down to the time of Nicaea, is one of hellenisation. Gnosticism marks an *acute* hellenisation, the difference in some sense being no more than one of degree. Towards the end of the nineteenth century, however, and in the course of the twentieth, a different view prevails. No longer are the Gnostics in the van of progress—on the contrary, they belong to the forces of reaction. They represent not the pioneers of Christian theology but almost the last resistance of the ancient world to the triumph of Christianity. Gnosticism, on this view, is not merely a deviation from Christianity but a recrudescence and resurgence of ancient Oriental religion, indeed a religion in its own right, invading the West as the rival and competitor of the Christian faith. And this view has claimed the allegiance of a considerable body of scholars, from Reitzenstein and Bousset down to Bultmann and his pupils.[13] But it has not gone without its opponents.

One difficulty lies in the fact that it has proved impossible to identify one single source from which the movement could be said to take its origin. A religion is normally the faith of a particular people, although in course of time it may come to be propagated also in other lands and among other peoples, as with Judaism or the mystery religions; or it may take its rise from a particular founder within an existing tradition, as with

[12] A. von Harnack, *History of Dogma*, i, (ET: London 1897), p. 226. Cf. R. P. Casey in *JTS* 36, (1935), pp. 45 ff.
[13] Cf. Carsten Colpe, *Die religionsgeschichtliche Schule*, (Göttingen 1961), and for Bultmann his *Primitive Christianity* [n. 10 above]. See also H. Langerbeck, *Aufsätze zur Gnosis*, (Göttingen 1967).

Buddhism, Christianity and Islam. In either case we can identify the milieu and the point of origin, but with Gnosticism this is not the case. Numerous candidates have been nominated—Egypt, Babylonia, Persia, the hellenised Judaism of Alexandria. The explanation has been sought in philosophy and in magic, in the mystery religions, and in the disappointed eschatological hopes of early Christians or of Qumran sectarians. All too often Reitzenstein's warning[14] has gone unheeded—that the individual scholar almost inevitably tends to fall victim to a kind of colour blindness, which makes him insensitive to important distinctions, and that according to the direction of his own specialised studies each tends to give undue significance to particular aspects; which can only mean a distorted picture of the whole. But few today in this age of specialisation can claim the necessary mastery in all the disciplines involved—classical and Biblical scholarship, Egyptology, *Iranistik*, the lore of ancient Babylon and Mesopotamia, not to mention the underworld of alchemy and magic, or the literatures of Qumran and Gnosticism, Manicheism and Mandeism. As Reitzenstein said, only the combined work of many can bring us to a real solution.

In point of fact, Gnosticism is fundamentally syncretistic, welding into a new synthesis elements from diverse cultures. It would be more correct to recognise the various 'spheres of influence' mentioned[15] as the *ultimate* sources of particular ideas, and proceed to the attempt to trace the channels by which they passed into the developed Gnostic systems. It should be added that, as Jonas pointed out,[16] Gnosticism is not *merely* syncretism, or syncretism Gnosis. To quote Bultmann again,[17] 'the essence of Gnosticism does not lie in its syncretistic mythology but rather in a new understanding—new in the ancient world—of man and the world.'

A second difficulty lies in our present lack of an agreed terminology. The terms *gnosis*, Gnostic and Gnosticism were for centuries employed to describe the Christian heresy—although even this was in fact an extension of the original meaning: it is

[14] R. Reitzenstein, *Poimandres*, (Leipzig 1904), p. 250; cf. C. H. Dodd, *The Bible and the Greeks*, (London 1935), p. xv.
[15] The phrase is van Unnik's (op. cit. p. 35).
[16] Hans Jonas, *Gnosis u. spätantiker Geist*, i, (Göttingen [2]1954), pp. 77 ff.
[17] Bultmann, *Theology of the NT*, i, (ET: London 1952), p. 165.

the *gnosis* falsely so called that Irenaeus assails, and only some of the heretical groups described by the early Fathers claimed the name. A *gnosis* falsely so called carries with it the implication that there is a true *gnosis*, so that we are faced at once with the problem of finding terms by which to distinguish them. In modern research the extension has been carried further still. German scholars in particular have widened the horizon, noting in the first place that the phenomena which appear in the Christian heresy do not stand alone, for similar phenomena can be seen elsewhere, outside of Christianity; and secondly that there are certain affinities earlier, for example in the New Testament itself, in the writings of Philo of Alexandria, or in the scrolls from Qumran. The consequence has been, inevitably, a certain amount of confusion and misunderstanding, arising from the use of the same terms in different senses. In the field of *Dogmengeschichte*, Gnosticism is still for many writers the heresy of the second century, whereas in that of *Religionsgeschichte* 'Gnosis' is something very much wider and more comprehensive, so much so indeed that some scholars appear unable to see anything but Gnosis when they investigate the background of the New Testament or even the New Testament documents themselves. A further complication arises from the use of the phenomenological as distinct from the historical approach. When we are studying the phenomena we have to note the similarities, the typical features, but these similarities do not necessarily guarantee any historical continuity, a point that has not always been borne in mind. From the phenomenological point of view it may be perfectly legitimate to group religious movements together on the basis of their common elements; but this does not necessarily mean that these movements stand in any genetic relationship, or that there is any direct connection between the earlier and the later.

English-speaking scholars on the whole have tended to adhere to the traditional definition. F. C. Burkitt for example urged that the best way in which to approach the second century systems was to regard them as Christian systems, and his arguments for the essential Christianity of Valentinus were accepted as convincing by C. H. Dodd.[18] Dodd in his turn explicitly

[18] F. C. Burkitt, *Church and Gnosis*, (Cambridge 1932); C. H. Dodd, *The Interpretation of the Fourth Gospel*, (Cambridge 1953), p. 100 n.4.

recognised that there is a sense in which the wider definition employed by German scholars is apposite, but he himself held to the narrower definition. Within recent years R. P. Casey[19] has developed a lengthy attack on the idea that a vaguely defined and widespread Gnosis had anything to do with the origins of Christianity. In this connection Dodd[20] noted three points which are worthy of being kept in mind:

1. There is no Gnostic document known to us which can with any show of probability be dated—at any rate in the form in which alone we have access to it—before the period of the New Testament.

2. The typical Gnostic systems all combine in various ways and proportions ideas derived from Christianity with ideas which can be shown to be derived from, or at least to have affinities with, other religious or philosophical traditions.

3. The various Gnostic systems differ widely in the way in which they introduce and combine these disparate elements, and each system has to be considered separately for what it is in itself. No general and all-embracing answer can be given to the question, What is the relation of Gnosticism to Christianity?

Nevertheless English-speaking scholars have tended more and more towards some acceptance of the German point of view—albeit with certain reservations. Thus in a recent article, published posthumously, the late A. D. Nock[21] can expressly recognise the existence of 'a gnostic way of thinking' in the period prior to the New Testament, although he also says that the relation of the Gospel of Truth and other recently discovered texts to the New Testament seems 'to vindicate completely the traditional view of Gnosticism as Christian heresy with roots in speculative thought.'

Our first requirement then at the present time is clarity and precision of definition, some measure of agreement as to what we mean by the terms we use. One possible solution is to distinguish

[19] *The Background of the NT and its Eschatology*, ed. W. D. Davies and D. Daube, (Cambridge 1956), pp. 52 ff.
[20] *Interpretation*, p. 98.
[21] *HTR* 57, (1964), pp. 255 ff. [quotation from p. 276].

between Gnosticism on the one hand and Gnosis on the other. By Gnosticism we mean the specifically Christian heresy of the second century A.D., by Gnosis, in a broader sense, the whole complex of ideas belonging to the Gnostic movement and related trends of thought. A difficulty here is the fact that we have only the one adjective 'Gnostic' to do duty for both purposes. Something can be done by use of modifications such as 'pre-gnostic', 'semi-gnostic' or 'gnosticising'; but here again such terms are not always clearly defined or precisely used. Worst of all, sometimes a term or concept, a theme or idea, is described as 'Gnostic' because as a matter of fact it does appear in Gnosticism as more narrowly defined. But having used the term *descriptively* and noted that this 'Gnostic' theme or concept occurs in the New Testament, the author then proceeds as if it had been used *derivatively*—to claim the point as evidence of Gnostic 'influence' upon some New Testament writer. We need to bear in mind here the warning, neatly phrased by E. Earle Ellis,[22] against the tendency 'to convert parallels into influences and influences into sources.' Also we need to pay greater attention to questions of chronology, for sometimes it would appear that scholars have formulated a synthesis on the basis of second or third century sources, and have then proceeded to force the New Testament writings into the resultant mould, on the assumption that the hypothetical pre-Christian gnosis which they postulate was identical with their reconstruction from the later documents.

This question of a pre-Christian Gnosticism is one that has been long and hotly debated. On the one hand Alan Richardson[23] says 'the objection to speaking of Gnosticism in the first century A.D. is that we are in danger of hypostatising certain rather ill-defined tendencies of thought and then speaking as if there were a religion or religious philosophy, called Gnosticism, which could be contrasted with Judaism or Christianity. There was of course no such thing.' On the other hand some scholars would argue that even if the tendencies of thought are rather ill-defined the very fact that similar motifs and conceptions appear in so many different areas, and in so many distinct systems, points to a common source on which they all depend.

[22] *Paul's Use of the Old Testament*, (Edinburgh 1957), p. 82.
[23] *An Introduction to the Theology of the NT*, (London 1958), p. 41.

B

Giovanni Miegge[24] writes 'pre-Christian Gnosticism may be, in reality, nothing more than an unknown something postulated by the science of religions, one of those invisible stars the position of which astronomers determine by calculating the deviations in the movements of neighbouring stars.'

On this two things require to be said: first, this is a brilliant analogy, but analogies can be misleading. The planet Uranus, which was actually discovered in the position calculated by the astronomers, is a solid mass which was already there and able to exert a gravitational pull upon its neighbours. We have no grounds for assuming that the analogy holds in the realm of thought and ideas for, secondly, Miegge goes on to quote a passage from Bultmann:[25] 'Even though the ideas have to be worked out in the mass and in detail from documents which are later than the Gospel according to St. John, that the ideas themselves date back to a period prior to the Gospel remains certain, beyond a shadow of doubt.' Now it is a fact that particular ideas can be traced far back into the pre-Christian period to ultimate origins in Egypt or Babylon or Persia. But were these ideas already Gnostic in the lands of their origin, or at what point do they become Gnostic? Here it seems there is a real possibility of clarifying our procedure if we think in terms of growth and development. The ideas admittedly are pre-Christian but the combination of these ideas, the way in which they are blended together, the associations which they come to have, these may only be Gnostic in the context of specifically Gnostic systems, which would mean that the ideas themselves are not necessarily Gnostic. The Gnostics adapted to their own ends the material they took over, and it is no small part of our problem to determine whether at any given point a particular term or concept carries the Gnostic connotation, whether in the New Testament, for example, a word which is a technical term in the second-century Gnostic systems should be given a Gnostic meaning, or whether this Gnostic meaning is in fact a secondary development.

At the present time there is a broad consensus of opinion over a fairly wide area of research. It is on points of detail that the

---

[24] *Gospel and Myth*, (ET: London 1960), p. 30.
[25] *Das Evangelium des Johannes*, pp. 11–12 [the translation is that of Miegge's translator, Bishop Stephen Neill].

differences emerge—on questions of origins and development, on the precise relation of one element to another. Where did this conception or that originate? How and why was it brought into its present context? What is its present significance and is this the significance it has always had, or has it at some point in the process undergone a change, and if so why and under what influences? Such are the questions which are being raised and must be raised; but sometimes we are not yet in a position to give a final answer.

To begin with Gnosticism as traditionally defined, we have long known enough about its general character for the purposes of the history of doctrine, enough to define it in a manual of Church history or in a dictionary of theology as the result of the amalgamation of Christianity and paganism, one consequence of the emergence of Christianity upon the stage of the wider world of the Roman empire, which carried with it the necessity for the reinterpretation of the original Palestinian gospel in language 'understanded of the people', in terms comprehensible to men and women of Gentile origin and background who had no real roots in the Old Testament and Jewish tradition. So much is clear and would be generally agreed. But was Gnosticism fundamentally Christian or essentially pagan? Does it owe more to the essential truths of the Gospel or to the ideas of the pagan world? Here there might be less agreement. If we think in terms of particular Gnostics and ask whether they were Christians who sought, as Burkitt said,[26] to present their faith in terms more acceptable to their own enlightened age, or pagans who sought to claim something of this new and potent Christian religion for their own purposes, we should have to say in general that some were one and some the other; when we endeavour to deal with Gnosticism in the abstract it is much more difficult. In the light of recent studies it is even open to question whether we should think in terms only of Christianity and paganism. As will appear, the Jewish element in Gnostic thought is sufficiently prominent to lead some scholars to think of a Jewish origin for the whole movement.

Again, how are we to distinguish between the Christian Gnosticism which is orthodox, or comparatively orthodox, in

[26] Cf. *Church and Gnosis*, pp. 27 f.

Clement of Alexandria and Origen, and the Christian Gnosticism which is heretical in Basilides or in Valentinus? What are we to make of the affinities which exist between the heretical Gnostic systems attacked by Irenaeus on the one hand and the Corpus Hermeticum on the other, or such fragments as we possess from the middle Platonism of the second century, or the neo-Platonism of Plotinus?[27] If these affinities suggest that the traditional theory is correct in seeing Gnosticism as the contamination of Christianity by philosophy, what of the affinities with the magical papyri, or with the mystery religions, or with astrology? If we are to think in terms of philosophy, again, at what stage did Christianity rise to such a level of society as to make influence from philosophy in the proper sense conceivable? It is scarcely within the New Testament period, for there is little there to compare with what we find in a Clement or an Origen —yet there are affinities with the later Gnostic heresy within the New Testament itself, as also in a contemporary writer like Philo of Alexandria.[28] When we add the indisputable similarities in Manicheism or in the Mandean literature, and at the other end what appear to be certain tendencies in the direction of Gnosticism in the Qumran texts, it becomes apparent that we can no longer think solely in terms of the second century or in terms of Gnosticism and Christianity. We have to set the whole problem in a very much wider context and consider it in the light of what we know or what we can learn about the whole religious situation and its developments in the early Christian centuries, and it is precisely here that the difficulties and the differences of opinion begin to emerge.

Manicheism, for example, originated in Persia in the third century A.D., although many elements in Manichean thought can be traced back a great deal further.[29] In particular the dualism that is so characteristic of Gnostic thinking may be very

---

[27] For Plotinus, cf. J. Zandee, *The Terminology of Plotinus and of Some Gnostic Writings*, (Ned. Hist.-Archaeol. Inst. Istanbul, 1961). Cf. also, for a wider field, E. R. Dodds, *Pagan and Christian in an Age of Anxiety*, (Cambridge 1965).

[28] For Philo, cf. Wilson, *The Gnostic Problem*; also the paper by M. Simon at the Messina Colloquium 1966 [see below].

[29] Cf. Geo. Widengren, *Mani and Manicheism*, (ET: London 1965); A. Adam in *Hbuch der Orientalistik*, viii. 2, (Leiden 1961), pp. 102 ff. H. C. Puech, *Le Manichéisme. Son fondateur, sa doctrine*, (Paris 1949).

plausibly linked with the dualism in the teaching of Zoroaster centuries before the birth of Christ. Hence when other elements in the Gnostic and Manichean tradition were also found in Zoroastrian texts it was but natural to think of a Persian origin for the whole movement and to attempt to trace the spread of its influence to the West. But, for one thing, there are different kinds of dualism, and a dualistic system is not for that reason necessarily Gnostic. For another, Zoroastrianism itself had a history. It is at least debatable whether some of these ideas already belonged to it in the pre-Christian period, or owe their presence to some extraneous influence. An idea, for example, which does not occur in the earliest Zoroastrian literature, but only in texts dating from the Sassanid period in the third century A.D. or later, cannot be seriously claimed in evidence for Zoroastrian influence on the thinking of an earlier age. Nor can we assume that the influence was always exerted from the one side and in the same direction. An example here is provided by a paper read at the Messina Colloquium on the origins of Gnosticism in 1966 by Dr. Edward Conze,[30] in which he drew attention to a number of parallels between Gnosticism and Mahayana Buddhism. At certain points, however, Dr. Conze was prepared to admit the possibility of Gnostic influence upon Buddhism, not the reverse. We have to allow for the possibility that influences moved in both directions, not only from East to West, but also from West to East. And we have further to consider whether the same words, the same phrases, the same concepts, have always and in every case the same associations and the same special meaning.

The Mandeans again still survive in the regions of Iraq and Iran, but their tradition claims an origin in the first century A.D. in the area of the Jordan valley.[31] We know something of 'Baptist' sects in that region in the early centuries,[32] and here

[30] For reports of the Colloqium see U. Bianchi, *Numen* 13, (1966), pp. 151 ff.; G. W. MacRae, *Catholic Biblical Quarterly* 28, (1966), pp. 322 ff. The papers submitted have now been published: *Le Origini dello Gnosticismo*, ed. U. Bianchi [Suppt. xii to *Numen*, (Leiden 1967)].

[31] See E. S. Drower, *The Secret Adam*, (Oxford 1960); K. Rudolph, *Die Mandäer*, (vol. 1, Göttingen 1960; vol. 2, 1961); id., *Theogonie, Cosmogonie und Anthropogonie in den mandäischen Schriften*, (Göttingen 1965).

[32] Cf. J. Thomas, *Le mouvement baptiste en Palestine et Syrie*, (Gembloux 1935).

again it was natural for scholars to seek an origin and an explanation for the whole movement on the basis of the Mandeans. It was this that occasioned the 'Mandean fever' of the twenties, a fever which abated when Lietzmann on the one hand pointed out that Mandean documents showed a knowledge of later Syrian liturgies and Burkitt on the other indicated their acquaintance with the Peshitta.[33] Thereafter interest in the Mandeans rather subsided, but recently it has been revived again. In several quarters it has been affirmed that the question is not yet closed, and this may well be so. Indeed the points made by Lietzmann and Burkitt may have a different significance—not as grounds for dismissing the Mandeans altogether, but as warnings of the need for care and caution in the drawing of our conclusions. It is perfectly possible that the Mandean tradition is correct, that the distant ancestors of this group did in fact migrate from the Jordan valley; but at some stage they were influenced by the Syrian church. We must therefore ask: to what other influences have they been subjected in the course of their lengthy history? How much of Mandean tradition as it now stands in the documents of their literature goes back in fact to the days of their origin, and how much is later accretion? Again, can we detect the stages at which such accretion took place? Manicheism and Mandeism have much to teach us, but we must beware of the facile assumption that what we find in them was there from the very outset. It is not difficult to imagine a group like that represented by the Dead Sea Scrolls migrating in the course of the first century, adopting some elements of the teaching of Marcion or of Gnosticism in the second, or of Manicheism in the third, reacting violently against persecution by more 'orthodox' neighbours at another stage, and finally emerging after several centuries with a collection of treasured documents which to some extent reflected their chequered history, but were no longer fully understood even by

---

[33] H. Lietzmann, *Kleine Schriften*, i, (*TU* 67, Berlin 1958), pp. 124 ff. (=SB Berlin 1930, pp. 596 ff.); F. C. Burkitt, *JTS* 29, (1928), pp. 235 ff., and *Church and Gnosis*, p. 106. Cf. W. F. Albright, *From the Stone Age to Christianity*, (Baltimore 1957), pp. 364 ff.; G. Bornkamm, *Jesus of Nazareth*, (ET: London 1960), p. 198 n.34; Cullmann, *Christology of the NT*, (ET: London 1963), p. 27 n.1, and the literature there cited.

the wisest of their number.[34] In such a case the problem would be to isolate the different stages, to recognise the influences which have operated at one period or another, and to determine when the common elements are to be taken as indications of extraneous influence upon our hypothetical group, when that group itself has influenced some other body, and when both groups are dependent not upon one another but upon some third source that lies behind them both.

Here attention should be drawn to a point that has not always received sufficient notice: that Gnosticism grew. It is, I believe, a fundamental mistake to think of the whole movement emerging in all the glory of its final development, or to assume that where one or two elements of later Gnostic thought, or even several elements, are present then the whole range is already there. To revert to the analogy of ingredients, already mentioned, a visit to the kitchen will soon disclose that even the assembling of all the necessary ingredients does not necessarily produce the finished dish. They may still require to be blended together in the proper proportions, and the mixture cooked; and the presence or absence of a single ingredient, or some variation in the quantities used, or in the method of mixing employed, may make a very considerable difference to the finished product. Gnosticism grew. Our problem therefore is to trace the process of its growth, from the earliest discernible origins to the full development in the sects of the second century and on to Manicheism and Mandeism, and from these again down through the related sects of the Middle Ages, the Bogomils, the Cathari, the Albigensians.[35] In so doing we shall have to recognise affinities outside the Gnostic tradition proper, in Christianity, for example, on the one hand, in Jewish mysticism on the other. There is a sense in which we may rightly speak of 'gnosis' as something much wider than the second century Christian

[34] Cf. R. Macuch, *TLZ* 1957, cols. 401 ff., 1965, cols. 649 ff.; K. Rudolph, *Die Mandäer*, i, pp. 252 ff.

[35] Cf. D. Obolensky, *The Bogomils*, (Cambridge 1948); S. Runciman, *The Medieval Manichee*, (Cambridge 1947), and for Jewish Cabbalism the works of G. Scholem. In this connection it may be as well to recall the warning voiced at the Messina Colloquium by H. Jonas against the assumption of a 'conveyor-belt' development. It is not merely a process of addition, but also of modification and adaptation, and sometimes of omission.

heresy, something of an atmosphere in which the people of the early Christian centuries lived and moved, but we must beware of assuming too readily that this 'gnosis' was in all respects and at all stages identical with the specifically heretical Christian Gnosticism of the second century schools, and we must give due regard to the mutual interaction of many different traditions.[36] We have to take account of Jews like Philo, Christians like Clement and Origen, Gnostics like Valentinus—and also of a host of others. Sweeping generalisations are out of place—on the contrary we have need of detailed and meticulous study of particular theories, of the ideas of individual thinkers, of the systems of particular schools.

Here in fact a great deal has already been done in the analysis and interpretation of the information provided by the early Fathers. There was a period at which it could be suggested that their evidence must be considered suspect, since it came from the opponents of the Gnostics, men whose concern it was to refute the Gnostic theories in the interest of what later came to be the Catholic faith; and indeed there are certain Fathers whose statements must occasionally be received with a due measure of caution. But the general reliability of Irenaeus, our earliest major witness, has been abundantly vindicated by the researches of Foerster and Sagnard,[37] and the conclusions of these scholars are now amply confirmed by such of the Nag Hammadi documents as have been published. Irenaeus may not always have understood his opponents, and certainly he was not always in sympathy with them, but it cannot be said that he deliberately misinterpreted them in the interest of his own polemic.

At this point further reference should be made to the Messina Colloquium in 1966, at which a large gathering of scholars and

[36] The late Johannes Munck suggested the substitution of 'syncretism' for 'gnosis' in this wider sense [*Current Issues in the NT*, ed. Klassen and Snyder, (London 1962), p. 236], but while I am in complete sympathy with his aim and purpose I cannot consider the suggestion satisfactory. The term 'syncretism' is already employed in two distinct though related senses, which has led to considerable confusion. To add a third shade of meaning would only make confusion worse confounded.

[37] W. Foerster, *Von Valentin zu Heracleon*, (Beiheft 7 zur *ZNW*, Giessen 1928); F. M. M. Sagnard, *La gnose valentinienne et le témoignage de S. Irénée*, (Paris 1947).

specialists from many countries met to discuss the problems of the origins of Gnosticism.[38] One feature of this meeting was a number of papers underlining the Jewish contribution to Gnostic thought. Another was the attempt made to formulate a definition of Gnosticism, to clarify the whole situation and eliminate the problems arising from failures of definition. This definition began from the classic Gnosticism of the second century and distinguished Gnosticism in this sense from 'gnosis', which is defined as 'knowledge of the divine mysteries reserved for an elect'. The Gnosticism of the second century sects 'involves a coherent series of characteristics which can be summed up in the idea of a divine spark in man, deriving from the divine realm, fallen into this world of fate, birth and death, and needing to be awakened by the divine counterpart of the self in order to be finally reintegrated.' It was noted that not every gnosis is Gnosticism, 'but only that which involves in this perspective the idea of the divine consubstantiality of the spark that is in need of being awakened and reintegrated. This gnosis of Gnosticism involves the divine identity of the *knower*, (the Gnostic,) the *known*, (the divine substance of one's transcendent self) and the *means by which* one knows (gnosis as an implicit divine faculty to be awakened and actualised.)' A further point made was a distinction between proto-Gnosticism and pre-Gnosticism. This distinction relates to the question of Gnostic origins. On the one hand the pre-Gnostic is prepared to recognise the existence of themes and motifs, concepts and ideas in the pre-Christian and pre-Gnostic period, which are preparing the way for the development of Gnosticism proper. The proto-Gnostic view however would find the essence of Gnosticism already in the centuries preceding the second century A.D. and also outside of the strictly Christian Gnosticism of the second century. This seems to be a useful distinction, because it sets out clearly the real issue of present discussion and debate. Those scholars who adhere to the proto-Gnostic point of view appeal especially to Iran, the Indo-Iranian world, to Platonism and to Orphism as evidence for their position; those who speak of pre-Gnosticism, on the other hand, emphasise rather Jewish apocalyptic, the Qumran Scrolls, Pharisaism, the atmosphere of crisis in Judaism following upon

[38] See above, n. 30. The proposals for clarification of the definition of terms are given in full by Bianchi, pp. 154 ff.

the fall of Jerusalem in A.D. 70, and also certain currents of Christian thought.

One problem in this connection has already been alluded to in passing, the problem of determining to what extent the same words, the same concepts, even the same statements, preserve their meaning in continuity right through the history of a tradition, and to what extent they may be modified and reinterpreted in course of time. This problem is the more difficult when it is a case not merely of one linguistic tradition, but of several. In a modern language the natural rendering of some term may be the same as that for a term in some other ancient tongue, but there is a danger for us of reading back associations which are not necessarily present in one or other of these ancient languages. Not every reference to 'knowledge' carries with it the special Gnostic significance associated in the Gnostic context with the Greek word *gnosis*, and *gnosis* itself does not in every case refer to 'Gnostic' knowledge. Again, there is a pssage in the Gospel of Truth which employs the Coptic word *mnt-rm-nhēt*.[39] The natural English rendering for this is in some cases 'wisdom', which in turn would suggest the Greek word *sophia*, but in point of fact there is no justification for identifying *mnt-rm-nhēt* and *sophia*. *Sophia* is not given as one of the equivalents for *mnt-rm-nhēt* in Crum's dictionary, nor is it ever used as the equivalent of *sophia* in the Coptic versions of the New Testament. Indeed there are two cases in which *mnt-rm-nhēt* and *sophia*, as a loan word, appear together in the same context, which indicates that they have a difference of meaning.[40] An interpretation based upon the understanding of this word in English could therefore very easily lead to mistranslation and misconception of the passage in the Gospel of Truth.

A further example of the same kind of thing comes with the reinterpretation of passages in a new context. The Epistle to the Hebrews for example quotes the eighth psalm:

> Thou hast made him a little lower than the angels,
> Thou hast crowned him with glory and honour.
>
> (Heb. 2 : 6 ff.)

The author applies this quotation to Jesus, taking 'a little lower' not in the sense of 'on a slightly lower level', but in a temporal

---

[39] Cf. *NTS* 9, (1963), p. 297 f.   [40] Col. 1.9, Eph. 1.8.

sense 'for a short space', which incidentally creates problems for the English translator. If the Gnostics were making such slight modifications and reinterpreting their texts, to what extent are we justified in carrying back the Gnostic interpretation into the original text?

A third example is provided by the motif of the pearl. In the Acts of Thomas we have the well-known Hymn of the Pearl, sometimes called the Hymn of the Soul, which most scholars would agree to interpret as a Gnostic allegory. Admittedly, there are in this hymn obscurities and apparent inconsistencies, which may perhaps suggest the adaptation of older material: is the prince of the story Everyman, sent into the world for a purpose which he fails to accomplish, until he is awakened and recalled to his task? This would be to interpret the pearl in the light of the Gospel parable of the Kingdom of God as a pearl of great price, worthy of the sacrifice of all a man's possessions; and in this case the hymn need not be Gnostic at all. Or is the prince the Saviour, descended to redeem the pearl which is the soul and at first for a time overcome by the deceit of this world, so that he himself has to be awakened—a Salvator salvandus? In some sense he is both, for the Saviour in his descent and ascent, as Bevan long ago observed, duplicates the destiny of the soul. For present purposes, however, these questions are subsidiary to the main point. Jonas[41] quotes a Manichean allegory in which the symbolism is spelt out to the last detail. Moreover the motif is found also in Mandeism, and further back there is the Naassene exegesis of Matt. 7 : 6, according to which this saying refers to 'the pearls of the Unformed One' (identified as 'words and minds and men') 'cast into the formation.' To carry this back to Matthew (Matt. 13 : 45 f.), and interpret the parable of the Pearl of great Price in the light of it, would be an obvious mistake. But what of logion 76 of the Gospel of Thomas, if Thomas is indeed a Gnostic work? Is it to be understood in terms of Matthew or of Gnosticism?

According to the Gospel of Philip (48) a pearl cast in the mud does not lose its value, nor is its worth enhanced by anointing with balsam oil. At an earlier point (Philip 22) the soul is

---

[41] *The Gnostic Religion*, (Boston 1958), pp. 112 ff., esp. p. 126 n.15; also his paper in *The Bible in Modern Scholarship*, ed. J. P. Hyatt, (Nashville 1965), pp. 279 ff.

described as a precious thing which has come to be in a despised body. The similar analogy of gold in mud is mentioned in Irenaeus' account of the system of Ptolemy, and also occurs in Plotinus.[42] The Gospel of Thomas speaks of spirit and flesh in terms of wealth and poverty (log. 29), a saying which readily recalls Paul's reference to 'treasure in earthen vessels' (2 Cor. 4 : 7). Are all these to be grouped together and classified as 'Gnostic'? Or should we not rather recognise the occurrence of a common motif, which may or may not have passed from one tradition to another, and proceed to examine the use that is made of it in different contexts? For it may be not the motif itself but the use that is made of it that is Gnostic. It is pertinent also to note the point made by Jonas,[43] that the Naassene exegesis appeals not to Matt. 13 : 45 f. but to Matt. 7 : 6. In short, it may be a serious error to assume that a motif or symbol always and in every case carries with it the same significance.

One feature of the Messina Colloquium, as already mentioned, was a number of papers in which stress was laid upon the Jewish contribution.[44] Reference has already been made to a number of spheres of influence, Egypt, Persia, Babylonia, Mesopotamia and so on. Of recent years it has been the Jewish element which has perhaps received the greatest emphasis. It was stressed for example by A. D. Nock, while R. M. Grant sought to find the origins of Gnosticism in the disappointed eschatological hopes of Qumran sectarians.[45] G. Quispel has stressed the contribution of heterodox Judaism, Gershom Scholem has noted Gnostic affinities in Jewish mysticism, in the whole tradition reaching right down to the Cabbala.[46] Again, there are certainly affinities with Gnosticism in Jewish apocalyptic, and in much of the writings of Philo, although it

[42] Plotinus, *The Enneads*, tr. Stephen McKenna, (²London 1956), p. 60 f. [Enn. I.6.5 ad fin.].

[43] *The Bible in Modern Scholarship*, p. 285 n.9. On the whole question of Christian and Gnostic language see S. Laeuchli, *The Language of Faith*, (Nashville 1962; London 1965).

[44] Cf. above, n. 30.

[45] Grant, *Gnosticism and Early Christianity*, (New York 1959).

[46] Cf. Quispel in *Eranos Jahrb*. XXII, (1953), pp. 195 ff.; *Evang. Theologie*, 1954, pp. 1–11; *The Bible in Modern Scholarship*, pp. 252 ff.; Scholem, *Jewish Gnosticism, Merkabah Mysticism, and Talmudic Tradition*, (New York 1960); *Ursprung und Anfänge der Kabbala*, (Berlin 1962).

should be emphasised that there are also differences. With regard to Scholem's position it must be asked: How far is Jewish mysticism really gnosis? Hans Jonas indeed has spoken of 'the semantic disservice which Scholem did to clarity when he called his Palestinian Hekhaloth mysticism a "gnosis".'[47] Jonas himself writes 'the recent Coptic discoveries are said to underline the share of a heterodox occultist Judaism, though judgement must be reserved pending the translation of the vast body of the material.'[48] In a footnote he adds 'nothing so far presented has to my mind proven the Judaistic thesis', and he continues 'some connection of Gnosticism with the beginnings of the Cabbala has in any case to be assumed, whatever the order of cause and effect. The violently anti-Jewish bias of the more prominent Gnostic systems is by itself not incompatible with Jewish heretical origin at some distance . . . The Jewish strain in Gnosticism is as little the orthodox Jewish as the Babylonian is the orthodox Babylonian, the Iranian the orthodox Iranian, and so on.' Finally, Kurt Rudolph[49] has drawn attention to the anti-Jewish strain in Mandeism—in this respect the Mandeans go with the Gnostics in the stricter sense of the word.

Now there is no question of the place of Jewish elements within the Gnostic systems. There are cases in which the Gnostic myth is little more than a reinterpretation of the Genesis creation story in Gnostic terms. This means that the Gnostics were somehow in contact with circles from which they could obtain the book of Genesis. The question is whether these circles were Jewish or Jewish-Christian,[50] or whether indeed the Gnostics knew no more of Judaism than the book of Genesis itself, whether in fact they were Gentiles who only had a more or less superficial knowledge of Jewish teaching. This is a further indication of the complexity of the problem. Again, in his Messina paper Alexander Böhlig underlined the *Umdeutung* which has taken place in the use of Jewish material in the new Coptic Gnostic texts; in a supplementary note he emphasises

[47] *The Bible in Modern Scholarship*, p. 291.
[48] *The Gnostic Religion*, pp. 33 f. Cf. also van Unnik in *Vig Chr.* 15, (1961), pp. 65 ff.
[49] *Die Mandäer*, 1.51 ff.
[50] Cf. J. Daniélou, 'Judéo-christianisme et gnose', in *Aspects du judéo-christianisme*, (Paris 1965); also his *Théologie du judéo-chrstianisme*, (Tournai 1958).

that whatever their original affiliation the men to whom we owe these texts were *Gnostics*, with a different understanding of human existence from that of other religions, a point borne out for example by some statements in the Gospel of Philip (cf. Philip 6 and 46). It is well to heed the warnings which have been uttered against undue reliance upon any particular theory as the complete and sufficient answer to the whole problem of Gnostic origins. 'What we must beware of in these championships of causes is the fallacy of exclusiveness, the lure of fashion, and the hasty identification of any one with the origin of Gnosticism.'[51]

The discussion thus far has inevitably ranged very far afield. It is time now to draw the threads together, and formulate the conclusions which seem to emerge.

1.   The starting point for all investigation must be the 'classical' Gnosticism of the second Christian century and after, for here we have a clearly-defined and manageable group of systems all showing certain common characteristics. It seems desirable to distinguish Gnosticism in this narrower sense from the wider and more nebulous 'Gnosis', although this does not by any means absolve us from the responsibility of investigating the relationship between them, the process of development from one to the other, the channels by which ideas were transmitted, the proximate and ultimate sources from which these ideas were derived.

2.   Gnosticism in this narrower sense must be regarded as a Christian heresy, but this is not the whole story. In the effort to understand the Christian heresy and explain its origins we have to take account of similar phenomena in other areas, religions and systems of thought which show affinities with Gnosticism proper, yet without exact correspondence in point of detail. It is here that the wider conception of Gnosis has its value. Manicheism and Mandeism are obvious cases in point. Related to Gnosticism, they must be reckoned with in any comprehensive study, yet they are sufficiently distinct from the 'classical' Gnosticism to be classified apart. Similarly Marcion shows certain affinities with Gnosticism, but it is open to question whether he should be classified simply as a Gnostic, without qualification. The Hermetica, again, are at least semi-Gnostic, and acquire a new importance from the inclusion of certain Hermetic docu-

[51] Jonas in *The Bible and Modern Scholarship*, p. 284.

ments in the Nag Hammadi library; but here there is no Christian influence. All these may legitimately be grouped under the general heading of Gnosis.

3.   In the same way, certain phenomena which appear in the writings of Philo or in the Dead Sea Scrolls, together with the 'Gnostic affinities' which have been found in various parts of the New Testament, may justifiably be included under this general head, although here it may be desirable to use some such term as 'pre-gnosis' to avoid any hasty generalisation or pre-judging of the issue. One problem here is to avoid the reading back into first-century terminology of associations and connotations which that terminology does have in the second century, and at the same time to recognise, already in the first century, the points of growth for second-century theories, or even the emergence in embryonic form of incipient Gnostic systems which only come to full development later.

A useful analogy here is provided by the figure of Wisdom, which in some of our documents is quite definitely and unmistakably hypostatised and personified. In other texts however wisdom is no less clearly just a quality or attribute, and personification does not enter in at all. In a third group, of which the Wisdom of Solomon is an outstanding example, it is a very difficult matter to determine when the reference is to the quality of wisdom and when to the hypostatised semi-divine figure. It may be that the author himself made no conscious distinction between the two, but the fact remains that a change has taken place, and that the Wisdom of Solomon represents a point of transition. It would be a mistake to read back the developed hypostatisation, or the Sophia of the Gnostic documents, into every occurrence of the word in this book, and a still more serious error to carry back these connotations to the earliest documents in which personification has in fact not yet taken place. Yet to understand the whole development we need to keep in mind the final outcome.

4.   The problem of Gnostic origins remains a crucial question, and one that is still in debate. In point of fact, it is not one single problem only but several, although not all are of equal significance.

(a) There is for example the problem of the date of the emergence of the Gnostic religion as a recognisable entity, distinct from the vaguely defined trends of thought subsumed under the broader heading of Gnosis. From some points of view this is not a vital question, but for the New Testament scholar and the student of Christian origins it is one of some importance, for it enters into the further question of the relation between Gnosticism and early Christianity. Some scholars confidently speak of Gnostic influence on the early Church, of Gnostic motifs in the New Testament itself; others show a very natural reluctance to admit any such influence. This question calls for more detailed treatment in a later chapter. For the present it may suffice to say that Gnosticism appears to be roughly contemporary with Christianity, or perhaps a little later, and that there are signs of an incipient Gnosticism in the New Testament period; but Gnosis in the broader sense is indisputably older. Hence in any consideration of alleged 'Gnostic influence' on the New Testament we have to ask whether the term 'Gnostic' is being employed *descriptively*, in the sense that the motif in question is Gnostic in the second century, although earlier and in a non-Gnostic context it might not be Gnostic at all; or whether the adjective is used in the sense of *derivation*, to indicate that the term, motif or concept involved was taken over from pre-Christian Gnosis.

(b) A second question is the relation of this pre-Christian Gnosis to the Gnostic Religion and to the second-century sects. To what extent is there continuity of development, and how far can we assume that what is clearly present in Gnosticism but suggested only vaguely, if at all, in Gnosis was already actually current at the earlier stage? The assumption that the full development of later Gnosticism is already present in pre-Christian Gnosis obviously involves a begging of the question, a reading of first-century texts with second-century spectacles, and this amply justifies the reluctance of some scholars, as already mentioned, to admit any widespread 'Gnostic influence' in the formation stages of early Christianity.

(c) A third problem is that of ultimate sources and proximate channels. It is now abundantly clear that the whole background of the late Hellenistic world has to be taken into account, and that attempts to derive the whole movement from one single source far back in the mists of antiquity are one-sided and misleading. To trace the ultimate origins of a particular idea is perfectly legitimate, but it is not the whole story. How, why, where and by whom was this particular idea brought into association with other ideas, often from very different sources, to take its place in the context of the developed Gnostic theories?

There is something undeniably attractive in the suggestion[52] that the unification of the Mediterranean world after the conquests of Alexander, the mingling of the peoples, the growth of cosmopolitanism, the increasing use of Greek as the common language, the emergence of a common philosophy, should all have prompted a drive towards a common religion, a religion for humanity; and the time was to come when Gnosticism and Christianity were competing for this position. But was there a deliberate and conscious effort to *create* such a religion, and if so when and by whom? Or was it a process of gradual development, which reached its culmination in the second Christian century? We do know of one attempt at a synthetic religion, the cult of Serapis, intended by the Ptolemies to form a bond of union for their Greek and Egyptian subjects, but a universal religion would be something on an altogether grander scale. We know also of the syncretism prevalent among the mystery cults, but syncretism is not yet Gnosis.

It would seem more profitable to seek the immediate sources, to try to find the points at which ideas are brought together, or new influences begin to operate. Where, for example, does Greek philosophy come in? Was the trend, in terms of the title of one of Jonas' volumes, 'from mythology to mystical philosophy'? In other words, was the philosophical element a later accretion, showing that Gnosticism like Christianity, and at almost the same period, had to come to terms with contemporary Greek philosophy? In that case, the affinities with Neo-Platonism, and with Middle Platonism earlier, and even with such a writer as Philo, should perhaps be discounted as evidence rather of the influence of philosophy upon Gnosticism than of Gnostic influence upon philosophy.

It is in this context that what Jonas calls 'the Judaistic thesis' calls for serious consideration. There is the undeniable Jewish

---

[52] Cf. Böhlig in *Koptische Kunst*, (Catalogue of the Exhibition of Coptic Art at the Villa Hügel, Essen, May-August 1963), pp. 42 ff., and the supplementary remarks to his Messina paper.

element in the Gnostic systems, even though the Jewish materials may be employed in a non-Jewish or even anti-Jewish way. There are the affinities in Philo. There is the prominence as centres of Gnosticism of areas which had a considerable Jewish element in the population, such as the city of Alexandria or the province of Asia Minor. There is the problem, familiar to the New Testament scholar, of determining whether the false teachers opposed in some letter were Jewish or Gnostic: Paul's opponents at Corinth, for example, or the heretics at Colossae; or we may recall the heresies hinted at in the letters of Ignatius. It may be that sometimes we have been too ready to make rigid and clear-cut distinctions where the situation was in fact rather fluid and the lines by no means clearly drawn. Finally, many specific motifs can be traced to a Jewish origin, or shown to have parallels in Jewish sources, and even where some particular motifs derive ultimately from other sources there may be grounds for thinking that it was through the medium of Judaism that they passed into Gnosticism.[53]

These points make up a strong case for the view that Judaism was at the very least an important factor in the development of Gnosticism, but Judaism itself, as we now know, was by no means uniform in the Hellenistic and Roman age. If Gnosticism is the result of an amalgamation of paganism and Christianity, the natural place to look for Jewish anticipations, a pre-Christian Jewish Gnosticism, would be the Diaspora; but there are Jewish elements in Gnosticism which are not to be found in the voluminous pages of Philo, although Alexandria was later to become one of the chief centres of Gnosticism. Again, some of the closest parallels to the Gospel of Thomas and the Gospel of Philip occur in Rabbinic sources, and the same holds for some of the material adduced by Böhlig in his Messina paper.[54] Does this mean that these elements are older, dating back before the split of Church and Synagogue, or are they evidence of a prolonged contact well into the second century, even after the revolt under Hadrian?

Finally, there are the parallels to which Scholem has drawn attention between Gnosticism and Jewish mysticism. Here it

[53] Cf. Rudolph, *Wiss. Zeitschr. Jena*, pp. 89 ff.
[54] *Der jüdische und judenchristliche Hintergrund in gnostischen Texten von Nag Hammadi.*

must be emphasised once again that while mysticism may be classed as Gnosis it is not necessarily Gnosticism. As Jonas puts it,[55] 'A Gnosticism without a fallen god, without benighted creator and sinister creation, without alien soul, cosmic captivity and acosmic salvation, without the self-redeeming of the Deity —in short: a Gnosis without divine tragedy will not meet specifications'. In contrast, the Jewish mystics with whom Scholem is concerned, for all their esotericism and 'gnosticising' tendencies, are in the last resort monotheistic and essentially orthodox, Jews rather than Gnostics, and the same must also be said of the Qumran sect. Sectarianism and heterodoxy do not necessarily amount to Gnosticism, although they may contribute to it and prepare the way.

R. M. Grant has traced the origins of Gnosticism to the disappointed eschatological hopes of Qumran sectarians,[56] which may be correct up to a point. I should prefer to say that *some* Gnostics may have formerly been Qumran sectarians, as others may have been former proselytes, both reacting in utter revulsion to the Fall of Jerusalem and the collapse of their hopes and expectations, and therefore degrading the God of Israel to the status of an inferior Demiurge. Others again might have been Christians: Mlle Pétrement has shown that some elements are explicable in terms of development within the Church, reflecting the conflict of Church and Synagogue.[57] Others might have been pagans, mocking at the Jews from whom they derived so much. But here we are in the realm of speculation. All we can say is that each is possible, but that probably none of them contains the whole story.

Little or nothing has yet been said in this chapter of the theory of the Gnostic Redeemer-myth, and this of set purpose. In the first place, this theory is no longer so central to the modern debate as it formerly was, and secondly Walter Schmithals, who has presented the fullest and most complete recent discussion, betrays its weakness when he writes that it is actually the result of a combination of two disparate myths; for he does not pause to ask when and by whom the combination was

---

[55] *The Bible in Modern Scholarship*, p. 293.
[56] *Gnosticism and Early Christianity*, (New York 1959).
[57] In her Messina paper; cf. more generally *Rev. de Métaphysique et de Morale* 65, (1960), pp. 385 ff.

effected. There were admittedly, in the ancient world, saviour-gods in abundance; Osiris is but one example. There were also myths, in various forms, of a Primal Man. But the full development of the theory in which the Heavenly Man descends into the realm of matter to be imprisoned there, and to leave behind on his deliverance something of himself which has to be recovered—this comes very much later as a synthesis of older ideas, probably incorporating also something of the *soma-sema* conception of the body as the tomb of the soul. As Carsten Colpe has put it,[58] we can document from known systems all the ideas embodied in the theory; nor is it simply to be dismissed as a modern mosaic constructed from materials of diverse origin, which largely coincides with the Manichean system. The real flaw is the idea that the myth of the Gnostic Redeemer originated at some time in dim antiquity, somewhere in the remoter East (vaguely conceived as 'Iran'), and then passed across the world and down the centuries, leaving behind scattered fragments in different circles of tradition until at last it was reconstituted as a unity in Manicheism and finally disintegrated into its several components in Mandeism. Rather should we conclude, with H. M. Schenke,[59] that there was no Redeemer-myth in the full sense before Manicheism. It is the climax and the culmination of the long process of development, not its original starting-point. Schenke's demonstration that the Gnostic Anthropos-doctrine owes its origin to speculation on Genesis 1.26 f. provides further confirmation of the importance of the Jewish element in the development of Gnosticism.

It is no exaggeration to say that Nag Hammadi marks the beginning of a new era in the study of Gnosticism.[60] Twenty years ago our resources consisted entirely of the Christian refutations written by the early Fathers, and of such Gnostic material as they chose to quote, together with the merest handful of original Gnostic documents, and these of late date, preserved in Coptic. Even ten years ago the three Gnostic texts

---

[58] Schmithals, *Die Gnosis in Korinth*, (Göttingen 1956), p. 82; Colpe, *Die religionsgeschichtliche Schule*, (Göttingen 1961), p. 191.

[59] *Der Gott 'Mensch' in der Gnosis*, (Göttingen 1962), p. 148.

[60] For the library in general cf. Doresse, *The Secret Books of the Egyptian Gnostics*, (ET: London 1960). Bibliography to 1963 by S. Giversen, *Studia Theologica* 17, (1963), pp. 139 ff.

in the Berlin Coptic papyrus had not yet been published, although their existence and their contents had been known for more than half a century; but that is another story.[61] Now we have from Nag Hammadi something like 1000 pages of Coptic text, much of it in a good state of preservation—more than forty documents hitherto quite unknown, to make no mention of the duplicates of texts in the Berlin Codex or of documents in the Nag Hammadi collection itself. So far a dozen have been edited and published, including three versions of the Apocryphon of John, already known from the Berlin text. If on the one hand progress appears disappointingly slow, there is this to be said on the other side: first that there were legal difficulties to be surmounted before publication could begin, not to speak of problems arising out of the political situation, and secondly that the preparation of a satisfactory edition requires time, for the number of people competent to undertake such a task is by no means large. Moreover most of us will be grateful for some interval between one document and the next—the prospect of the release of 1000 pages of Coptic text at one fell swoop is, to say the least, somewhat daunting for anyone who may have to deal with them!

As already noted, the texts so far published led Nock to express the opinion that they confirm the traditional view of Gnosticism as a Christian heresy. This is not in the least surprising, since these texts in fact belong to the Christian era and derive from the second century or later. Some of them indeed fit neatly into the accounts of the Gnostic systems provided by Irenaeus. It remains to be seen whether all the remaining texts are of the same character, or whether some of them may admit of the detection of an older *Grundschrift*. As it happens, the editor of one of the latest volumes claims to have found a pre-Christian document among his texts,[62] and there are cases in which it has been maintained that we can see the hand of a Christian redactor.[63] Here much has still to be done, first in the way of publication, then in the study and comparison and analysis of

---

[61] See W. C. Till, *Die gnostischen Schriften des koptischen Papyrus Berolinensis 8502* (*TU* 60, Berlin 1955).

[62] Böhlig, *Koptisch-gnostische Apokalypsen aus Codex V von Nag Hammadi*, (Halle-Wittenberg 1963); see below on the Apocalypse of Adam.

[63] See below on the Apocryphon of John and the Sophia Jesu Christi.

the texts. Even if they do not supply the answer to our questions about Gnostic origins, these texts still have their value, for they will enable us to study the development of Gnostic ideas, the elaboration of Gnostic documents, the ways in which themes and concepts were adopted and adapted, possibly even to establish the course of the development in chronological sequence. Above all they will give us an insight into the meaning which Gnosticism possessed for the Gnostic. Reference has already been made to Bigg's disparaging comment, with which most of those who have concerned themselves with the subject must at some time have felt themselves in agreement. Yet this queer farrago of nonsense does have a meaning, when the clues are known, and there are passages of genuine religious feeling in such documents as the Gospel of Truth or the Gospel of Philip.

To sum up, the broad picture is fairly clear, particularly where we are concerned with the developed Gnosticism of the second century and later, but there are still many gaps in our knowledge: the precise relationship of different groups, the ways in which they influenced one another, the sources upon which they drew. In the earliest stages in particular much is still uncertain. We can indeed speak of an incipient Gnosticism in the New Testament period, but how much of the developed later Gnosticism was already present at any given stage is still obscure. It has been said that we can see two attitudes in the New Testament writings, one of tolerance in a period of mutual interpenetration, and one of rejection and resistance,[64] and this may probably be considered as broadly accurate. It is not uncommon for 'heretic' and 'orthodox' to live in peaceful co-existence for a period before the lines of division become distinct, or for the men of one generation to tolerate with equanimity ideas which a later age would denounce. This means that in our investigations we must constantly pay heed to accurate definition, and ask whether a word or concept in any given case must necessarily carry the associations which it has in a different context of ideas. Sometimes, again, we need to consider whether we are in fact asking the proper questions, or drawing the correct conclusions from our data. And when it comes to assessing the possibility of influence from one source or another due attention must be given to considerations or chronology.

[64] Haenchen in *RGG*³ II, col. 1652.

II

'Gnosticism' in the New Testament

IN the light of the discussion in the previous chapter, the above title must appear to be erroneous. If Gnosticism is defined as the Christian heresy of the second century, then obviously there can be no such thing as Gnosticism in the New Testament, and to think in these terms is to run the risk of interpreting first-century documents in the light of second-century ideas. The title has however been deliberately chosen, and for various reasons.

In the first place, the preceding discussion has explicitly recognised (a) that Gnosis in the broader sense is pre-Christian, and may therefore have exercised some influence on the New Testament; and (b) that there are indications of an incipient Gnosticism, in the narrower sense of that term, within the New Testament period. The aim of this chapter is to explore this question in greater detail, to make some attempt to define and delimit the areas of 'gnostic' influence, in the wider sense of the term, in the New Testament literature, and to trace so far as possible the emergence and, it may be, the development of this incipient Gnosticism. Secondly, the alternative title 'Gnosticism *and* the New Testament' would also be misleading, since it could cover not only the subject of the present chapter but also that of the chapter following. In examining the relationship between Gnosticism and the New Testament we have to take account not only of the 'gnostic motifs' and 'gnostic influences' which scholars have claimed to find in the New Testament, but also of the clear and indisputable use that was made by the Gnostics of the New Testament itself. The relationship in fact is not a simple one, with the debt always and wholly on the side of the New Testament and of Christianity. Whatever the date of the emergence of Gnosticism as a fully-developed religion in its own right, we have to think rather of a period of mutual inter-pretation in which Christianity was confronted first by the older vaguely-defined Gnosis, and later by the initial stirrings of an incipient Gnosticism, and in which each in some measure reacted to and was influenced by the other.

At this stage the situation is still fluid, the lines of division not yet clearly drawn. As has already been said, it is by no means uncommon for 'heretic' and 'orthodox' to live in peaceful coexistence for a period, for the men of one generation to tolerate with equanimity ideas and conceptions, theories and doctrines, which a later generation will denounce as heretical. It is only in the light of subsequent developments that we can determine which was to become the 'orthodox' position and which the 'heretical'. We have therefore to guard against the danger of judging by the standards of a later age, of transferring the clear distinctions of a later period back into a situation in which the final cleavage had not yet taken place and the full implications of a particular theory had not yet been realised. This, it need hardly be said, only adds to the delicacy and complexity of our task.

A further problem concerns the method of approach. One possible line of procedure would be to ransack the commentaries and ancillary literature and cull from them every passage, ever motif, every term which has at any time been classified as 'Gnostic'. We should then have to examine each in turn, to determine whether it is in fact Gnostic, and in what sense: whether it derives from the vaguer pre-Christian Gnosis, or is only Gnostic in the narrower sense because it appears in the theories of the second-century sects. In the former case we should have to enquire whether it is a specifically gnostic influence upon Christianity, or derives from some other movement, be it some school of Greek philosophy, or Jewish apocalyptic, or some other field of ancient thought. In the latter case it is open to question whether in the New Testament such a motif should be classed as 'Gnostic' at all, or whether we should not think in terms of Gnostic borrowing and adaptation from the New Testament itself. A third possibility of course is that of parallel development, ideas and concepts of a similar character being utilised in the same way in Christianity and in Gnosis, or later in Gnosticism proper. And a fourth possibility is that ideas from the vaguer Gnosis may have been taken over and adapted to their own purposes by the New Testament writers, and then later adopted from Christianity by the Gnostics, who re-interpreted them in the light of their own ideas.

Such theoretical possibilities could no doubt be multiplied, and only serve to increase the complexity of the problem. How are we to distinguish one kind of motif from another, the 'parallel developments' from those derived by Gnosticism and Christianity alike from Platonism or Stoicism or Judaism? Nor are our difficulties lightened by the fact that, when we try to push back, the vague pre-Christian Gnosis tends to become even vaguer and more nebulous, indeed to evaporate until it is little more than an attitude of mind which comes to expression in the documents of various schools of thought. It is this that prompts the outright denial of the very existence of a 'pre-Christian Gnosticism' by such writers as Alan Richardson. But it must be remembered that we are probing back in search of the first tentative beginnings of a movement which came to full flower only later.

Desirable as it might be to have this line of approach followed up, and the whole range of material brought under scrutiny, the weaknesses and disadvantages are obvious. In the first place, there is the sheer amount of labour involved, not to mention problems of space and documentation, or of the avoidance of duplication. Nor is it even certain that the results would be commensurate. And secondly the problem would be complicated by the need to investigate at every turn the precise conception of Gnosis or of Gnosticism held by the modern scholars concerned.

The present chapter accordingly proposes something a great deal less ambitious: first, an attempt to clarify the situation within the New Testament itself, to identify those areas in which an incipient Gnosticism may with some confidence be detected in the background, and distinguish them on the one hand from those which present no such phenomena, and on the other from those where the Gnostic element or Gnostic influence is either hypothetical or debated; and secondly, an examination of some of the motifs which have been claimed as Gnostic, bearing in mind the various possibilities outlined above, with a view to their classification so far as may be possible under the proper heads.

By way of further introduction, reference may be made to

two contrasting examples of the modern approach. Bultmann
in his *Theology* has a whole section under the heading 'Gnostic
Motifs',[1] in which he affirms that Paul's anthropological concepts had already been formed under the influence of Gnosticism, and that Paul himself 'regards the Gnostic terminology as
the appropriate form of expression for the Christian understanding of existence.' In his little book *Primitive Christianity in
its Contemporary Setting*[2] he lists a number of terms which, he
affirms, are mythological and derived from Gnosticism. Alan
Richardson on the other hand, in words already quoted,[3] says
'The objection to speaking of Gnosticism in the first century
A.D. is that we are in danger of hypostatising certain rather
ill-defined tendencies of thought and then speaking as if there
were a religion or religious philosophy, called Gnosticism,
which could be contrasted with Judaism or Christianity. There
was, of course, no such thing.' Further on he says 'when scholars
like Bultmann describe a Gnostic doctrine they take their first-
century "evidence" from the New Testament itself. But this is a
question-begging proceeding, since the New Testament is sus-
ceptible of a very different interpretation.' And finally, 'those
scholars who readily find Gnostic influences at work in the New
Testament argue that the beginnings of this type of thought
must have been fairly well defined in the first century; they then
set out to look for evidences of it in the New Testament, and are
then in peril of interpreting the earlier by means of the later
writings.'

Here then we have a direct and head-on collision, but it
should be observed that this conflict is due at least in part to
difference of definition. Richardson on the one hand is working
with the traditional definition, on which obviously there can be
no talk of Gnosticism in the New Testament, except in such
parts as we may see fit to date in the second century. The
movement is in one direction only, from the first century to the
second, from the New Testament to Gnosticism; and the only
question concerns the use that was made by the Gnostics of the
New Testament documents. Now so long as we confine our
attention to the Christian sphere, within the limits of the history

[1] *Theology of the NT*, i, (ET: London 1952), pp. 164 ff.
[2] *Primitive Christianity*, (ET: London 1956), p. 190.
[3] *Introduction to the Theology of the NT*, (London 1958), pp. 41 ff.

of Christian doctrine, this position is both tenable and valid; but it leaves two questions outstanding: first, how are we to account for this curious second-century deviation? Was it purely a development *within* Christianity, or were extraneous factors at work? In the latter case, what other factors were in fact influential? And secondly, how are we to account for elements in the New Testament itself, and in contemporary or even earlier documents, which seem to bear a distinct resemblance to certain aspects of the second-century Gnosticism?

Bultmann on the other hand is working with the wider definition. As it happens, both his translators in the English editions of the books cited make use of the English word 'Gnosticism', but this with the adjective 'Gnostic' is to say the least misleading; for Bultmann himself consistently speaks of *die Gnosis*.[4] It is for this reason that an attempt was made above to reach a clearer definition by distinguishing between Gnosis in the wider sense and Gnosticism proper. We have to recognise the affinities, even the anticipations, which are undoubtedly present, or we cannot fully understand the development of the Christian heresy. On the other hand, Richardson's criticisms present a necessary warning, which must be borne in mind: (a) we probably should not claim as 'Gnostic influence' those elements in the New Testament which are capable of another interpretation *as well as the Gnostic*. Here the issue should rather be left open. And (b) we must constantly beware of the danger of reading back.

Taking the field of Gnostic studies as a whole, we can distinguish three fairly well defined and clear-cut stages, two of them sufficiently well documented for us to speak with some confidence. These are the second and third, the traditional Gnosticism of the second century and later, and the further developments in Manicheism and Mandeism. The first stage is the period of the New Testament itself, and it is here that the burning questions arise. For that very reason it is incumbent upon us to move with caution. Nothing is easier than to formulate an *Arbeitshypothese*, that because some term or concept is Gnostic at the second stage it may in the New Testament be a case of influence from Gnosis; then to apply the theory to the

[4] The same holds at some points in W. G. Kümmel's *Introduction to the NT*, (ET: London 1966).

New Testament occurrences, ignoring the possible alternatives and explaining away the inconvenient evidence; and so to emerge with the 'proof' of 'Gnostic influence'. It is much more difficult to take all the evidence into account, to discriminate between the various possibilities, to distinguish those cases in which the influence of Gnosis must be considered certain, because there is no alternative explanation, from those in which such an influence is merely possible. Our results in the latter case may be much less conclusive, our solutions much less neat and tidy, but it is only by following this more difficult procedure that we can achieve any real and lasting progress.

A convenient starting-point for our investigation is provided by Ernst Haenchen's article in *Die Religion in Geschichte und Gegenwart*,[5] in which he distinguishes two stages in the relationship between New Testament Christianity and Gnosis, using the latter term, of course, in the wider sense. In the first, 'gnostic' ideas and concepts are employed, but any further penetration of Gnosis is resisted, whereas in the second Gnosis is treated simply as false doctrine, and any *Auseinandersetzung* with it is forbidden. These two periods incidentally overlap to some extent in time. This seems to point in the right direction, although there are places at which we may feel called upon to differ from Haenchen's assessment. For example, it is at least open to question whether Paul's opponents in Corinth rejected a future resurrection of the body in favour of a present one in the Spirit; that is, whether the heresy of 2 Tim. 2.18, that the resurrection has already passed, was already current in Corinth in Paul's life-time. Again, it may well be that the Pastorals are directed against Gnosticism, but does this justify the assumption that 1 Tim. 5.23 'hints at a Gnostic prohibition of wine'? Are all forms of asceticism, or abstinence of any kind, to be claimed without more ado as Gnostic, or are there other possibilities? Thirdly, it is again open to question whether we should see a Christianisation of Gnostic material in the contrast of νήπιοι and τέλειοι at Heb. 5.14, or in the identification at Heb. 10.20 of the veil with the flesh of Jesus. The contrast certainly fits the pattern of later Gnostic thinking, but surely it is one that would readily come to mind, without the necessity of any

5 *RGG*[3] II, cols. 1652 ff.

'Gnostic' influence. The two references listed by Bauer[6] from Philo (*Leg. all.* 1.94; *De sobr.* 9) do not demand a Gnostic interpretation, and even if Philo is to be assigned to the realm of Gnosis in the wider sense, what of Polybius?

> For while they (the Aetolians) had hoped to find a helpless infant in Philip (παίδιον νήπιον), owing to his tender years and inexperience, they really found him to be a grown-up man (τέλειος ἀνήρ), both in his projects and in his performances.
> (Polyb. 5.29.2, tr. W. R. Paton in Loeb Classical Library)

To reckon Polybius as Gnostic would be *Pangnostizismus* indeed!

This contrast, then, should rather be regarded as a very natural metaphor which *in a Gnostic context* could take on a technical sense, but which is not for that reason to be claimed as Gnostic at every occurrence.[7] The case of the veil is more difficult, and should perhaps be left an open question. On the one hand, the idea of a barrier between the higher and the lower realms does play a part in the later Gnostic systems, and in the Gospel of Philip this barrier is symbolised by the veil (76, 125; cf. *SJC* 118.7 ff.); but one of the passages in Philip (125) presents a combination of motifs which appear in Hebrews itself and in the Synoptic Passion Story, so that some influence *from Hebrews* upon Gnostic thinking is not to be ruled out. On the other hand the motif of the Celestial Veil itself goes back to late Jewish speculation,[8] and may have passed directly into Gnosticism from there. Indeed it may already have figured in the older and vaguer Gnosis, in which case only the motif of the *rending* of the veil could be claimed as Christian influence.

There is also, however, a problem of exegesis here.[9] It is certainly natural to take the final words Τοῦτ' ἐστιν τῆς

---

[6] *Wörterbuch*, (4Berlin 1952), col. 1470; cf. also col. 975 and note Matt. 11.25.

[7] Cf. also Bertram in Kittel, *TWB*, iv, pp. 913 ff.; P. J. du Plessis, ΤΕΛΕΙΟΣ. *The Idea of Perfection in the NT*, (Kampen n.d.).

[8] Cf. A. Adam, *Die Psalmen des Thomas* . . . , (Beiheft 24 zur *ZNW*, Berlin 1959), p. 35 n.15, and more fully G. W. MacRae, (Cambridge thesis 1966).

[9] Michel [*Hebräerbrief*, (Göttingen 1966), p. 345 n. 2] quotes Käsemann as seeing here a connection with Gnostic mythology; but cf. also the commentaries of Westcott, (1909), Spicq, (1952), Héring, (1954), Montefiore, (1964) for other views.

σαρκὸς αὐτοῦ as standing in apposition to, and explanatory of, the preceding τοῦ καταπετάσματος, which produces the identification mentioned above. If the flesh is the barrier which separates man from God, we are certainly in the realm of 'Gnostic' ideas. This interpretation is however widely recognised to be difficult, on various grounds. One alternative, not generally favoured, is the deletion of the final words as a gloss; another, frequently adopted, is to take them as explanatory not of the veil but of the way. Yet even if we accept the identification it is by no means certain that we have to do with Gnosticism, or even with Gnosis in the wider sense. Moffatt[10] writes 'instead of saying that (Jesus') sacrificial death meant the rending of the veil (like the author of Mark 15.38), *i.e. the supersession of the Old Testament barriers between God and man,* he allegorises the veil here as the flesh of Christ; this had to be rent before the blood could be shed, which enabled him to enter and open God's presence for the people. It is a daring, poetical touch, and the parallelism is not to be prosaically pressed into any suggestion that the human nature in Jesus hid God from men' (italics mine). Such allegorisation is by no means alien to the author's mind, as can be seen from numerous other examples in the Epistle. Here then no assumption of Gnostic influence is necessary, but it can readily be seen how a Gnostic later could re-interpret the passage in the sense not of the Old Testament barriers of sin and the law but in that of the barrier between the realms of flesh and spirit. The motif of the veil thus provides an excellent example of the way in which Gnostic thinking developed, but it is by no means certain that we ought to think of Gnostic influence upon the author of Hebrews. There are other possibilities which must also be considered.

With the motif of the veil Haenchen links that of the 'middle wall of partition' in Eph. 2.14, on which he has earlier said 'The Gnostic idea of the dividing wall which hinders the ascent of the soul to the Pleroma becomes at 2.14–16 the μεσότοιχον between Jews and Gentiles, removed by Christ.' Here again the commentaries are at variance. English-speaking commentators generally cite the wall in the Temple at Jerusalem, between the Court of the Gentiles and the inner precincts, and the warning inscriptions which have been discovered. Not so the German

[10] *Hebrews*, (*I.C.C.*, Edinburgh 1924), p. 143.

scholar—Dibelius[11] asks if the Ephesians would have understood the reference, and claims that this conception belongs to the Gnostic world of thought: the wall is the division between man and God, the firmament that separates this world from the heavenly realm above. But the earliest parallel he quotes is from Ignatius, and the closest is Mandean. Schlier,[12] as it happens, quotes a series of passages from Qumran and Jewish Apocalyptic—but it is surely legitimate to ask if the Ephesians would have understood these references! In point of fact, a preacher in search of a vivid illustration for the reconciliation of Jew and Gentile could hardly have found one better, and Paul who had lived in Jerusalem might well have used it often enough in Ephesus for the readers to recognise it, or for some disciple to recall it as one of the hall-marks of Paul's preaching. This is not to deny the possibility that the Gnostic conception of the dividing wall may have developed from other roots, or that the germ of the idea may already have been in existence in the time of Paul—it is simply to question the assumption that the Gnostic conception and this alone provides us with the clue to the meaning of this passage in Ephesians. The problem is much more complex. We have in fact a number of distinct but similar ideas which are certainly pre-Christian, and indeed go back to various forms of primitive cosmology, but which could readily be combined. One form of the combination appears in the Gnostic theory, but how far this combination had taken place when Ephesians was written, and whether it had any influence upon the author, is very much open to question.

Haenchen very properly deals with the New Testament documents in roughly chronological order, beginning with Paul and passing in turn to the Synoptics, John, Acts, the deutero-Paulines and the later books. For present purposes however it would seem more appropriate to begin where the situation is fairly clear, to work out, as it were, from the well-lit area immediately beneath the spot-light, recognising that as we move outward the light grows progressively weaker until it merges completely into the darkness. Correspondingly it becomes more and more difficult to see distinctly and clearly as we progress.

Working back from the well-defined systems of the second

11 *Hbuch zum NT* 12, (Tübingen 1953), p. 69.
12 *Epheserbrief,* ad loc.

century, we have in the first instance the fairly clear incipient Gnosticism combatted in 1 John. The two key-notes here are the Docetic Christology, denying that Jesus is come in the flesh (4.2: every spirit which confesses that Jesus Christ has come in the flesh is of God, and every spirit which does not confess Jesus is not of God), perhaps also denying the crucifixion (5.6: not with water only but with the water and the blood), and a certain indifference to morality in matters of conduct. It is not really possible to identify this heresy with any known Gnostic group, but it is close to the teaching of Cerinthus so far as we know it. In the light of the significance later given by the Gnostics to the chrism, as for example in the Gospel of Truth and the Gospel of Philip, it is probable that we should see a polemic edge to the two references in this letter (2.20,27), which contain the only three occurrences of the word in the New Testament.[13] In this case the author would be turning the vocabulary of his opponents against them. On the other hand, the evidence for anointing with oil in other contexts (e.g. James 5.14) makes it impossible to regard this as a *primary* argument here, and further we must beware of assuming that the developed Gnostic theory of a later period is already present.[14]

Jude likewise denounces 'ungodly persons who pervert the grace of our God into licentiousness and deny our only Master and Lord, Jesus Christ.' Nothing very specific is said about the nature of their teaching, but a later reference to Balaam's error might perhaps be linked with the references in Revelation (2.14) to Balaam 'who taught Balak to put a stumbling-block before the sons of Israel, that they might eat food sacrificed to idols and practise immorality.' Balaam however is only one of three Old Testament figures mentioned in Jude 11, and may therefore be merely a typical example; nor are idolatry and immorality in themselves adequate criteria for the identification of Gnostics, otherwise we should have to regard Gnosticism as very much older and more widely spread than we have any reason to believe. The reference to Balaam in 2 Peter 2.15

[13] Cf. Dodd, *The Johannine Epistles*, (London 1946), pp. 58 ff.; Schnackenburg, *Die Johannesbriefe*, (Freiburg 1963), 152 f.

[14] On the use of chrismation in the early Church cf. G. W. H. Lampe, *The Seal of the Spirit*, (London 1951); L. L. Mitchell, *Baptismal Anointing*, (London 1966).

would lend itself more readily to association with the passage in Revelation, but the dependence of 2 Peter on Jude, now widely recognised, must give us pause; the author may have had reasons of his own for selecting only one of the three Old Testament figures for mention. Finally, the Nicolaitans who appear in the same context in Revelation may have stood under the same condemnation; but their relation on the one hand to the Nicolaus of Acts 6.5 and on the other to the later sect of the name is by no means clear.

The Pastoral Epistles provide the famous admonition 'avoid the godless chatter and contradictions of what is falsely called knowledge' (1 Tim. 6.20), which supplied Irenaeus with his term—and is at the bottom of our whole problem! Here controversy with the false teachers is discouraged, as leading only to useless strife and controversy, and certainly there are elements which suggest a Gnostic character for the opposition (e.g. 2 Tim. 2.18—the resurrection past already; possibly also a Docetic Christology, cf. 2 Tim. 2.8; 1 Tim. 2.5 ff., 3.16); but sometimes a specifically *Gnostic* character has to be inferred, and is not necessary stated—are the 'myths and genealogies' of 1 Tim. 1.4 (cf. Titus 3.9) necessarily to be identified, in Haenchen's words, with 'Gnostic sequences of the powers in the Pleroma, in the manner of Irenaeus *haer.* I.30,5'? The description in 1 Tim. 4.3 of people who forbid marriage and enjoin abstinence from certain foods would fit some Gnostics; but were these Gnostics the only people to practise such asceticism? The demand for celibacy as a pre-requisite for baptism in the early Syrian Church[15] may be the result of Gnostic influence, and such later documents as the Acts of Thomas would certainly appear to have been at least influenced by Gnosticism, but what of an earlier period? In Pythagoreanism celibacy, if not required, was at least highly esteemed; some Essenes at any rate were celibate, and Matthew Black has traced this ascetic element in Essenism to the ancient Israelite institution of the Nazirate.[16] Moreover a

[15] A. Vööbus, *Celibacy. A Requirement for Admission to Baptism in the Early Church*, (Stockholm 1951). A. F. J. Klijn, *The Acts of Thomas*, (Leiden 1962), pp. 192 ff., doubts Vööbus' view that a promise of virginity was required. Cf. more generally H. Chadwick, art. Enkrateia in *RAC* 5, (1962), cols. 343 ff.; F. Bolgiani, 'La tradizione eresiologica sull' encratismo', *Atti Acad. Torino* 96, (1962), pp. 1–128.

[16] *The Scrolls and Christian Origins*, (London 1961), pp. 27 ff.

D

passage quoted by Black from Schürer[17] suggests the advisability of caution here: 'Since the act of marriage as such made an individual unclean and necessitated a Levitical bath of purification, the effort to attain to the highest degree of purity might well lead to the entire repudiation of marriage.' It is not difficult to believe that such conceptions of purity and holiness were not confined to the Jews alone, but may have been widely current. Here again, then, we have something which may be Gnostic *in a Gnostic context*, but is not necessarily to be employed as a primary criterion for the detection of Gnostic influence.

At this point we seem to be near the border-line where things become obscure and hard to identify with precision. All the documents so far mentioned contain attacks on false teaching, but the precise nature of the heresy is nearly always difficult to grasp. 1 John perhaps presents the clearest picture, but even here we are not told much that we should like to know. It is the cumulative effect of a number of features shared with the later Gnostics by the opponents attacked in these documents which makes us think of an incipient Gnosticism as the heresy in view. But there is nothing, in the first place, to suggest that this incipient Gnosticism had as yet advanced very far in the direction of later developments; nor in the second place are we given any clear indication as to whether it was the result of the meeting of Christianity with something from outside, already more or less fully developed, or whether we have to do only with a more or less sporadic outbreak of false teaching in different areas, but within Christianity itself.

A further point to be noted is that in Titus 1.14 the 'myths' are described as Jewish, and are linked with 'the commands of men who overturn the truth.' The same letter earlier speaks of insubordinate men, empty talkers and deceivers, *especially the circumcision party*' (1.10). According to 1 Tim. 1.7, the opponents wish to be 'teachers of the law'. There was therefore, to say the least, a considerable Jewish element in the false teaching, which provides additional confirmation of what has already been said about the significance of the Jewish contribution to the development of Gnosticism. As will appear later, there are passages in other documents where it is sometimes extremely difficult to say

[17] *History of the Jewish People*, II.ii, (ET: Edinburgh 1885), p. 211 [Black, p. 29 n. 4].

whether the false teaching was Jewish or Gnostic, the Colossian heresy providing a good example. If we could assume that Paul's opponents were always of the same uniform character, and that the Pastoral Epistles and Colossians are authentic Pauline letters, we could then claim that Paul throughout was contending against Jewish Gnostics or Gnosticising Jewish Christians, and this in turn would involve pushing back the origins of Gnosticism to an earlier period. It is obvious, however, that this involves a number of assumptions which are at least doubtful, and which many scholars would regard as without real foundation. The evidence seems rather to suggest a gradual development. In Galatians we seem to have to do with Judaisers who may have made room in their theories for some of the speculations which later came to be known as Gnostic.[18] In the Colossian heresy this 'Gnostic colouring' is more prominent, in the Pastorals perhaps more prominent still; but even here, as Kelly puts it,[19] it is 'something much more elementary' than the developed Gnostic systems of the second century.

One obvious problem is that of dating, another that of authenticity; and in neither case can it be claimed that scholars generally are in complete agreement.[20] There may be a wide consensus of opinion that the Pastorals are post-Pauline, but there are nonetheless still some who would maintain their authenticity, and that on grounds which are not simply to be dismissed without further ado. Now if these documents are dated late, somewhere into the early second century, we can reasonably contemplate the possibility of Gnostic influence on the false teaching they attack; but we cannot claim them as valid evidence for an earlier period. There is too an obvious danger of arguing in a circle here, by using the 'Gnostic' element to prove the Pastorals late, and then using the Pastorals as evidence for Gnosticism in the New Testament. It is however worthy of note that those scholars who claim the existence of a pre-Christian

[18] I cannot accept the theory advanced by Schmithals, *Paulus und die Gnostiker*, (Hamburg-Bergstedt 1965), pp. 9 ff. Cf. my paper at the Oxford NT Congress 1965 [in the press], and see Kümmel, *Introd. to the NT*, (ET: London 1965), pp. 194 f.

[19] J. N. D. Kelly, *The Pastoral Epistles*, (London 1963), p. 12.

[20] Contrast, for example, Kelly's commentary and that of C. K. Barrett, (Oxford 1963).

Gnosticism have not to my knowledge attempted to date the Pastorals early and use them as evidence for Paul's own lifetime. Where so much is uncertain, the safest procedure is one of cautious reserve. Perhaps all we can say is that these documents provide evidence (a) for certain trends in a Gnostic direction, and (b) for a considerable Jewish element in this development. I John seems to indicate that the process was fairly well advanced, though not yet fully developed, by the end of the first century. How much further back we can trace its origins is still obscure.

In the Synoptics Haenchen finds but one echo, the famous 'Johannine thunderbolt' in Matt. 11.27 and its Lucan parallel. This is in striking contrast with Leisegang's assertion[21] that 'the Christian Gospels, which appeared in the Hellenistic world in the Greek language, were all more or less full of or pervaded by Gnostic motifs'. Unfortunately Leisegang provides neither examples nor documentation, so that it is not clear which Gospels he means. Possibly he actually had only John in mind, since the Synoptic passages listed in his index all appear to be passages re-interpreted by the Gnostics later for their own purposes. A further point to be noted here is the curious fact that Matt. 11.27 is not cited in the Gospel of Thomas, although this document does contain a version of the verses immediately following (log. 90). What is beyond question is that the Synoptic Gospels later provided the material for much Gnostic speculation, and also that Thomas at times shows a special affinity with Luke; but this of course does not make the Synoptics themselves 'Gnostic', or prove that they were subject to Gnostic influence.

A recent study of Luke's purpose in writing takes up another aspect. Starting from the fact that earlier scholars have called attention to items in Luke and Acts which 'seem to imply Luke's awareness of and response to a Gnostic problem', Charles H. Talbert[22] argues that these two works were written 'for the express purpose of serving as a defense against Gnosticism.' The main arguments rest upon the emphasis placed by Luke on the authenticity of the apostolic witness, the legitimacy of the Church's interpretation of Scripture, and the succession of tradition—the three bulwarks of the later Church's defence

[21] H. Leisegang, *Die Gnosis*, (Stuttgart 1955), pp. 2 f.
[22] *Luke and the Gnostics*, (Nashville 1966); but cf. Kümmel, *Introd.*, p. 114.

against the Gnostics. Taken in association with the points noted
by earlier scholars, such as the materialisation of Jesus' form in
the resurrection narrative or the emphasis upon his eating and
drinking with his disciples after the Resurrection, this amounts
to a strong case. The one question is whether this is the whole of
Luke's purpose in writing. Jeremias for example regards the
anti-Docetic use of the post-Resurrection meal as secondary to
its significance as a mark of forgiveness, of the disciples' restoration to fellowship with their Master.[23] It is indeed probably a
mistake to narrow down Luke's aim in writing to a single
purpose, as if he had but one object in mind and no other; it is
more likely that he had several aims in view, and even that
some of the factors which influenced his writing were not
consciously present to his mind. The important points for our
purpose are the resemblances to the situation reflected in the
Pastorals, and the difference from the approach of the Fourth
Evangelist to much the same problem.[24]

The Fourth Gospel raises questions which have been warmly
debated. On the one hand, some scholars are naturally reluctant
to admit any suggestion that a Gospel so beloved might be
tainted with even the least suspicion of the Gnostic heresy. On
the other hand there are many, from different schools of
thought, who are prepared to recognise at least some affinity
between John and the Gnostics. F. C. Grant, for example,
suggests that the author 'may have been a Gnostic—a "converted" Gnostic, perhaps.'[25] C. H. Dodd wrote[26] 'there is a
sense in which orthodox Christian theologians like Clement of
Alexandria and Origen, on the one hand, and Hellenistic Jews
like Philo, and pagan writers like the Hermetists, on the other,
should be called Gnostics . . . *In this sense* the Gospel according to
John should be classed as Gnostic,' (italics mine). And this of
course takes no account as yet of Bultmann and his school. More
recently, C. K. Barrett has said 'That there exists a relation of
some kind between the Fourth Gospel and non-Christian Gnosticism is scarcely open to question; exactly what this relation is,

[23] *The Eucharistic Words of Jesus*, (ET: London 1966), p. 204 n. 3.
[24] Cf. Talbert, pp. 46 f.; C. K. Barrett, *Luke the Historian in Recent Study*,
(London 1961), pp. 62 f.
[25] *The Gospels. Their Origin and their Growth*, (London 1959), p. 160.
[26] *The Interpretation of the Fourth Gospel*, p. 97.

is one of the most disputed problems in current New Testament scholarship.'[27]

Here it is well to get back to established facts. (1) The earliest known commentary on the Fourth Gospel was written by the Gnostic Heracleon, and it is the Gnostics who provide us with the first clear traces of a knowledge of John. On the other hand, as Barrett pertinently remarks, it cannot be claimed that their use of the Gospel notably affected their systems, since their interest was largely cosmological and concentrated on the Prologue. 'It is difficult to resist the view that the Gnostics used John because out of it, by exegesis sound or unsound, they were able to win support and enrichment for preconceived theories and mythologies.'[28] Gnostic use of a document does not make the document itself Gnostic.

(2) As already noted, the First Epistle of John provides some of the clearest traces in the New Testament of an incipient Gnosticism. Whether or not the Epistle and the Gospel come from the same author, they certainly derive from the same school. Hence it is probable that the evangelist was aware of the kind of thinking and way of life which are attacked in the Epistle. Recent investigations however have focused attention upon three points which require to be taken into account in this connection: (a) the parallels and resemblances between John and the Dead Sea Scrolls have shown that much which formerly was thought to be Hellenistic was in fact current also in Palestine, at least in certain circles. It would of course be going too far to relate John simply and solely to Palestine and the Qumran sect, but it is no longer possible to treat the Gospel as a purely Hellenistic document. (b) It has been observed that Bultmann's commentary, which attempts to interpret the Gospel against the background of Gnostic dualism, shows 'that at every crucial point the Gospel is in tension with the Gnostic point of view, indeed repudiates it',[29] and indeed this is confirmed by the relevant sections of Bultmann's *Theology*. The Gospel therefore ought *not* to be described as Gnostic without qualification. (c)

[27] *Current Issues in NT Interpretation*, ed. Klassen and Snyder, (London 1962), p. 210.

[28] C. K. Barrett, *The Gospel according to St. John*, (London 1958), p. 55.

[29] Stephen Neill, *The Interpretation of the New Testament 1861–1961*, (London 1964), p. 310.

In a comparison of the theological vocabulary of John with that of the Gospel of Truth, C. K. Barrett[30] brings out the differences between the two works. The eschatological motif, for example, is missing from the Gnostic Gospel, which also diagnoses the human situation in terms of ignorance rather than of sin.[31] The differences indeed 'show the fundamentally biblical and anti-Gnostic content of John.' Similarly Haenchen, after noting the affinities between John and Gnosis, also points out certain differences: if the presentation of Jesus as one who comes from God and returns to God, and whose work consists in his proclamation of the unknown Father, recalls the Gnostic 'emissary'; if it is only those who come to know God in Jesus who are saved; yet on the other side John knows nothing of a fall of divine sparks into matter, and above all there are two major points of variance: the linking of salvation not to a mythical incarnation of the Gnostic cry of awakening but to the word of the historical Jesus, and the fact that Jesus proclaims not the identity of a divine spark in man with God, so that knowledge of God and knowledge of the self become identical, but the gracious God himself.

John then is not Gnostic, although there are certain affinities and the precise relationship is difficult to define. In particular, there is the problem of the evangelist's 'Gnostic' terminology. On this two things require to be said: (1) regard must be paid to the distinction drawn above between the descriptive use of this term and the use which implies derivation. Is this terminology described as Gnostic because it *later* becomes current in the Gnostic systems, or was it already Gnostic, and in what sense, before it was used by John? (2) As already noted, Dodd and others have recognised that there is a sense, a broad and comprehensive sense, in which John *can* be called 'Gnostic'. Indeed, this is one of the points at which the distinction made earlier between Gnosis and Gnosticism is of value. But this broader sense itself requires investigation and more careful definition. Some elements in the Hellenistic Gnosis can be, and should be, more precisely identified as Stoic or Platonic,

---

[30] *Current Issues*, [see n. 27] pp. 210 ff.
[31] ibid., p. 214. On Bultmann's elimination of the futuristic element from the Johannine eschatology cf. P. Ricca, *Die Eschatologie des vierten Evangeliums*, (Zürich 1966), p. 50 n. 124.

Babylonian, Iranian or Jewish constituents in the contemporary syncretism. Allowance must be made for the convergence of ideas, for the natural tendency to assimilate or even identify similar features in distinct cultural traditions, as was done by those who claimed that the Greeks borrowed from Moses. In short, we must ask whether John's Gnostic terminology is Gnostic only in the descriptive sense, in which case the later Gnostics may have borrowed from John; or implies derivation, either in the sense that John is combatting the incipient Gnosticism of his opponents with their own weapons or, more generally, and more vaguely, that he is using the language of his period, a language marked by the tendencies broadly characterised as Gnosis. And further, we must consider whether John's use of such terminology is in fact Gnostic, or whether this terminology only becomes Gnostic in a strictly Gnostic context.

The burning problem in discussion of Gnosticism and the New Testament always comes with John—and with Paul. The latter indeed presents the more intricate problem, since we have evidence from other sources to indicate that by the end of the first century, the probable date of the Fourth Gospel, an incipient Gnosticism was already developing. As Barrett notes, 'it is for many reasons unlikely that a non-Christian Gnosticism arose full-grown between the writing of John and the writing of the Gospel of Truth in such a way as to influence the author of the latter.'[32] Even if we admit the view that the Gospel of Truth pre-supposes the developed Valentinian theory (see Chapter IV), and must therefore be dated somewhat later, we still have the space of barely half a century between John and Valentinus, and into this we should have to compress the whole development of Ophitism and of the teachings of such men as Saturninus and Basilides, some of which manifestly influenced the development of Valentinianism. It therefore seems a legitimate inference that the origins of Gnosticism proper are pre-Johannine, although here we are moving into the shadowy no-man's-land between Gnosticism proper and the vaguer Gnosis. The problem is to determine how much further back we must go.

If Haenchen's argument could be sustained,[33] that Simon

[32] ibid., p. 223.
[33] *Gott und Mensch*, (Tübingen 1965), pp. 265 ff. [$=ZTK$ 49, (1952), pp. 316 ff.]. But cf. Wilson, *The Gnostic Problem*, (London 1958), p. 99.

Magus was already a Gnostic before he came into contact with Christianity, then the problem would be resolved; for in Acts the episode of Simon precedes the conversion of Paul. This however involves (a) assumptions regarding the reliability of Acts which not every scholar would be prepared to entertain; and (b) the ever-present problem of definition, for while Simon may reasonably be described as a Gnostic in the sense of Gnosis it is by no means clear that he was a Gnostic in the sense of the later developed Gnosticism. We cannot for example assume that the Megale Apophasis, cited by Hippolytus but apparently unknown to Irenaeus, is a genuinely Simonian document in the sense that it derives from Simon himself; we have to allow for developments within the Simonian school, so that this document may reflect the influences of a much later period.

We are thus reduced to the examination of Paul's own writings in the effort to determine to what extent he reflects or is influenced by Gnosis, as more broadly defined, or even perhaps provides indications of the existence in his life-time of the germ of what later blossomed into Gnosticism. Since Ephesians and Colossians present a special problem, quite apart from questions of authenticity, consideration of these will be deferred for the moment.

At this point attention should be drawn to the careful wording of Haenchen's article: Paul's teaching about the fall of Creation (Rom. 8.19–22) and of Adam (Rom. 5.12–17), about the contrast of ψυχικοί and πνευματικοί (1 Cor. 2.14 f.; 15.21, 44–49), about φῶς and σκότος (Rom. 13.11–13; 1 Thess. 5.4–6) and the demonic rulers of this age (1 Cor. 2.6–8; 2 Cor. 4.4) and the dangers of marriage (1 Cor. 7.32–4, 38) shows 'traits akin to Gnosis'. Again, his doctrine of the Redeemer 'is in contact with the Gnostic doctrine', in that Jesus is presented as a heavenly being who descends unknown (1 Cor. 2.8) from God and returns again to Him (2. Cor. 8.9; Phil. 2.6–11). Other features 'recall' Gnostic theories. The spirit-ruled Christians of 1 Cor. 3.16 and Rom. 8.9 'look like' the Gnostic πνευματικοί.

What does this mean? What do these 'traits akin to Gnosis' signify—that they are derived from Gnosis, or merely like it, or starting-points for it? What is meant by 'contact with Gnostic doctrine'—a fully-developed Gnostic Redeemer-myth? These features certainly 'recall' Gnostic ideas, but was Gnosticism or

even Gnosis the source from which they came? Or have we to do
with Gnostic influence, or merely with Gnostic parallels? Or is
it even possible that at some points reflection on Paul's own
teaching may have led later Gnostics to embellish their own
theories with choice stones quarried from his letters? It should
be noted that, whatever careless readers may have made of his
words, Haenchen does not affirm that these traits *are* Gnostic.
Clearly we have here a task as yet unfinished, calling for careful
exploration and evaluation on sound principles of exegesis. A
wholesale and sweeping incorporation of Paul, and the New
Testament writers generally, into the sphere of 'Gnosticism' is
not adequate; nor is an equally wholesale and sweeping rejection of any kind of contact whatsoever. Our task calls for long
and patient evaluation and assessment. Some features, like the
contrast of light and darkness, may be more or less common-
place in Hellenistic thought; others, like that of the demonic
rulers of this age, may have links with Jewish apocalyptic;
others again may perhaps be documented from Greek philosophy. All these may legitimately be classed for convenience of
reference under the general head of Gnosis; but this is not yet
Gnosticism.

Paul in short stands at a point of inter-play and inter-action,
where ideas from various distinct cultural traditions were in
circulation. In some cases the conceptions in two different
traditions might in fact be identical, and therefore readily
assimilated. In other cases however the conceptions though
similar were not identical, and their assimilation produced a
modification, sometimes profound, on one side or the other; or
the associations which clustered around a conception in one
tradition introduced a new element into the understanding of
the corresponding conception in a different tradition. The
Septuagint, to come to a concrete example, presents the Hebrew
Scriptures in a Greek dress but, says Dodd, 'the words of the
Hebrew Scriptures, in passing into Greek, partly lost one set of
associations, and partly gained a new set, while at the same
time the Greek words used in translation may have acquired
something of the value of the Hebrew words they represent.'[34]
This, as Dodd shows, is of some significance for the understanding of the Old Testament, and of the Jewish religion, by

[34] *The Bible and the Greeks*, (London 1935), p. xi.

Diaspora Jews who read their Scriptures in Greek, or for that matter by Gentiles who may have had no other means of access to the Jewish faith. The process however did not affect the Jews alone, or their religion. It has long been noted that the only mystery religions from the East which enjoyed any large measure of success in the Graeco-Roman world were those which were capable of some degree of Hellenisation. We have only to envisage two men of different cultural backgrounds and different language, whose only common medium of communication was Greek, comparing and discussing their respective religions, to realise the extent of the possibilities for assimilation and syncretism. And on its entry upon the stage of the wider world Christianity had to be 'translated' from its original Palestinian thought-forms and terms of reference into those comprehensible in its new environment. It is not in the least surprising that there should have been some people who in the process lost the essence of the Gospel in 'the maelstrom of Hellenistic syncretism.' For convenience in study and analysis, we have to talk in terms of ideas, trends and currents of thought; but in fact we are dealing with ideas in the minds of *people*, which introduces a highly complicating factor into all our investigations.

A further point to be noted arises in connection with Haenchen's discussion of the Corinthian correspondence. Paul, he says, combats the Gnostics in Corinth because they denied a future resurrection of the body in favour of a present resurrection in the Spirit. Citing as evidence 1 Cor. 15.29–32 and 2. Cor. 5.1–5, he adds that Paul 'at first misunderstood the Gnostic teaching because of inadequate information.' This in the present context, assuming for the moment that Paul *was* dealing with Gnostics, is a legitimate inference. There is a difference in the positions held in the two letters, although C. F. D. Moule[35] has recently argued a different exegesis, that there was a change in Paul's own ideas on the subject: in 1 Corinthians he is thinking of the spiritual body as a kind of overcoat, to be put on *on top of* the existing material body, whereas in 2 Corinthians he is contemplating the more painful, drastic and demanding prospect that the material must be annihilated before the spiritual body can be put on. In the latter case Paul would be approaching

[35] *NTS* 12, (1966), pp. 106 ff.

the Gnostic conception which seems to underlie a passage in the Gospel of Philip, although it should be added that this passage starts from Paul's own teaching.

The point for our present purpose is however that while Haenchen's inference may be legitimate here it is not universally valid. To hold a mirror up to Paul, in the hope of detecting Gnostic leanings in his opponents, is one thing. To decide, when the evidence is not forthcoming, that Paul misunderstood his opponents and was entertaining Gnostics unawares, is quite another; for this may involve the reading into the theories deduced from Paul's refutations of the very Gnostic teachings for which we are looking. 'Gnostic influences' which have first to be read into the evidence are a very insecure foundation on which to build.

In the above discussion it has been assumed for the moment that Paul was dealing with Gnostics, but this is precisely the point at issue. Here the perennial problem of definition rises once again. In the broad and comprehensive sense of the term Gnosis, it is perfectly correct to speak of Gnosis at Corinth; but this is not really very helpful unless we can determine the relation between this Gnosis and the later developed Gnosticism. To speak of Gnosis in Corinth, and then to interpret the teaching of Paul's opponents by a wholesale introduction of ideas from the second-century systems, is to run the risk of seriously distorting the whole picture. There *are* points of contact, and indeed the very least that can be said is probably Robert Law's remark[36] that 1 Corinthians shows 'into how congenial a soil the seeds of Gnosticism were about to fall.' Yet prior to the sowing, and even when the sowing has been completed, the most fertile field may be some way short of being ripe for the harvest. It is therefore necessary to ask whether those features of the Corinthian 'heresy' which are claimed as Gnostic are in fact already Gnostic in the stricter sense of the term, whether they are the germs out of which the later Gnosticism developed, or whether they admit of some other explanation. These alternatives, of course, are not all mutually exclusive.

To take but two examples: (a) it is frequently affirmed that on the question of the resurrection Paul's opponents, like the

[36] *The Tests of Life*, (Edinburgh 1909), p. 28.

heretics of the Pastorals, maintained that it had already taken place.[37] This may be so; but on the other hand this interpretation may be no more than a reading back from the Pastorals into the situation at Corinth. The most natural rendering of 1 Cor. 15.12 is not that some say there will be no resurrection (because it is already past), but that in their view there is no such thing. The verb is in the present tense, not the future. In other words, Paul's opponents would be maintaining the 'Greek' view of the immortality of the soul over against a resurrection of the body, as indeed Paul's whole argument seems to imply, with its emphasis on the fact of the resurrection of Jesus. Robertson and Plummer[38] appositely quote a passage from Aeschylus (Eum. 648): οὔτις ἔστ᾽ ἀνάστασις. Moreover it is possible to see how the heresy of the Pastorals could have developed from a misunderstanding of Paul's own teaching: in Rom. 6 he speaks of the Christian being buried with Christ in Baptism, of the old man being crucified, of walking in newness of life. In this context Paul speaks of our being σύμφυτοι καὶ τῆς ἀναστάσεως in the future (Rom. 6.5), but it is not difficult to see how the conclusion could have been drawn that the resurrection had already taken place.

(b) It has been argued that the 'wisdom' section in 1 Cor. 1–2 reflects a pre-Christian Gnostic Sophia myth.[39] Now the figure of Sophia does play a prominent part in the later Gnostic systems, and there are grounds for carrying the beginnings of such speculation back at least to the Jewish Wisdom literature of the inter-testamental period. This does not however necessarily mean that Paul had any such myth consciously in mind as he wrote, or even that he was unconsciously influenced by it. This is a point where Jonas' warning against the conveyor-belt analogy is highly apposite: we cannot assume that if a theory is older than Paul it was therefore known to him, and must have been alluded to whenever he touched on the subject. Modern

[37] Cf. e.g. Kümmel, *An die Korinther,* (*Hbuch z. NT,* Tübingen 1949), pp. 192 f., and contrast Lietzmann's own view in the original commentary [ibid., p. 79].

[38] *1 Corinthians,* (*ICC,* Edinburgh 1953), p. 347.

[39] Cf. U. Wilckens, *Weisheit und Torheit,* (Tübingen 1959), with Köster's review in *Gnomon* 33, (1961), pp. 590 ff.; also Wilckens' art. σοφία in Kittel *TWB,* vii, pp. 465 ff., 497 ff. For critical assessment see K. Prümm in *ZKT* 87, (1965), pp. 399 ff.; 88, (1966), pp. 1 ff.

scholars, with a much greater concern for fullness of documentation and adequate coverage of the relevant material, have been known to overlook discussions which they had actually read, or pieces of evidence of which they knew. In Paul's case, such an occurrence is the more likely in that he was writing less formally and not trying to explore every avenue. Moreover his whole discussion begins from an Old Testament quotation which seems to have no connection with any Sophia myth, and it can be quite adequately expounded, without introducing a hypostatised Wisdom at all, in terms of the wisdom upon which men pride themselves and the 'foolishness' of God which yet is superior to all the wisdom of this world. It is only the identification of Christ as 'the power of God and the wisdom of God' which prompts the question of 'Gnostic' influence, in the sense that Paul is claiming for Christ the titles and attributes applied by his opponents to their hypostatised Sophia; but the alternative surely bears examination, that the identification arises naturally out of the context of the whole discussion.

Space does not permit of detailed discussion of the whole Corinthian question, but these examples may suffice to show that while there may at Corinth have been certain affinities with the later Gnosticism a thorough-going 'Gnostic' interpretation of the situation may involve some begging of the question. A further problem arises with 2 Corinthians: is Paul dealing with the same opponents? Or is he dealing in one case with opponents of a Gnostic type, in the other with Jewish Christians, or with Judaisers?[40] Can we assume that Paul throughout his career was confronted with the same kind of opposition, or did he at different periods and in different areas have to face attack from different quarters? The Tübingen school saw the whole history of the early Church in terms of a conflict between the Judaising and the Hellenistic wings. More recently the attempt has been made, particularly by W. Schmithals,[41] to identify Paul's opponents in almost every case as Gnostics. In the broad sense of the term, perhaps they were; even in Galatia, where all the evidence suggests rather a Judaising opposition, there are

[40] See D. Georgi, *Die Gegner des Paulus im 2 Korintherbrief*, (Neukirchen 1964).
[41] *Die Gnosis in Korinth*, (Göttingen 1956); *Paulus und die Gnostiker*, (Hamburg-Bergstedt 1965).

certain elements of a 'Gnostic' type.[42] But to describe all Paul's opponents as Gnostic without further qualification is to ignore distinctions which both can and ought to be made, and to run the risk of interpreting the embryonic and undeveloped in the light of the mature and fully developed systems of a later age. It seems much nearer to the facts to recognise Judaisers in Galatia, with perhaps some 'Gnostic' leanings, opponents of a more Gnostic type at Corinth, with perhaps a Jewish Christian element which may have entered into the situation at a later stage.

Ephesians and Colossians present special problems, in the matter of date and authenticity as well as in regard to possible 'Gnostic' influences. Some scholars regard both as Pauline, others consider them both deutero-Pauline, others again accept the one but not the other, Colossians as a rule being given the stronger claim. Obviously, our decision on such questions must affect our interpretation of developments in Paul's own lifetime and in the succeeding generation; but here again we must beware of arguing in a circle. Again, if Günther Bornkamm can write[43] 'Of the fact that behind the Colossian heresy there stands a Jewish or Judaistic Gnosis, strongly infected by Iranian ideas, there can scarcely be any doubt', Ernst Percy argues[44] that this heresy *lacks* the characteristic and essential features of Gnosticism, and A. S. Peake long ago[45] roundly denied any Gnostic influence, declaring it improbable that we have Gnosticism here even in a rudimentary form. 'We are certain,' he

---

[42] Cf. Paul's references to 'the weak and beggarly elements' [Gal. 4.3 ff.; but see also *The Gnostic Problem*, p. 93 n. 111], and his warnings against transforming liberty into licence. The facts which led Lütgert, Ropes, Schmithals and others to see Gnosticism in some form in Galatia require explanation, but do they indicate a developed *system* or merely the raw material out of which such systems were to be built? See further A. Oepke, *Der Brief an die Galater*, (Berlin 1957), pp. 93 ff. The reference to 'this present evil age' [Gal. 1.4] should be linked with Jewish apocalyptic rather than with Gnosticism [cf. Oepke p. 19; Burton, *Galatians*, (*ICC*, Edinburgh 1921), pp. 426 ff.; Sasse in *TWB*, i, p. 206].

[43] *Das Ende des Gesetzes*, (Munich 1958), p. 150.

[44] *Probleme der Kolosser- und Epheserbriefe*, (Lund 1946), pp. 176 ff.

[45] *Expositor's Greek Testament*, iii, (London 1903), pp. 484 ff. See further H. Hegermann, *Die Vorstellung vom Schöpfungsmittler im hellenistischen Judentum und Urchristentum*, (*TU* 82, Berlin 1961); H. M. Schenke in *ZTK* 61, (1964), pp. 391 ff.

says, 'of the Jewish nature of the teaching, and if it can be explained from Judaism alone have no warrant for calling in other sources.' A further complication is introduced by the contacts noted between the Colossian heresy and Qumran.[46] Close on a century ago J. B. Lightfoot[47] linked the Colossian heresy with the Essenes, a view which Peake was to reject. Were the Essenes Gnostic after all? Or have we at Qumran and at Colossae still only 'Gnosticism in the making', or even nothing more than the first tentative experiments in combining the raw materials? It should be noted also that passages from both Ephesians and Colossians were later re-interpreted by the second-century Gnostics to suit their own purposes. One passage in Irenaeus' account of Valentinianism (adv. Haer. 1.1.4) looks very like an adaptation of Col. 1.19,[48] and others will be noted in the next chapter.

According to Haenchen,[49] Colossians 'probably pre-supposes a Jewish-Christian Gnosis, which did indeed ascribe to Christ the work of redemption but demanded the worship of the elemental powers (στοιχεῖα τοῦ κόσμου 2.8,20) who with him form the Pleroma (cf. 1.19; 2.9 f.).' In none of the verses cited, however, is it expressly said that these powers form part of the Pleroma—this is an inference in the light of later Gnostic thought. Indeed, the Valentinian technical use of this term for the totality of the higher aeons is sometimes extended, for convenience, to describe the spiritual world in systems which do not themselves make use of the word. It is at least open to question whether the 'Gnostic' interpretation of such passages in Colossians would ever have been suggested but for our prior knowledge of the use of the term in Valentinianism; and consideration of the range of possible meanings would suggest that this is not the only possible interpretation.[50] On the other hand the word does seem to be used in a technical sense at some points in Ephesians and Colossians, and there seems to be

[46] Cf. W. D. Davies, *Christian Origins and Judaism*, (London 1962), p. 157. For Ephesians cf. K. G. Kuhn, *NTS* 7, (1961), pp. 334 ff.

[47] *St. Paul's Epistles to the Colossians and Philemon*, (London 1875), esp. pp. 83 ff.

[48] Cf. Sagnard, *La gnose valentinienne*, (Paris 1947), p. 605.

[49] RGG³ II, col. 1654.

[50] Cf. Bauer, *Wörterbuch* and *TWB* s.v.; also C. F. D. Moule, *Colossians and Philemon*, (Cambridge 1957), pp. 164 ff.

justification for the view suggested by Ernest Best,[51] that the Hellenistic philosophical conception of the universe as filled by God was at this time passing into the Gnostic conception of a divine *pleroma*, at once the abode of the aeons and the aggregate of them. In this case we should have in this conception one of the 'points of growth' for the later Gnosticism.

Again, Haenchen speaks of the use in Colossians, in a Christianised form, of 'the Gnostic idea of the Redeemer as the Urmensch, identical with the cosmos.' In Ephesians 4.8–10 he finds 'the Gnostic doctrine of the descent and ascent of the Redeemer', who at 2.15 appears as the 'new Man' and at 4.13 as ἀνὴρ τέλειος, which Haenchen identifies as the Urmensch. Further traces of the Gnostic Anthropos doctrine are found in the statements about Christ as the head of the body (Eph. 4.3 f., 12; 5.23), while the description of the Church as a heavenly building (2.20–22) and its relation to Wisdom (3.8–10) are 'akin to Gnostic ideas'. Once again it is advisable to call a halt and ask what precisely is meant. Does kinship with Gnostic ideas imply derivation from Gnosticism, or merely that the same kind of imagery is employed on one side and on the other? Ideas of a Heavenly Man or Primal Man are admittedly pre-Christian, but a considerable leap of faith is involved in the assumption that these pre-Christian ideas already carried with them the full implications of the alleged Gnostic Redeemer-myth. Summing up recent studies, P. Pokorny[52] writes that an original pre-Gnostic Urmensch-Redeemer myth cannot be proved, and that the use of Gnostic texts for the exegesis of Ephesians and Colossians, especially in regard to the conception of the Body, has become problematical. Building on the researches of Schenke and others, he develops a theory of an Anthropos-myth, based on Jewish speculation about Gen. 1.26 f., which is quite another matter than the old Redeemer-myth hypothesis. Here again we may have one of the points of growth for later Gnostic thinking. As Best puts it,[53] 'once Paul had attached the metaphor of the body and its members to Christ, it was only to be expected that Gnosticism would attach it to the Heavenly Man and so produce the references we have to it.' The Pauline use of the

[51] *One Body in Christ*, (London 1955), p. 148, cf. p. 140.
[52] Petr Pokorný, *Die Epheserbrief und die Gnosis*, (Berlin 1965), p. 40.
[53] op. cit., p. 87 n. 1 [see generally pp. 85 ff.].

E

metaphor in his earlier epistles may have provided a part of the stimulus which led to later developments, although this is not to say that it was by any means the only factor.

This survey is by no means exhaustive, but may serve for present purposes. It is evident that if we approach from the side of the second Christian century, and interpret in the light of the later Gnostic systems, there is much in the New Testament that may be claimed as 'Gnostic'. When we begin at the other end, however, and endeavour to trace the historical development, it is another matter. In most cases the 'Gnostic' features admit of another interpretation, and seldom if ever is the Gnostic explanation absolutely demanded as the one explanation which alone is possible. If we think in terms of the wider definition of Gnosis, again, the New Testament belongs in the 'Gnostic' sphere; but this is to obscure distinctions which ought to be made. On the one hand, 'Gnosis' may be a convenient label for the general trend, but frequently it is possible to identify more precisely the source from which a particular idea is derived. 'Gnosis' thus tends to become little more than an attitude, finding expression in ideas drawn from various sources, and it is frequently difficult in the extreme to determine to what extent this attitude is actually present at all. On the other hand, the New Testament reveals a variety of response and re-action to what appears to be a developing movement. Unless we begin by pre-supposing Gnostics at every turn, there is nothing Paul's letters to Thessalonica or Philippi which demands a 'Gnostic' explanation. Nor is there in James or 1 Peter. Galatians shows some vague traces of the kind of thinking later characteristic of Gnosticism, but it is by no means beyond question that the warning against license in the closing chapters was directed against anti-cosmic libertarian Gnostics; it is obviously quite possible that some could have misinterpreted freedom from the law to mean complete absence of moral restraint, without actually being Gnostics. Corinth supplies a better case, and at least reveals how easily Gnostic ideas could develop. Somewhat clearer signs appear in Ephesians and Colossians, but even here much is still vague and ambiguous. It is still in debate whether the false teaching in view is Gnostic or Jewish, or both. And this seems to hold in general for Paul's life-time and the immediately succeeding period.

Greater clarity and assurance comes only when we approach the end of the century. In 1 John and the Pastorals we find for the first time real traces of what may be called Gnosticism proper, although even here, and in the Pastorals particularly, the evidence is not always so firm as one might wish. The implication seems to be that Gnosticism in the proper sense developed alongside Christianity in the course of the first century, and that this was a time of considerable ferment, during which nothing was in any sense final or clear-cut. The fact that so often it is difficult to decide whether some feature is Gnostic or Jewish, and the marked Jewish element in later Gnostic thinking, may suggest that there was a Jewish Gnosticism before there was a Christian, and hence that the origins of Gnosticism proper go back to the pre-Christian period; but here we are moving beyond what can be established on the basis of the New Testament evidence into the realm of conjecture. In terms of the distinction drawn at the Messina Colloquium, it may be said that there is ample justification for the pre-Gnostic position, that there were in existence in pre-Christian times various themes and motifs, conceptions and ideas, which later were incorporated into Gnosticism proper, but that at this stage they cannot be said to constitute 'Gnosticism' in the strict sense.

In this connection it has finally to be noted that the identification of 'Gnostic terminology' is a dubious expedient.[54] The examples cited, and in particular such words as πλήρωμα and τέλειος, show that while they did acquire a technical sense in later Gnosticism this sense is not the only one possible, and sometimes is not even probable, when the word occurs in the New Testament. To import into a New Testament passage the interpretation given to it by the Gnostics may be to distort the meaning, and the same holds for the terminology. Of the seventeen New Testament occurrences of πλήρωμα, as examination of the concordance will reveal, only a few are capable of interpretation in Gnostic terms, and none absolutely require it to the exclusion of all other meanings. We have to distinguish those areas in which 'Gnostic influence' is clear and unmistakable from those in which it is merely possible, and from those again in which the possibility is distinctly remote.

[54] Cf. S. Laeuchli, *The Language of Faith*, (Nashville 1962; London 1965).

III

Gnostic Use of the New Testament

THE preceding chapter has clearly shown that the relation between the New Testament on the one hand and the Gnostic movement on the other is by no means a simple one. If we approach the New Testament from the side of the second century, there is much that is familiar, much that lends itself to interpretation in the light of the developed Gnostic theories; and it is then very natural to assume, as the explanation for these phenomena, a pre-Christian Gnosticism which has exercised an extensive influence upon the New Testament writers. On the other hand, (1) there is no conclusive proof of the existence of a fully-developed Gnosticism in the pre-Christian period; (2) some of the material quoted as evidence for Gnostic influence does not in itself demand an exclusively Gnostic interpretation, but can equally be understood in quite non-Gnostic terms; and (3) some of this material can be traced back to other movements of thought, to the Old Testament or to the Jewish apocalyptic or wisdom literature, to some school of Greek philosophy, be it Platonism, Stoicism, or Pythagoreanism, or to one or another of the religious traditions of the ancient East. It is therefore essential to consider at every point whether the Gnostic connotation is necessary to any given term or concept, inherent in it from the beginning, or is the result of a later re-interpretation imposed upon it within a Gnostic context. It may indeed be convenient to use some such term as Gnosis as a general label for the whole phenomenon, but use of the adjective Gnostic without qualification is frankly dangerous.

In this connection it may be objected that to distinguish between Gnosticism proper and Gnosis in this wider and vaguer sense is to introduce unnecessary complications, and that to insist on identifying particular elements specifically as Stoic, Platonic or Jewish rather than Gnostic is merely to complicate matters further. On this it must be said in the first place that while there is a continuity between the vaguer Gnosis and the developed Gnosticism, the two are not identical in such a way that what is true of the second may also be predicated, without qualification, of the first. There are elements in the developed second-century systems for which we have as yet no evidence in the early wider Gnosis, in particular the marked anti-cosmic strain, the conception of the Demiurge as a subordinate deity hostile to man, the hostility to the Jewish God. To understand the growth of Gnosticism proper, and of the later Gnosis, we have to investigate the reasons for the developments which have taken place.

Secondly, while the Stoic, Platonic, Jewish or other elements do indeed become Gnostic at a later stage, indiscriminate use of this label tends to deprive it of any real significance. Everything in the thought of the early Christian centuries becomes Gnostic, regardless of the fact that some of the writers concerned were outspokenly opponents of Gnosticism. Philo, Paul, John, Clement of Alexandria, Origen and Plotinus are grouped together under the same head as Valentinus, Basilides, Marcion and the writers of the Nag Hammadi documents. Yet to ignore the differences is quite as serious an error as neglect of similarities. It may appear to be simpler to use a single label, glossing over the finer academic distinctions, but when appeal is made to the principle of Occam's razor that principle is not always cited in full: *entia non sunt multiplicanda praeter necessitatem*. It is not the multiplication of hypothetical sources which is to be avoided, but their *unnecessary* multiplication; and in the present instance it is open to question whether application of the principle is even valid; for Platonism, Stoicism and the rest are not hypothetical sources, but are already present and can be shown to be the sources of particular ideas. The only hypothetical entity, in fact, is the pre-Christian Gnosticism which is so often held to have been so widely influential. Gnosis may serve as a convenient and legitimate label for a whole complex of related phenomena; but Gnosis is not yet Gnosticism. If there is continuity and development, there has also been modification and re-interpretation.

A further point to emerge is that in the New Testament period we have to take account not only of influence from this vaguer Gnosis but also of reaction against it, and against the incipient forms of the later Gnosticism. How far we can really speak of Gnosticism in the first half-century after the Crucifixion is very much open to question, although the 'points of growth' are certainly present. Much depends here on our interpretation of the situation at Corinth, and on the date and authenticity of Ephesians and Colossians. Were the latter genuine letters of Paul, and the false teachers opposed in them recognisably Gnostic, we should have stronger grounds for dating the origins of Gnosticism proper into Paul's own life-time. As it is, the earliest clear indications of the emergence of an incipient Gnosticism appear to fall in the last quarter of the first century. This fits well with Grant's theory of the disappointed hopes of Qumran sectarians after the Fall of Jerusalem in A.D. 70, although as already noted this is probably not the whole answer. There were other developments still to take place.

The first century, then, presents a rather confused picture, with an emergent Christianity seeking to establish itself on the stage of a wider world, endeavouring to understand and express its faith in language comprehensible to the people of that world, defending itself first against enemies from without and later also against the subversive activities of enemies within. Which was eventually to become the orthodox tradition, and which the heretical, was still an open question. Equally open for us is the further question, whether there was anything so distinct that it can be called a movement, in competition with Christianity and with the other religions of the time, which later developed into the classical Gnosticism; or whether the precursor of Gnosticism at this stage was no more than a number of varied trends and tendencies. To use the distinction drawn at the Messina Colloquim, the proto-Gnostic view would affirm the first, while the pre-Gnostic would regard either position as tenable. In the second century however the lines of cleavage become gradually more distinct, the Gnostic religion is more and more clearly recognised as a rival to the Christian faith, the more dangerous in that it has so much in common and yet is so fundamentally different. At this stage part of the common element is provided by the New Testament itself, for it was used by 'orthodox' and Gnostic alike, although sometimes with very different results.

The history of exegesis is as yet to a large extent a field uncultivated, in certain areas indeed almost virgin soil. We have of course studies of particular themes and concepts, or of particular texts, as they are handled by various expositors down the centuries. We have also discussions of the allegorical method, generally in the context of an examination of the exegesis of a Philo of Alexandria or an Origen, and we have studies of the exegetical methods of particular Fathers in the context of surveys of their life and work. But much of this material is dispersed in numerous volumes, if not buried in periodicals and *Festschriften*, where it is difficult even for the specialist to trace it. It would be difficult to name one volume which provides at once a comprehensive survey of the whole history of biblical exegesis and sufficient detailed discussion of specific points.[1] Yet this is surely a field of genuine importance for those whose task it is to expound the Scriptures. How was it done by the men of the past? What can we learn from them, from their errors as well as from their achievements? What are the canons of sound exegesis, how and when were they arrived at, to what extent have they been observed or neglected in days gone by? It is encouraging to learn that a new series of publications recently launched in Germany is devoted to this very purpose.[2]

It is not of course the aim of this chapter to supply the need. All that is attempted here is a preliminary and of necessity rather cursory survey of one small corner of a very extensive field. Tertullian in a famous dictum once declared that the heretic Marcion practised Biblical Criticism with a pen-knife, cutting away all that did not conform with his own conception of the Christian faith; but the accusation brought against the Gnostics was a different one, not that they truncated Scripture but that they distorted it to serve their own ends and purposes.[3] This, incidentally, provides further reason for a certain reserve about classifying Marcion unambiguously as a Gnostic.

To bring things into some sort of perspective at the outset, we may begin with two studies published in the present century,

[1] A few relevant works are: R. M. Grant, *A Short History of the Interpretation of the Bible*, (New York 1964; London 1965); R. P. C. Hanson, *Allegory and Event*, (London 1959); Beryl Smalley, *The Study of the Bible in the Middle Ages*, (Oxford 1941); W. G. Kümmel, *Das Neue Testament*, (Munich 1958); Stephen Neill, *The Interpretation of the NT 1861–1961*, (London 1964).

[2] *Beiträge zur Geschichte der biblischen Exegese*, (Tübingen: J. C. B. Mohr). There is also a similar series on Hermeneutics.

[3] Cf. H. E. W. Turner, *The Pattern of Christian Truth*, (London 1954), pp. 168 f., 194.

singling out only a few points to serve as guiding lines for our examination of the texts themselves. The first is Carola Barth's study of the interpretation of the New Testament in Valentinian Gnosticism, published in 1911.[4] Here, following upon a survey of the formulae employed in citation, it is noted that for the Valentinians Christ and his apostles speak to reveal the hidden mysteries to the disciples. Their words have an absolute and incontrovertible validity. The formulae of citation already make it clear that it is the Saviour's function as a teacher and revealer of Gnosis which stands in the forefront of his activity. It is also notable that the words of Paul are introduced in the same manner as those of the Lord. Further on it is observed that certain passages show characteristic variations, in which we can detect genuinely Valentinian tendentious modifications. Again, it is noted that events in the life of Jesus, the birth, the baptism, the temptation and so on, are so interpreted as to include more than appears to earthly sight—for parallel with them are *heavenly* events, part of the process of eternal salvation. At later points reference is made to allegorical interpretation, not only of the parables and other words of Jesus but of events from his life, and also of the words of Paul; to the further development of the cosmological statements of the New Testament; and to the use of number-symbolism. There are cases of straightforward simple application of the text, but there are also cases of apologetic interpretation. Towards the end we have this comment: that these exegetes made use of the rules of interpretation current in their time, as we can see by comparing them with Paul, or the interpreters of Homer, or Philo of Alexandria. It is only rarely that we can charge them with arbitrary procedure. The literal interpretation is usually to be found in sections dealing with cosmology or soteriology, or in purely ethical sections. And these Valentinian interpreters have no interest in attaining to a historical grasp of the life of Jesus. This last sentence, incidentally, reflects one of the dominant interests of New Testament scholarship in the period when Barth's book was written.

The picture drawn by Barth is broadly confirmed by the outline of Gnostic exegesis presented by H. E. W. Turner in *The*

---

[4] *Die Interpretation des Neuen Testaments in der valentinianischen Gnosis* (*TU* 37.3, Leipzig 1911).

Pattern of Christian Truth.[5] He notes that there are few references to incidents of Jesus' life, but much use of parables and hard sayings. Passages from the Fourth Gospel are of frequent occurrence, but it is used as a source-book rather than a source, raided for proof-texts without any real attempt to treat it as a whole—a point confirmed in its turn by the remarks of C. K. Barrett quoted in the previous chapter.[6] In Paul, selection is made of the more mysterious passages, and here Turner adds a noteworthy comment: 'Those who like Bultmann find Gnostic motifs already present in St. Paul would hold that here they were merely receiving their own with usury, but it is more probable that they were selecting isolated "numinous expressions" or perhaps even bridge words with little regard for what lay on the other side.' To look at it from another angle, there is no question, as we have already seen, that the terminology and many of the ideas employed in Gnosticism were already current in the pre-Christian period, and even certain combinations of these ideas; but we still have to ask if they already possessed a Gnostic connotation.

Here the European visitor to America has a useful analogy at hand, although of course no analogy is ever complete or perfect. The traveller cannot fail to observe various customs, usages and other aspects of American life which are already familiar, for the simple reason that they are part of the heritage from the settlers of a by-gone age. One cannot however understand 'the American way of life' merely by tracing back particular elements to their ultimate origins in Europe or elsewhere—due allowance has to be made for the country itself, its climate, the heritage of its history. Many factors have contributed to the moulding of something that is in many ways unique, however close its affinities with the ways of certain other peoples. Some elements again have been developed further than in the lands of their origin, or united with elements from other sources to form something new; and sometimes the similarities are due not to European influence upon America but to American influence upon Europe. So it is with Gnosticism—we must beware of the

---

[5] *The Pattern of Christian Truth*, pp. 232 ff. Cf. also Norbert Brox, *Offenbarung, Gnosis u. gnostischer Mythos bei Irenäus von Lyon*, (Salzburg 1966), esp. pp. 56 ff.

[6] See above, p. 46.

facile assumption that the occurrence of a single element, or even a group of elements, is sufficient to demonstrate the existence of anything that may truly be called Gnostic. Where the New Testament is concerned we have to explore not one but many possibilities: direct indebtedness on one side or the other, dependence on some common background of thought and ideas, mutual influence, and so on. In particular we have to allow for the convergence of ideas, for the tendency to assume that what is similar is in fact the same. The Jewish doctrine of the Two Ages, for example, is not identical with the Platonic distinction between the visible world and the intelligible, but the two could be and were confused, and not only in the ancient world.

Further on, Turner notes the Gnostic penchant for numerical symbolism, and 'the flight from history which characterises their systems as a whole'. 'The factual side of the Biblical record is systematically undervalued. Hence arises their persistent neglect of the context in which their quotations are set. Their references to Biblical incident spiritualise away the basis upon which it rests.' Turner later quotes the extract from Theodotus[7] which deals with the teaching method of Jesus: first mystically and typically, secondly by parables and dark sayings, and finally in open revelation. Here it should be noted that the Gnostics were not the only ones to find the parables and sayings obscure: 'for the Primitive Church,' writes Otto Piper,[8] 'the story of Jesus presented no special problem, while they discovered a depth of meaning in his sayings, which was not easily probed.' As words of the Lord, these sayings were significant and important; was it not written 'You have the words of eternal life' (John 6.68)? But detached from the context in which they were originally spoken, sometimes without even a clue to the situation to which they were addressed, they presented a problem to the would-be interpreter. Indeed there are indications of such a situation as early as the canonical Gospels themselves, for example in Mark's section on the significance of the parables (Mk. 4). Transported from Palestine in the time of Jesus into a wider world, and into the situation of a later age, the parables and sayings inevitably became mysterious and enigmatic; but

[7] Clem. Alex., *Excerpta ex Theodoto*, (ed. Casey, London 1934; Sagnard, Paris 1948).
[8] *Princeton Seminary Bulletin* 53, (1959), pp. 19 f.

they were the words of the Lord and words of life, and therefore demanded explanation. 'He who finds the interpretation of these words,' says the Gospel of Thomas (log. 1), 'shall not taste of death.' The same attitude could readily have been adopted by others, not simply towards the sayings recorded in Thomas but towards the teaching of Jesus generally.

At another point Turner compares the methods of Heracleon and Origen.[8a] They are, he says, 'fundamentally at one in their use of symbolic interpretation', but 'the significant feature in the work of Heracleon is not the employment of allegory but the standard of reference which determines its application . . . His chief defect lay in importing his own doctrinal pre-suppositions into the text instead of applying himself to the elucidation of the real meaning of his author.' Despite the centuries that have passed, there is something here that is still of relevance. The Warrack lecturer on preaching at the University of St. Andrews in 1964 devoted one of his lectures to '*The Homiletic Sin of Eisegesis*'.[9]

So much for general background. What do the texts reveal— in particular the latest discoveries? At the outset we are faced with a problem of identification. Some of these texts belong quite definitely and unmistakably to *Christian* Gnosticism, and the number of New Testament quotations which they certainly contain makes it the more probable that the doubtful cases should be classed at least as allusions. But what of those texts in which the Christian element is comparatively slight? The Apocalypse of Adam, for example, has a passage about a child born of a virgin who was driven out of his city with his mother and taken to a desert place.[10] Here the editor notes that one might think of Rev. 12.5, or rather of its mythological background. One's instinctive reaction may be to ask 'Why not just Rev. 12.5 alone?'; but this would be to beg the whole question. There are points at which one might be inclined to discover Christian influence in this document, echoes of or allusions to New

[8a] Cf. M. Simonetti, *Vetera Christianorum* 3, (1966), pp. 3–75.
[9] James T. Cleland, *Preaching to be Understood*, (Nashville 1965), pp. 59 ff.
[10] Böhlig-Labib, *Koptisch-gnostische Apokalypsen aus Codex V von Nag Hammadi*, (Halle-Wittenburg 1963), p. 111. It should be noted that this is but one of fourteen successive statements about the coming of the Phoster [see Böhlig's discussion, op. cit., pp. 91 ff.].

Testament material, but in no case is such influence incontrovertible; and to limit our attention to possible Christian influence is to commit the very error against which warning was given above in relation to alleged Gnostic influence on the New Testament. The motif of 'the man born to be king', in one form or another, is both old and widespread. In Greek mythology, to go no further afield, there are the stories of Jason and Perseus; and so far as the background of Rev. 12 is concerned there is the legend of the birth of Apollo.[11] From a later age one might also recall, as a parallel to the Apocalypse of Adam, the story in the life of John the Baptist according to Serapion,[12] while in the Old Testament there is the episode of Hagar and Ishmael. But while each of these may show certain points of contact with the passage in the Apocalypse of Adam it would be too much to claim any one of them as its source. Nor should we lay too much stress on the occurrence in this Apocalypse of the word παρθένος, which incidentally does not appear in Rev. 12. If it is to be taken strictly, in the sense of virginity, it would presumably be applicable to Danae, the mother of Perseus; but whether it is to be taken strictly is itself matter for discussion.[13] In short, while we may perhaps suspect an allusion to Rev. 12.5 in the Apocalypse of Adam, we cannot be certain; we have to make allowance for the possibility of other influences.

The Gospel of Thomas presents a different problem, for here our approach will differ according to our decision as to the nature of this document. If we assume it to be based on our Gospels, then it becomes a source of information for Gnostic use of the Gospels; but if we have reason to suspect that any given saying goes back to an independent tradition, then it is another matter. Again, even when we have clear evidence for the use of our New Testament, the allusions may not be easy to detect, or it may be impossible to affirm with confidence that the author had a particular passage in mind when he wrote. When we read in the Gospel of Philip, for example, the words 'Then the slaves

---

[11] On the interpretation of this passage see P. Prigent, *Apocalypse 12. Histoire de l'exégèse*, (Tübingen 1959).

[12] Hennecke-Schneemelcher, *NT Apocrypha*, i, (ET: London 1963), pp. 414 ff.

[13] Cf. Delling, *TWB*, v, pp. 824 ff.; J. M. Ford, *NTS* 12, (1966), pp. 293 ff.

will be free, and the captives delivered', are we to think of Luke
4.8? Or Romans 7.23? Or Ephesians 4.8? Does a contrast of
slave and son, with a reference to inheritance in the context,
necessarily imply a knowledge of Gal. 4.7? Finally, we must be
careful about the conclusions we draw, for example with reference to the history of the Canon. Do such references and
allusions, or even direct quotations, indicate that the books in
question were already of canonical status, or merely that they
were known and accorded a certain recognition? Are we justified
in forming an estimate of the date of one of these documents and
then, on the basis of this dating, drawing from the quotations in
that document the conclusion that the development of the
Canon was rather more rapid than was formerly believed; or
should we argue conversely that the use of the New Testament,
reflecting as it does a later stage in the development of the
Canon, must be held to show that the document cannot be so
early? When it comes to Textual Criticism, should we quote
these texts as evidence for variant readings in New Testament
passages, or as possible indications of the source of these variants? The Gospel of Thomas again is a case in point: if it is
dependent on our Gospels, then its variants rank with the
patristic quotations (with of course due regard to the possibility
of tendentious modification) as evidence for the text of the
Gospels in a particular area at a particular time; but if it is
independent, then Thomas may itself have been the source of
certain variants in the manuscript tradition. The problem is of
course complicated by the further question of the relation
between Thomas and the Diatessaron: which came first? Did
Tatian use Thomas, or Thomas Tatian, or did both independently draw on the same older source?

To turn to specific instances, one example of the kind of thing
that could happen is not precisely Gnostic, although it stands in
the Gnostic tradition. Orosius says of Priscillian that he sought
to establish his dualistic doctrine 'from a certain book entitled
Memoria Apostolorum, wherein the Saviour appears to be questioned by the disciples in secret, and to show from the Gospel
parable which has 'The sower went forth to sow' that he was not
a good sower, asserting that if he had been good he would not
have been neglectful, or cast seed 'by the wayside' or 'on stony
places' or 'in untilled soil'; wishing it to be understood that the

sower is he who scatters captive souls in diverse bodies as he wills.[14] Here the interpretation supplied in Mark is completely ignored, and the parable is interpreted in the light of Gnostic doctrine.

The parable of the Good Samaritan is quoted in the Gospel of Philip (111) in the context of a difficult passage, the point of which appears to be that the fragrance of a perfume is enjoyed not only by those who wear it but by others in their company, so long as the wearers are present. So the Gnostic imparts something of his own fragrance, but only so long as he is in this world. When he returns to the Pleroma, merely material men are left to their own evil odour. Then comes the reference: 'The Samaritan gave nothing to the wounded man except wine and oil. It is nothing other than the ointment. And he (or it?) healed the wounds. For love covereth a multitude of sins.' Here of course we may recall the allegorisation of the parable in Origen and Augustine;[15] but in Philip the wine and the oil are specifically identified with the ointment of the chrism. The prominence given in Philip to this sacrament, incidentally, sheds a new light on the references to a chrism in 1 John, although here again it is all too easy to read too much into the text.[16] The way in which the term is introduced in 1 John does suggest polemic against a false claim to the possession of a superior 'unction' on the part of the opposition; but we have no evidence at this stage for a sacrament with oil, such as was practised by the later Gnostic sects. On the other hand the metaphorical use of the term surely implies some reality which might serve as the basis for the metaphor. Another feature of the passage in Philip is of course the introduction of a verse from 1 Peter—one of those sayings which evidently became proverbial at an early stage, as they still are with us.

Such association and combination of texts drawn from diverse sources is characteristic. The Treatise on the Resurrection, for example, says:

[14] Hennecke-Schneemelcher, i, p. 266.
[15] Origen, *Hom. in Luc.*, xxxiv, [*GCS*, ix, p. 201 f.]; Augustine, *Quaest. Evang.*, ii.19; already in germ in Iren. *adv. haer.* 3.18.2 Harvey. Cf. Daniélou, *Origen*, (ET: London 1955), pp. 196 f., *Sacramentum Futuri*, (Paris 1950), pp. 246 f.
[16] Cf. Schnackenburg, *Die Johannesbriefe*, (Freiburg 1963), pp. 152 f.

As the Apostle said, we suffered with him and we arose with him, and we went to heaven with him.

(45.24–28)

Here the Apostle is manifestly Paul, the Apostle *par excellence* for the second century, but this is not an exact quotation; it is an amalgam of Pauline texts which, as it happens, implies the heresy refuted in the Pastorals, that the resurrection is already past.[17] In such cases it is sometimes exceptionally difficult to determine whether the writer is consciously selecting the material to suit his own purposes, giving a Pauline ring to what is actually Gnostic doctrine; or whether he is quoting loosely and from memory; or finally whether he is merely echoing the Pauline words and phrases, without any intention of accurately reproducing Paul's statements or his teaching. Anyone familiar with the Bible knows how readily its language springs to mind, offering an appropriate word or phrase, even in quite non-theological and even non-religious contexts; and it is clearly evident that many of the Gnostics were thoroughly steeped in the New Testament literature.

One of the more remarkable examples of this kind of association occurs in the Gospel of Thomas (log. 79):

A woman in the crowd said to him: Blessed is the womb which bore thee, and the breasts which nourished thee. He said to her: Blessed are they who have heard the word of the Father, and have kept it in truth. For there shall be days when you will say: Blessed is that womb which has not conceived, and those breasts which have not given suck.[18]

The first part of this logion has a parallel in Luke 11.27–28, but Thomas adds the words 'in truth' and substitutes 'which nourished thee' for 'which thou hast sucked'. The parallel to the second part is Luke 23.39, where as it happens some manuscripts read ἔθρεψαν, 'nourished', and others ἐθήλασαν, 'given suck'. There is room here for discussion as to the bearing of the readings in Thomas on the textual question in Luke: what is the significance of agreement between Thomas on the

---

[17] Cf. Rom. 8.17; Col. 3.1–4; Eph. 2.5–6 [see Malinine etc., *De Resurrectione*, (Zürich 1963), p. 27].

[18] See most recently W. Schrage, *Das Verhältnis des Thomas-Evangeliums zur synoptischen Tradition*, (Beiheft 29 zur *ZNW*, Berlin 1964), pp. 164 ff.

one hand and a whole series of witnesses to Luke on the other, including agreements at one point with the Sahidic version of Luke 23.29, at another with the Bohairic of Luke 11.27? A more important and indeed prior question is that of the relation between Thomas and Luke itself. The natural assumption is that Thomas drew upon Luke, but there is a danger here of assuming at the outset the very conclusion which has to be proved. Both the Lucan parallels belong to Luke's special tradition, so that we have no direct evidence for the form in which they came to Luke. In Thomas the passage as a whole fits so well together that it is legitimate to question whether *without the Lucan parallels* we should ever have suspected that the two parts did not originally belong together. We have therefore to reckon with the possibility that the passage was originally a unity, and raise the further questions: Is Thomas in fact combining two passages from Luke, or does this logion perhaps go back to tradition independent of Luke? Could it be that it was Luke who was responsible for the separation of the two parts, and not Thomas who combined them?

A decision here must rest upon what we can discover about the methods of the two authors. We know from comparison with Matthew that Luke generally adheres to the order of Q, keeping separate sayings which in Matthew are assembled together. Similarly, where Matthew tends to conflate Mark and Q, Luke keeps the material separate, resuming Mark's order again after introducing Q material. The implication is that it is Matthew's habit to conflate, whereas Luke retains the order of his sources. Only on the assumption that Luke used Matthew could it be argued that it was his practice to break up what was already combined, but against this assumption there are serious objections. On the other hand, there is in Thomas evidence in abundance for the compiler's tendency to combine material from different sources. Accordingly, the probability at this point favours the originality of Luke, but it should be noted (a) that it is a probability, and not an absolute certainty; the alternative, that it is Thomas who preserves the original form, remains at least a possibility; and (b) that conclusions drawn from this one saying are not necessarily valid for all the sayings in the Gospel of Thomas.

At the Crucifixion, according to the Gospels, 'the veil of the

Temple was rent in twain, from top to bottom.' In one apocryphal Gospel it is the lintel of the Temple which falls, but in the Epistle to the Hebrews the rending of the veil is made the basis of theological interpretation: it symbolises the free and unhindered access to God achieved for all through the death of Christ. Now the Gospel of Philip has two references to the veil. The first unfortunately occurs in a badly damaged passage, and all that we can really say is that the Gospel text is quoted, with the words 'For it was fitting for some from below to go upward.' The second passage however is extant in full:

> The veil at first concealed how God controlled the creation, but when the veil is rent and the things within are exposed this house will be left deserted, or rather will be [destroyed]. But the whole deity will not flee [from] these places again into the holy of the holy [ones], for it will not be able to mix with the [unmixed light and] the [flawless] pleroma, but will be under the wings of the Cross [and under its] arms. This ark will be [for them] deliverance when the flood of water becomes powerful over them. If some are in the tribe of the priesthood, these will be able to go within the veil with the high priest. Because of this the veil was not rent at the top only, since it would be open only for those above; nor was it rent at the bottom only, since it would be revealed only to those below; but it was rent from top to bottom. Those above opened to us who are below, in order that we might go in to the secret of the truth . . .
>
> (Philip 125)

Here a whole speculation has been spun out of the apparently quite subsidiary point that the veil was rent 'from top to bottom'. The veil itself has become the firmament which separates the material world from the higher realms. The 'whole deity' is the Demiurge with his powers, who cannot ascend into the Pleroma but only to the region immediately beneath it, separated from it by the barrier of the Cross—a feature of the Valentinian system. As R. M. Grant has put it, 'This passage is significant for Valentinian exegesis of the New Testament. It shows that these Gnostics were busy at work combining various New Testament passages, especially the more mysterious ones, in an effort to produce new mysteries and fit them into their system. It is also significant for the study of exegesis in general,

F

for it shows the dangers of allegorisation without the controls provided either by common sense or by some dogmatic system with roots on earth.'[19] It may be worth recalling the words of C. H. Dodd:[20] 'In the controversy with Gnosticism in the second and third centuries the main point at issue was whether the Christian faith could be detached from its biblical and historical basis and presented as a form of Hellenistic theosophy', or those of Bultmann:[21] 'Insofar as Christian preaching remained true to the tradition of the Old Testament and Judaism and of the earliest Church, *definitive contrasts between it and Gnosticism* are straightway apparent.'

In this passage of Philip, the 'house left desolate' comes from one passage of Matthew, 'destroyed' from another, 'under the wings' from a third; the ark recalls Hebrews 11.4 if we are thinking in terms of the Temple, but a more obvious reference is to the ark of Noah. Grant suggests that the author 'moves imaginatively from one ark to the other'. In any case we may refer to 1 Peter 3.20. Here, then, we have a whole series of New Testament texts woven together and pressed into the service of Valentinian theory.

Another example deals with the problem of the resurrection:[22]

> Some are afraid lest they rise naked. Because of this they wish to rise in the flesh, and they do not know that those who bear the flesh [it is they who are] naked; those who . . . themselves to unclothe themselves [it is they who are] not naked. 'Flesh [and blood shall] not inherit the Kingdom [of God].' What is this which will not inherit? This which we have. But what is this which will inherit? That which belongs to Jesus with his blood. Because of this he said: He who shall not eat my flesh and drink my blood has no life in him. What is it? His flesh is the logos, and his blood is the Holy Spirit. He who has received these has food and drink and clothing. For myself, I find fault with the others who say that it will not rise. Then both of these are at fault. Thou sayest that the flesh will not

[19] *Journal of Biblical Literature* 79, (1960), p. 8. On the whole passage cf. Wilson, *The Gospel of Philip*, (London and New York 1962), pp. 190 ff.

[20] *According to the Scriptures*, (London 1952), pp. 136 f.

[21] *Theology of the NT*, i, (ET: London 1952), p. 168.

[22] Cf. J. Zandee, *Nederlands Theol. Tijdschr.* 16, pp. 361 ff.; Wilson, op. cit., pp. 87 ff.

rise; but tell me what will rise, that we may honour thee. Thou sayest the spirit in the flesh, and it is also this light in the flesh. But this too is a logos which is in the flesh, for whatever thou shalt say thou sayest nothing outside the flesh. It is necessary to rise in this flesh, in which everything exists.

(Philip 23)

At first sight, the author is frankly inconsistent here: first he denies the doctrine of the resurrection of the flesh, then he defends it. But when we compare the Treatise on the Resurrection and other parts of the Gospel of Philip it becomes plain that the situation is rather more complicated. A later passage (72) seems to make a distinction between the flesh of Jesus, which is 'true' flesh, and a flesh which is only an image of the true— which is a simple inversion of Paul's words in Romans about 'the likeness of sinful flesh'. The Letter of James in the Codex Jung makes Jesus say *after the Resurrection*: 'from now I shall unclothe myself in order that I may be clothed'. And there is a passage in the Ascension of Isaiah (9.9) in which the prophet sees 'Enoch and all who were with him' stripped of their earthly garments and arrayed in their heavenly robes, like the angels in glory.

It is commonly said that the Gnostics denied the resurrection of the flesh, on the ground that the flesh (being material) was evil and could have no part in the world of the spirit. This may be true of some Gnostics, but not for the group with which we are here concerned; or rather, while it is indeed *ultimately* true they introduced a further stage in the process. The idea here seems to be that the Gnostic must rise in the flesh, but only in order to be stripped of the garment of the flesh and put on his heavenly robe—in other words, they affirmed the Pauline doctrine but gave to it a twist of their own. In this case, the author of Philip first rejects the idea of a mere resurrection of the flesh, and then the 'Greek' conception that only the soul or spirit is immortal. In any event we have here allusions to three New Testament texts: 2 Cor. 5.3, 1 Cor. 15.50 and John 6.53 ff.—all once more pressed into the service of Gnostic theory. The exposition of the Johannine passage presents another feature of Gnostic exegesis in its identification of the flesh and blood there mentioned with the Logos and the Holy Spirit. That such methods were not confined to the Gnostics is shown by Ignatius, who identifies the flesh with faith and the blood with love (*Trall.* 8; cf. Ign. *Rom.* 7.3).

This passion for identification appears also in the Gnostic penchant for number-symbolism, neatly summarised by Turner:[23] 'The total number of Valentinian aeons is prefigured in the thirty years of the hidden life of our Lord and the total of the hours at which the labourers were called into the Vineyard. These divide into two groups of twelve and eighteen. The former are found in the number of disciples, the age at which our Lord paid His visit to the Temple, and the duration of the illness of the woman with the issue of blood. The Fall of Sophia corresponds with the Fall of the last disciple. The remaining group are represented in the eighteen months after the Resurrection during which, according to one tradition, our Lord taught Gnosis to his disciples. It is also the numerical value of the first two letters of the name of Jesus. Six was the number of evil and forty of the spiritual seed. Thus the forty-six years in which the Temple was built (John 2.20) bears the composite meaning of the indwelling of the spiritual seed in matter. The six husbands of the Samaritan woman also represent matter.' And so one could go on. There is justification for the comment of Henry Chadwick,[24] that the trouble with the Gnostics was not that they tried to apply reason to the Scriptures, but that they did not apply it enough. They are prone to allegory, but they can be literalists when it suits them, when a literal interpretation provides the means for adapting some scriptural passage to their own theories. Indeed, the distinction commonly drawn between literal and allegorical interpretation requires some modification here, for literalism and allegory can go hand in hand. The Gnostics often adhere to the literal *words* of Scripture, but have no regard for the literal *meaning* of the text as it stands. The words are accepted, but they are made to signify something quite different. The essential point is that it is the Gnostic theories which are dominant, and not the plain meaning of the Biblical text.

[23] *The Pattern of Christian Truth*, p. 236.

[24] In a lecture at St. Andrews. Cf. his *Early Christian Thought and the Classical Tradition*, (Oxford 1966), p. 9, and Brox, *Offenbarung, Gnosis u. gnostischer Mythos*, p. 17. The Gnostic texts often show a negative attitude to philosophy [cf. Quispel, *Gnosis als Weltreligion*, (Zürich 1951), pp. 23 f. and see further the texts discussed below].

Once again, however, it has to be noted that the Gnostics were not alone. Matthew, for example, frequently cites Old Testament passages the fulfilment of which he claims to find in New Testament events. The Epistle of Barnabas has a famous passage (9.8) in which the number of Abraham's servants in Gen. 14.14 is interpreted in terms of Jesus and the Cross (18 in Greek is *IH*, the first two letters of the name of Jesus; 300 is *T*, the symbol of the Cross). Philo of Alexandria devotes considerable attention to number symbolism, especially in relation to the numbers six, seven and ten; the first of these, incidentally, is given a very different interpretation from that of the Gnostics, for to Philo it is a perfect number (*Leg. alleg.* 1.3 ff.). It is not surprising that Gnostic exegesis provoked the early Fathers to exasperation, for the Gnostics were using the Church's books and employing the self-same methods of interpretation, but producing very different results.

In this connection it may be observed, as Barth already noted, that the Gnostics did not feel themselves bound to any one exegesis of any particular passage. On the Cry of Dereliction, for example, Barth notes that for the Gnostic it had on the lips of the Redeemer a blasphemous ring, and was therefore assigned to Sophia;[25] but the Gospel of Philip quotes it (72) with the express statement 'He said these words on the Cross'. Luke 1.35 appears to have been differently interpreted by Philip on the one hand (17; cf. 82) and the Excerpta ex Theodoto on the other (59–60). Barth draws a contrast between the ethical tension of Paul's words in Rom. 7.18 f. and the 'intellectualism' of John 8.32; but both these passages are echoed in Philip, and in the same context (Philip 123). And we have two divergent interpretations of the parable of the Lost Sheep. The Gospel of Truth finds an explanation in terms of number-symbolism:

He is the Shepherd who abandoned the ninety-nine sheep which had not gone astray. He went in search of that one which had strayed. He rejoiced when he found it. For ninety-nine is a number which is in the left hand, which encompasses it. But as soon as the one is found the whole number passes over to the right. Thus it is with him who lacks the one, that is to say, the entire right hand, which attracts that which is

[25] *Die Interpretation des Neuen Testaments*, p. 68; cf. Wilson, *The Gospel of Philip*, p. 135.

lacking and takes it away from the left side, and passes over to the right; and in this way the number becomes a hundred.

(31.35 ff.)

In the Gospel of Thomas, however, we find:

> The Kingdom is like a shepherd who had a hundred sheep. One of them, the biggest, went astray. He left the ninety-nine and sought after the one till he found it. When he had laboured, he said to the sheep: I love thee more than the ninety-nine.

(log. 107)

It is at least open to question whether we ought to use the one to explain the other.

Another of the parables in Thomas is that of the treasure (log. 109):

> The Kingdom is like a man who had in his field a [hidden] treasure about which he did not know; and [after] he died he left it to his [son. The] son also did not know; he took (possesson of) that field and sold it. The man who bought it came to plough, and [found] the treasure. He began to lend money at interest to whomsoever he chose.

The differences from Matthew's parable are considerable, and the whole point has been changed. In Matthew the treasure, like the pearl of great price, is something so precious that a man will go to any lengths to obtain it. Here in Thomas various explanations are possible: we may have the Gnostic classification of men into material, psychic and spiritual; or it may be that the man and his son represent Jews and Christians, who possess the treasure of Gnosis in the Scriptures without knowing it—only the Gnostic is able, in the words of the opening saying in Thomas, to find the interpretation of these words, hidden and secret words.[26] Or again the treasure, like the leaven or the grain of mustard-seed, may signify the divine self within man. Most men do not suspect what a treasure is laid up within them, and hence do not find 'the treasure in their field'; that is, they do not attain to a recognition of their true divine nature.[27] This

[26] A suggestion made by Dr. R. E. Taylor.

[27] Gärtner, *The Theology of the Gospel of Thomas*, (London 1961), p. 237; Haenchen, *Die Botschaft des Thomas-Evangeliums*, (Berlin 1961), p. 47; Schrage op. cit. [n. 18 above] pp. 196 ff.

third interpretation is supported by the fact that Hippolytus says the Naassenes identified the Kingdom with the treasure and the leaven (*Ref.* V.8.8) and with the mustard-seed (ibid. V.9.6); but this does not necessarily mean that other interpretations are either impossible or irrelevant. A further point is that a closer parallel than Matthew is to be found in a second-century Rabbinic text, and in one of Aesop's fables. The Gnostics here are elaborating their scriptural interpretation with the help of extraneous material.

The Gospel of Thomas, of course, presents the problem: is it or is it not Gnostic? It is perfectly possible to show how many of these mysterious sayings take on a meaning when they are translated into Gnostic terms, or rather interpreted in the light of our knowledge, from other sources, of Gnostic symbolism; but does this mean that this was their meaning from the outset? Was Thomas a Gnostic composition, or should we not reckon with the possibility that in its present form it is the result of a process of adaptation, and that much of the material originally had nothing to do with Gnosticism at all? Here we are confronted again with the problem which has already risen in connection with the New Testament: does the fact that a passage, or a document, can be read and understood in terms of Gnosticism mean that it is simply to be labelled Gnostic? To take but one example, the parable of the pearl:

> The Kingdom of the Father is like a merchant who had a load (of goods) and found a pearl. That merchant was wise. He sold the load, and bought for himself the pearl alone. You also, seek after his treasure which does not perish but endures, where moth does not enter to devour, nor does worm destroy.
> (log. 76)

Here again we have the combination of sayings from different passages, but the question for the present concerns the interpretation of the pearl.[28] In Matthew the pearl, like the treasure, is a symbol of the Kingdom, something of such surpassing value that a man will give up all he has to win it. But the Naassenes, interpreting the Matthaean saying about casting pearls before swine (Matt. 7.6, cf. Thomas 93), said that 'understanding and intelligences and men' (i.e. in Jonas' words, the 'living' elements

[28] Cf. above, pp. 19f.

in the physical cosmos) were 'the pearls of that Formless One cast into the formation (i.e. the body).' Later on in the Acts of Thomas, we have the famous Hymn of the Pearl, and in the Manichean Kephalaia there is an allegory which identifies the pearl with the soul. The question is: are we to interpret Thomas in terms of Matthew, or of the Manichean Kephalaia?

The Naassenes provide some justification for the latter procedure, the more especially in view of the parallels which have been noted; but here again we must ask: What is the significance of these parallels? Do they imply a Naassene origin for Thomas, or merely that the Naassenes used this document? It has been observed above that Hippolytus' account of the Naassenes seems to provide a clue to the understanding of some of these sayings. Grant and Freedman[29] note a number of similarities: 'significant examples of Gnostic interweaving' in the Naassene use of the Gospels, 'a tendency to combine words found in different contexts in order to bring out their Gnostic meaning.' Almost one might conclude that Thomas is a Naassene document, but Grant and Freedman merely say that the Naassenes knew and used Thomas, and that they 'quote several gospel sayings in a way which seems to reflect Thomas'. The point for their purpose is the similarity of method. More recently Haenchen[30] has given warning against an over-hasty association of Thomas with the Naassenes, affirming that it is *not* a Naassene gospel. There was of course nothing at all to prevent one school of Gnostics from using, quoting or adapting a document composed by another school, unless it was strictly reserved for members of the school of its origin; and we know that they did make use of 'orthodox' documents such as the New Testament writings themselves.

The point here is that it is by no means difficult to establish a table of correspondences: the robbers are the planetary powers who rule the destinies of men and hold the soul in subjection in the prison of the body; little children are the Gnostics; sleep and intoxication represent man's unregenerate state in this life, apart from the saving Gnosis, and so on. But we are left again and again with the question whether this table is in fact applicable in any given situation, whether for example it is even legitimate to apply it to the study of a New Testament text, to

[29] *The Secret Sayings of Jesus,* (London 1960), pp. 92 ff.
[30] *Botschaft,* p. 10.

the exclusion of what must seem the plain and natural meaning. To employ such a table of correspondences where it is not applicable is to find Gnosis and Gnosticism where none in fact exists, and to commit the very error of which the Gnostics themselves were guilty. Yet at times it is exceptionally difficult to be sure.

It was noted in the previous chapter that the references to the Gospels in Leisegang's index appear in most cases to relate to Gnostic re-interpretation of Gospel material. Basilides for example, according to Hippolytus,[31] says 'That everything has its own appointed seasons is sufficiently proved by the Saviour when he says "My hour is not yet come" (John 2.4), and by the Magi who saw the star (Matt. 2.1–2).' This of course is not specifically Gnostic; but a little earlier we have the passage:

The light which came down from the Ogdoad above to the son of the Hebdomad descended from the Hebdomad upon Jesus, the son of Mary, and he was enlightened, being set on fire by the light which shone into him. This is that which was spoken, 'Holy Spirit will come upon you', that which came down from the Sonship through the intermediate spirit upon the Ogdoad and the Hebdomad, as far as to Mary, 'and power of the Most High will overshadow you', the power of judgment from the height above through the demiurge as far as the creation, that which is of the son.[32]

This interpretation of Luke 1.35 does have some connection with the literal meaning of the verse, but it has been completely transposed into a Gnostic context and adapted to the needs of Basilides' system. A few lines further on there is an echo of Romans (8.19 and 22): the creation groans until now and is tormented and awaits the revelation of the sons of God, in order that all the men of the Sonship may ascend hence. Basilides evidently is weaving New Testament texts together into new patterns of his own design. Other examples of a similar kind may be found in abundance.

One point of some interest in this connection is that the same

[31] Hippol. *Ref.*, vii. 27.5 [Völker, *Quellen zur Geschichte der christlichen Gnosis*, (Tübingen 1932), p. 55].
[32] ibid., vii.26.8 f. [Völker, *Quellen*, p. 54]. For the use of Luke 1.35 cf. Philip 17 [Wilson, *The Gospel of Philip*, pp. 80 ff.], and *Exc. ex Theodoto* 59–60.

kind of use is made of Ephesians and Colossians. According to Ptolemy,[33] Christ on his return to the Pleroma was unwilling to descend a second time at the appeal of the abandoned Sophia, and sent the Paraclete, that is, the Saviour, 'the Father giving to him all power and handing over all under his authority, and the Aeons likewise, that "in him all things might be created, visible and invisible, thrones, deities, lordships",' (Col. 1.16). According to the Peratae,[34] 'the man Christ, who descended in the times of Herod, had a threefold nature, three bodies and three powers, since he contained in himself all the compounds and powers of the three parts of the cosmos. "And this is the meaning of the saying: He resolved that the whole fullness should dwell in him bodily, and that the whole Godhead should be in him" (Col. 2.9, cf. 1.19).' The Naassenes[35] in their exposition of the myth of Attis refer to the eternal essence 'where there is neither male nor female, but a new creation, a new man' (cf. Gal. 3.28, 6.15, 2 Cor. 5.17, Eph. 2.15, 4.24). As Leisegang puts it,[36] 'The motif of the castration of Attis is interpreted to mean that the originally bisexual Logos breaks apart within the Creation, and on earth through contact with matter is separated into a male and a female sex, only to be restored to heaven through the redemption of the male part alone. This motif is rediscovered in the Ephesians passages' (which are then quoted). It is evident from these examples that the New Testament material is here re-interpreted, sometimes with great ingenuity, to support some quite different kind of theory.

The point for present purposes is however that in these last instances we have Gnostic adaptation of passages from documents which are often claimed to have themselves been subject to the influence of Gnosticism. To argue that Paul, or his disciple, took such motifs from existing Gnostic theories which he did not understand and employed them for his own ends, and that the Gnostics later in apparently adapting Paul were in fact restoring the real and original meaning, is to make a whole series of assumptions for which there is no justification. On the contrary, the Gnostic adaptation of such passages must surely

[33] Ap. Iren. *Adv. haer.*, i.1.8 [Harvey 1, p. 38].
[34] Hippol. *Ref.*, v.12.5.
[35] Hippol. *Ref.*, v.7.15 [Völker, *Quellen*, p. 13].
[36] *Die Gnosis*, (Stuttgart 1955), p. 134.

be held to weaken the theory that such motifs were truly Gnostic in the first place. At the very least these examples suggest the need for caution in the identification of Gnostic influence in the New Testament. The simplest and most obvious explanation is that the Gnostics were using the New Testament itself.

A more difficult question is whether it was the New Testament which was the basis for such speculations, or whether the New Testament allusions, echoes and quotations are merely secondary embellishment. There are cases in which a particular motif appears to have developed out of speculation based on a New Testament passage, but there are also cases where the New Testament element can be removed from a document without essential damage to its structure. A notable example is the Naassene document,[37] where Reitzenstein separated a 'purely pagan document' from the Christian commentary with which it is interwoven; however, as Goppelt says, 'the Christian traits prove to be later interpolation, but the Old Testament ones cannot be detached', which may be a further pointer to a Jewish form of Gnosticism lying behind the Christian. Other examples are the Berlin Gospel of Mary, perhaps also the Apocryphon of John, and also the Sophia Jesu Christi.[38] We can therefore claim with some confidence the Christianisation of certain texts, but whether these texts were originally not only non-Christian but pre-Christian is another question.

Approaching this question from another angle, C. H. Dodd[39] long ago pointed out that the Hermetic *Poimandres* shows no dependence on Christian writings, although its thought does have affinities with some aspects of early Christian thought, and more particularly with Gnosticism. Indeed 'the Valentinian system, apart from its definitely Christian elements, has the aspect of an elaboration of a system very like that of the *Poimandres*', and conversely the Poimandres 'has the aspect, not of a simplification of something more elaborate, but of an

---

[37] Cf. Reitzenstein, *Poimandres*, (Leipzig 1904), pp. 81 ff., but see also Burkitt in *JTS* 26 (1925) 117 ff.; L. Goppelt, *Christentum u. Judentum*, (Gütersloh 1954), p. 134 [= *Jesus, Paul and Judaism*, (New York 1964), p. 179].

[38] See chapter 5 below.

[39] *The Bible and the Greeks*, (London 1935), pp. 208–9.

experiment in the direction in which Valentinus travelled to a further stage.' The date of the Corpus Hermeticum is by no means certain, and in its present form the collection may be comparatively late, but some of the documents may date from the second Christian century and 'give the impression of being the deposit of many years of oral teaching, as well as of reflection and mystical meditation.'[40] If this be so, then the Hermetica would serve to show something of the kind of speculation current in certain circles already in the first century, and there would be full justification for Dodd's conclusion, that at an early stage in its career 'Christianity attracted the attention of thinkers who stood in the line of development of which the *Poimandres* is a representative', and who introduced the figure of Christ, with a varying measure of other Christian elements, into their speculations to produce the Gnostic systems.

It is no wonder that such fathers as Irenaeus waxed wroth with the Gnostics, for they were mishandling the Church's scriptures, and moreover they were doing so on principles and methods which the 'orthodox' themselves employed; for we can observe the use of the same methods and the same principles even in the works of the opponents of Gnosticism. The vital difference lay not so much in the methods as in the controlling factor: such a writer as Irenaeus is governed by the Church's Rule of Faith, whereas the Gnostics endeavour to mould the Scriptures to suit their own theories. The distinction is still relevant, and still merits consideration by exponents of modern theologies. There is all the difference in the world between an interpretation that is brought to the text from without and one which emerges from the text itself.

[40] C. K. Barrett, *The New Testament Background: Selected Documents,* (London 1956), p. 80.

IV

The New 'Gospels'

PRIOR to the publication of the Berlin Gnostic Codex by W. C. Till in 1955, our knowledge of Gnosticism was almost entirely based on the Christian refutations of the heresy by such Fathers as Irenaeus and Hippolytus, together with such extracts from Gnostic sources as they and other writers chose to quote: the excerpts from Theodotus among the writings of Clement of Alexandria, the fragments of Heracleon's commentary on the Fourth Gospel quoted by Origen, the letter of Ptolemy to Flora preserved by Epiphanius.[1] Since this material came through the hands of the opponents of Gnosticism, it was obviously open to some suspicion as the propaganda of the side which emerged victorious, deliberately selected to expose the weaknesses of Gnostic theory and to present the Gnostics themselves in the worst possible light. The only original Gnostic documents at our disposal were the three books of Pistis Sophia and an older unnamed work in the Askew Codex, and the two books of Jeu and another anonymous work in the Bruce Codex, all in Coptic and all dating from a period when Gnosticism was already in an advanced state of decline.[2] To these the Berlin Codex added another three, the Gospel of Mary, the Apocryphon of John, and the Sophia Jesu Christi.

It is this that gives the Nag Hammadi library its significance, for here we have more than forty different documents of various kinds, some of them in two or three copies, and presenting types of Gnosticism much nearer than the first group of texts above mentioned to those attacked by the Christian Fathers.[3] As A. D.

---

[1] *Excerpta ex Theodoto* ed. Casey, (London 1934), ed. Sagnard, (Paris 1948); *The Fragments of Heracleon* ed. Brooke, (Cambridge 1891), cf. Völker, *Quellen*, pp. 63 ff.; *Ptolemy to Flora* ed. Quispel, (Paris 1949).

[2] Cf. W. C. Till, *La Parola del Passato* 4, (1949), pp. 230 ff.

[3] Cf. Doresse, *The Secret Books of the Egyptian Gnostics*, (ET: London 1960). Bibliography to 1963 by S. Giversen in *Studia Theologica* 17, (1963), pp. 139 ff.

Nock wrote, 'The historical importance of this discovery may fairly be set on a level with that of the Dead Sea Scrolls. The latter throws new light on inter-testamental Judaism and on Christian beginnings; the former does something comparable for subsequent Christian development.'[4] To go no further, the texts so far published serve to confirm the conclusions reached through the researches of Foerster and Sagnard as to the essential reliability of Irenaeus, our earliest patristic authority.[5] Whatever its interest for the scholar, however, the Nag Hammadi discovery has not as yet attracted nearly the same public interest as the Scrolls, for reasons which are not far to seek. For one thing, the Gnostic texts have so far produced no sensation comparable to the suggestion that the Scrolls present the clue to the origins of Christianity, or even an anticipation of the faith itself. They belong quite definitely to the Christian era, and most of those so far published show very clear signs of Christian influence. For another, the records of a heresy long outmoded, a lost cause of a bygone age, cannot exert the same romantic appeal as the discovery of a whole field of thought and speculation hitherto unknown and well-nigh unsuspected; although Gnosticism too may have its lessons for the modern world. Again, the number of those who know Coptic, and hence can deal with these documents at first hand, is even smaller than in the case of Hebrew. And finally the publication of the texts has been beset by protracted and vexatious delays of one kind or another. The library was found in 1945 or 1946, but several years were to elapse before the main part of it finally passed into the possession of the Coptic Museum in Cairo. A photographic edition of some of this material was published in 1956, and translations of its contents were speedily made into German and later, in some cases, into other modern languages.[6] One codex meanwhile had been brought out of Egypt, and eventually found a resting place in the Jung Institute in Zürich. One of the

---

[4] *JTS* 9, (1958), p. 315.

[5] Foerster, *Von Valentin zu Heracleon*, (Beiheft 7 zur *ZNW*); Sagnard, *La gnose valentinienne*, (Paris 1947).

[6] P. Labib, *Coptic Gnostic Papyri in the Coptic Museum at Old Cairo*, (Cairo 1956); German translations in *TLZ* 1958–1959, most of them collected in Leipoldt-Schenke, *Koptisch-gnostische Schriften aus den Papyrus-Codices von Nag Hammadi*, (Hamburg-Bergstedt 1960).

documents it contains was published in 1957,[7] another in 1963.[8] The three Cairo texts of the Apocryphon of John appeared in 1962,[9] as did an anonymous treatise from Codex II,[10] and four apocalypses from Codex V in 1963.[11]

From one point of view it is regrettable that after the lapse of twenty years only thirteen documents, including the three in the Berlin Codex, have been adequately published out of more than forty, but the important thing is that progress is being made. Thirteen documents since 1955 represent a rather more favourable rate of progress than appears at first sight. After all, close on sixty years elapsed between the first announcement of the Berlin Codex and its eventual publication.[12]

It is commonly assumed that the collection was the library of a Gnostic group, and Doresse[13] suggests that it was hidden 'at the latest, about the beginning of the fifth century, at the time when the Pachomian monasteries . . . finally extended their influence over the region.' This is entirely plausible, but assumes the accuracy of the information supplied to Doresse regarding the location of the discovery. An alternative, suggested by T. Säve-Söderbergh,[14] is that the collection was made for heresiological purposes, in which case it may never have been owned as a whole by any single Gnostic group. This would materially affect our conclusions, for example as to the significance of the presence in the collection of a number of Hermetic texts, or of three versions of the Apocryphon of John; but in the present state of our knowledge it is impossible to decide. The strict orthodoxy of the Pachomian monks however suggests a reason for the concealment of the texts by a diminishing minority in the face of their growing influence, and the common view may therefore be allowed to stand.

[7] *Evangelium Veritatis*, ed. Malinine, Puech, Quispel, (dated Zürich 1956).

[8] *De Resurrectione*, ed. Malinine, Puech, Quispel, Till, (Zürich 1963).

[9] M. Krause and P. Labib, *Die drei Versionen des Apocryphon des Johannes*, (Wiesbaden 1962).

[10] A. Böhlig and P. Labib, *Die koptisch-gnostische Schrift ohne Titel aus Codex II von Nag Hammadi*, (Berlin 1962).

[11] Böhlig-Labib, *Koptisch-gnostische Apokalypsen aus Codex V von Nag Hammadi*, (Halle-Wittenberg 1963).

[12] W. C. Till, *Die gnostischen Schriften des koptischen Papyrus Berolinensis 8502*, (*TU* 60, Berlin 1955).

[13] *Secret Books*, p. 135.   [14] See his paper at the Messina Colloquium.

Of the documents so far available three, despite their differences, are sufficiently akin to be grouped together: the Gospel of Truth, the Gospel of Thomas and the Gospel of Philip. At least, they are all called 'Gospels'! Moreover all three have now been accessible long enough to allow of their intensive study, although it must be said that on some questions we are still a long way from any final conclusions. In particular, the publication of the remaining texts may yet entail considerable modification of prevailing opinions.

These three documents comprise in all some eighty pages of Coptic text. Even to present them in translation, without comment, interpretation or discussion, would require more than the space at our disposal; and as it happens each of them has had more than one complete book devoted to it. All that can be done here is to present a summary and even superficial outline of their contents and their significance, and of the problems they have helped to solve, or have themselves created.

It should be made clear at the outset, even at the present stage of research, that these documents are not 'Gospels' at all, in the sense in which this word is used as applying to the four canonical Gospels contained in our New Testament. They do not record the story of Jesus, nor do they give a connected account of his life and teaching, his death and resurrection. Two of them, the Gospel of Thomas and the Gospel of Philip, are so called because these are the names which are given to them in the manuscript in which they are contained. The third, the Gospel of Truth, owes its title to its opening words, and to the fact that Irenaeus in his refutation of the Gnostics speaks of a Gospel of Truth which was current among the Valentinians.[15] For this text begins 'The Gospel of Truth is joy for those who have received from the Father of Truth the grace of knowing Him.' It was but natural that the scholars who first examined the document should identify it with the treatise mentioned by Irenaeus, the more especially since it appears to be of a Valentinian character.

Formally the three texts are very different. The Gospel of Truth is a rather rambling treatise, aptly described as a meditation or homily on the theme of 'the Gospel', but for all its meandering it is a continuous text. Thomas on the other hand

---

[15] *Adv. haer.*, iii.11.12, [Harvey 2, p. 52].

is a collection of 'sayings' ascribed to Jesus, some very brief and others, especially the parables, of somewhat greater length, but all simply set down one after another with little apparent connection between them. Philip at first sight appears to be equally disjointed, but here there are some lengthy sections which cannot be properly classified as 'sayings', nor are they presented as sayings of Jesus. Moreover there are indications here that some of the units are linked by catch-words or by association of ideas, while another feature is the constant recurrence of a number of favourite themes.

The first of the three to appear was the Gospel of Truth, published in a very sumptuous edition dated 1956 and containing not only introduction, text, commentary and a full set of photographs but also French, German and English translations.[16] Four pages missing from the middle of the work were subsequently found among the Cairo fragments, and published in a supplementary volume.[17] An English translation with commentary was published by Kendrick Grobel in 1960, a French version with an attempt to put the text back into Greek by J. E. Ménard in 1962.[18] The latter also has a very comprehensive bibliography (pp. 21 ff.) for the Nag Hammadi library as a whole.

Publication of the text was anticipated by a number of articles and lectures, three of which were translated by F. L. Cross in the volume *The Jung Codex* (London 1955). In one of these W. C. van Unnik argues that the author was Valentinus himself, the founder of the Valentinian school, and that the work was written at Rome round about A.D. 140–145, before the development of the typically Gnostic dogmas. The main points of his argument are (a) the absence of 'the distinct and typical points of Valentinianism' in a document whose origin in the Valentinian circle is beyond question; (b) certain agreements with the surviving fragments of Valentinus; and (c) a certain reserve in the attitude of the document towards Docetism. In this opinion van Unnik has the general concurrence of Kendrick

[16] See n. 7 above.
[17] *Evangelium Veritatis* (Supplementum), ed. Malinine etc., (Zürich and Stuttgart 1961).
[18] Grobel, *The Gospel of Truth. A Valentinian Meditation on the Gospel*, (London 1960); Ménard, *L'Evangile de Vérité*, (Paris 1962).

G

Grobel and of R. M. Grant,[19] although they do not agree on points of detail; but the editors of the published edition, although they mention the theory with respect, are prepared to go no further than to say that the composition of the document may go back to about A.D. 150, and that the author may have been Valentinus or one of his immediate disciples.

The factors underlying the more general ascription of the document to the Valentinian school are (a) that with one possible exception all the texts included in this particular codex appear to be Valentinian, and (b) that the document itself shows agreement in language and in doctrine with the Valentinian system. It refers to aeons, to the Pleroma, to the place of rest, to the classification of mankind into spiritual, psychic and material, and so on—all terms familiar from the accounts of Valentinianism given by Irenaeus and other early Fathers. But the author makes a quite unique use of these terms, and his teaching as a whole does not coincide with any known form of Valentinianism. In particular there is no detailed list of the aeons, no account of the way in which they emanated from the primal deity; there is no myth of the fall of Sophia, so prominent in the Valentinian doctrine as previously known; and there is no mention of the Demiurge, or of the distinction between him and the supreme God.

This general 'Valentinian' ascription has been challenged from different angles. H. M. Schenke[20] claimed that the Gospel of Truth shows nothing specifically Valentinian at all, and that its central ideas are more akin to those of the Odes of Solomon; but the origins and associations of these Odes are themselves disputed, and when they were first published they were claimed by many scholars as Valentinian! Ernst Haenchen,[21] again, declared that the differences between the Gospel and Valentinianism were such that to pass from one to the other consti-

---

[19] Grant, *Gnosticism and Early Christianity*, (New York and London 1959), pp. 128 ff. Cf. also the discussion by H. C. Puech in Hennecke-Schneemelcher, *NT Apocrypha*, i, pp. 233 ff.

[20] *Die Herkunft des so-genannten Evangelium Veritatis*, (Berlin 1958). Links with the Odes of Solomon were also noted by F. M. Braun, *Rev. Thomiste* 57, (1957), pp. 597 ff. [cf. his *Jean le Théologien*, (Paris 1959), pp. 235 ff.], and R. M. Grant, *Vig. Chr.* 11, (1957), pp. 149 ff.

[21] *ZKG* 67, (1955–56), p. 154; cf. also his survey in *ThR* 30, (1964), pp. 47 ff.

tuted a *metabasis eis allo genos*; but this is to ignore the possibility of growth and development within the Valentinian system. For example, the suggestion has been made, though never fully explored, that the Gospel of Truth represents a primitive stage, and that the developed Valentinianism known to Irenaeus results from the subsequent assimilation of some such theory as that represented by the Apocryphon of John. It must be remembered that what we have in Irenaeus is not the system of Valentinus himself but that of his disciples—and their disciples.

At this point attention should be drawn to the ambiguity of the term 'Valentinian' in this connection, for it is not always clear whether it should be taken to refer to Valentinus himself or to his school. Some scholars would be prepared to accept a Valentinian origin in the latter sense but not, with van Unnik, in the former. Again, due heed should be paid to Haenchen's warning[22] against hasty ascription of authorship. Much as we should like to identify the authors of our documents, and greatly as it would simplify our task, the fact remains that often we simply do not know, nor have we any adequate basis for making such identifications. As it is, Valentinus has been credited with the authorship both of the Gospel of Truth and of the Epistle to Rheginus, and more recently Mademoiselle Pétrement[23] has suggested that he may also be the author of the Epistle to Diognetus, or part of it. The arguments advanced in such cases may carry considerable weight, but they must always be received with a due measure of reserve.

A third challenge is that of Hans Jonas,[24] who argues that the Gospel of Truth does not ante-date but presupposes the developed Valentinian system, that in other words it does not mention the missing elements just because they are taken for granted. This question is important because upon it depends our estimate of the place of this Gospel in the development of Valentinianism. If van Unnik is correct, we can trace something of the growth of the theory, in particular a movement away from Christianity—which would serve to confirm, so far as the Valentinians are concerned, the traditional view of Gnosticism

---

[22] *ThR* 30, (1964), p. 57.
[23] *Rev. Hist. Phil. Rel.*, (1966), pp. 34 ff.
[24] Cf. his review in *Gnomon* 32, (1960), pp. 327 ff., also *Studia Patristica*, vi, (Berlin 1962), pp. 96 ff.

as a Christian heresy; and moreover we should be able to identify one at least of the influences which were operative, namely the Barbelognostic system described by Irenaeus and now more fully available in the Coptic Apocryphon of John. On the other hand, if Jonas is right we have to assume that the full Valentinian system is already present behind even so comparatively early a document as the Gospel of Truth. In point of fact it is not difficult to extract from it numerous passages which fit neatly into the system described by Irenaeus, but *does* this mean that the whole system was already present? Or was the Gospel perhaps the work of some unknown Valentinian, who sought to work out a closer rapprochement with Christian doctrine? Here obviously much remains to be done.

In regard to the character of the document, Puech and Quispel in their pioneer article regarded it as a fifth Gospel, intended to supplement or supersede the canonical form, but they themselves subsequently accepted van Unnik's argument, now generally adopted, that it is rather a meditation on the theme of the Gospel, 'a sermon, a devotional contemplation, or, if one will, a dogmatic or mystical tractate.'[25] Some Scandinavian scholars would be even more specific and claim it as a baptismal or confirmation homily, and in this they are followed by Sasagu Arai, a Japanese scholar whose well-documented study of the Christology of the Gospel of Truth represents the latest contribution to research on this text.[26] Baptismal elements are certainly present but, as in the more familiar case of 1 Peter, not every scholar is quite confident that we have to do with a baptismal homily.

Since 1959 this text has been rather overshadowed by the Gospel of Thomas.[27] This is only natural, in view of the charac-

[25] Puech-Quispel, *Vig. Chr.* 8, (1954), pp. 22 ff.; van Unnik in *The Jung Codex*, p. 95 [cf. p. 106 n. 1].

[26] T. Säve-Söderbergh, *RoB* 17, (1958), cited by Segelberg, thinks it a baptismal homily. E. Segelberg (*Orientalia Suecana*, Uppsala 1960; cf. *Studia Patristica*, v, (Berlin 1962), pp. 118 ff.) calls it rather a confirmation homily, and stresses not the kinship but the differences between it and the Odes of Solomon. See also S. Arai, *Die Christologie des Evangelium Veritatis*, (Leiden 1964), p. 14.

[27] First published in P. Labib's photographic edition, *Coptic Gnostic Papyri in the Coptic Museum at Old Cairo*, (Cairo 1956), and subsequently the subject of a very extensive literature. For the earlier studies, cf. Puech in Hennecke-Schneemelcher, i, pp. 278 ff.

ter of the latter document: a collection of sayings, some of them parallel to sayings already familiar, others entirely new; and more particularly because of the possible significance of this collection for the development of the early Gospel tradition. Yet the Gospel of Truth is a more comprehensible document. It has of course its difficulties and obscurities, and the author meanders, turning his theme about and approaching it now from one angle, now from another. But there is some continuity in his meandering, whereas in Thomas there seems to be nothing of the sort. On the contrary, sayings and parables which in our Gospels appear in the same context are in Thomas widely separated, or are brought into association with other sayings from completely different contexts. Familiar sayings appear in unfamiliar forms and unfamiliar groupings, while others again have no canonical parallels but are cited by early Fathers as occurring in the Gospel of the Hebrews or the Gospel of the Egyptians; and still others are entirely new.

Phenomena such as these inevitably give rise to questions: What is the relation between Thomas and our Gospels—is it dependent on them, or independent? What is its background, its origin, what are its sources? Here as so often we are confronted by problems of method and approach. There are at least two distinct approaches, which lead to two divergent results.[28] On the one hand there are those scholars who begin with the question of the relation of Thomas to the Synoptics, and who may or may not conclude that it is largely independent. On the other hand an approach from the angle of theology, from the point of view of an analysis of the doctrine which the document contains, leads on the whole to the conclusion that it is a Gnostic text, and secondary to our Gospels.[29] Now there is no question that we can put a Gnostic theology into Thomas, that if we approach it with Gnostic theory in mind we can find a meaning for much that is otherwise obscure. But is this the whole answer?[30] Or are we not once more faced by the danger of

[28] E. Haenchen, *Die Botschaft des Thomas-Evangeliums*, (Berlin 1961), pp. 37 f., makes a similar but slightly different distinction in relation to the *interpretation* of the document.

[29] Cf. Haenchen, op. cit.; B. Gärtner, *The Theology of the Gospel of Thomas*, (London and New York 1961).

[30] Cf. for example K. Grobel in *NTS* 8, (1962), pp. 367 ff., and on the other side Y. Janssens, *Le Muséon* 75, (1962), pp. 301 ff.

imposing on the text a preconceived interpretation? Granted that the gospel as it now stands can be read as a Gnostic document, does this mean that it was Gnostic from the first, that it was composed by a Gnostic and with the full Gnostic theory present to his mind? Or should we not consider, here as in other respects, the possibility of growth, the possibility that a document originally non-Gnostic has been taken over, adapted and embellished, to serve a Gnostic purpose?[31]

Broadly speaking, the earlier studies on Thomas all tended to favour some degree of independence from our Gospels, but the more recent trend has been towards the view that Thomas used the canonical books.[32] The first book published in English on the subject, by R. M. Grant with David Noel Freedman, does indeed touch on the possibility of independent tradition, but no more. The evidence provided by Papias, they say, is not such as to inspire confidence in the reliability of the oral tradition in that period—in fact 'we may wonder whether oral tradition, by his time, was not getting rather garbled.'[33] So they conclude (p. 102) that while Thomas *may* have used traditions underlying our Gospels it is more likely, if he wrote towards the middle of the second century, that he relied on written documents.

The chief protagonist of the theory of independence has been G. Quispel, although a somewhat similar theory has also been advanced by Oscar Cullmann.[34] Starting from the fact that one logion in Thomas is quoted by Clement of Alexandria as from the Gospel of the Hebrews, and that others show affinities with citations from the Gospel of the Egyptians, Quispel argues that these were the original sources from which Thomas drew, and goes on to trace the influence of this independent tradition in

[31] Thus G. Quispel argues [e.g. in *The Bible in Modern Scholarship*, (Nashville 1965), pp. 256 f.] that Thomas is not Gnostic but Encratite.

[32] For details see R. McL. Wilson, *Studies in the Gospel of Thomas*, (London 1960), where full references are given to the earlier literature.

[33] Grant and Freedman, *The Secret Sayings of Jesus*, (London 1960), p. 26. A somewhat different picture of the survival of oral tradition emerges from Helmut Köster's *Synoptische Überlieferung bei den apostolischen Vätern*, (*TU* 65, Berlin 1957).

[34] Quispel's earlier papers are listed in my *Studies in the Gospel of Thomas*. Cf. more recently by the paper cited in n. 31. Cullmann's articles appeared in *TLZ*, (1960), cols. 321 ff. [ET: in *Interpretation* 16, (1962), pp. 418 ff.; cf. also *Universitas* 4, (1961), pp. 141 ff., *Hibbert Journal* 60, (1961), pp. 116 ff.].

the Diatessaron of Tatian, in the pseudo-Clementines, and elsewhere in early Christian literature. Not all his arguments are
equally cogent, and some may be considered frankly weak. In
particular there is the difficulty that we possess so little either of
the Gospel of the Hebrews or of the Gospel of the Egyptians,
which makes any far-reaching conclusions relating to either
precarious in the extreme. Nevertheless, the case is not one to be
lightly swept aside without more ado. Could it but be substan-
tiated in detail, it would shed fresh light on the whole development of early Christianity, particularly in Syria.[35]

On the positive side, one thing is certain, that Thomas
includes all the sayings contained in the three famous Oxyrhynchus Logia papyri. Even here however there are differences
which make it dangerous to assume that the papyri present the
original Greek from which the Coptic Thomas was translated.
One saying in POx.1 is in Thomas divided into two, with some
forty other logia between. We therefore have to reckon with the
possibility of development between the Greek fragments in the
third century and the Coptic Gospel in the fourth or fifth; and
once this is granted it becomes necessary to enquire whether
such development may not also have taken place even earlier.
It is not difficult to imagine, although it would be very difficult
to prove, a process in which some elements were taken from the
oral tradition (sometimes at a later stage than that represented
in our Gospels), while others are in some measure dependent on
the canonical books, and others again are purely 'Gnostic' or at
least Encratite constructions. In such a case, proof of the
dependence of any given saying would have no significance for
any other saying; each would require to be considered on its own
merits.

The latest contribution here, by W. Schrage,[36] sets out the
Coptic text of the relevant sayings with the Sahidic version of

---

[35] Support for some of Quispel's views is provided by A. Baker, *Vig. Chr.*
18, (1964), pp. 215 ff. [cf. Quispel ibid., 226 ff.]; *JTS* 16, (1965), pp.
449 ff.; *NTS* 12, (1965), pp. 49 ff. On the other hand his attempt to link
Thomas with the Anglo-Saxon *Heliand* has met with determined resistance,
from the side of *Germanistik*, from W. Krogmann [see most recently *Vig. Chr.*
18, (1964), pp. 65 ff.].

[36] W. Schrage, *Das Verhältnis des Thomas-Evangeliums zur synoptischen
Tradition und zu den koptischen Evangelienübersetzungen*, (Beiheft 29 zur *ZNW*,
Berlin 1964). Cf. my review in *Vig. Chr.* 20, (1966), pp. 118 ff.

the Synoptic parallels below. Schrage claims that Thomas shows not only a knowledge of our Gospels, but also an astonishing familiarity with the Coptic versions thereof. This might seem decisive, but unfortunately he proves too much; for Thomas shows agreements not only with the Sahidic but with the Bohairic, sometimes separately and in the same saying; elsewhere he is actually closer to the Greek than the Coptic versions are. Nor has Schrage taken sufficient account of the question how far the words used in common were the obvious and even the inevitable words for a translator to employ. Moreover there are a few logia for which no parallels are supplied because the differences are too great. Evidently the problem is more complex than appears at first sight, and much still remains to be done.

The Gospel of Philip is still something of an enigma. For one thing it is only recently that the Coptic text has been made available in convenient form, or an English translation provided, although we have had a German version for some years past.[37] We are still at the stage of clarifying, explaining and emending obscure passages in the text, and collecting the necessary parallels and comparative material.[38] Nor is it clear what should be said as to the character of this document. H. M. Schenke, who did the pioneer work, described it as a kind of Gnostic florilegium, and divided it into 127 'Sprüche'. But here already we must pause for reflection: was he perhaps unduly influenced by the example of Thomas? Some of these 'sayings', even on Schenke's division, are extremely long, and there are cases where he seems to have put asunder what was originally

[37] First published in Labib's photographic edition (see n. 6). German version by H. M. Schenke in *TLZ* 1959, reprinted in Leipoldt-Schenke, *Koptisch-gnostische Schriften aus den Papyrus-Codices von Nag-Hammadi*, (Hamburg-Bergstedt 1960), pp. 33–65 and 81 f. English translation by C. J. de Catanzaro, *JTS* 13, (1962) pp. 35 ff. and (independently, with commentary) by R. McL. Wilson, *The Gospel of Philip*, (London and New York 1962). Text with German translation by W. C. Till, *Das Evangelium nach Philippos*, (Berlin 1963).

[38] Cf. J. W. B. Barns' review of Wilson in *JTS* 14, (1963), pp. 496 ff., and M. Krause's review of Till in *ZKG* 75, (1964), pp. 168 ff., the latter based on more adequate photographs than those available to earlier contributors. See also A. Helmbold, *NTS* 11, (1964/5), pp. 90 ff., and W. C. van Unnik, ibid., 10, (1963/4), pp. 465 ff.

joined.[39] The most recent editor, J. E. Ménard, takes a different line.[40] Noting that some of these sections appear to be linked by catchwords, he suggests that this is the clue to the continuity and progression of the thought, and that sometimes we should take two or even three of Schenke's sections together. But Ménard himself cannot carry the process through from beginning to end of the work. If this is the Ariadne thread to guide us through the labyrinth, there are places where it has been broken.

If the structure and plan of the book are still obscure, its Gnostic character is beyond dispute. It is definitely and unambiguously a Gnostic work, nor does it raise any such interesting and attractive theories as does Thomas, with the possibility of independent tradition lying behind it. The question here is one of fitting it into its proper place in the development of Gnosticism. There are clear links with the Valentinian theory, in particular with the Marcosian version as described by Irenaeus, and with the Excerpta ex Theodoto of Clement of Alexandria. In fact there are passages which can only be understood in the light of what Irenaeus tells us; but curiously there are others where the closest parallels are to be found not in Irenaeus' discussion of Gnostic theories but in his own Demonstration of the Christian faith. This is a reminder that the Gnostics were not always so far removed from 'orthodox' Christianity. In the early stages especially there was a good deal of common ground, and it was only gradually that the lines of division emerged.

One point of special interest is the considerable number of allusions, tantalising in that they are only allusions and not full descriptions, to Gnostic sacraments. Baptism and the Eucharist of course are shared with the Great Church, but there are references also to the Chrism, which for the author ranks as superior to Baptism; to the Apolutrosis which appears to be characteristic of the Marcosians, and finally to one which appears to rank above them all but is never precisely defined: the bridal chamber. We know the Valentinians gave a special place to marriage, regarding human marriage as symbolic of the union of the aeons in the heavenly realm; but is it to marriage that Philip refers, or to some ceremony akin to the 'sacred

---

[39] In a survey of research published in *TLZ* 90, (1965), cols. 321 ff., Schenke now adopts the more general term 'paragraph'.

[40] J. E. Ménard, *L'Evangile selon Philippe*, (Montreal and Paris 1964).

marriage' of which we read in connection with some ancient religions of the Middle East?

Another point of interest in this document is its use of the New Testament, whether by direct quotation or in its Gnostic interpretation of New Testament themes and ideas.[41] Here a word of warning is required: it is all very well to list the references and allusions, but what do they signify for the history of the Canon? Full canonicity, or merely knowledge of the books in question? For example, van Unnik argued from the Gospel of Truth that almost the whole of our New Testament was already recognised as authoritative in Rome by about A.D. 150, but the argument could be reversed: the stage of development here reflected might be claimed to show that this document cannot possibly be so early. The dates of all these documents, it must be said, are still rather conjectural. Van Unnik dates the Gospel of Truth about A.D. 140–145, Grobel and Grant slightly later. If Jonas is right, it may be perhaps a generation later, which might agree better with the state of the Canon here reflected. Puech puts the earliest redaction of Thomas about A.D. 140, but the problem here is very complex, since we have to allow for the possibility of growth. The Oxyrhynchus Logia are dated between A.D. 200 and 250, but are they fragments of Thomas, or were they later incorporated into it? Or are the Logia on the one hand and Thomas on the other both versions of some earlier document? Again, if Thomas is dependent on Tatian, this provides a *terminus a quo*; but if Tatian is dependent on Thomas it is a *terminus ante quem*. The closest affinities of Philip appear to be with the Marcosians and the Excerpta ex Theodoto, which would put this document near the time of Irenaeus (c. A.D. 170–180). Ménard lists a number of themes which can be found in the later forms of Gnosis: in Mandeism, the Pistis Sophia and Manicheism. He accordingly places the origin of Philip in this milieu, and takes the third century as the *terminus a quo* for this document. The question is however whether Philip presupposes the doctrines of such groups, as Ménard seems to assume, or anticipates them. At all events, we can hardly put this gospel before the final quarter of the second century or the beginning of the third. Nor do the three texts provide any adequate basis for constructing a relative chrono-

[41] Cf. R. McL. Wilson, *NTS* 9, (1963), pp. 291 ff.

logy. Mademoiselle Y. Janssens[42] has recently suggested that Philip and Thomas derive from different, although perhaps parallel, currents of thought, and hence it is impossible to say which is the older, since they do not follow the same line. The same would appear to be true of the Gospel of Truth: unless it is by Valentinus himself, in which case it is certainly the oldest of the three, we have no real basis for determining whether it is older than the other two or not.

One passage in particular in Philip is of interest as showing how a Gnostic could take over and adapt Paul's teaching on the resurrection[43]—which may help to explain Tertullian's emphasis on resurrection not only of the body but of the flesh; for Paul's doctrine may have served Gnostic interests all too well. Another passage presents a curious and, so far as yet known, unique piece of speculation about the Cross:

> Philip the apostle said 'Joseph the carpenter planted a garden because he needed the wood for his trade. It was he who made the Cross from the trees which he planted. And his seed hung on that which he planted. His seed was Jesus, but the planting was the Cross.'
>
> (Philip 91)

Finally, there is the contribution which this text can make to the study of Gnostic imagery and symbolism.

This review is of course very far from being exhaustive—a recent survey on Thomas alone lists ninety titles[44]—but it may serve to give some indication of the progress made, the problems encountered, and the tasks remaining.

[42] *Byzantion* 35, (1965), p. 454.
[43] Philip 23 [see above, pp. 74 ff.].
[44] H. Quecke, in *La Venue du Messie*, (1962), pp. 271 ff.

V

The other Published Documents from Nag Hammadi

SOME twelve years ago our materials for the study of Gnosticism proper consisted almost entirely of the Christian refutations, with such fragments of original Gnostic documents as they contain, and a handful of original texts preserved in Coptic, all of them comparatively late. The Berlin Coptic papyrus had long been known, and had indeed to some extent been utilised, but only in the autumn of 1955 was it finally published, thus making three further texts available: the Gospel of Mary, the Apocryphon of John, and the Sophia Jesu Christi. Since then nine of the Nag Hammadi documents have been published in text and translation, with commentaries more or less detailed and comprehensive: the three Gnostic gospels discussed in the previous chapter, the Treatise on the Resurrection (otherwise known as the Epistle to Rheginus), four Gnostic apocalypses, and the anonymous treatise contained in Codex II. In addition the three Nag Hammadi versions of the Apocryphon of John, which vary at sundry times and in divers manners from the Berlin text, are now at our disposal, and the Hypostasis of the Archons has been translated into German.

The primary concern of the present chapter is with the eight remaining Nag Hammadi documents in the above list. The library however contains copies not only of the Apocryphon of John but also of the Sophia Jesu Christi and of a related document, which were used by Dr. Till in his edition of the Berlin text, and it therefore seems appropriate to include some discussion of these also, and of the relevant problems, even though the Nag Hammadi copies have not yet appeared. It is then rather pointless to omit the comparatively short Gospel of Mary, even though it does not strictly belong to the new discovery. With this accordingly we begin.

1. *The Gospel of Mary (Berlin Codex)*.[1] This is the first of the three texts in the Berlin Codex, but six pages are missing at the beginning and a further four later on (pp. 11–14), so that of the original eighteen pages little more than eight remain. The final pages are extant in Greek in a papyrus in the John Rylands collection in Manchester.[2] The document falls into two distinct parts, of which the first is a conversation between the Saviour and his disciples. It begins in the middle of a question about the destiny of matter, to which the Saviour replies 'All natures, all formations, all created things exist in and with one another and will again be resolved into their own roots. For the nature of matter is dissolved into the roots of its nature alone.' Peter then asks 'What is the sin of the world?', and receives the reply 'There is no sin, but it is you who make sin when you do what is of the nature of fornication, which is called "sin".' Then follows a brief farewell address, composed largely of a tissue of New Testament quotations and allusions, and the Saviour takes his departure. At this the disciples are plunged into despair, but they are comforted and encouraged by Mary.

Here one might expect the document to end, but in fact it continues with a request from Peter to Mary, that she impart to them the revelations given to her by the Saviour, which she therefore knows and they do not. The reply is interrupted by the four-page lacuna already mentioned, but includes an account of a vision and, after the lacuna, part of a description of the ascent of a soul and its conversations with a succession of hostile powers. Andrew however bluntly expresses his disbelief, and is supported by Peter, and at this Mary is reduced to despair. Levi comes to her defence, and wins over the others. The text ends with the statement that they 'began to go out to preach and proclaim'.

As Puech observes,[3] there is a contrast between the dominant role which Mary plays in the second part of the work and the modest place which she assumes in the first, and this together

---

[1] Text in Till, *TU* 60, pp. 62 ff.; English translation in Grant, *Gnosticism. An Anthology*, (London 1961), pp. 65 ff. See also Puech in Hennecke-Schneemelcher, i, pp. 340 ff.

[2] C. H. Roberts, *Catalogue of the Greek and Latin Papyri in the John Rylands Library*, iii, (Manchester 1938), pp. 18 ff. [P Ryl. 463].

[3] op. cit., p. 344.

with the diversity of the content suggests that two originally independent documents have been artificially combined. This conclusion, also drawn by Till, appears to be confirmed by the fact that the New Testament allusions almost all occur either at the beginning or in the suture between the two parts.[4] The second part, however, forms a fairly coherent whole, and it is difficult to believe it the result of a redaction which consisted only in the substitution of New Testament names for those in the original document. Consideration must therefore be given to the possibility that we have here not the combination of two earlier *documents* but a Christian Gnostic composition into which earlier and non-Christian material has been incorporated. At all events, we do seem to have in this document evidence of the Christian Gnostic redaction of older material, although it should be added that even if this material was non-Christian it was not necessarily also *pre*-Christian. The age and character of this material still requires to be examined.

Another point of interest is the opposition encountered by Mary from the side of Andrew and Peter. As Puech notes,[5] this has its parallels in the Pistis Sophia, and more particularly in the Gospel of Thomas (log. 114). Mary Magdalene of course occupies a privileged position in Gnostic literature (cf. also Philip 32, 55), but what are we to make of Peter's hostility? Is it merely an echo, or a development, of the unbelief with which, according to our Gospels (Mark 16.11, Luke 24.11), the disciples greeted the news of the Resurrection,[6] or is there another significance? The Church of Rome, as Kelly puts it, 'regarded itself and was regarded by many, as in a special sense the appointed custodian and mouthpiece of the apostolic tradition.'[7] When Irenaeus seeks to defend the authentic apostolic doctrine against Gnostic innovations, it is to the tradition of Rome that he appeals, the church founded by Peter and Paul (*adv. haer.* III.3.1 Harvey). Is Peter then in the Gnostic gospels representative of the church of Rome? The suggestion is certainly

[4] Cf. *NTS* 3, (1957), pp. 233 ff.
[5] op. cit., p. 343.
[6] Cf. the *Epistula Apostolorum* 10 ff. [Hennecke-Schneemelcher, i, pp. 195 ff.]
[7] *Early Christian Doctrines*, (London 1958), p. 44. Cf. R. P. C. Hanson, *Tradition in the Early Church*, (London 1962), pp. 144 ff.

attractive, but it may also be misleading. At what stage, for example, did Peter become so identified with the Roman church that he could stand as its representative? Or would such an interpretation not involve a rather later period for these Gnostic documents than the second-century date hitherto suggested? Such questions call for further and more detailed investigation. As Hanson notes,[8] Irenaeus (unlike Cyprian later) 'consistently speaks of both Peter and Paul as founding the Roman church and never connects the importance of the Roman church with our Lord's words to Peter recorded in the gospels.'

2. *The Apocryphon of John.*[9] In the Berlin Codex the Apocryphon of John follows immediately on the Gospel of Mary. Indeed Carl Schmidt at first thought they formed a single document, a mistake which he later corrected but which is still occasionally perpetuated by those who have not consulted either his later writings or the published edition of the Codex. In addition, we now have no fewer than three copies in the Nag Hammadi library,[10] one of them close to the Berlin text and collated by Dr. Till for his edition, the others rather longer, although one of them unfortunately is in a somewhat fragmentary condition.

Part of the interest in this document lies in the fact that the first section, containing the account of the origin of the world, tallies very closely with the account of the Barbelognostics given by Irenaeus (*adv. haer.* I.27 Harvey) and that, as Sagnard notes,[11] we are here touching upon the sources of the Valentinian Gnosis. Schmidt[12] many years ago claimed this document as the source of Irenaeus' account, arguing that the original used by Irenaeus extended beyond his excerpt. In the following chapter Irenaeus presents in detail an extract from another source, which overlaps with the material in the Apocryphon. Hence he breaks off where he does simply to avoid repetition.

[8] op. cit., p. 145.
[9] Text in Till, pp. 78 ff.; English translation in Grant, *Anthology*, pp. 69 ff. See also Puech in Hennecke-Schneemelcher, i, pp. 314 ff.
[10] Cf. Krause-Labib, *Die drei Versionen des Apocryphon des Johannes*. The Codex II version has been published with an English translation by S. Giversen, *Apocryphon Johannis*, (Copenhagen 1963).
[11] *La gnose valentinienne*, pp. 445 f.
[12] In *Philotesia*, (Berlin 1907), pp. 317 ff.

On this view we should have to date the Apocryphon at any rate before A.D. 180.

The situation now, however, is rather less simple. We now have four versions, two short and closely similar and two rather longer. We therefore have to ask which of them is the older, the 'long recension' or the short, and what is their relation one to another, before we can go on to examine the relationship between them and Irenaeus. Is the long recension the original, or is it an expansion of the shorter? Did Irenaeus know the longer or the shorter, or did he perhaps use something that lay yet further back? Werner Foerster,[13] for example, finds it impossible to believe that the Apocryphon in its shorter version presents an original form of a Gnostic system, or could have served as the basis for Irenaeus' account: it presents only part of the underlying system; there are contradictions and inconsistencies; and there are points at which the account in Irenaeus is clearer and more comprehensible than the Apocryphon. Similarly, Puech[14] writes that if the shorter version is the older it would be difficult to identify it with the original version of the work; but he shows some reserve with regard to the view earlier advanced by Doresse,[15] that the original document was a short treatise of non-Christian character, identical with Irenaeus' source, which later formed the basis on which our Apocryphon was constructed. Finally H. M. Schenke[16] argues that the Apocryphon is not Irenaeus' source, but a composite work the second part of which shows certain parallels with the Sophia Jesu Christi (see below). Among other things, he notes the striking fact that Irenaeus ends his extract precisely at a point where the Apocryphon shows a clear suture: thus far the exposition has taken the form of connected discourse and deals with cosmogony; from this point on it takes the form of question and answer, and the subject is soteriology. The document used by Irenaeus contained a variant form of the cosmogony presented in the Apocryphon, not that cosmogony itself.

For reasons of space it is not possible to discuss in detail the arguments advanced by these four scholars, or the divergencies between their respective views. It is however clear that Schmidt's

---

[13] In *Gott und die Götter*, (Festgabe E. Fascher, Berlin 1958), p. 141.
[14] op. cit., p. 330.　　　　　　[15] *Vig. Chr.* 2, (1948), p. 158.
[16] *ZRGG* 14, (1962), pp. 57 ff.

opinion of the relationship between Irenaeus and the Apocryphon is no longer tenable in the form in which it was first advanced. We certainly have in both cases the same system, but whether Irenaeus' source was an earlier version of the Apocryphon itself, or another document which served as the basis for it, is still an open question. As Schenke notes,[17] comparison of other pairs of documents from Nag Hammadi, the Sophia Jesu Christi and the Epistle of Eugnostos or the Hypostasis of the Archons and the anonymous treatise in Codex II, together with the long and short recensions of the Apocryphon itself, shows that the Gnostics were in the habit of adapting and revising their documents. We have therefore to reckon with the possibility that the Coptic versions of the Apocryphon of John stand at some remove from the document used by Irenaeus.

That the Apocryphon is composite is suggested not only by the suture detected by Schenke, with the differences in form and subject-matter between the two parts, but also by the curious fact that it begins by referring to John in the third person, switches on the first page to the *first* person, and finally reverts again at the end to the third person. This suggests that the narrative framework is a later addition to a text already complete, and prompts a search for clear and unmistakable Christian elements, such as New Testament quotations or allusions. Extensive and direct quotations are conspicuous by their absence, and even such allusions as have been detected must be considered doubtful. In Till's edition only four are noted: (a) The formula 'that which is, that which has been, and that which shall be' (22.4 f.) recalls Rev. 1.19; but as W. C. van Unnik writes in a study of this formula, 'the relation between these two texts is not inevitably so that AJ depends on Apoc. 1.19'.[18] (b) At 26.18 there is a reference to 'the fount of the water of life, the light full of purity', with which Till compares Rev. 22.1; but again the parallel is scarcely so close as to suggest dependence. (c) At 59.9 ff. it is said that the ἐπίνοια of light is unattainable, and that 'although the darkness pursued her, it could not grasp her'. Here there does appear to be an echo of John 1.5, but direct dependence on John is another matter. It would seem nearer the mark to suggest a speculation inspired by John, in

[17] ibid., p. 63 n. 20. [18] *NTS* 9, (1963), p. 93.

H

which the light which came into the world has been re-inter-preted and identified with the ἐπίνοια; but then we are plunged into the problem of priorities. Was John the inspiration for this speculation, or could it be independent and the similarity quite fortuitous? Or does the Apocryphon point to some older specu-lation upon which John is dependent? (d) The strongest claim-ant is probably a saying of the Revealer: 'I am the one who is with you always' (21.19; cf. Matt. 28.20).

Grant in his *Anthology*[19] adds a few more: John 'went up to the temple' (19.9 f.; cf. Acts 3.1); the Revealer says 'John, why do you doubt?' (21.14 f.; cf. Matt. 28.17), and speaks of instruct-ing him 'about the perfect Man' (22.9; cf. Eph. 4.13). The supreme God is 'invisible, because no-one has seen him' (23.21–24.1; cf. John 1.18). The fount of the Spirit 'flowed out of the living water of light' (26.19 ff.; cf. John 7.38); here Grant passes over Till's reference to Rev. 22 for the previous line, but on 'he told it to us' (26.14) cites John 1.18. At 32.13 f., 'the invisible Spirit appointed him as God over the All', Grant quotes Rom. 9.5; but no-one seems to have noticed the closer parallel in the following lines: 'The true God gave him all power' (cf. Matt. 28.18). Rom. 8.22 is adduced at 53.10 ff., 'This is she who works at the whole creature [Adam] since she labours with the crea-ture', but here caution is necessary. This translation certainly suggests the Romans passage, and the latter may indeed be somewhere in the background; but examination of the parallel versions and of the translations by Till, Giversen and Krause suggests that in these the similarity is not so close. It may indeed be one of those cases in which conclusions based on a particular modern translation can be misleading without some explana-tory comment.

At 61.12 ff. Ialdabaoth is said to be 'ignorant of the mystery which originated from the decree of the holy Height'; for 'mystery' Grant refers to Eph. 5.32. A closer parallel appears at 66.8, with its reference to those who 'endure all things and suffer all things (1 Cor. 13.7) so that they may pass through the struggle and inherit eternal life'. Finally, at 70.11 ff. Grant identifies a whole cluster of allusions: 'They will go to the place where the angels of impoverishment (cf. Gal. 4.9) will with-draw, for whom there is no portion of repentance (cf. Heb.

[19] *Gnosticism. An Anthology*, pp. 69 ff.

12.17). They will all be preserved for the day on which they will be punished. All who have blasphemed against the Holy Spirit (Matt. 12.31) will be tormented in eternal punishment' (cf. Heb. 6.4–8).

The significance of these parallels will of course be variously estimated. In a document of Christian Gnosticism they are most naturally taken as allusions to the New Testament itself, but some of them are very faint echoes indeed. Now in its present form the Apocryphon *is* a Christian Gnostic document, as the narrative framework is enough to show; but was it entirely of Christian Gnostic origin, or are these 'New Testament elements' signs of a Christianising redaction of a non-Christian text? At any rate there is a striking contrast between the comparatively spasmodic introduction of such New Testament allusions and the thorough-going re-interpretation of the Genesis creation story which forms the basis of the cosmogonical section.

A further point relates to the occurrences of the name 'Christ', which in the cosmogony is assigned to a 'spark of light' to which Barbelo gives birth and which is also called Monogenes and the First-born Son of the All. At the first appearance of this figure, and in a passage including the first occurrence of the name, it is said that the Invisible Spirit 'anointed him with his goodness, so that he became perfect, faultless, and Christ, for he anointed him with the goodness of the Invisible Spirit.' Here again there are New Testament echoes, and in addition a play on the Greek words χριστός and χρηστός, known also from other sources.[20] There is however some variation in the texts at this point, and the Codex II version eliminates the name Christ altogether. This makes the later statement that the next aeon, Nous, 'stood up together with Christ' very sudden and abrupt, and it would certainly appear that the Berlin text is more original here, since in it the way is prepared. Consideration must however be given to the possibility that the introduction of the name is part of a process of Christianisation. Certainly there are points (e.g. 32.20 Till) at which it seems to be added almost as an afterthought. Here then is a problem which awaits closer investigation: Can it be shown that the Apocryphon as we now have it presents a Christianisation of an

[20] Cf. Bauer, *Wörterbuch*, col. 1610; Böhlig however [*Titelloses Werk*, p. 46] translates the Apocryphon passage differently.

older text, or an older system, or do the various versions suggest a movement *away from* Christianity? What, for example, is the significance of the addition at the very end of the long recension, both in Codex II and in Codex IV, of the words 'Jesus Christ. Amen', which are missing both from the Berlin text and from Codex III?

The revelation takes the form of a continuous discourse down to p. 45 of the Berlin text, where a question by John affords the opportunity for the Revealer to correct a 'false' interpretation of Gen. 1.2. Schenke, as already noted, detected a suture here, but this is open to question, although the same view was taken also by Doresse.[21] The discourse resumes for a further thirteen pages, until it is interrupted on p. 58 by two similar questions which again provide occasion for the correcting of false interpretations. It is only at p. 64 that the form changes to a dialogue, and the questions relate to soteriology. In the space of eight pages we have seven questions, the last of which leads to another long discourse, which in the Codex II version runs into the account of 'the deeds of the Redeemer', missing from the Berlin text. Does the 'new' section begin only at p. 64, or is the whole of the material from the point where Irenaeus breaks off to be regarded as later addition, perhaps in several stages? In all ten questions John in the Berlin text addresses the Revealer as 'Christ', but in each case Till notes that Codex III (CG I in Till) has the reading 'Lord', a reading supported in nine cases by Codex II, and in several also by the fragmentary Codex IV. The variant is easily explained as due to confusion of two Coptic letters in the contracted form of the word, but which was the original?

Giversen[22] notes that in the description of the deeds of the Redeemer 'it is conspicuous that the redeemer is nowhere referred to as Christ, nor as Jesus or Saviour or Lord'. Working on the basis of the Berlin text, van Unnik[23] had already written 'the role of Jesus is clearly no more than that of mediator of the true Knowledge, which is the real saving power. Jesus has no central place in the work of redemption. The figure of Jesus could come right out of the book without changing its character in any essential respect.' He found plenty of evidence that the

[21] *Secret Books*, p. 210.   [22] *Apocryphon Johannis*, p. 270.
[23] *Newly Discovered Gnostic Writings*, pp. 76 ff.

author (or redactor?) knew his New Testament intimately, for there are references at several points. 'But they are woven into an entirely different context of thought from that in which they occur in the New Testament.' In sum, 'because of its peculiar combination of ideas drawn from sharply divergent systems of thought, this document throws a special light on the rise of Gnosticism. Everything points to its having originated outside Christianity and to the enrichment of an existing system at a later stage with Christian material.'[24] It is only when we recall the role played by Hermes as mediator of *gnosis* in the Corpus Hermeticum, and the conclusions drawn by Dodd in his study of the Hermetica,[25] that such a judgment is given its full weight.

There is, then, ground for the view that the Apocryphon of John presents a Christianisation of an older non-Christian text, or at least of a non-Christian system, but is this confirmed by comparison of the different versions? Can we arrange them in chronological order and show a progressive Christianisation, or is the movement in the opposite direction? The latter conclusion would of course entail revision of van Unnik's judgment, but investigation of this question has scarcely begun, nor can it be entered into here. It must suffice to outline some aspects of the problem.

There are cases in which one of the two shorter versions uses a Greek word, the other its Coptic equivalent; but the usage is not consistent, for sometimes it is the first which uses the Coptic word and the second the Greek. And there are cases in which there seems to be an alteration in the meaning. In the longer versions, again, some of the apparent expansion fits so well into the context that we should never have suspected anything but for its absence in the shorter versions. Which direction did the development take—expansion of the shorter versions, or abridgement of the longer?

Here already two opinions have been advanced. Giversen[26] thinks Codex II more original and holds the shorter versions to be abridgements, although he admits (a) that the latter are sometimes more reliable in terms of content, and (b) that Codex

[24] ibid., p. 79.
[25] *The Bible and the Greeks*, p. 248; cf. above, p. 83 f.
[26] *Apocryphon Johannis*, p. 277.

II also has some insertions, some of them fairly lengthy. Kasser[27] on the other hand argues that it is rare for a text to be shortened, and that examination of the material peculiar to the long recension shows it to be a development of the shorter. The Berlin text he considers nearest to the original, but he considers its parallel in Codex III comparatively late.

One passage which Giversen admits to be an interpolation occurs in the account of the creation of man—a passage (Codex II, 63.29–67.10) which identifies and names the angels responsible for the making of each part of the body, the right eye and the left, for example, or the right foot and the left—there is a separate angel for the toes of each foot, and another for the toe-nails! Now it might appear that in conceding the presence of insertions Giversen has given his case away, but we must be more subtle. It is not sufficient simply to dismiss the longer version as secondary because of this passage, or other such insertions. We have to leave such sections out of the reckoning and compare the rest, in the effort to see *why* the changes have been made. If we can find the explanation for an alteration in one direction or another, this may help to solve the problem. If there are grounds for thinking that one version has been consistently modified to bring it into conformity with a particular theory, then we also have reason for considering that version to be the later. Here obviously much remains to be done.

Two final points of interest are (a) the reference at 67.10 in Codex II, at the end of the long insertion mentioned above, to the 'book of Zoroaster', which Giversen[28] suggests may indicate not only where further information may be found but also the source upon which the Apocryphon has drawn at this point, and (b) the possible significance of the document for the development of Valentinianism. Irenaeus places the Barbelognostics among the precursors of Valentinus, and comparison with known Valentinian documents may help us to trace the growth of that system. This, as we have already seen, is a point at which the Gospel of Truth may be of significance: is it possible to trace a line of development from that Gospel to the full Valentinian system, such as to show that knowledge of Barbelognostic theory in general, and the Apocryphon of John in particular, has contributed to the process? How much of the Valentinian theory

---

[27] *Rev. Theol. et Phil.*, 1964, pp. 144 f.   [28] *Apocryphon Johannis*, p. 281.

remains if we remove the Barbelognostic elements? Here again
are problems still awaiting investigation.

3. *The Sophia Jesu Christi*.[29] Of this document two versions are
extant in Coptic, one complete in the Berlin Codex and a
second, of which two leaves are missing, in the Nag Hammadi
library. The latter has not yet been published, but its variant
readings are noted in Dr. Till's edition of the Berlin text. Part of
the interest of this document lies in the fact that it has in the
Nag Hammadi library a very close parallel, the Epistle of
Eugnostos, so close indeed as to raise the question of literary
dependence. Now the Sophia is a book of revelation, in fact a
'gospel' of the Gnostic type, containing a conversation between
Jesus and the disciples upon a mountain after the Resurrection.
Much of it is in the form of answers given by Jesus in response to
the questions put by his hearers. Eugnostos on the other hand is
a straightforward dogmatic epistle, in the form not of a dialogue
but of continuous discourse, and according to some accounts
without any distinctly Christian features. The question is
whether Eugnostos is a development from the Sophia, by the
elimination of the dialogue and of the Christian elements; or the
Sophia created out of Eugnostos by the breaking up of the
discourse and the insertion of the questions. In fact, this might
appear to be a test case for the relation of Gnosticism to
Christianity, for on the first alternative obviously we should
have evidence of a movement away from Christianity, a process
of de-Christianisation; whereas on the second view we should
have the Christianising of a previously non-Christian text. Unfortunately, as so often happens, the issue is not quite so simple,
nor are the problems so readily solved.

   Doresse in one of the earliest studies of the Nag Hammadi
documents[30] argued for the dependence of the Sophia upon
Eugnostos, and even at one point for the view that it was composed in Coptic on the basis of Eugnostos. In this he was
followed by Werner Foerster,[31] but both wrote before the publication of the Berlin text, which at the points in question varies

[29] Text in Till, pp. 194 ff. See also Puech in Hennecke-Schneemelcher, i,
pp. 243 ff.
[30] *Vig. Chr.* 2, (1948), pp. 150 ff. Cf. Till, op. cit., p. 305.
[31] *TLZ* 79, (1954), col. 379.

to some extent from that of Nag Hammadi. Moreover Puech[32] had shown in the interval that two pages of the *Greek* text of the Sophia are preserved in one of the Oxyrhynchus papyri (POx.1081). It is more probable that translation was from Greek into Coptic than the other way, and moreover the Oxyrhynchus fragment is dated at least half a century before the Coptic texts, so that Doresse's earlier conclusion as to the original language is incorrect; in his book he has accordingly abandoned it.[33] The facts which led him to this conclusion, however, remain to be explained, as does the precise relationship of the two Coptic versions of the Sophia. This example provides an excellent illustration of the way in which apparently sound deductions may be overtaken by events, and shown to be in fact erroneous by subsequent discovery.

Eugnostos unfortunately has not yet been published, and our information has to be dug out of the apparatus to the Berlin edition of the Sophia. A final judgment on the relation between them must therefore await publication of the text of Eugnostos, but it may be noted that so far those who have gone into the matter differ in their conclusions. Doresse, as already remarked, argued for the priority of Eugnostos, but Till in his edition says 'It seems to me much more probable that SJC was the source of Eug. and not the contrary.'[34] Puech notes that the Sophia is a little longer, and 'contains here and there passages which are peculiar to it.'[35] Like Doresse, he maintains that the Sophia is only a recasting of the epistle. It should perhaps be noted here that while some of the peculiar passages are quite short and consist of a few lines only, containing a question from a disciple and words to the effect that the Saviour answered, there are one or two which extend to two or three pages; moreover there are over two pages of text before the parallel with Eugnostos begins, and some ten pages at the end where the Sophia is again quite independent.

Perhaps the fullest discussions as yet are those of H. M. Schenke and M. Krause,[36] who again take opposite sides.

---

[32] Cf. Hennecke-Schneemelcher, i, p. 245.
[33] *Secret Books*, p. 196.   [34] op. cit., p. 54.
[35] Hennecke-Schneemelcher, i, p. 248.
[36] Schenke, *ZRGG* 14, (1962), pp. 264 ff.; Krause in *Mullus*, Jahrb. f. Antike u. Christentum, Ergänzungsband 1, (Münster 1964), pp. 215 ff.

Schenke states and refutes the arguments advanced by Doresse, and notes as the decisive argument in his opinion the fact that Eugnostos also contains peculiar material, one section of which lists six pairs of aeons originating from the Saviour and Pistis Sophia. These, he argues, considerably increase and complicate the number of the heavenly beings present in the Sophia, and can be recognised from their names to be the product of secondary elaboration of the original system. Moreover Eugnostos, to judge by Doresse's account of its contents, gives the impression of being put together from fragments detached from their original setting, and indeed there are points at which one can still detect the breaks. A further argument advanced by Schenke is directly countered by Krause. Schenke wrote that it is scarcely credible that any-one, even a Gnostic, should have forced a systematically ordered whole into a scheme of question and answer which destroys the run of thought. The subsequent systematisation of what was formerly unsystematic is on the other hand perfectly comprehensible. Krause affirms that this argument is not valid for the Gnostic texts, since experience repeatedly shows how clear systems through the incorporation of further ideas become ever more complicated and obscure. He cites the Apocryphon of John by way of example, and the Pistis Sophia as generally recognised to be the final product of such a process.

Previous scholars, as Schenke had already noted,[37] were not in possession of all the evidence. Doresse did not know the Berlin text of the Sophia or the Greek fragment, and while he knew the version of Eugnostos in Codex III he did not have access to the second version in Codex V. Schenke knew both the Greek fragment and the Berlin text of the Sophia, but the Nag Hammadi version was available to him only through Till's apparatus and Eugnostos only in so far as it was parallel to the Sophia or from Doresse's account of its contents. Krause's case is strengthened by the fact that it is based on the whole of the material.

His method is to examine the material peculiar to each of the documents and compare it with the material common to both. 'The document whose special material agrees in content with the text common to both is probably the primary document,

[37] op. cit., p. 265; cf. Krause, p. 217 n. 27.

the one whose special material obviously does not fit the common text is probably the secondary.'[38] Now the special material in the Sophia is more extensive than that of Eugnostos, and it does not agree with the common material. When we compare the questions of the disciples (special material) with the answers given by the Saviour (common material), we find that so far as they are not cast in general terms the questions do not fit the answers. Again, the special material breaks up sections which belong together, and there are points at which the special material does not agree with statements contained in the common matter. On the other hand the special material in Eugnostos does fit the common material. Finally, there are points at which the Sophia is confusing, because the introduction of the special material has interrupted the train of thought. When this special material is removed, we obtain an intelligible text which is close to that of Eugnostos. Eugnostos therefore is the older and the Sophia the secondary document.

Final judgment must of course await the detailed checking which can only be done when the text of Eugnostos becomes available. There is however a further point to be considered. According to Krause[39] the special material in Eugnostos, like the material common to both documents, contains no Christian ideas. Schenke[40] on the other hand affirms that Christian motifs are firmly rooted in the teaching of Eugnostos. On this point Till's edition provides an adequate basis for preliminary discussion.

In the first place it has to be noted that, apart from the common formula 'He who has ears to hear, let him hear!' (Matt. 11.15 par.), the clearest New Testament allusions in Till's brief list occur on p. 79 of the Berlin Codex, that is, in the preamble to the Sophia. Here there is a clear reference to the Transfiguration, which is however located on the Mount of Olives—in Galilee! Again, when the risen Jesus comes in his glory to the disciples, he greets them with the words 'Peace be with you! The peace which is mine I give you' (cf. Lk. 24.36; John 20.19,21,26; 14.27). The Matthean formula mentioned above occurs at four points (89.4 f., 90.13–14, 107.18–108.1 Till; the reference to 98.10–12 in Till's index is a mistake for 100.10–12), but on closer inspection every one of them proves to

[38] op. cit., p. 218.   [39] ibid.   [40] op. cit., p. 265.

be in material peculiar to the Sophia. The same holds also for the three other citations listed by Till: 'To you it is given to know, and to those who are worthy to know' (82.9–10; cf. Matt. 13.11); a reference to 'those who were born of the seed of the unclean impulse' (82.14; cf. John 1.13); and a further reference to those who were sent 'like a drop from the light into the world' (103.10–14; cf. John 1.9). The Christian element in the Sophia is therefore to this extent stronger than is the case in Eugnostos; but was Eugnostos itself completely non-Christian?

Dr. Krause very kindly placed his synopsis of the texts of Eugnostos at my disposal for a few days, and the following points are drawn from his transcription. Most of them can be readily verified from Till's edition. Codex III (77.20 ff., cf. SJC 95.17 ff. Till) refers to the creation of 'gods and archangels and angels for service' (cf. also 81.3, SJC 100.1). This recalls Heb. 1.14, although the Greek loan-word in the Coptic texts is not the one used in Hebrews. On the following page (96.10 f. Till) the titles 'God of gods' and 'King of kings' may reflect knowledge of Rev. 17.14, 19.16, but here of course the Old Testament also has to be taken into account (cf. Deut. 10.17, Dan. 2.47); nor can it be assumed that even the Old Testament is necessarily the source of these titles. Codex III (81.5–6; not in Till) refers to 'the church of the saints of light', and the word ἐκκλησία recurs later in the material common to both documents (Codex III 86.16,22 and p. 82; SJC 110.11 and p. 111). It is doubtful how much weight should be placed on such words as ἀσπάζεσθαι, ἀσπασμός and πίστις, but ἀγάπη occurs not only three times in the special material of the Sophia (88.3, 99.14, 124.3), but also once in material peculiar to Eugnostos (Codex III 82.24). Finally, there is a reference to 'the kingdom of the Son of man' (Codex III 81.13; SJC 101.6 f.), and the title 'Son of man' appears later in conjunction with the other title 'Saviour' (Codex III 81.21 ff.; SJC 102.15 ff.). The phrase 'from the foundation of the world' (SJC 80.7 f., 83.11; common material) is common in the New Testament, and there is a passage in Codex V of Eugnostos (8.11) which with its reference to a 'form' and a 'name' may recall Phil. 2; but again too much should not perhaps be built on the latter point. There is a similar passage in the special material of the Sophia (97.17–

98.4) which will require to be compared when Codex V eventually becomes available.

Once again, the significance of these resemblances will be variously estimated. At the very least, however, they seem to demand a due measure of caution over against assertions that Eugnostos is entirely non-Christian or shows no sign of Christian influence. There is nonetheless a further possibility: is the Epistle of Eugnostos itself a Christianised version of an earlier document? Here a further suggestion by Krause[41] calls for examination. He suggests that the original basis was a cosmogonical text, intended to refute three different philosophical theories regarding the origin of the world and to present in their stead a system which began with a description of the true and unbegotten God and extended down through three successive emanations to the manifestation of Chaos. This system contained some Jewish but no Christian elements, and no soteriology. The document was transformed by Eugnostos into an epistle through the addition of the appropriate framework, and one of the versions of this epistle was subsequently worked over and given the Christian framework which we now find in the Sophia.

Such a process is not in itself improbable, although confirmation of the theory must await the publication of all the texts. The very existence of differing versions of certain documents in the Nag Hammadi library shows that such redactional activity did take place, but on the other hand there must always be an element of speculation in the reconstruction of hypothetical 'basic documents' from existing texts when we have no originals to work on. Two points however may be significant: (a) if Krause is correct, and Eugnostos or its *Grundschrift* contained Jewish but no Christian elements, we should have a further pointer to some connection between Judaism and Gnostic origins; and (b) if the *Grundschrift* was of a philosophical character we may have to revise some of our ideas as to the development of Gnosticism. Was it from mythology to philosophy, or did systems originally philosophical degenerate into myth and finally into fantasy? Or should we think of a development from mythology to philosophical mysticism, followed by a degeneration? Conclusions on this point would obviously have a bearing

[41] op. cit., p. 222.

on the place of particular documents in the whole process of development.

Two further points may be noted in conclusion: (a) if Eugnostos or its *Grundschrift* is non-Christian, this does not necessarily mean that it is *pre*-Christian, at least in the sense that it dates back before the Christian era. It is entirely possible for Gnosticism in some of its forms to have developed parallel to but independently of Christianity, in approximately the same period, and for some of its documents to have been subsequently Christianised by the more specifically Christian Gnostics. (b) As Schenke observes,[42] we have to reckon in the history of Gnosticism not only with Christianisation but also with de-Christianisation. It is probably a mistake to envisage the development as moving always and consistently in the one direction, and the same may be true also of the relation between Gnosticism and philosophy. Here again a great deal needs to be done in the way of detailed investigation before we can attempt to formulate general conclusions.

4. *De Resurrectione (The Epistle to Rheginus)*.[43] The double title in this case calls for explanation: De Resurrectione is the Latin form of the title 'the Treatise concerning the Resurrection' which appears in the manuscript at the end of the text. The final leaf containing the title was not however among the leaves of this Codex which were brought to Zürich, but was subsequently discovered among the Cairo fragments published by Labib.[44] Working on the Zürich portion only, Puech and Quispel in their pioneer study took the document to be a letter to Rheginus, otherwise unknown, who is addressed in the opening lines and at two other points in the text. The discovery and identification of the missing leaf later revealed the real title, which was accordingly adopted for the edition of the text; but the other title had already to some extent become established.

This document is the third of those contained in the Jung Codex, and follows immediately on the Gospel of Truth.

[42] op. cit., p. 266.
[43] Text with French, German and English translations in Malinine, Puech, Quispel and Till, *De Resurrectione*, (Zürich and Stuttgart 1963). Cf. Puech-Quispel, *Vig. Chr.* 8, (1954), pp. 40 ff.
[44] *Coptic Gnostic Papyri*, plates 1 and 2.

Comparatively short, it extends to seven pages only and belongs unmistakably to the documents of Christian Gnosticism, or more particularly the Valentinian school. As yet it has not attracted a great deal of attention, and apart from the pioneer article mentioned above and the material assembled in the edition only a few articles have been devoted to it. J. Zandee[45] has compared its teaching with that of the Gospel of Philip, and noted some striking similarities which serve to confirm its general Valentinian character. W. C. van Unnik[46] made it the subject of two lectures, and C. F. D. Moule[47] has drawn upon it in a study of Paul's teaching.

The first point to be observed is the difference, indeed the contrast, between this document and such works as the Apocryphon of John, the Sophia Jesu Christi, or the Epistle of Eugnostos. As we have seen, there is some possibility that the three latter works may go back to older documents, or to an older system, which has in them been Christianised. The De Resurrectione however has not as yet prompted any such intriguing speculations. On the contrary, the author clearly takes his stand within the Church. As van Unnik notes, 'He quotes the Gospel and St. Paul; his ideas have parallels in non-Gnostic authors and are based solely on the work of Jesus Christ.' Indeed the centrality of Jesus is a notable feature of the document, and this not only as a Teacher or as the Revealer of Gnosis: the resurrection of believers is firmly based upon what has happened in Christ. The resurrection is not an illusion but the truth, a reality, and 'came into being through our Lord the Saviour Jesus Christ' (48.10–19). The Son of God was also Son of Man, in order that as Son of God he might vanquish death and that 'through the Son of Man the restoration into the Pleroma might take place' (44.21–33).

As these last words show, it is a Gnostic document; 'restoration' and 'pleroma' are both technical terms in the vocabulary of Valentinianism, and there are other indications also of its Gnostic character elsewhere in the text. Yet this is a form of Gnosticism much nearer to what we know as 'orthodox' Christainity. This may serve to warn against undue readiness to formulate sweeping and comprehensive generalisations about

---

[45] *Nederlands Theol. Tijdschr.* 16, pp. 361 ff.
[46] *JEH* 15, (1964), 141 ff., 153 ff.   [47] *NTS* 12, (1966), pp. 106 ff.

the nature of Gnosticism. If some of the Nag Hammadi texts still unpublished present 'purely Gnostic' revelations, as Doresse[48] affirms, and others may be described as 'Gnostics disguised as Christians', there were other Gnostic thinkers who started from some point of Christian doctrine and developed it, or re-interpreted it, in a Gnostic direction.

A second feature is the emphasis placed in this text upon faith, and in particular upon faith in contrast to philosophical argument:

'If there is anyone who does not believe, it is not possible to persuade him, for it is the place of faith, and does not belong to persuasion' (46.2–7).

'We came to know the Son of Man, and we came to believe that he rose again from the dead, and this is he of whom we say that he became the destruction of death, so that it is a great one on whom they believe. Those who believe are immortal' (46.14–21). On the other hand, as the editors justly note,[49] the author 'shows a certain animosity with regard to the endless discussions to which the philosophers devoted themselves, these eternal *disputationes in utramque partem* on such subjects as the immortality of the soul' (cf. 43.25–35). For him Christianity is the absolute truth, the final answer to all the vain discussions of the philosophical schools. In this, as they observe, he is akin to Justin or the Clement of the Recognitions, a man trained in Greek philosophy, and especially in Platonism, who has yet abandoned it because it did not satisfy his deepest needs.

Not only is there this emphasis upon faith, but it is clearly the Christian faith which after his own fashion the author desires to commend. As we have seen, he speaks of 'our Lord the Saviour Jesus Christ', and describes him as both Son of God and Son of Man. There is a reference to the Transfiguration:

For if thou remember reading in the Gospel that Elias appeared and Moses with him, do not think that the resurrection is an illusion. It is no illusion, but it is the truth. Nay rather it is fitting for us to say that the world is an illusion rather than the resurrection.

(48.6–16)

Finally there is a reference to 'the Apostle', who is clearly Paul,

[48] *Secret Books*, p. 146.   [49] *De Resurrectione*, p. xviii.

for it is followed by a catena of quotations from the Pauline epistles (45.23–9).

Other New Testament echoes and allusions can be detected at various points, but this Christian material is built up into something quite different. In particular, as Puech and Quispel noted in their pioneer study,[50] the Pauline mysticism has been interpreted in terms of solar theology:

> As the Apostle said, we suffered with him, and we arose with him, and we went to heaven with him. But if we are made manifest in this world wearing him, we are his beams and we are encompassed by him until our setting, which is our death in this life. We are drawn upward by him like the beams by the sun, without being held back by anything. This is the spiritual resurrection which swallows up the psychic alike with the fleshly.
>
> (45.24–46.2)

Here we touch upon one of the most interesting and intriguing, yet sometimes also frustrating, aspects of the study of these new texts: the detailed tracing out of the connections, the influences which were at work, the way in which these writers thought, the reasons which led them to a particular interpretation, or re-interpretation, of the passages before them. The question here is not whether they were right or wrong, 'orthodox' or 'heretical', but how and why they came to their conclusions. In most cases there is a certain logic about their procedure, even if by 'orthodox' standards it is a perverse logic. Given a particular interpretation of a passage from Paul, its association with particular interpretations of other passages, and in some cases a link with some philosophical or other motif in the contemporary world, and the whole theory begins to fall into place. In other words, intensive study of these texts may help to show not only what the Gnostics thought but why and how they developed their theories. Here however we are still only at the beginning of our investigations.

A further point relates to the 'solar theology' mentioned above. There is no question that the first beginnings of this kind of thinking go far back before the Christian period. Wendland[51]

---

[50] *Vig. Chr.* 8, (1954), pp. 43 f.; cf. *De Resurrectione*, p. xiv.
[51] *Die hellenistisch-römische Kultur*, (Tübingen 1912), p. 158.

for example long ago wrote that the Chaldean solar and astral theology, already combined in the second century B.C. with advanced astronomical knowledge and with the Stoic philosophy, was united in Posidonius with the stream of Greek mysticism and the conception of the substantial unity of the soul with the realm of the stars. It was however only in the second Christian century and later that this solar theology reached the peak of its influence. The references adduced by the editors of our document[52] are significant: Plutarch, Philostratus, Proclus, the emperor Julian. And this is the very period which saw the rise of Gnosticism proper. It may be that such passages as Eph. 5.14 show these ideas already in currency at an earlier period, but here in Ephesians we have a definitely Christian hymn, and moreover we have to allow for the probable influence of the Old Testament (cf. Is. 60.1). It is not unusual, again, for something which began as poetic metaphor to be later hardened into a prosaic statement of fact. The point is that whatever the ultimate origins, and whatever the anticipations and adumbrations which we may detect, it was the second century which saw the real explosion, in Gnosticism, in Mithraism and other solar religions, in certain aspects of contemporary philosophy. We must of course endeavour to trace the whole chain of connection back to the ultimate origins, but it is dangerous in the extreme to assume that the entire content of later speculation was already present at earlier stages. We have also to try to understand the 'explosion' in the context and setting of its own period. Why was this kind of thinking so widely prevalent at this particular time?

It would be too much to say that the De Resurrectione is a masterly study; indeed at first sight it appears rather a rambling discourse. Certainly it falls far short of the massive and comprehensive treatment of Tertullian's treatise on the subject, and the author seems to stand on a rather different intellectual level from a Paul or a John, or from the best of the early Fathers. This may however be due in part to the difficulties of the subject, which the author expressly mentions (44.39–45.2), and in part to the fact that it is a comparatively early attempt to deal with these problems. The editors have provided a clue to the structure which shows that the work is in fact composed to a deliberate pattern: after a general introduction (43.25–44.3),

[52] *De Resurrectione*, pp. xiv–xv.

I

the theme is stated (44.3–12) and the main argument follows (44.12–47.1), rounded off by a brief summary (47.1–4); the following section deals with objections (47.4–49.9), and then comes a paraenetic conclusion (49.9–36), the document ending with an epilogue and greetings (49.37–50.16).

In the argument there are some remarkable contrasts with what is usually considered the 'Gnostic' attitude; for example, there is apparently no rejection of the resurrection of the flesh:

> For if thou wert not in the flesh, thou didst take on flesh when thou didst come into this world. Wherefore shouldst thou not take on the flesh when thou goest up into the aeon? That which is better than the flesh is for it the cause of life.
>
> (47.4–10)

This however appears to be contradicted later (the passage unfortunately is damaged):

> ... the members which are visible (but) dead will not be saved, for it is only the living (members?) that are within them which were to rise again. What then is the resurrection? It is the revelation at every moment of those who have arisen.
>
> (47.38–48.6)

Here we have to keep in mind the various theories which were current about the resurrection in the second century.[53] It was not simply a question of acceptance of the doctrine, or of its rejection in favour of belief in the immortality of the soul alone. It was a question also of the interpretation placed upon the doctrine, what it was held to signify; for there were those who affirmed that 'death' meant ignorance of God, and that in coming to knowledge of the truth, in accepting the Gospel, the believer was raised from death to walk in newness of life. Or it could be held that resurrection was deliverance from the tomb of the body, or again that it involved a transformation of the physical body into a spiritual one. It is not difficult to see how at one point or another an appeal could be made to Paul's teaching, but the combination of different elements of Pauline thought into a new synthesis, and the association of such

---

[53] Cf. *Vig. Chr.* 8, (1954), pp. 40 ff.; *De Resurrectione*, pp. x ff.; *JEH* 15, (1964), pp. 153 ff.

elements with other ideas from very different sources, might well lead to conclusions which Paul himself would not have countenanced.

The interest of the De Resurrectione lies (a) in its presentation of the doctrine—not perhaps an epoch-making treatment, yet one that is instructive as showing the thought of the period; (b) in its presentation of a Gnostic discussion of a theme which attracted the attention of other writers also—Justin, Athenagoras, Theophilus, Tertullian. As van Unnik notes,[54] the doctrine does not appear on the whole to have been a centre of debate in the first century, while it was already a fixed element in the Creed by the third; but in the second century it was a highly controversial subject. Finally the document is of interest (c) for the persistence and utilisation of Pauline themes and echoes. It enables us to see how a thinker of the second century could understand and interpret Paul from the point of view of his own later tradition.

That it is a Valentinian document has been sufficiently shown by Puech and Quispel.[55] It makes use of technical terms from the Valentinian vocabulary, and quotes a passage from Colossians with a variant characteristic of that school; and in addition to the Valentinian elements in point of content there are also the similarities to the Gospel of Philip, to which Zandee has drawn attention.[56] Whether we can identify the author more precisely is however another question. Puech and Quispel would date it after the Gospel of Truth, and suggest that the author was either a leader of the 'oriental' school of Valentinianism or Valentinus himself; and they incline to favour the latter alternative.[57] For van Unnik, on the other hand, this remains uncertain.[58] It is not impossible that the same man wrote both the De Resurrectione and the Gospel of Truth, and other works too for that matter, but the fact remains that we have no really adequate basis for a decision; and over-hasty identifications tend to be overtaken by later events. It

---

[54] *JEH* 15, (1964), p. 156.
[55] *Vig. Chr.* 8, (1954), pp. 46 ff.; *De Resurrectione*, pp. xx ff.
[56] *Ned. Theol. Tijdschr.* 16, pp. 361 ff.
[57] *Vig. Chr.* 8, (1954), p. 50; *De Resurrectione*, p. xxxiii.
[58] *JEH* 15, (1964), p. 144. Cf. Haenchen, *ThR* 30, (1964), p. 57 on the difficulty of assigning both this work and the Gospel of Truth to Valentinus.

would seem therefore advisable to describe the De Resurrectione simply as a work of the Valentinian school, although the possibility does exist that it may go back to Valentinus himself. In the present state of our knowledge we can say no more on this point.

5. *The Hypostasis of the Archons and the Anonymous Treatise from Codex II.* These two documents may be taken together, since there is a certain connection between them. Passages from the one can be adduced to shed light upon the other, although it should at once be added that there are also considerable differences. A further question, which has yet to be examined in detail, is the relation between these documents, or the system which they presuppose, and the system presented in such works as the Apocryphon of John, the Sophia Jesu Christi and Eugnostos.

The Hypostasis and the anonymous treatise were first made available in the photographic edition published by Labib, and were translated into German by H. M. Schenke.[59] In the case of the anonymous treatise, Schenke thought that he had almost the whole document in the fourteen pages accessible to him. It would then have been slightly longer than the immediately preceding Hypostasis. The full text however has now been published by Böhlig and Labib,[60] and a further seventeen pages have been added. As the Nag Hammadi library amply shows, it is dangerous to attempt a calculation of the probable length of a fragmentary Gnostic text unless there is some kind of external evidence upon which to work; we cannot tell what modifications, expansions or elaborations may have taken place, and the fact that, for example, a particular episode or motif occurs near the end in one document does not mean that it was also near the end in another. It should be added that Schenke was prompt to publish a correction when he learned the facts.[61]

[59] Labib, *Coptic Gnostic Papyri*, plates 134 ff., 145 ff.; Schenke, *TLZ* 1958, cols. 661 ff. [Hypostasis]; 1959, 243 ff.

[60] *Die koptisch-gnostische Schrift ohne Titel aus Codex II von Nag Hammadi*, (Berlin 1962).

[61] Leipoldt-Schenke, *Koptisch-gnostische Schriften aus den Papyrus-Codices von Nag-Hammadi*, (Hamburg-Bergstedt 1960), p. 84. This volume includes the Hypostasis, but not the anonymous treatise. An edition of the Hypostasis by R. A. Bullard is in preparation.

Between them these texts extend to some forty pages, so that space does not admit of detailed discussion here. The Hypostasis, after an introductory sentence which might almost be a title, begins with a quotation of Eph. 6.12, ascribed to 'the great Apostle Paul', and professes to be a reply to a question about the powers. There appear to be no obvious Christian elements until near the end, where we find a reference to 'the Spirit of truth whom the Father has sent' (144.35; cf. John 14.26), and to 'the unction of life eternal' (145.2). On the other hand the document is clearly a re-interpretation of Genesis of the Barbelo-gnostic type. It begins with the boast of Jaldabaoth, quoting Is. 46.9, and continues roughly parallel with the Apocryphon of John, but in summary form and with variations of detail, through the narrative of the creation of man to the birth of Cain and Abel, here the children of Adam and Eve. The statement that God looked upon the gifts of Abel, and later spoke to Cain, may be due to a failure to revise this section in a Gnostic sense; or it might possibly reflect a closer proximity to the original Genesis story. The narrative continues to the story of the Flood, where it introduces the figure of Norea, here apparently the wife of Noah (elsewhere she is the wife of Seth or Shem[62]). At this point questions arise as to the relation of our document to a 'Book of Norea' mentioned by Epiphanius (Pan. 26.1,3–9), which has the same story but with some variations. Refused admission to the ark, Norea destroys it, according to Epiphanius three times over. Menaced by the archons, she appeals for help, and an angel comes down from heaven—and proceeds to reveal to her the story of the origin of things as it had already been recorded above. Near the end the Hypostasis reports the fettering of Jaldabaoth and his imprisonment in Tartarus, and the repentance of his son Sabaoth, who is set over the seventh heaven and called 'god of the powers'. Following the reference mentioned above to 'the unction of life eternal', the document closes: 'Then they will cast away from them blind thought, and trample down the death of the powers (cf. SJC 125.19–126.11), and go up to the infinite light where this seed is. Then the powers will leave their seasons, and their angels weep over their destruction, and their demons over their death. Then all the sons of light (cf. Qumran!) shall know the truth, their true root,

[62] Cf. Leipoldt-Schenke, p. 70; Böhlig, op. cit., pp. 31 f.

the Father of the All and the Holy Spirit. They will all say with one voice: Righteous is the truth of the Father, and the Son is over all and through all for ever and ever. Holy, holy, holy. Amen.' (pl. 145 Labib).

There is evidently a slight Christian element in this document, but it is only slight, which once again raises the question of the possible Christianisation of older material. Again, why the repentance and rehabilitation of Sabaoth? What is the relation of this motif to the Hippolytan account of the theory of Basilides, where the Great Archon has a son much wiser than himself, who sits beside him, upon whom the light of the Gospel descends, and who is subsequently identified as Christ? According to Epiphanius, again, Noah put his trust in the archon, the god of this world, whereas Norea revealed the higher powers; but in the Hypostasis, in Schenke's view, Noah relies upon the righteous God who stands between the evil Demiurge and the realm of light, and this is one of Schenke's reasons for rejecting the identification of the Hypostasis with the Book of Norea. In the latter view he may be correct, but *is* the Hypostasis at variance with Epiphanius? Or has Schenke himself been misled through the identifying the ἄρχων of the powers (140.8) as Sabaoth, who is *later* given the title 'god of the powers' (143.23)? If the archon is Jaldabaoth, the two texts are in complete harmony on this point.

The anonymous work has been described by some writers as an apocalypse, but Böhlig takes a different view. He claims that the document is a polemical tract directed against the theory found in Hesiod's Theogony: that Chaos lay at the origin of all things. 'The gods of this world,' it begins, 'and men too, all say that nothing existed before Chaos, but I will demonstrate that they are all in error.' Chaos, to summarise, is darkness, a shadow—and a shadow pre-supposes something to cast the shadow. But if Chaos is thus secondary, what is the primal beginning? As Böhlig says,[63] 'the author does not have an easy task in answering this question. In the closely related Hypostasis of the Archons all this is much more clearly handled.'

Briefly, through the action of Pistis Sophia a veil is interposed between the higher and lower regions, and Chaos is the shadow created by this veil. Pistis Sophia is disturbed at the conse-

[63] *Wiss. Zeitschr. Halle* 10, (1961), pp. 1065 f.

quences of her action, and creates an archon from Chaos to set it in order. This is Jaldabaoth, and the document continues with the exposition of a system like that of the Apocryphon of John. Here however it is not a simple and straightforward exposition, for the course of the narrative is interrupted again and again by the introduction of mythological motifs. Böhlig justly speaks of *Kompilationsfreudigkeit*, and expresses the opinion that we are here at a later stage of the mythology. There is at one point a shaking of the heavens, which seems to reflect the myth of the Titans; later the legend of Cupid and Psyche is drawn upon, and later still there are references to the legend of the phoenix, to the crocodile, and to 'the bulls of Egypt' which have as a mystery the sun and moon. At several places Böhlig notes the possibility of an interpolation, notably in the transference of the repentance of Sabaoth to an earlier point in the system. The general impression left is that an originally simple system has been elaborated and expanded by the incorporation of additional material, which has not always been successfully assimilated into the context. Sometimes indeed the result is quite incongruous: one wonders how the seven virgins (153.32 ff.) contrived to handle thirty zithers, with harps and trumpets in addition! But Böhlig plausibly suggests that the virgins represent the planets (and the days of the week) and the instruments the days of the month.

As already noted, Böhlig rejects the view that this document is an apocalypse, and argues that it is a polemical tract. On this I am happy to agree, the more especially since I shall have cause to differ at a later point. It certainly begins as a polemical tract, but it develops into something more: a cosmogony running into a description of the final *apocatastasis*; and there are certainly elements of an 'apocalyptic' character in the description of the last things, the coming of the new aeon and the annihilation of evil.

Christian elements are present, but they are by no means prominent.[64] Jesus is mentioned twice only, and in a subordinate role. On the other hand Böhlig remarks 'That the Christian influences in the Gnostic thought of our text at least are greater than they might sometimes appear is shown by the introduction of New Testament words at important points.' There are quotations of New Testament passages, but they are re-interpreted

[64] Böhlig-Labib, p. 33.

and even on occasion textually modified. In many cases the Christian form is present, but that is all: 'for our Gnostics the Christian form was a form without content; for it was empty when Jesus Christ no longer formed its centre.' Lest these last words be thought too great a concession to the view which would see Gnosticism as entirely a movement away from Christianity, it should be added that Böhlig suggests that one of the references to Jesus (153.26) may be a secondary addition. The process in fact was not a simple one, for we have evidence in other texts both for Christianisation and for de-Christianisation.

The significance of these two documents lies first in the fact that they present affinities with other documents, as well as differences from them, and thus show how the Gnostics could adapt and modify their teachings to meet particular situations. Here there is need for a detailed comparison of these texts with one another, and with such other documents as the Apocryphon of John, to determine their mutual relationships and relative dates. In the process we may find much to learn about the development of Gnostic theory. Secondly, there are a number of points at which they may shed light on ideas contained in texts outside this immediate group. For example, the Hypostasis (140.1–3) uses the words 'the virgin whom the powers did not defile', and the same phrase is used in the Gospel of Philip (103.31 Labib). Here we have Gnostic use of an older motif, going back to Jewish legend. Now the Hypostasis provides an explanation earlier (137.20 ff.) in the story of the archons' abortive attempt upon Adam's 'spiritual' wife, although the phrase itself refers neither to this spiritual wife nor to Eve, but to Eve's daughter. Are we then at liberty to use the Hypostasis to explain Philip? Or have we a motif which has come to them along different lines of tradition? Is it possible to trace these developments? Again, Philip speaks of a veil or curtain (132.21 ff.), and both the Hypostasis (142.5 ff.) and the anonymous work set at the beginning of the whole cosmic (and supra-cosmic) process an act of Pistis Sophia which results in the coming into being of a veil between the higher and the lower regions. Perhaps we may also link with these the rather obscure passage at the beginning of the Gospel of Truth (17.9 ff.) concerning the operations of Error. A further example is a passage in the anonymous work about the trees in paradise (158.6 ff.), at which Böhlig compares log. 19 of the Gospel of Thomas. In each of these cases we have the same or a similar motif utilised in different documents. It would obviously be a mistake to assume without further ado that one document explains another, especially when the former is the later of the two; but comparison and analysis may provide valuable insights into the use of such motifs, the ways in which they were adapted and re-interpreted. At present we are still scarcely beyond the stage of noting the similarities and collecting the material.

Thirdly, Böhlig at a number of points draws attention to Manichean parallels, and remarks that we may see in the myths of our texts preliminary forms which furnished the materials for Mani. Here again we have evidence for developments within the Gnostic movement, in the ways in which the Manicheans took over, and sometimes adapted to their own ideas, materials already in use among the older sects. Fourth, both the Hypostasis and the anonymous treatise refer to other documents, the Book of Norea, the Book of Solomon, the Sacred Book, and so on, which may with some justice be assumed to be among their sources—and some of these may yet prove to be included among the other documents in the Nag Hammadi collection. This however remains to be seen. It is dangerous to assume from similarity of title that we have the actual book—we have as it is three different Apocalypses associated with the name of James in the Nag Hammadi library alone, two works associated with Thomas, distinct from the Infancy Gospel previously known, and a Gospel of Philip which has nothing to do with the one mentioned by Epiphanius. Also the Gospel of the Egyptians from Nag Hammadi appears to have no connection with the document of the same title quoted by Clement of Alexandria. Finally, there is the fact that while the Christian element in these documents is often slight and sometimes appears to be secondary, the Jewish is integral to the whole structure, for these works are in large measure re-interpretations of Old Testament material. Indeed there are points (e.g. the anonymous work 161.21 ff.) at which the whole speculation seems to be built upon a play on Hebrew or Aramaic words. This confirms, were confirmation needed, the significance of the Jewish contribution to the development of Gnosticism, although as already noted in an earlier chapter the fact that the material is Jewish does not necessarily mean that the people who moulded it into these systems were themselves Jews. We have also to take account of the introduction in the anonymous treatise and elsewhere of motifs derived from Greek mythology; a passage in the Gospel of Truth (29.11–14) appears to be inspired by the Iliad of Homer; and there are various reactions to and attitudes towards philosophy. These texts in short provide some insight into a period of considerable intellectual ferment, in which an emergent Christianity was striving to find a foothold and maintain itself, and experiments in syncretism of one kind or another were a common feature.

6. *Gnostic Apocalypses: The Apocalypse of Adam.* As already noted, Böhlig rejects the view that the anonymous treatise in Codex II is an apocalypse. An apocalypse, he says, 'is a revelation, whose actual or fictitious recipient is normally named.' This literary form was frequently employed in late Judaism and in early Christianity, and the vision which belongs to the very nature of this category makes the use of myth readily comprehensible. But the mythical content of a work does not necessarily make it an apocalypse. Böhlig's point is certainly valid, but as we have seen there are elements of an 'apocalyptic' character in the work, in the section dealing with the End, the coming of the new aeon, and the final *apocatastasis*. Some consideration of the nature of 'apocalypse' would therefore seem to be called for at the outset.

A convenient starting-point is provided by the comprehensive introduction to the section 'Apocalypses and Related Subjects' in the Hennecke-Schneemelcher *NT Apocrypha*.[65] Here a distinction is made between different types of apocalypse within the Jewish tradition, those for example which report a vision and on the other hand those which profess to relate a farewell discourse by Enoch, Moses, or some other such figure from the past. The Jewish apocalypses contain revelations not only about the last things but also on the Beyond, on heaven and hell, and so on; their main interest however is not in problems of cosmology or theodicy but in eschatology. Among the characteristic features noted are the doctrine of the two ages, the 'apocalyptic

[65] Hennecke-Schneemelcher, ii, (ET: London 1965), pp. 581 ff.

pessimism' with its extreme devaluation of this present age, and the corresponding intensification of hope for and speculation about the age to come. Another feature is the use of surveys of history in the form of prophecy, which frequently give a clue to the date of these works: 'the point at which the history loses precision and accuracy is the moment of writing'.[66]

Early Christianity to a large extent shared the thought-world and temper of Jewish Apocalyptic, and took over much of the older Jewish material, whether in the form of concepts or imagery or in that of actual documents, which were Christianised by more or less extensive editing. The Church also produced its own Christian apocalypses, some of which were to exercise a considerable influence upon the literature and art of later centuries. There is however a shift of emphasis, through the concern of Christian apocalyptic with the Parousia and later with anti-Christ and the after-life. The latter, says Vielhauer,[67] while in the New Testament subsidiary to the Parousia expectation, 'are the two main themes around which Christian Apocalyptic revolves from the middle of the second century.'

The Gnostic apocalypses with which we are here concerned were not yet available to Vielhauer, and he could do no more than refer to the survey provided by Doresse.[68] He did however note two points: (a) that the contents of the works entitled 'Apocalypse' appear to be 'extensively cosmological and soteriological, and not of an eschatological-apocalyptic nature'; and (b) that on the other hand apocalyptic material is to be found in documents which carry other labels. 'The designations of form which these writings often carry in their titles should not be understood in the traditional sense as literary characterisations.'[69]

The 'apocalyptic pessimism' with its devaluation of this present age provides of course an obvious affinity with Gnosticism, and is indeed a part of the evidence to which appeal is made in support of the theory of a pre-Christian Jewish Gnosticism. Gnosticism and Apocalyptic are not however identical; difficult as it may be to distinguish them, the effort must nevertheless be made, and one criterion is already available in the

[66] Quoted from C. K. Barrett, *The NT Background*, (London 1956), p. 231.
[67] op. cit., p. 600.
[68] op. cit., p. 599, referring to Doresse, *Secret Books*, pp. 146–248.
[69] ibid.

first point noted above from Vielhauer. Jewish apocalyptic has beyond question contributed to the development of Gnosticism, but here again there has been a transposition of older material into a different key.

Of the apocalypses which immediately concern us, three may be briefly dealt with. As Böhlig notes, the Apocalypse of Paul and the two Apocalypses of James form a fairly homogeneous group, linked with two leading figures of the early Church. The Apocalypse of Adam, he thinks, was associated with them only because it belongs to the same literary type, for here he finds Jewish and Hellenistic Gnosis indeed, but not Christian.[70] A third Apocryphon of James in the Jung Codex has no connection with the two in Codex V.[71]

The brief *Apocalypse of Paul* is an account of Paul's ascent into the heavens, evidently inspired by 2 Cor. 12.2. It begins on the way to Jericho, and indeed as later appears 'on the mountain of Jericho' (19.11 ff.), which is of course a purely artificial setting; a mountain is the conventional place for a revelation. The actual ascent begins at the third heaven, and passes at once to the fourth, where a soul is under examination. Condemned at the mouth of three witnesses (cf. Deut. 19.15), it is cast down into a body. Entering the fifth and sixth heavens, Paul sees his 'fellow-apostles' going with him. In the seventh he meets an old man, with whom he has a long discussion, and who only allows him to go further on presentation of a sign. The further ascent up to the tenth heaven is merely related, with but little in the way of description.

This apocalypse is not the one known to Dante,[72] although there are links: in the fourth heaven Paul is told to look down on the earth (19.25 ff.; cf. Apoc. Pauli 13); that Apocalypse also introduces an old man (Apoc. Pauli 20), there identified as Enoch. This however would not fit our apocalypse, where the old man appears to be a 'guardian'; Böhlig suggests Sabaoth. Finally there are the judgment scenes, but these in the

[70] Böhlig-Labib, *Apokalypsen*, p. 11.
[71] Cf. Puech in Hennecke-Schneemelcher, i, pp. 333 ff.; van Unnik, *Newly Discovered Gnostic Documents*, pp. 80 ff.; Zandee, *Ned. Theol. Tijdschr.* 17, (1963), pp. 401 ff. An edition of this document is in preparation.
[72] Böhlig-Labib, *Apokalypsen*, p. 18; cf. Hennecke-Schneemelcher, ii, pp. 755 ff.

Apocalypse are much more fully elaborated. Any attempt to trace a connection between the two documents must be highly speculative.

The first *Apocalypse of James* is of a different type, and takes the form of a dialogue between James and Jesus, the first part of which (24.10–30.11) falls before the death of Jesus, the second (31.5–42.19) after the Resurrection. Between these sections is an account of James's sorrow at the sufferings of Jesus, of his ascent of 'the mountain called Gaugela' with his disciples, and of his ignorance that there is a Comforter (cf. John 14.16 etc.). James is given the name 'James the Just' (32.2 f.) and is addressed as 'my brother', although it is said that he is not a brother materially (24.12–15); in other words he is regarded as an adoptive brother. Jesus is regularly addressed as 'Rabbi'.

The document does not lend itself readily to presentation in summary form, and only a few points can be noted. The risen Lord says 'Never have I endured any kind of suffering, nor was I tormented. And this people did not do me any evil' (31.18–22). Rather does the responsibility rest with the archons. Here we seem to have something of a Docetic Christology, and certainly the responsibility, which in the canonical tradition tends to be transferred from the Romans to the Jews, is here transferred from the Jews to the heavenly powers who rule this world (cf. 1 Cor. 2.8). Again, suffering is prophesied for James, and at this he is sorely disturbed; but he is comforted by Jesus (32.10 ff.), who then instructs him how to reply to the questions of the 'guardians' (33.6 ff.). To this section, as Böhlig notes, corresponds a passage in Irenaeus, the Greek text of which is preserved by Epiphanius.[73] References to Sophia and Achamoth, among other details, point to Valentinianism. The text unfortunately is damaged towards the end. A point of interest here, however, is the connection of this text, and through it of the Valentinian school, with the Jewish Christianity which gave so high a place to James. A possible link with the Hypostasis of the Archons is provided by a reference to casting away 'blind thought, the fetter of the flesh which surrounds thee' (27.3–6; cf. HA 145.5 ff.). This *may* reflect a certain antipathy towards philosophy, such as we know to have been a characteristic of some groups of Gnostics, but here again care is necessary. The

[73] *Adv. haer.* i.14.4 Harvey; Epiph. *Pan.* 36.3.2–6.

apocalypse uses the Greek word διάνοια, the Hypostasis a Coptic equivalent, and this word has a wide range of meaning. If some of its meanings would favour the suggestion of an antipathy to philosophy, others could be so understood only indirectly, if at all. We have therefore first to examine what the word meant for the Gnostics, but this cannot be undertaken here.

Links with Jewish Christianity may be detected also in the *second Apocalypse of James*, which is formally a speech delivered by James in Jerusalem prior to his martyrdom (Böhlig aptly compares the case of Stephen in Acts). In the account of the martyrdom, strict attention is paid to the Jewish regulations regarding stoning, and the description recalls the tradition reported by Hegesippus.[74] There are also links with the account of the death of James in the pseudo-Clementines.[75] Such features strengthen Daniélou's case for a connection between Jewish Christianity and Gnosticism, and might seem to entail also a reconsideration of H. J. Schoeps' claim that the Ebionites of the Clementines were not Gnostic but anti-Gnostic. Here again however caution is required. It has become abundantly clear that whatever the source from which they drew their material the Gnostics made of it something new. Pseudo-Clementine parallels to a Gnostic text do not therefore make either the Clementines Gnostic or the Gnostics Jewish-Christian; they merely indicate that at some point there is a connection, whether through borrowing on one side or the other, or through re-action against the 'false' teaching of the other group, or through their common dependence on older tradition, which each may have adapted to its own ends. Here once again there is need for careful and detailed analysis and comparison. Sweeping generalisations based on superficial resemblances are out of place, and merely confuse the issue.

The content of the document has been analysed in detail by Böhlig. Formally, after the introduction, it is a speech by James delivered from the fifth step of the Temple, and includes such statements as: 'Now am I rich in *gnosis* and have a single Father' (47.7 ff.); 'I am the first son who was begotten . . . the beloved, . . . the righteous, . . . the son of the Father' (49.5 ff.). As Böhlig notes,[76] this gives James a position little inferior to

---

[74] Cf. Kittel, *TWB*, iv, pp. 961 ff.   [75] Böhlig-Labib, *Apokalypsen*, p. 64.
[76] ibid., p. 28 and the notes to the text.

that of Jesus himself. The speech goes on to relate an appearance of Jesus, who as in the first apocalypse greets James as 'my brother', an address immediately explained by Mary (50.11 ff.). Then follows a revelation given by Jesus expounding the Gnostic doctrine of the Father and the Demiurge, and explaining the place and function of James: 'Thy father is not my Father, but my Father is become a father to thee' (51.19 ff.); 'Thou art not the redeemer and helper of strangers; thou art a redeemer and helper of those who are mine, but now are thine' (55.15 ff.). At the close, in response to Jesus' command to embrace him, James stretches out his arms but finds nothing; he hears Jesus say 'Know and embrace me!', which Böhlig reasonably suggests is intended to express the idea that it is not the stretching out of the hands but gnosis which brings one to Jesus. Accordingly James rejoices (57.10 ff.).

James continues his speech, now directly addressing his judges. Condemned to death, he is flung down from the pinnacle of the Temple (cf. Euseb. HE ii.23) and stoned. The document ends with his dying prayer (62.12 ff.). The points of interest in this text are obviously first the connections with Jewish Christianity already noted, and the use which is made of them in a Gnostic context; and secondly the frequent New Testament echoes and allusions; but there are also affinities with the martyrdoms in some of the apocryphal Acts. Here again detailed comparisons have still to be made.

The last of the documents to be considered in the present context is the *Apocalypse of Adam*. In contrast to the three preceding texts, which all have a distinct Christian colouring, this document shows at most only slight traces of Christian influence, and indeed in Böhlig's opinion derives from a pre-Christian Gnosis. Here lies its significance, for if Böhlig is correct we now have for the first time a genuine document of this Gnosis.

Externally, it is a revelation transmitted by Adam and his son Seth 'in the 700th year', which Böhlig takes to be the 700th year of Seth's life, 100 years before the death of Adam (Gen. 5.1–5). This revelation however contains within itself an account of a revelation made *to Adam* by three men, with whom Böhlig compares the three men who appeared to Abraham at Mamre on the one hand (Gen. 18.1), and the three Uthras of Mandeism on the other. Böhlig's analysis of the contents is as follows:

Introduction 64.2–4.

I. Adam's account of his own and Eve's experiences 64.5–67.14.

II. The Apocalypse proper 67.14–85.15.

    1. The Flood as an attack upon all mankind; preservation of the Men of Seth and of Noah 67.22–73.24.

    2. The destruction by fire as an attack on the Men of Seth and their dependants, and their preservation 73.25–76.7.

    3. The coming of the Phoster for the deliverance of the Sons of Noah 76.8–77.27.

Excursus: The fourteen statements about the origin of the Phoster 77.27–83.4.

    4. Repentance of the Peoples and sentence of judgment 83.4–85.18.

Conclusion 85.19–31.

Part I, relating the experiences of Adam and Eve, again falls into three sections, each of which speaks first of a manifestation of glory and then of an act of the Demiurge. In the first, Adam and Eve walk in glory, like the great eternal angels, and are taught 'a word of gnosis of God the eternal'. It is expressly stated that they were superior to the Demiurge, 'higher than the God who created us, and the angels that were with him', and he in his wrath divides them—Böhlig here aptly cites the Gospel of Philip (71, 78). This leads to the loss both of glory and of gnosis. The gnosis does not however perish, but passes into a new race of men, 'the seed of great aeons'.

Having lost the eternal gnosis of the true God, Adam and Eve are now instructed concerning dead works, come to know the God who made them (i.e. the Demiurge) and serve him in fear and slavery. In his sleep, three men appear to Adam—who do not belong to the powers of the Demiurge. They arouse him from the sleep of death, but the Demiurge takes note. The text here is damaged, but among his devices apparently is the creation of sexual desire. Weakness falls upon man, and the days of his life are shortened. Adam recognises that he is now come under the power of death. Now he will proclaim to Seth the revelation given him by the three. The theme is the promise of salvation, and the discourse describes the way in which the race of Seth, with those others who confess him, will be preserved and delivered from harm. The whole section is cast in the future tense, for this is after all an apocalypse. For present purposes however it will be more convenient to use the present throughout. An interesting feature here is the use of the Old Testament history in a *Gnostic* apocalypse.

First the Demiurge (here called the Pantocrator) brings a flood to destroy all flesh and in particular those to whom the revelation of gnosis had come down (i.e. through Seth). The plan is thwarted, because angels descend and carry them off in clouds (cf. AJ 73.4 ff. Till on Noah). Then the Demiurge will relent and take pity on Noah (expressly identified with Deucalion), and in conformity with the Biblical account set him and his family on the land. The men of Seth, who 'were separated through the knowledge of the great aeons and the angels', once more make their appearance, which arouses the wrath of the Demiurge. Noah protests his innocence, and they are then apparently brought into a land appropriate for them, where they build a holy dwelling-place.

Noah now divides the earth among his sons, Shem, Ham and Japhet, urging upon them and their seed obedience to the Pantocrator. But 400,000 men of the seed of Ham and Japhet join with the men of gnosis, and these are protected from all evil works and unclean desire.

The seed of Ham and Japhet now form twelve kingdoms, and call on the Demiurge (here called Saklas), emphasising that the seed of Noah has fulfilled his will, but that the race of Seth with its allies has not. The Demiurge now sends his powers to destroy them with fire. (Here as at other points Böhlig notes Mandean parallels, but surely both the Mandeans and these Gnostics are dependent on the Old Testament (the Flood, Sodom and Gomorrah)? It is of course at some distance.) Once again the men of gnosis are delivered.

The third epoch brings on the scene the figure of the *Phoster*, who comes to deliver men sunk in the power of death. This word had already occurred on the previous page (75.14 f.), where it seems to refer to the heavenly luminaries. It is after all the word used in Genesis (1.14) for the two great lights in the firmament (cf. also the four great lights in the Apocryphon of John 33.1 ff. Till. The Codex II version uses the Greek word here). He does signs and wonders, which alarm the Demiurge, who stirs up

K

wrath against him. And, it is said, 'the glory will come and dwell in holy houses which it has chosen for itself' (is this an echo of Paul's 'temples of the Holy Spirit'?). The powers cannot see him, hence they punish his fleshly manifestation (cf. Asc. Is. 9.14 f.).

This is the point at which we must call a halt. Böhlig remarks that at first one might think of an allusion to the sufferings of Jesus, but goes on to observe that this would be the only mention of Jesus in the text, and that even here the name is not once mentioned. Hence he thinks the assumption of a pre-Christian idea nearer to hand, and turns to Iranian religion, which 'definitely exercised an influence on the late-Jewish Gnosis'.[77]

Three points may be raised in objection, although Böhlig's argument has convinced at least one scholar:[78] first, that the narrative, brief and summary as it is, appears too closely tailored to the figure of Jesus to be entirely independent; second, that there is, as already noted, something that looks very like a New Testament echo in this very passage; and third, that at the close of the treatise there is a reference to 'the holy baptism of those who know the eternal gnosis through the logos-born (*logogenes*) and the incorruptible *phosteres* which have come forth from the holy seed, Jesseus, /Maz/areus, /Jesse/dekeus . . .' Jesseus Maza-reus—thus restored by Böhlig—might well be a corruption of Iesous Nazareus, and I suspect that Jessedekeus might originally have had something to do with Melchizedek. The Christian element is certainly slight, but is it completely non-existent? Böhlig himself draws attention to Revelation 12.5–6 as a parallel to 78.18 ff.—which speaks of a virgin mother and her child driven into the wilderness. But as already noted in an earlier chapter he prefers to think of the mythology lying behind Revelation. In any case, if it *is* from Revelation, it has been thoroughly worked over! Moreover, we need some further information about the Iranian parallels to which Böhlig appeals, their date and so forth. For if they are first attested in comparatively late Iranian texts they cannot be called into account here. In short, this is an interesting but not yet absolutely certain suggestion.

[77] ibid., p. 58.
[78] Cf. G. W. MacRae, *Heythrop Journal* 6, (1965), pp. 27 ff. See also Böhlig in *Oriens Christianus* 48, (1964), pp. 44 ff.

The text is in fact a curious mixture—we have references to Deucalion and the Pierides, together with Sodom and Gomorrah, the Flood, and Solomon apparently rather out of context. It is clearly a witness to a syncretism no longer controlled by exact knowledge of the texts, and recalls the eagerness of native guides to associate all kinds of events with their own particular sites. In view of this, and of the Mandean and other parallels to which Böhlig has drawn attention, I should be inclined (but very tentatively!) to disagree with him and suggest that this document represents not a pre-Christian Gnosis but a later stage.[79] This however is a question which remains to be explored.

And what shall I more say? For the time would fail me—these ancient words are still apposite, especially when there is such a mass of material to discuss, and more yet to come. Yet perhaps even so cursory and superficial account may serve to indicate something of the significance of these texts, and of the tasks that still await attention.

[79] More confidently Schenke in *OLZ* 61, (1966), col. 32.

Epilogue and Conclusion

THE discussion of the question of definition, in the first chapter, had already been drafted before the appearance of two recent contributions by H. M. Schenke, in which he also deals with the question, but from a somewhat different angle of approach.[1] Comparison may serve to show the extent of our agreement, and to bring the points at issue into sharper focus.

1. In the first place, Schenke uses the term Gnosis for preference, rather than Gnosticism, and he includes under this head the following figures or groups:

a. Simon Magus, Menander, Cerinthus, Saturnilus, Basilides, Valentinus, Marcion, Mani, with their respective disciples and adherents.

b. the Carpocratians; the Naassenes, Peratae and Sethians (in Hippolytus); the Nicolaitans, Ophites, Sethians and others (in Epiphanius); the Ophians in Origen; the Gnostics of Plotinus; the Mandeans.

c. two systems in Irenaeus, *Adv. haer.* i.29 and 30 (27 and 28 Harvey); the Gnostic Justin; the Poimandres and other Hermetic documents; Coptic Gnostic texts.

From this it will immediately be evident that for Schenke Gnosis is both wider than Gnosticism as defined above, and narrower than Gnosis in the wider and vaguer sense in which the term has been used in this book. On closer inspection it will be seen that Schenke's Gnosis, as here defined, is the 'classical' Gnosticism with the addition in group (a) of Marcion and Mani, in group (b) of the Mandeans and in group (c) of the Hermetica. All of these, beyond question, must be taken into account in any comprehensive treatment of the question, but as we have seen there is reason for some reserve about classifying Marcion as a Gnostic without qualification; Schenke himself speaks of Manicheism as a second major wave of the Gnostic movement, swamping the older systems;[2] the precise relation of the Her-

---

[1] *Kairos* 2, (1965), pp. 114 ff.; *Umwelt des Christentums*, i, (Berlin 1965), pp. 371 ff.

[2] *Kairos*, p. 121.

metica to Gnosticism in the strict sense is not yet fully settled; and finally Schenke himself traces a three-stage development of the Mandeans, who were originally a heretical Jewish Baptist sect, exposed *at a second stage* to the Gnostic *Weltanschauung*.[3] Both Manicheism and Mandeism are important for the understanding of the nature of the Gnostic phenomenon, and may legitimately be drawn upon to *illustrate* the significance of terms and concepts in the earlier Gnosticism and even in the New Testament. There is however an ever-present danger (of which Schenke is fully aware) that such illustration may pass over into derivation, that in words already quoted parallels may be converted into influences and influences into sources. Both Manicheism and Mandeism present enough in the way of distinctive features of their own to be classed apart, as related to but still to some extent distinct from the systems of the second century. It is for this reason among others that the wider definition of Gnosis has been employed above, and these two groups included under it.

A second point of difference relates to the inclusion of Simon Magus in group (a). This of course has the authority of Irenaeus in support, but how far is it true to say that Simon himself taught in Samaria in the first half of the first Christian century 'a typically Gnostic *Weltanschauung*'?[4] How much of the developed Simonian system known to Irenaeus was actually held by Simon himself, and how much was fathered upon him by later adherents? To ascribe to Simon a developed Gnostic system *may* be to read back Gnosticism into a period earlier than is justified by the texts at our disposal.

2.   Negatively, Schenke affirms that Gnosis is not a degenerate Christianity, as Harnack held; nor is it the direct continuation of an oriental (or Iranian) popular religion, as maintained by the school of *Religionsgeschichte* and their modern adherents; nor is it simply the spirit of late antiquity, as Jonas holds. On the first two points here we are in complete agreement, but on the third the wider definition given in this book to the term Gnosis brings us closer to the position of Jonas. Schenke would no doubt claim that this wider definition is too vague to be of any value, but the fact remains that we require some term by which

[3] *Umwelt*, p. 401. See the whole excursus pp. 396 ff., and cf. above, p. 14 f.
[4] *Kairos*, p. 130.

to describe the whole complex of phenomena which show some affinity with Gnosticism proper but cannot yet be considered fully Gnostic in the second-century sense. Moreover Schenke himself goes on to claim that his Gnosis came into being shortly before Christianity or coevally with it, but independently of it, and traces its origins to unorthodox and unofficial Jewish circles in the pre-Christian period.

3. At first sight there is some inconsistency between Schenke's statement[5] that a derivation of Gnosis from Judaism is no better or more plausible than any other derivation, from Christianity or Hellenism, from Egypt or from Persia, and his subsequent argument[6] that Jewish people had a fundamental share in the origins of Gnosticism and in its earliest dissemination. This however is a situation familiar to anyone who has tried to write about the subject. The Jewish contribution to Gnosticism is unmistakable, as we have seen, and it is therefore probable that Jews had some part in the process of development. But Gnosis and Gnosticism are not to be derived from Judaism alone, for other cultures also have made their contribution. And we have the problem raised by Jonas:[7] what could have led Jews to trample on all that was holy in their ancestral faith? Schenke suggests the reaction of an unofficial group to persecution by their 'orthodox' neighbours, but other explanations are also possible.

Schenke rightly notes the possibility that certain Jewish elements in Christian Gnostic systems may have found their way thither through the medium of Christianity, but where the Christian elements are often a mere veneer the Jewish are generally integral to the system.[8] Here the discussion of the Nag Hammadi documents in the two preceding chapters may suggest that we can make a distinction within Gnosticism proper between those systems and documents which are only superficially Christianised, and hence admit the hypothesis of a non-Christian Jewish-Gnostic basis, and those in which the Christian elements are more fundamental. Generalisation here could be misleading, since what is true of the one group may not be true of the other. Non-Christian, moreover, need not necessarily mean pre-Christian.

[5] ibid., p. 125.   [6] ibid., p. 133.
[7] *The Bible in Modern Scholarship*, pp. 289 f.   [8] *Kairos*, p. 127.

Schenke places the origin of his Gnosis shortly before or contemporary with the rise of Christianity. The discussion in previous chapters of this book has recognised the existence of trends and tendencies in this period which have been classed as Gnosis in the wider sense, or perhaps better as pre-Gnosis. Examination of the New Testament evidence takes us back at least to the last quarter of the first century for the first signs of incipient Gnosticism, and there are indications, although the question is much debated, that the beginnings of the movement go back still further; but the process of transition from Gnosis (or pre-Gnosis) to Gnosticism proper is still obscure.

Not all investigators into the problems of Gnosis and Gnosticism would entirely agree with all the positions noted in this discussion, but the extent of the agreement between two scholars of differing training, background and approach may perhaps suggest that a consensus of opinion on these questions is not so remote a prospect as is sometimes thought.

To sum up: the problems of Gnosticism, and in particular the problem of Gnostic origins, are more complex than is sometimes recognised. Particular motifs and concepts can be traced far back into the pre-Christian period, but it is not clear that such motifs can be truly classed as Gnostic except in the context of the developed Gnostic systems. Attempts to derive the whole movement from any single source come to grief, for no one of the various theories propounded is completely adequate. Moreover, as Schenke notes,[9] Gnosticism (or on his definition Gnosis) is not merely the sum of its constituent elements. We have to take account also of the fact stressed by Jonas, and others after him, that here we have a new attitude, a new outlook upon life, a radical acosmism which repudiates this world and man's existence in it. Gnosticism is not however a religion of despair, for it offers a hope in the prospect, for the elect at least, of return to the realm of light to which man essentially belongs.

The Jewish element in the developed Gnosticism is unmistakable. In some of our documents the Christian element appears to be only a superficial veneer, whereas the Jewish is integral to the whole. Again, there are cases, as with the Hermetica and Mandeism, in which we find theories of a Gnostic type with Jewish elements but little if any sign of

[9] ibid., p. 126.

Christian influence. These and other facts suggest that the earliest beginnings of the movement are to be sought in Jewish circles, probably in Palestine or Syria rather than Alexandria, for there are Jewish elements in Gnosticism of which there is no trace in Philo. If this be so, the Iranian and Mesopotamian elements may have been mediated through Judaism, and the contribution of Greek philosophy may belong to a later stage of the development; but here we are largely in the realm of speculation.

Christianity emerged on the stage of history in much the same period. It is therefore reasonable to assume that the factors which promoted the development of Gnosticism also had some influence on the emergent Christian faith. Such influence however need not have operated in the same way, or produced the same results. We have to note the differences as well as the similarities.

A further question is that of the stage at which Christianity and Gnosis came into contact, whether it was already early in the New Testament period or only later. Here there has been a widespread tendency to speak of Gnostic influence upon the New Testament, but the fact is that at a later stage the Gnostics were to adopt and adapt the New Testament to their own ends. The influence therefore was not altogether on the one side, and it would be better to envisage a period of mutual interpenetration and interaction. Here an analogy used by A. M. Hunter[10] may be relevant: Shakespeare, he writes, 'is indebted to the past in every play. His plots he often took from others. Now he recast an old play, now he turned to Plutarch or to Holinshed. Yet, though he borrowed, though in a score of ways he owed a debt to the past, Shakespeare stands out, unapproached and unapproachable, as the most original literary genius in the English language.'

This analogy is capable of wider application. In our present context, it is not the ultimate source of a theme or concept which finally matters, but the use that is made of it. And it is here that the distinctive character of the New Testament and Christian tradition, over against the Gnostic, begins to emerge. Paul, for example, can accept the contemporary *Weltanschauung* of his time, but he rejects the Gnostic interpretation of it. It is

[10] *Paul and his Predecessors*, (London 1961), p. 113.

right and proper to set the New Testament in the context of its contemporary environment, to study its documents in the light of what we can learn about the world of that time; but we must beware of drawing the wrong conclusions from our study. Gnosticism is another response to the problems of the age, at some points in close agreement with Christianity, but at others completely at variance. A balanced assessment of their mutual relationships must give to each its due.

Index

The more important references are shown in bold type.